Insurance Risk and Ruin

The focus of this book is on the two major areas of risk theory: aggregate claims distributions and ruin theory. For aggregate claims distributions, detailed descriptions are given of recursive techniques that can be used in the individual and collective risk models. For the collective model, the book discusses different classes of counting distribution, and presents recursion schemes for probability functions and moments. For the individual model, the book illustrates the three most commonly applied techniques. Beyond the classical topics in ruin theory, this new edition features an expanded section covering time of ruin problems, Gerber-Shiu functions, and the application of De Vylder approximations. Suitable for a first course in insurance risk theory and extensively classroom tested, the book is accessible to readers with a solid understanding of basic probability. Numerous worked examples are included and each chapter concludes with exercises for which complete solutions are provided.

DAVID DICKSON is Professor of Actuarial Studies at the University of Melbourne. His main research interest is ruin theory, and he has published many papers in the leading international actuarial journals. He is a Fellow of the Institute and Faculty of Actuaries in the UK and the Institute of Actuaries of Australia, and has twice been awarded the H.M. Jackson Prize of the Institute of Actuaries of Australia, most recently for the first edition of this book. He is also a co-author of *Actuarial Mathematics for Life Contingent Risks*, the recommended text for the Society of Actuaries MLC exam.

INTERNATIONAL SERIES ON ACTUARIAL SCIENCE

The *International Series on Actuarial Science*, published by Cambridge University Press in conjunction with the Institute and Faculty of Actuaries, contains textbooks for students taking courses in or related to actuarial science, as well as more advanced works designed for continuing professional development or for describing and synthesizing research. The series is a vehicle for publishing books that reflect changes and developments in the curriculum, that encourage the introduction of courses on actuarial science in universities, and that show how actuarial science can be used in all areas where there is long-term financial risk.

A complete list of books in the series can be found at www.cambridge.org/statistics. Recent titles include the following:

Insurance Risk and Ruin (2nd Edition)
David C. M. Dickson

Predictive Modeling Applications in Actuarial Science, Volume 2: Case Studies in Insurance
Edited by Edward W. Frees, Glenn Meyers & Richard A. Derrig

Computation and Modelling in Insurance and Finance
Erik Bølviken

Predictive Modeling Applications in Actuarial Science, Volume 1: Predictive Modeling Techniques
Edited by Edward W. Frees, Richard A. Derrig & Glenn Meyers

Actuarial Mathematics for Life Contingent Risks (2nd Edition)
David C. M. Dickson, Mary R. Hardy & Howard R. Waters

Solutions Manual for Actuarial Mathematics for Life Contingent Risks (2nd Edition)
David C. M. Dickson, Mary R. Hardy & Howard R. Waters

Risk Modelling in General Insurance
Roger J. Gray & Susan M. Pitts

Financial Enterprise Risk Management
Paul Sweeting

Regression Modeling with Actuarial and Financial Applications
Edward W. Frees

Insurance Risk and Ruin

Second Edition

DAVID C. M. DICKSON
University of Melbourne

CAMBRIDGE
UNIVERSITY PRESS

CAMBRIDGE
UNIVERSITY PRESS

University Printing House, Cambridge CB2 8BS, United Kingdom

One Liberty Plaza, 20th Floor, New York, NY 10006, USA

477 Williamstown Road, Port Melbourne, VIC 3207, Australia

4843/24, 2nd Floor, Ansari Road, Daryaganj, Delhi – 110002, India

79 Anson Road, #06–04/06, Singapore 079906

Cambridge University Press is part of the University of Cambridge.

It furthers the University's mission by disseminating knowledge in the pursuit of education, learning and research at the highest international levels of excellence.

www.cambridge.org
Information on this title: www.cambridge.org/9781107154605

First published 2017

Printed in the United Kingdom by Clays, St Ives plc

A catalogue record for this publication is available from the British Library

Library of Congress Cataloguing in Publication data
Names: Dickson, D. C. M. (David C. M.), 1959– author.
Title: Insurance risk and ruin / David C.M. Dickson, University of Melbourne.
Description: Cambridge, United Kingdom : Cambridge University Press, 2017. |
Series: International series on actuarial science | Earlier edition: 2010.
| Includes bibliographical references and index.
Identifiers: LCCN 2016019813 | ISBN 9781107154605 (hardback : alk. paper)
Subjects: LCSH: Risk (Insurance)
Classification: LCC HG8781 .D53 2017 | DDC 368–dc23 LC record available at
https://lccn.loc.gov/2016019813

ISBN 978-1-107-15460-5 Hardback

To Robert and Janice

Contents

Preface

Preface to the Second Edition

The major themes of the first edition were aggregate claims distributions and ruin theory. Since the publication of the first edition, there have been significant developments in ruin theory, most notably in the study of Gerber-Shiu functions. Consequently, the major change in this second edition is that Chapter 8, Advanced Ruin Theory, has been substantially expanded to reflect recent developments.

The other major change from the first edition is the inclusion of full solutions to exercises, which I hope will make the book more useful to undergraduate students. There are also some new exercises.

Work on this second edition was largely completed during study leave at Heriot-Watt University in the second half of 2015, and I am again grateful for the hospitality shown to me there. Thanks also to my colleague Shuanming Li for feedback on the changes to Chapters 7 and 8.

David C. M. Dickson
Melbourne, March 2016

Preface to the First Edition

This book is designed for final year university students taking a first course in insurance risk theory. Like many textbooks, it has its origins in lectures delivered in university courses, in this case at Heriot-Watt University, Edinburgh, and at the University of Melbourne. My intention in writing this book is to provide an introduction to the classical topics in risk theory, especially aggregate claims distributions and ruin theory.

The prerequisite knowledge for this book is probability theory at a level such as that in Grimmett and Welsh (1986). In particular, readers should be familiar with the basic concepts of distribution theory and comfortable in the use of tools such as generating functions. Much of Chapter 1 reviews distributions and concepts with which the reader should be familiar. A basic knowledge of stochastic processes is helpful, but not essential, for Chapters 6 to 8. Throughout the text, care has been taken to use straightforward mathematical techniques to derive results.

Since the early 1980s, there has been much research in risk theory in computational methods, and recursive schemes in particular. Throughout the text recursive methods are described and applied, but a full understanding of such methods can only be obtained by applying them. The reader should therefore by prepared to write some (short) computer programs to tackle some of the examples and exercises.

Many of these examples and exercises are drawn from materials I have used in teaching and examining, so the degree of difficulty is not uniform. At the end of the book, some outline solutions are provided which should allow the reader to complete the exercises, but in many cases a fair amount of work (and thought!) is required of the reader.

Some references are given at the end of each chapter for the main results in that chapter, but it was not my intention to provide comprehensive references, and readers are therefore encouraged to review the papers and books I have cited and to investigate the references therein.

Work on this book started during study leave at the University of Copenhagen in 1997 and, after much inactivity, was completed this year on study leave at the University of Waterloo and at Heriot-Watt University. I would like to thank all those at these three universities who showed great hospitality and provided a stimulating working environment. I would also like to thank former students at Melbourne: Jeffrey Chee and Kee Leong Lum for providing feedback on initial drafts, and Kwok Swan Wong who devised the examples in Section 8.6.7. Finally, I would like to single out two people in Edinburgh for thanks. First, this book would not have been possible without the support and encouragement of Emeritus Professor James Gray over a number of years as teacher, supervisor and colleague. Second, many of the ideas in this book come from joint work with Howard Waters, in both teaching and research, and I am most appreciative of his support and advice.

David C. M. Dickson

Melbourne, August 2004

1
Probability Distributions and Insurance Applications

1.1 Introduction

This book is about risk theory, with particular emphasis on the two major topics in the field, namely risk models and ruin theory. Risk theory provides a mathematical basis for the study of general insurance risks, and so it is appropriate to start with a brief description of the nature of general insurance risks. The term general insurance essentially applies to an insurance risk that is not a life insurance or health insurance risk, and so the term covers familiar forms of personal insurance such as motor vehicle insurance, home and contents insurance, and travel insurance.

Let us focus on how a motor vehicle insurance policy typically operates from an insurer's point of view. Under such a policy, the insured party pays an amount of money (the premium) to the insurer at the start of the period of insurance cover, which we assume to be one year. The insured party will make a claim under the insurance policy each time the insured party has an accident during the year which results in damage to the motor vehicle, and hence requires repair costs. There are two sources of uncertainty for the insurer: how many claims will the insured party make, and, if claims are made, what will the amounts of these claims be? Thus, if the insurer were to build a probabilistic model to represent its claims outgo under the policy, the model would require a component that modelled the number of claims and another that modelled the amounts of these claims. This is a general framework that applies to modelling claims outgo under any general insurance policy, not just motor vehicle insurance, and we will describe it in greater detail in later chapters.

In this chapter we start with a review of distributions, most of which are commonly used to model either the number of claims arising from an insurance risk or the amounts of individual claims. We then describe mixed distributions before introducing two simple forms of reinsurance arrangement and describing these in mathematical terms. We close the chapter by considering a problem that is important in the context of risk models, namely finding the distribution of a sum of independent and identically distributed random variables.

1.2 Important Discrete Distributions

1.2.1 The Poisson Distribution

When a random variable N has a Poisson distribution with parameter $\lambda > 0$, its probability function is given by

$$\Pr(N = x) = e^{-\lambda}\frac{\lambda^x}{x!}$$

for $x = 0, 1, 2, \ldots$. The moment generating function is

$$M_N(t) = \sum_{x=0}^{\infty} e^{tx} e^{-\lambda}\frac{\lambda^x}{x!} = e^{-\lambda}\sum_{x=0}^{\infty}\frac{(\lambda e^t)^x}{x!} = \exp\{\lambda(e^t - 1)\} \tag{1.1}$$

and the probability generating function is

$$P_N(r) = \sum_{x=0}^{\infty} r^x e^{-\lambda}\frac{\lambda^x}{x!} = \exp\{\lambda(r-1)\}.$$

The moments of N can be found from the moment generating function. For example,

$$M_N'(t) = \lambda e^t M_N(t)$$

and

$$M_N''(t) = \lambda e^t M_N(t) + (\lambda e^t)^2 M_N(t)$$

from which it follows that $E[N] = \lambda$ and $E\left[N^2\right] = \lambda + \lambda^2$, so that $V[N] = \lambda$.

We use the notation $P(\lambda)$ to denote a Poisson distribution with parameter λ.

1.2.2 The Binomial Distribution

When a random variable N has a binomial distribution with parameters n and q, where n is a positive integer and $0 < q < 1$, its probability function is given by

$$\Pr(N = x) = \binom{n}{x} q^x (1-q)^{n-x}$$

for $x = 0, 1, 2, \ldots, n$. The moment generating function is

$$M_N(t) = \sum_{x=0}^{n} e^{tx}\binom{n}{x} q^x (1-q)^{n-x}$$

$$= \sum_{x=0}^{n} \binom{n}{x} (qe^t)^x (1-q)^{n-x}$$
$$= \left(qe^t + 1 - q\right)^n,$$

and the probability generating function is

$$P_N(r) = (qr + 1 - q)^n .$$

As

$$M_N'(t) = n\left(qe^t + 1 - q\right)^{n-1} qe^t$$

and

$$M_N''(t) = n(n-1)\left(qe^t + 1 - q\right)^{n-2} \left(qe^t\right)^2 + n\left(qe^t + 1 - q\right)^{n-1} qe^t,$$

it follows that $E[N] = nq$, $E\left[N^2\right] = n(n-1)q^2 + nq$ and $V[N] = nq(1-q)$.

We use the notation $B(n, q)$ to denote a binomial distribution with parameters n and q.

1.2.3 The Negative Binomial Distribution

When a random variable N has a negative binomial distribution with parameters $k > 0$ and p, where $0 < p < 1$, its probability function is given by

$$\Pr(N = x) = \binom{k+x-1}{x} p^k q^x$$

for $x = 0, 1, 2, \ldots$, where $q = 1 - p$. When k is an integer, calculation of the probability function is straightforward as the probability function can be expressed in terms of factorials. An alternative method of calculating the probability function, regardless of whether k is an integer, is recursively as

$$\Pr(N = x + 1) = \frac{k+x}{x+1} q \Pr(N = x)$$

for $x = 0, 1, 2, \ldots$, with starting value $\Pr(N = 0) = p^k$.

The moment generating function can be found by making use of the identity

$$\sum_{x=0}^{\infty} \Pr(N = x) = 1. \tag{1.2}$$

From this it follows that

$$\sum_{x=0}^{\infty} \binom{k+x-1}{x} (1 - qe^t)^k (qe^t)^x = 1$$

provided that $0 < qe^t < 1$. Hence

$$\begin{aligned} M_N(t) &= \sum_{x=0}^{\infty} e^{tx} \binom{k+x-1}{x} p^k q^x \\ &= \frac{p^k}{(1-qe^t)^k} \sum_{x=0}^{\infty} \binom{k+x-1}{x} (1-qe^t)^k (qe^t)^x \\ &= \left(\frac{p}{1-qe^t}\right)^k \end{aligned}$$

provided that $0 < qe^t < 1$, or, equivalently, $t < -\log q$. Similarly, the probability generating function is

$$P_N(r) = \left(\frac{p}{1-qr}\right)^k.$$

Moments of this distribution can be found by differentiating the moment generating function, and the mean and variance are given by $E[N] = kq/p$ and $V[N] = kq/p^2$.

Equality (1.2) trivially gives

$$\sum_{x=1}^{\infty} \binom{k+x-1}{x} p^k q^x = 1 - p^k, \tag{1.3}$$

a result we shall use in Section 4.5.1.

We use the notation $NB(k, p)$ to denote a negative binomial distribution with parameters k and p.

1.2.4 The Geometric Distribution

The geometric distribution is a special case of the negative binomial distribution. When the negative binomial parameter k is 1, the distribution is called a geometric distribution with parameter p and the probability function is

$$\Pr(N = x) = pq^x$$

for $x = 0, 1, 2, \ldots$. From above, it follows that $E[N] = q/p$, $V[N] = q/p^2$ and

$$M_N(t) = \frac{p}{1-qe^t}$$

for $t < -\log q$.

This distribution plays an important role in ruin theory, as will be seen in Chapter 7.

1.3 Important Continuous Distributions

1.3.1 The Gamma Distribution

When a random variable X has a gamma distribution with parameters $\alpha > 0$ and $\lambda > 0$, its density function is given by

$$f(x) = \frac{\lambda^\alpha x^{\alpha-1} e^{-\lambda x}}{\Gamma(\alpha)}$$

for $x > 0$, where $\Gamma(\alpha)$ is the gamma function, defined as

$$\Gamma(\alpha) = \int_0^\infty x^{\alpha-1} e^{-x} dx.$$

In the special case when α is an integer the distribution is also known as an Erlang distribution, and repeated integration by parts gives the distribution function as

$$F(x) = 1 - \sum_{j=0}^{\alpha-1} e^{-\lambda x} \frac{(\lambda x)^j}{j!}$$

for $x \geq 0$. The moments and moment generating function of the gamma distribution can be found by noting that

$$\int_0^\infty f(x) dx = 1$$

yields

$$\int_0^\infty x^{\alpha-1} e^{-\lambda x} dx = \frac{\Gamma(\alpha)}{\lambda^\alpha}. \tag{1.4}$$

The nth moment is

$$E\left[X^n\right] = \int_0^\infty x^n \frac{\lambda^\alpha x^{\alpha-1} e^{-\lambda x}}{\Gamma(\alpha)} dx = \frac{\lambda^\alpha}{\Gamma(\alpha)} \int_0^\infty x^{n+\alpha-1} e^{-\lambda x} dx,$$

and from identity (1.4) it follows that

$$E\left[X^n\right] = \frac{\lambda^\alpha}{\Gamma(\alpha)} \frac{\Gamma(\alpha+n)}{\lambda^{\alpha+n}} = \frac{\Gamma(\alpha+n)}{\Gamma(\alpha)\lambda^n}. \tag{1.5}$$

In particular, $E[X] = \alpha/\lambda$ and $E\left[X^2\right] = \alpha(\alpha+1)/\lambda^2$, so that $V[X] = \alpha/\lambda^2$.

We can find the moment generating function in a similar fashion. As

$$M_X(t) = \int_0^\infty e^{tx} \frac{\lambda^\alpha x^{\alpha-1} e^{-\lambda x}}{\Gamma(\alpha)} dx = \frac{\lambda^\alpha}{\Gamma(\alpha)} \int_0^\infty x^{\alpha-1} e^{-(\lambda-t)x} dx\,, \tag{1.6}$$

application of identity (1.4) gives

$$M_X(t) = \frac{\lambda^\alpha}{\Gamma(\alpha)} \frac{\Gamma(\alpha)}{(\lambda - t)^\alpha} = \left(\frac{\lambda}{\lambda - t}\right)^\alpha . \tag{1.7}$$

Note that in identity (1.4), $\lambda > 0$. Hence, in order to apply (1.4) to (1.6) we require that $\lambda - t > 0$, so that the moment generating function exists when $t < \lambda$.

A result that will be used in Section 4.8.2 is that the coefficient of skewness of X, which we denote by $Sk[X]$, is $2/\sqrt{\alpha}$. This follows from the definition of the coefficient of skewness, namely third central moment divided by standard deviation cubed, and the fact that the third central moment is

$$\begin{aligned} E\left[\left(X - \frac{\alpha}{\lambda}\right)^3\right] &= E\left[X^3\right] - 3\frac{\alpha}{\lambda}E[X^2] + 2\left(\frac{\alpha}{\lambda}\right)^3 \\ &= \frac{\alpha(\alpha+1)(\alpha+2) - 3\alpha^2(\alpha+1) + 2\alpha^3}{\lambda^3} \\ &= \frac{2\alpha}{\lambda^3}. \end{aligned}$$

We use the notation $\gamma(\alpha, \lambda)$ to denote a gamma distribution with parameters α and λ.

1.3.2 The Exponential Distribution

The exponential distribution is a special case of the gamma distribution. It is just a gamma distribution with parameter $\alpha = 1$. Hence, the exponential distribution with parameter $\lambda > 0$ has density function

$$f(x) = \lambda e^{-\lambda x}$$

for $x > 0$, and has distribution function

$$F(x) = 1 - e^{-\lambda x}$$

for $x \geq 0$. From equation (1.5), the nth moment of the distribution is

$$E\left[X^n\right] = \frac{n!}{\lambda^n},$$

and from equation (1.7) the moment generating function is

$$M_X(t) = \frac{\lambda}{\lambda - t}$$

for $t < \lambda$.

1.3.3 The Pareto Distribution

When a random variable X has a Pareto distribution with parameters $\alpha > 0$ and $\lambda > 0$, its density function is given by

$$f(x) = \frac{\alpha\lambda^\alpha}{(\lambda + x)^{\alpha+1}}$$

for $x > 0$. Integrating this density we find that the distribution function is

$$F(x) = 1 - \left(\frac{\lambda}{\lambda + x}\right)^\alpha$$

for $x \geq 0$. Whenever moments of the distribution exist, they can be found from

$$E[X^n] = \int_0^\infty x^n f(x)dx$$

by integration by parts. However, they can also be found individually using the following approach. Since the integral of the density function over $(0, \infty)$ equals 1, we have

$$\int_0^\infty \frac{dx}{(\lambda + x)^{\alpha+1}} = \frac{1}{\alpha\lambda^\alpha},$$

an identity which holds provided that $\alpha > 0$. To find $E[X]$, we can write

$$E[X] = \int_0^\infty xf(x)dx = \int_0^\infty (x + \lambda - \lambda)f(x)dx = \int_0^\infty (x + \lambda)f(x)dx - \lambda,$$

and inserting for f we have

$$E[X] = \int_0^\infty \frac{\alpha\lambda^\alpha}{(\lambda + x)^\alpha}dx - \lambda.$$

We can evaluate the integral expression by rewriting the integrand in terms of a Pareto density function with parameters $\alpha - 1$ and λ. Thus,

$$E[X] = \frac{\alpha\lambda}{\alpha - 1}\int_0^\infty \frac{(\alpha - 1)\lambda^{\alpha-1}}{(\lambda + x)^\alpha}dx - \lambda, \tag{1.8}$$

and since the integral equals 1,

$$E[X] = \frac{\alpha\lambda}{\alpha - 1} - \lambda = \frac{\lambda}{\alpha - 1}.$$

It is important to note that the integrand in equation (1.8) is a Pareto density function only if $\alpha > 1$, and hence $E[X]$ exists only for $\alpha > 1$. Similarly, we can find $E\left[X^2\right]$ from

$$E\left[X^2\right] = \int_0^\infty \left((x+\lambda)^2 - 2\lambda x - \lambda^2\right) f(x)dx$$
$$= \int_0^\infty (x+\lambda)^2 f(x)dx - 2\lambda E[X] - \lambda^2.$$

Proceeding as in the case of $E[X]$ we can show that

$$E\left[X^2\right] = \frac{2\lambda^2}{(\alpha-1)(\alpha-2)}$$

provided that $\alpha > 2$, and hence that

$$V[X] = \frac{\alpha\lambda^2}{(\alpha-1)^2(\alpha-2)}.$$

An alternative method of finding moments of the Pareto distribution is given in Exercise 5 at the end of this chapter.

We use the notation $Pa(\alpha, \lambda)$ to denote a Pareto distribution with parameters α and λ.

1.3.4 The Normal Distribution

When a random variable X has a normal distribution with parameters μ and σ^2, its density function is given by

$$f(x) = \frac{1}{\sigma\sqrt{2\pi}} \exp\left\{-\frac{(x-\mu)^2}{2\sigma^2}\right\}$$

for $-\infty < x < \infty$. We use the notation $N(\mu, \sigma^2)$ to denote a normal distribution with parameters μ and σ^2.

The standard normal distribution has parameters 0 and 1 and its distribution function is denoted Φ, where

$$\Phi(x) = \int_{-\infty}^{x} \frac{1}{\sqrt{2\pi}} \exp\left\{-z^2/2\right\} dz.$$

A key relationship is that if $X \sim N(\mu, \sigma^2)$ and if $Z = (X - \mu)/\sigma$, then $Z \sim N(0, 1)$.

The moment generating function is

$$M_X(t) = \exp\left\{\mu t + \tfrac{1}{2}\sigma^2 t^2\right\} \tag{1.9}$$

from which it can be shown (see Exercise 7) that $E[X] = \mu$ and $V[X] = \sigma^2$.

1.3.5 The Lognormal Distribution

When a random variable X has a lognormal distribution with parameters μ and σ, where $-\infty < \mu < \infty$ and $\sigma > 0$, its density function is given by

$$f(x) = \frac{1}{x\sigma\sqrt{2\pi}} \exp\left\{-\frac{(\log x - \mu)^2}{2\sigma^2}\right\}$$

for $x > 0$. The distribution function can be obtained by integrating the density function as follows:

$$F(x) = \int_0^x \frac{1}{y\sigma\sqrt{2\pi}} \exp\left\{-\frac{(\log y - \mu)^2}{2\sigma^2}\right\} dy,$$

and the substitution $z = \log y$ yields

$$F(x) = \int_{-\infty}^{\log x} \frac{1}{\sigma\sqrt{2\pi}} \exp\left\{-\frac{(z - \mu)^2}{2\sigma^2}\right\} dz.$$

As the integrand is the $N(\mu, \sigma^2)$ density function,

$$F(x) = \Phi\left(\frac{\log x - \mu}{\sigma}\right).$$

Thus, probabilities under a lognormal distribution can be calculated from the standard normal distribution function.

We use the notation $LN(\mu, \sigma)$ to denote a lognormal distribution with parameters μ and σ. From the preceding argument it follows that if $X \sim LN(\mu, \sigma)$, then $\log X \sim N(\mu, \sigma^2)$.

This relationship between normal and lognormal distributions is extremely useful, particularly in deriving moments. If $X \sim LN(\mu, \sigma)$ and $Y = \log X$, then

$$E\left[X^n\right] = E\left[e^{nY}\right] = M_Y(n) = \exp\left\{\mu n + \tfrac{1}{2}\sigma^2 n^2\right\},$$

where the final equality follows by equation (1.9).

1.4 Mixed Distributions

Many of the distributions encountered in this book are mixed distributions. To illustrate the idea of a mixed distribution, let X be exponentially distributed with mean 100, and let the random variable Y be defined by

$$Y = \begin{cases} 0 & \text{if } X < 20 \\ X - 20 & \text{if } 20 \le X < 300 \\ 280 & \text{if } X \ge 300 \end{cases}.$$

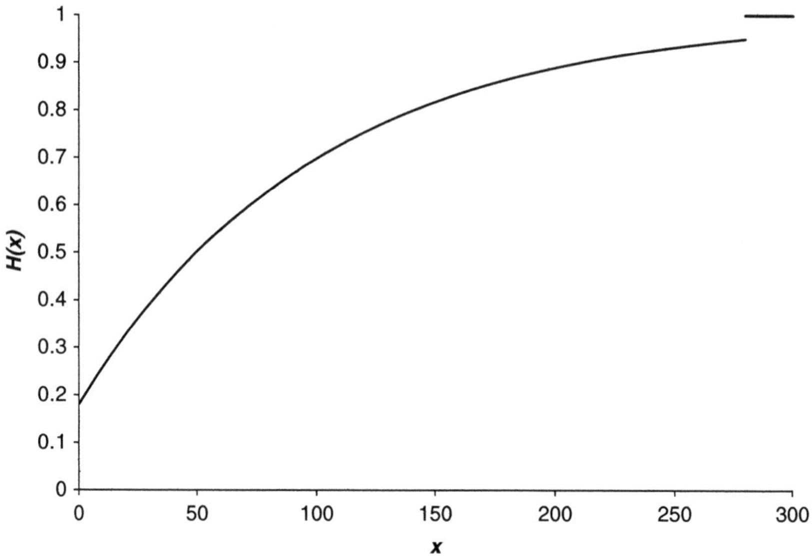

Figure 1.1 The distribution function H.

Then

$$\Pr(Y = 0) = \Pr(X < 20) = 1 - e^{-0.2} = 0.1813,$$

and similarly $\Pr(Y = 280) = 0.0498$. Thus, Y has masses of probability at the points 0 and 280. However, in the interval $(0, 280)$, the distribution of Y is continuous, with, for example,

$$\Pr(30 < Y \leq 100) = \Pr(50 < X \leq 120) = 0.3053.$$

Figure 1.1 shows the distribution function, H, of Y. Note that there are jumps at 0 and 280, corresponding to the masses of probability at these points. As the distribution function is differentiable in the interval $(0, 280)$, Y has a density function in this interval. Letting h denote the density function of Y, the moments of Y can be found from

$$E\left[Y^r\right] = \int_0^{280} x^r h(x)dx + 280^r \Pr(Y = 280).$$

At certain points in this book, it will be convenient to use Stieltjes integral notation, so that we do not have to specify whether a distribution is discrete, continuous or mixed. In this notation, we write the rth moment of Y as

$$E\left[Y^r\right] = \int_0^{\infty} x^r dH(x).$$

More generally, if $K(x) = \Pr(Z \leq x)$ is a mixed distribution on $[0, \infty)$, and m is a function, then

$$E[m(Z)] = \int_0^\infty m(x)dK(x),$$

where we interpret the integral as

$$\sum_{x_i} m(x_i) \Pr(Z = x_i) + \int m(x)k(x)dx,$$

where summation is over the points $\{x_i\}$ at which there is a mass of probability, and integration is over the intervals in which K is continuous with density function k.

1.5 Insurance Applications

In this section we discuss some functions of random variables. In particular, we focus on functions that are natural in the context of reinsurance. Throughout this section we let X denote the amount of a claim, and let X have distribution function F. Further, we assume that all claim amounts are non-negative quantities, so that $F(x) = 0$ for $x < 0$, and, with the exception of Example 1.7, we assume that X is a continuous random variable, with density function f.

A reinsurance arrangement is an agreement between an insurer and a reinsurer under which claims that occur in a fixed period of time (e.g. one year) are split between the insurer and the reinsurer in an agreed manner. Thus, the insurer is effectively insuring part of a risk with a reinsurer and, of course, pays a premium to the reinsurer for this cover. One effect of reinsurance is that it reduces the variability of claim payments by the insurer.

1.5.1 Proportional Reinsurance

Under a proportional reinsurance arrangement, the insurer pays a fixed proportion, say, a, of each claim that occurs during the period of the reinsurance arrangement. The remaining proportion, $1 - a$, of each claim is paid by the reinsurer.

Let Y denote the part of a claim paid by the insurer under this proportional reinsurance arrangement, and let Z denote the part paid by the reinsurer. In terms of random variables, $Y = aX$ and $Z = (1 - a)X$, and trivially $Y + Z = X$. Thus, the random variables Y and Z are both scale transformations of the random variable X. The distribution function of Y is given by

$$\Pr(Y \leq x) = \Pr(aX \leq x) = \Pr(X \leq x/a) = F(x/a),$$

and the density function is

$$\tfrac{1}{a} f(x/a).$$

Example 1.1 *Let $X \sim \gamma(\alpha, \lambda)$. What is the distribution of aX?*

Solution 1.1 *As*

$$f(x) = \frac{\lambda^\alpha x^{\alpha-1} e^{-\lambda x}}{\Gamma(\alpha)},$$

it follows that the density function of aX is

$$\frac{\lambda^\alpha x^{\alpha-1} e^{-\lambda x/a}}{a^\alpha \Gamma(\alpha)}.$$

Thus, the distribution of aX is $\gamma(\alpha, \lambda/a)$.

Example 1.2 *Let $X \sim LN(\mu, \sigma)$. What is the distribution of aX?*

Solution 1.2 *As*

$$f(x) = \frac{1}{x\sigma\sqrt{2\pi}} \exp\left\{-\frac{(\log x - \mu)^2}{2\sigma^2}\right\},$$

it follows that the density function of aX is

$$\frac{1}{x\sigma\sqrt{2\pi}} \exp\left\{-\frac{(\log x - \log a - \mu)^2}{2\sigma^2}\right\}.$$

Thus, the distribution of aX is $LN(\mu + \log a, \sigma)$.

1.5.2 Excess of Loss Reinsurance

Under an excess of loss reinsurance arrangement, a claim is shared between the insurer and the reinsurer only if the claim exceeds a fixed amount called the retention level. Otherwise, the insurer pays the claim in full. Let M denote the retention level, and let Y and Z denote the amounts paid by the insurer and the reinsurer respectively under this reinsurance arrangement. Mathematically, this arrangement can be represented as the insurer pays $Y = \min(X, M)$ and the reinsurer pays $Z = \max(0, X - M)$, with $Y + Z = X$.

The Insurer's Position

Let F_Y be the distribution function of Y. Then it follows from the definition of Y that

$$F_Y(x) = \begin{cases} F(x) & \text{for } x < M \\ 1 & \text{for } x \geq M \end{cases}.$$

Thus, the distribution of Y is mixed, with a density function $f(x)$ for $0 < x < M$, and a mass of probability at M, with $\Pr(Y = M) = 1 - F(M)$.

As Y is a function of X, the moments of Y can be calculated from

$$E\left[Y^n\right] = \int_0^\infty (\min(x, M))^n f(x)dx,$$

and this integral can be split into two parts since $\min(x, M)$ equals x for $0 \leq x < M$ and equals M for $x \geq M$. Hence

$$\begin{aligned} E\left[Y^n\right] &= \int_0^M x^n f(x)dx + \int_M^\infty M^n f(x)dx \\ &= \int_0^M x^n f(x)dx + M^n \left(1 - F(M)\right). \end{aligned} \tag{1.10}$$

In particular,

$$E[Y] = \int_0^M xf(x)dx + M\left(1 - F(M)\right),$$

so that

$$\frac{d}{dM}E[Y] = 1 - F(M) > 0.$$

Thus, as a function of M, $E[Y]$ increases from 0 when $M = 0$ to $E[X]$ as $M \to \infty$.

Example 1.3 *Let $F(x) = 1 - e^{-\lambda x}$, $x \geq 0$. Find $E[Y]$.*

Solution 1.3 *We have*

$$E[Y] = \int_0^M x\lambda e^{-\lambda x}dx + Me^{-\lambda M},$$

and integration by parts yields

$$E[Y] = \tfrac{1}{\lambda}\left(1 - e^{-\lambda M}\right).$$

Example 1.4 *Let $X \sim LN(\mu, \sigma)$. Find $E[Y^n]$.*

Solution 1.4 *Inserting the lognormal density function into the integral in equation (1.10) we get*

$$E\left[Y^n\right] = \int_0^M x^n \frac{1}{x\sigma\sqrt{2\pi}} \exp\left\{-\frac{(\log x - \mu)^2}{2\sigma^2}\right\} dx + M^n \left(1 - F(M)\right). \tag{1.11}$$

To evaluate this, we consider separately each term on the right-hand side of equation (1.11). Let

$$I = \int_0^M x^n \frac{1}{x\sigma\sqrt{2\pi}} \exp\left\{-\frac{(\log x - \mu)^2}{2\sigma^2}\right\} dx.$$

To deal with an integral of this type, there is a standard substitution, namely $y = \log x$. *This gives*

$$I = \int_{-\infty}^{\log M} \exp\{yn\} \frac{1}{\sigma\sqrt{2\pi}} \exp\left\{-\frac{(y-\mu)^2}{2\sigma^2}\right\} dy.$$

The technique in evaluating this integral is to write the integrand in terms of a normal density function (different to the $N(\mu, \sigma^2)$ *density function). To achieve this we apply the technique of "completing the square" in the exponent, as follows:*

$$\begin{aligned} yn - \frac{(y-\mu)^2}{2\sigma^2} &= \frac{-1}{2\sigma^2}\left[(y-\mu)^2 - 2\sigma^2 yn\right] \\ &= \frac{-1}{2\sigma^2}\left[y^2 - 2\mu y + \mu^2 - 2\sigma^2 yn\right] \\ &= \frac{-1}{2\sigma^2}\left[y^2 - 2y(\mu + \sigma^2 n) + \mu^2\right]. \end{aligned}$$

Noting that the terms inside the square brackets would give the square of $y - (\mu + \sigma^2 n)$ *if the final term were* $(\mu + \sigma^2 n)^2$ *instead of* μ^2, *we can write the exponent as*

$$\begin{aligned} &\frac{-1}{2\sigma^2}\left[(y - (\mu + \sigma^2 n))^2 - (\mu + \sigma^2 n)^2 + \mu^2\right] \\ &= \frac{-1}{2\sigma^2}\left[(y - (\mu + \sigma^2 n))^2 - 2\mu\sigma^2 n - \sigma^4 n^2\right] \\ &= \mu n + \tfrac{1}{2}\sigma^2 n^2 - \frac{1}{2\sigma^2}(y - (\mu + \sigma^2 n))^2. \end{aligned}$$

Hence

$$I = \exp\left\{\mu n + \tfrac{1}{2}\sigma^2 n^2\right\} \int_{-\infty}^{\log M} \frac{1}{\sigma\sqrt{2\pi}} \exp\left\{-\frac{1}{2\sigma^2}(y - (\mu + \sigma^2 n))^2\right\} dy,$$

and as the integrand is the $N(\mu + \sigma^2 n, \sigma^2)$ *density function,*

$$I = \exp\left\{\mu n + \tfrac{1}{2}\sigma^2 n^2\right\} \Phi\left(\frac{\log M - \mu - \sigma^2 n}{\sigma}\right).$$

Finally, using the relationship between normal and lognormal distributions,

$$1 - F(M) = 1 - \Phi\left(\frac{\log M - \mu}{\sigma}\right),$$

so that

$$E\left[Y^n\right] = \exp\{\mu n + \tfrac{1}{2}\sigma^2 n^2\}\Phi\left(\frac{\log M - \mu - \sigma^2 n}{\sigma}\right) + M^n\left(1 - \Phi\left(\frac{\log M - \mu}{\sigma}\right)\right).$$

The Reinsurer's Position

From the definition of Z it follows that Z takes the value zero if $X \leq M$, and takes the value $X - M$ if $X > M$. Hence, if F_Z denotes the distribution function of Z, then $F_Z(0) = F(M)$, and for $x > 0$, $F_Z(x) = F(x + M)$. Thus, F_Z is a mixed distribution with a mass of probability at 0.

The moments of Z can be found in a similar fashion to those of Y. We have

$$E\left[Z^n\right] = \int_0^\infty (\max(0, x - M))^n f(x)dx,$$

and since $\max(0, x - M)$ is 0 for $0 \leq x \leq M$, we have

$$E\left[Z^n\right] = \int_M^\infty (x - M)^n f(x)dx. \tag{1.12}$$

Example 1.5 *Let* $F(x) = 1 - e^{-\lambda x}$, $x \geq 0$. *Find* $E[Z]$.

Solution 1.5 *Setting* $n = 1$ *in equation (1.12) we have*

$$\begin{aligned} E[Z] &= \int_M^\infty (x - M)\lambda e^{-\lambda x}dx \\ &= \int_0^\infty y\lambda e^{-\lambda(y+M)}dy \\ &= e^{-\lambda M}E[X] \\ &= \tfrac{1}{\lambda}e^{-\lambda M}. \end{aligned}$$

Alternatively, the identity $E[Z] = E[X] - E[Y]$ *yields the answer with* $E[X] = 1/\lambda$ *and* $E[Y]$ *given by the solution to Example 1.3.*

Example 1.6 *Let* $F(x) = 1 - e^{-\lambda x}$, $x \geq 0$. *Find* $M_Z(t)$.

Solution 1.6 *By definition,* $M_Z(t) = E\left[e^{tZ}\right]$ *and as* $Z = \max(0, X - M)$,

$$\begin{aligned} M_Z(t) &= \int_0^\infty e^{t\max(0,x-M)}\lambda e^{-\lambda x}dx \\ &= \int_0^M e^0\lambda e^{-\lambda x}dx + \int_M^\infty e^{t(x-M)}\lambda e^{-\lambda x}dx \end{aligned}$$

$$= 1 - e^{-\lambda M} + \lambda \int_0^\infty e^{ty-\lambda(y+M)} dy$$
$$= 1 - e^{-\lambda M} + \frac{\lambda e^{-\lambda M}}{\lambda - t}$$

provided that $t < \lambda$.

The above approach is a slightly artificial way of looking at the reinsurer's position since it includes zero as a possible "claim amount" for the reinsurer. An alternative, and more realistic, way of considering the reinsurer's position is to consider the distribution of the non-zero amounts paid by the reinsurer. In practice, the reinsurer is likely to have information only on these amounts, as the insurer is unlikely to inform the reinsurer each time there is a claim whose amount is less than M.

Example 1.7 *Let* X *have a discrete distribution as follows:*

$$\begin{aligned}\Pr(X = 100) &= 0.6\\ \Pr(X = 175) &= 0.3\\ \Pr(X = 200) &= 0.1\end{aligned} .$$

If the insurer effects excess of loss reinsurance with retention level 150, *what is the distribution of the non-zero payments made by the reinsurer?*

Solution 1.7 *First, we note that the distribution of* Z *is given by*

$$\begin{aligned}\Pr(Z = 0) &= 0.6\\ \Pr(Z = 25) &= 0.3\\ \Pr(Z = 50) &= 0.1\end{aligned} .$$

Now let W *denote the amount of a non-zero payment made by the reinsurer. Then* W *can take one of two values:* 25 *and* 50. *Since payments of amount* 25 *are three times as likely as payments of amount* 50, *we can write the distribution of* W *as*

$$\begin{aligned}\Pr(W = 25) &= 0.75\\ \Pr(W = 50) &= 0.25\end{aligned} .$$

The argument in Example 1.7 can be formalised, as follows. Let W denote the amount of a non-zero payment by the reinsurer under an excess of loss reinsurance arrangement with retention level M. The distribution of W is identical to that of $Z|Z > 0$. Hence

$$\Pr(W \le x) = \Pr(Z \le x | Z > 0) = \Pr(X \le x + M | X > M)$$

from which it follows that

$$\Pr(W \leq x) = \frac{\Pr(M < X \leq x + M)}{\Pr(X > M)} = \frac{F(x+M) - F(M)}{1 - F(M)}. \tag{1.13}$$

Differentiation gives the density function of W as

$$\frac{f(x+M)}{1 - F(M)}. \tag{1.14}$$

Example 1.8 *Let $F(x) = 1 - e^{-\lambda x}$, $x \geq 0$. What is the distribution of the non-zero claim payments made by the reinsurer?*

Solution 1.8 *By formula (1.14), the density function is*

$$\frac{\lambda e^{-\lambda(x+M)}}{e^{-\lambda M}} = \lambda e^{-\lambda x},$$

so that the distribution of W is the same as that of X. (This rather surprising result is a consequence of the "memoryless" property of the exponential distribution.)

Example 1.9 *Let $X \sim Pa(\alpha, \lambda)$. What is the distribution of the non-zero claim payments made by the reinsurer?*

Solution 1.9 *Again applying formula (1.14), the density function is*

$$\frac{\alpha\lambda^\alpha}{(\lambda + M + x)^{\alpha+1}} \left(\frac{\lambda + M}{\lambda}\right)^\alpha = \frac{\alpha(\lambda + M)^\alpha}{(\lambda + M + x)^{\alpha+1}},$$

so that the distribution of W is $Pa(\alpha, \lambda + M)$.

1.5.3 Policy Excess

Insurance policies with a policy excess are very common, particularly in motor vehicle insurance. If a policy is issued with an excess of d, then the insured party pays any loss of amount less than or equal to d in full, and pays d on any loss in excess of d. Thus, if X represents the amount of a loss, when a loss occurs the insured party pays $\min(X, d)$ and the insurer pays $\max(0, X - d)$. These quantities are of the same form as the amounts paid by the insurer and the reinsurer when a claim occurs (for the insurer) under an excess of loss reinsurance arrangement. Hence there are no new mathematical considerations involved. It is important, however, to recognise that X represents the amount of a loss, and not the amount of a claim.

1.6 Sums of Random Variables

In many insurance applications we are interested in the distribution of the sum of independent and identically distributed random variables. For example, suppose that an insurer issues n policies, and the claim amount from policy i, $i = 1, 2, \ldots, n$, is a random variable X_i. Then the total amount the insurer pays in claims from these n policies is $S_n = \sum_{i=1}^{n} X_i$. An obvious question to ask is what is the distribution of S_n? This is the question we consider in this section, on the assumption that $\{X_i\}_{i=1}^{n}$ are independent and identically distributed random variables. When the distribution of S_n exists in a closed form, we can usually find it by one of the methods described in the next two sections.

1.6.1 Moment Generating Function Method

This is a very neat way of finding the distribution of S_n. Define M_S to be the moment generating function of S_n, and define M_X to be the moment generating function of X_1. Then

$$M_S(t) = E\left[e^{tS_n}\right] = E\left[e^{t(X_1+X_2+\cdots+X_n)}\right].$$

Using independence, it follows that

$$M_S(t) = E\left[e^{tX_1}\right]E\left[e^{tX_2}\right]\cdots E\left[e^{tX_n}\right],$$

and as the X_i's are identically distributed,

$$M_S(t) = M_X(t)^n.$$

Hence, if we can identify $M_X(t)^n$ as the moment generating function of a distribution, we know the distribution of S_n by the uniqueness property of moment generating functions.

Example 1.10 *Let X_1 have a Poisson distribution with parameter λ. What is the distribution of S_n?*

Solution 1.10 *As*

$$M_X(t) = \exp\left\{\lambda(e^t - 1)\right\},$$

we have

$$M_S(t) = \exp\left\{\lambda n(e^t - 1)\right\},$$

and so S_n has a Poisson distribution with parameter λn.

Example 1.11 *Let X_1 have an exponential distribution with mean $1/\lambda$. What is the distribution of S_n?*

Solution 1.11 *As*

$$M_X(t) = \frac{\lambda}{\lambda - t}$$

for $t < \lambda$, we have

$$M_S(t) = \left(\frac{\lambda}{\lambda - t}\right)^n,$$

and so S_n has a $\gamma(n, \lambda)$ distribution.

1.6.2 Direct Convolution of Distributions

Direct convolution is a more direct, and less elegant, method of finding the distribution of S_n. Let us first assume that $\{X_i\}_{i=1}^n$ are discrete random variables, distributed on the non-negative integers, so that S_n is also distributed on the non-negative integers.

Let x be a non-negative integer, and consider first the distribution of S_2. The convolution approach to finding $\Pr(S_2 \leq x)$ considers how the event $\{S_2 \leq x\}$ can occur. This event occurs when X_2 takes the value j, where j can be any value from 0 up to x, and when X_1 takes a value less than or equal to $x - j$, so that their sum is less than or equal to x. Summing over all possible values of j and using the fact that X_1 and X_2 are independent, we have

$$\Pr(S_2 \leq x) = \sum_{j=0}^{x} \Pr(X_1 \leq x - j) \Pr(X_2 = j).$$

The same argument can be applied to find $\Pr(S_3 \leq x)$ by writing $S_3 = S_2 + X_3$, and by noting that S_2 and X_3 are independent (as $S_2 = X_1 + X_2$). Thus,

$$\Pr(S_3 \leq x) = \sum_{j=0}^{x} \Pr(S_2 \leq x - j) \Pr(X_3 = j),$$

and, in general,

$$\Pr(S_n \leq x) = \sum_{j=0}^{x} \Pr(S_{n-1} \leq x - j) \Pr(X_n = j). \tag{1.15}$$

The same reasoning gives

$$\Pr(S_n = x) = \sum_{j=0}^{x} \Pr(S_{n-1} = x - j) \Pr(X_n = j).$$

Now let F be the distribution function of X_1 and let $f_j = \Pr(X_1 = j)$. We define

$$F^{n*}(x) = \Pr(S_n \leq x)$$

and call F^{n*} the n-fold convolution of the distribution F with itself. Then by equation (1.15),

$$F^{n*}(x) = \sum_{j=0}^{x} F^{(n-1)*}(x-j)f_j \,.$$

Note that $F^{1*} = F$, and, by convention, we define $F^{0*}(x) = 1$ for $x \geq 0$ with $F^{0*}(x) = 0$ for $x < 0$. Similarly, we define $f_x^{n*} = \Pr(S_n = x)$, so that

$$f_x^{n*} = \sum_{j=0}^{x} f_{x-j}^{(n-1)*} f_j$$

with $f^{1*} = f$.

When F is a continuous distribution on $(0, \infty)$ with density function f, the analogues of the above results are

$$F^{n*}(x) = \int_0^x F^{(n-1)*}(x-y)f(y)dy$$

and

$$f^{n*}(x) = \int_0^x f^{(n-1)*}(x-y)f(y)dy. \tag{1.16}$$

These results can be used to find the distribution of S_n directly.

Example 1.12 *What is the distribution of S_n when $\{X_i\}_{i=1}^n$ are independent exponentially distributed random variables, each with mean $1/\lambda$?*

Solution 1.12 *Setting $n = 2$ in equation (1.16) we get*

$$\begin{aligned} f^{2*}(x) &= \int_0^x f(x-y)f(y)dy \\ &= \int_0^x \lambda e^{-\lambda(x-y)} \lambda e^{-\lambda y} dy \\ &= \lambda^2 e^{-\lambda x} \int_0^x dy \\ &= \lambda^2 x e^{-\lambda x}, \end{aligned}$$

so that S_2 has a $\gamma(2, \lambda)$ distribution. Next, setting $n = 3$ in equation (1.16) we get

$$\begin{aligned} f^{3*}(x) &= \int_0^x f^{2*}(x-y)f(y)dy \\ &= \int_0^x f^{2*}(y)f(x-y)dy \\ &= \int_0^x \lambda^2 y e^{-\lambda y} \lambda e^{-\lambda(x-y)} dy \\ &= \tfrac{1}{2}\lambda^3 x^2 e^{-\lambda x}, \end{aligned}$$

so that the distribution of S_3 is $\gamma(3, \lambda)$. An inductive argument can now be used to show that for a general value of n, S_n has a $\gamma(n, \lambda)$ distribution.

In general, it is much easier to apply the moment generating function method to find the distribution of S_n.

1.6.3 Recursive Calculation for Discrete Random Variables

In the case when X_1 is a discrete random variable, distributed on the non-negative integers, it is possible to calculate the probability function of S_n recursively. Define

$$f_j = \Pr(X_1 = j) \quad \text{and} \quad g_j = \Pr(S_n = j),$$

each for $j = 0, 1, 2, \ldots$. We denote the probability generating function of X_1 by P_X, so that

$$P_X(r) = \sum_{j=0}^{\infty} r^j f_j\,,$$

and the probability generating function of S_n by P_S, so that

$$P_S(r) = \sum_{k=0}^{\infty} r^k g_k\,.$$

Using arguments that have previously been applied to moment generating functions, we have

$$P_S(r) = P_X(r)^n,$$

and differentiation with respect to r gives

$$P_S'(r) = nP_X(r)^{n-1}P_X'(r).$$

When we multiply each side of the above identity by $rP_X(r)$, we get

$$P_X(r)rP'_S(r) = nP_S(r)rP'_X(r),$$

which can be expressed as

$$\sum_{j=0}^{\infty} r^j f_j \sum_{k=1}^{\infty} kr^k g_k = n \sum_{k=0}^{\infty} r^k g_k \sum_{j=1}^{\infty} jr^j f_j \,. \tag{1.17}$$

To find an expression for g_x, we consider the coefficient of r^x on each side of equation (1.17), where x is a positive integer. On the left-hand side, the coefficient of r^x can be found as follows. For $j = 0, 1, 2, \ldots, x-1$, multiply together the coefficient of r^j in the first sum with the coefficient of r^{x-j} in the second sum. Adding these products together gives the coefficient of r^x, namely

$$f_0 x g_x + f_1(x-1)g_{x-1} + \cdots + f_{x-1}g_1 = \sum_{j=0}^{x-1} (x-j) f_j g_{x-j} \,.$$

Similarly, on the right-hand side of equation (1.17) the coefficient of r^x is

$$n\left(g_0 x f_x + g_1(x-1)f_{x-1} + \cdots + g_{x-1}f_1\right) = n \sum_{j=1}^{x} j f_j g_{x-j} \,.$$

Since these coefficients must be equal we have

$$x g_x f_0 + \sum_{j=1}^{x-1} (x-j) f_j g_{x-j} = n \sum_{j=1}^{x} j f_j g_{x-j}$$

which gives (noting that the sum on the left-hand side is unaltered when the upper limit of summation is increased to x)

$$g_x = \frac{1}{f_0} \sum_{j=1}^{x} \left((n+1)\frac{j}{x} - 1 \right) f_j g_{x-j} \,. \tag{1.18}$$

The important point about this result is that it gives a recursive method of calculating the probability function $\{g_x\}_{x=0}^{\infty}$. Given the values $\{f_j\}_{j=0}^{\infty}$ we can use the value of g_0 to calculate g_1, then the values of g_0 and g_1 to calculate g_2, and so on. The starting value for the recursive calculation is g_0 which is given by f_0^n since S_n takes the value 0 if and only if each X_i, $i = 1, 2, \ldots, n$, takes the value 0.

This is a very useful result as it permits much more efficient evaluation of the probability function of S_n than the direct convolution approach of the previous section.

We conclude with three remarks about this result:

(i) Computer implementation of formula (1.18) is necessary, especially when n is large. It is, however, an easy task to program this formula.
(ii) It is straightforward (see Exercise 12) to adapt this result to the situation when X_1 is distributed on $m, m+1, m+2, \ldots$, where m is a positive integer.
(iii) The recursion formula is unstable. That is, it may give numerical answers which do not make sense. Thus, caution should be employed when applying this formula. However, for most practical purposes, numerical stability is not an issue.

Example 1.13 *Let $\{X_i\}_{i=1}^4$ be independent and identically distributed random variables with common probability function $f_j = \Pr(X_1 = j)$ given by*

$$f_0 = 0.4 \qquad f_2 = 0.2$$
$$f_1 = 0.3 \qquad f_3 = 0.1.$$

Let $S_4 = \sum_{i=1}^4 X_i$. Recursively calculate $\Pr(S_4 = r)$ for $r = 1, 2, 3$ and 4.

Solution 1.13 *The starting value for the recursive calculation is*

$$g_0 = \Pr(S_4 = 0) = f_0^4 = 0.4^4 = 0.0256.$$

Now note that as $f_j = 0$ for $j = 4, 5, 6, \ldots$, equation (1.18) can be written with a different upper limit of summation as

$$g_x = \frac{1}{f_0} \sum_{j=1}^{\min(3,x)} \left(\frac{5j}{x} - 1 \right) f_j g_{x-j},$$

and so

$$g_1 = \frac{1}{f_0} 4 f_1 g_0 = 0.0768,$$

$$g_2 = \frac{1}{f_0} \left(\tfrac{3}{2} f_1 g_1 + 4 f_2 g_0 \right) = 0.1376,$$

$$g_3 = \frac{1}{f_0} \left(\tfrac{2}{3} f_1 g_2 + \tfrac{7}{3} f_2 g_1 + 4 f_3 g_0 \right) = 0.1840,$$

$$g_4 = \frac{1}{f_0} \left(\tfrac{1}{4} f_1 g_3 + \tfrac{3}{2} f_2 g_2 + \tfrac{11}{4} f_3 g_1 \right) = 0.1905.$$

1.7 Notes and References

Further details of the distributions discussed in this chapter, including a discussion of how to fit parameters to these distributions, can be found in Hogg and Klugman (1984). See also Klugman et al. (1998).

The recursive formula of Section 1.6.3 was derived by De Pril (1985), and a very elegant proof of the result can be found in his paper.

1.8 Exercises

1. A random variable X has a logarithmic distribution with parameter θ, where $0 < \theta < 1$, if its probability function is

$$\Pr(X = x) = \frac{-1}{\log(1-\theta)} \frac{\theta^x}{x}$$

for $x = 1, 2, 3, \ldots$. Show that

$$M_X(t) = \frac{\log(1-\theta e^t)}{\log(1-\theta)}$$

for $t < -\log\theta$. Hence, or otherwise, find the mean and variance of this distribution.

2. A random variable X has a beta distribution with parameters $\alpha > 0$ and $\beta > 0$ if its density function is

$$f(x) = \frac{\Gamma(\alpha+\beta)}{\Gamma(\alpha)\Gamma(\beta)} x^{\alpha-1}(1-x)^{\beta-1}$$

for $0 < x < 1$. Show that

$$E\left[X^n\right] = \frac{\Gamma(\alpha+\beta)\Gamma(n+\alpha)}{\Gamma(\alpha)\Gamma(n+\alpha+\beta)}$$

and hence find the mean and variance of X.

3. A random variable X has a Weibull distribution with parameters $c > 0$ and $\gamma > 0$ if its density function is

$$f(x) = c\gamma x^{\gamma-1}\exp\{-cx^\gamma\}$$

for $x > 0$.

(a) Show that X has distribution function

$$F(x) = 1 - \exp\{-cx^\gamma\}$$

for $x \geq 0$.

(b) Let $Y = X^{\gamma}$. Show that Y has an exponential distribution with mean $1/c$. Hence show that

$$E\left[X^n\right] = \frac{\Gamma(1+n/\gamma)}{c^{n/\gamma}}.$$

4. Let $\gamma_n(x) = \beta^n x^{n-1} e^{-\beta x}/\Gamma(n)$ denote the Erlang(n, β) density function, where n is a positive integer. Show that

$$\gamma_n(x+y) = \frac{1}{\beta}\sum_{j=1}^{n} \gamma_{n-j+1}(x)\,\gamma_j(y).$$

5. The random variable X has a generalised Pareto distribution with parameters $\alpha > 0$, $\lambda > 0$ and $k > 0$ if its density function is

$$f(x) = \frac{\Gamma(\alpha+k)\lambda^{\alpha}x^{k-1}}{\Gamma(\alpha)\Gamma(k)(\lambda+x)^{k+\alpha}}$$

for $x > 0$. Use the fact that the integral of this density function over $(0, \infty)$ equals 1 to find the first three moments of a $Pa(\alpha, \lambda)$ distribution, where $\alpha > 3$.

6. The random variable X has a $Pa(\alpha, \lambda)$ distribution. Let M be a positive constant. Show that

$$E[\min(X, M)] = \frac{\lambda}{\alpha-1}\left(1 - \left(\frac{\lambda}{\lambda+M}\right)^{\alpha-1}\right).$$

7. Use the technique of completing the square from Example 1.4 to show that when $X \sim N(\mu, \sigma^2)$, $M_X(t) = \exp\left\{\mu t + \frac{1}{2}\sigma^2 t^2\right\}$. Verify that $E[X] = \mu$ and $V[X] = \sigma^2$ by differentiating this moment generating function.

8. Let the random variable X have distribution function F given by

$$F(x) = \begin{cases} 0 & \text{for } x < 20 \\ (x+20)/80 & \text{for } 20 \le x < 40 \\ 1 & \text{for } x \ge 40 \end{cases}.$$

Calculate

(a) $\Pr(X \le 30)$,
(b) $\Pr(X = 40)$,
(c) $E[X]$ and
(d) $V[X]$.

9. The random variable X has a lognormal distribution with mean 100 and variance 30,000. Calculate
   (a) $E[\min(X, 250)]$,
   (b) $E[\max(0, X - 250)]$,
   (c) $V[\min(X, 250)]$ and
   (d) $E[X|X > 250]$.
10. Let $\{X_i\}_{i=1}^n$ be independent and identically distributed random variables. Find the distribution of $\sum_{i=1}^n X_i$ when
    (a) $X_1 \sim B(m, q)$ and
    (b) $X_1 \sim N(\mu, \sigma^2)$.
11. $\{X_i\}_{i=1}^4$ are independent and identically distributed random variables. X_1 has a geometric distribution with

$$\Pr(X_1 = x) = 0.75(0.25^x)$$

for $x = 0, 1, 2, \ldots$. Calculate $\Pr\left(\sum_{i=1}^4 X_i \leq 4\right)$
    (a) by finding the distribution of $\sum_{i=1}^4 X_i$ and
    (b) by applying the recursion formula of Section 1.6.3.
12. Let $\{X_i\}_{i=1}^n$ be independent and identically distributed random variables, each distributed on $m, m+1, m+2, \ldots$, where m is a positive integer.
    Let $S_n = \sum_{i=1}^n X_i$ and define $f_j = \Pr(X_1 = j)$ for $j = m, m+1, m+2, \ldots$ and $g_j = \Pr(S_n = j)$ for $j = mn, mn+1, mn+2, \ldots$. Show that

$$g_{mn} = f_m^n,$$

and for $r = mn + 1, mn + 2, mn + 3, \ldots$,

$$g_r = \frac{1}{f_m} \sum_{j=1}^{r-mn} \left(\frac{(n+1)j}{r - mn} - 1 \right) f_{j+m} g_{r-j}.$$

2
Utility Theory

2.1 Introduction

Utility theory is a subject which has many applications, particularly in economics. However, in this chapter we consider utility theory from an insurance perspective only. We start with a general discussion of utility, then introduce decision making, which is the key application of utility theory. We also describe some mathematical functions that might be applied as utility functions, and discuss their uses and limitations. The intention in this chapter is to provide a brief overview of key results in utility theory. Further applications of utility theory are discussed in Chapters 3 and 9.

2.2 Utility Functions

A utility function, $u(x)$, can be described as a function which measures the value, or utility, that an individual (or institution) attaches to the monetary amount x. Throughout this book we assume that a utility function satisfies the conditions

$$u'(x) > 0 \quad \text{and} \quad u''(x) < 0. \tag{2.1}$$

Mathematically, the first of these conditions says that u is an increasing function, while the second says that u is a concave function. Simply put, the first states that an individual whose utility function is u prefers amount y to amount z provided that $y > z$, i.e. the individual prefers more money to less! The second states that as the individual's wealth increases, the individual places less value on a fixed increase in wealth. For example, an increase in wealth of 1,000 is worth less to the individual if the individual's wealth is 2,000,000 compared to the case when the individual's wealth is 1,000,000.

An individual whose utility function satisfies the conditions in (2.1) is said to be risk averse, and risk aversion can be quantified through the coefficient of risk aversion defined by

$$r(x) = \frac{-u''(x)}{u'(x)}. \tag{2.2}$$

Utility theory can be used to explain why individuals are prepared to buy insurance, and to pay premiums which, by some criteria at least, are unfair. To illustrate why this is the case, consider the following situation. Most homeowners insure their homes against events such as fire on an annual basis. Although the risk of a home being destroyed by a fire in any year may be considered to be very small, the financial consequences of losing a home and all its contents in a fire could be devastating for a homeowner. Consequently, a homeowner may choose to pay a premium to an insurance company for insurance cover as the homeowner prefers a small certain loss (the premium) to the large loss that would occur if their home was destroyed, even though the probability of this event may be small. Indeed, a homeowner's preferences may be such that paying a premium that is larger than the expected loss may be preferable to not effecting insurance.

2.3 The Expected Utility Criterion

Decision making using a utility function is based on the expected utility criterion. This criterion says that a decision maker should calculate the expected utility of resulting wealth under each course of action, then select the course of action that gives the greatest value for expected utility of resulting wealth. If two courses of action yield the same expected utility of resulting wealth, then the decision maker has no preference between these two courses of action.

To illustrate this concept, let us consider an investor with utility function u who is choosing between two investments which will lead to random net gains of X_1 and X_2 respectively. Suppose that the investor has current wealth W, so that the result of investing in Investment i is $W + X_i$ for $i = 1$ and 2. Then, under the expected utility criterion, the investor would choose Investment 1 over Investment 2 if and only if

$$E\left[u(W+X_1)\right] > E\left[u(W+X_2)\right].$$

Further, the investor would be indifferent between the two investments if

$$E\left[u(W+X_1)\right] = E\left[u(W+X_2)\right].$$

Example 2.1 *Suppose that in the above discussion,* $u(x) = -\exp\{-0.002x\}$, $X_1 \sim N(10^4, 500^2)$ *and* $X_2 \sim N(1.1 \times 10^4, 2000^2)$. *Which of these investments does the investor prefer?*

Solution 2.1 *For Investment 1, the expected utility of resulting wealth is*

$$\begin{aligned} E[u(W+X_1)] &= -E\left[\exp\{-0.002(W+X_1)\}\right] \\ &= -\exp\{-0.002W\}E\left[\exp\{-0.002X_1\}\right] \\ &= -\exp\{-0.002W\}\exp\left\{-0.002 \times 10^4 + \tfrac{1}{2}0.002^2 \times 500^2\right\} \\ &= -\exp\{-0.002W\}\exp\{-19.5\}, \end{aligned}$$

where the third line follows from the fact that the expectation in the second line is $M_{X_1}(-0.002)$. *Similarly,*

$$E[u(W+X_2)] = -\exp\{-0.002W\}\exp\{-14\}.$$

Hence, the investor prefers Investment 1 as $E[u(W+X_1)]$ *is greater than* $E[u(W+X_2)]$.

Note that the expected utility criterion may lead to an outcome that is inconsistent with other criteria. This should not be surprising, as different criteria will, in general, lead to different decisions. For example, in Example 2.1 above, the investor did not choose the investment which gave the greater expected net gain.

We end this section by remarking that if a utility function v is defined in terms of a utility function u by $v(x) = au(x) + b$ for constants a and b, with $a > 0$, then decisions made under the expected utility criterion will be the same under v as under u since, for example,

$$E[v(W+X_1)] > E[v(W+X_2)]$$

if and only if

$$aE[u(W+X_1)] + b > aE[u(W+X_2)] + b.$$

2.4 Jensen's Inequality

Jensen's inequality is a well-known result in the field of probability theory. However, it also has important applications in actuarial science. Jensen's inequality states that if u is a concave function, then

$$E[u(X)] \le u(E[X]) \tag{2.3}$$

provided that these quantities exist.

We now prove Jensen's inequality on the assumption that there is a Taylor series expansion of u about the point a. Thus, writing the Taylor series expansion with a remainder term as

$$u(x) = u(a) + u'(a)(x-a) + u''(z)\frac{(x-a)^2}{2},$$

where z lies between a and x, and noting that $u''(z) < 0$, we have

$$u(x) \le u(a) + u'(a)(x-a). \tag{2.4}$$

Replacing x by the random variable X in equation (2.4) and setting $a = E[X]$, we obtain equation (2.3) by taking expected values.

We can use Jensen's inequality to obtain results relating to appropriate premium levels for insurance cover, from the viewpoint of both an individual and an insurer. Consider first an individual whose wealth is W. Suppose that the individual can obtain complete insurance protection against a random loss, X. Then the maximum premium that the individual is prepared to pay for this protection is P, where

$$u(W-P) = E\left[u(W-X)\right]. \tag{2.5}$$

This follows by the expected utility criterion and the fact that $u'(x) > 0$, so that for any premium $\bar{P} < P$,

$$u(W-\bar{P}) > u(W-P).$$

By Jensen's inequality,

$$E\left[u(W-X)\right] \le u\left(E\left[W-X\right]\right) = u\left(W - E\left[X\right]\right),$$

so by equation (2.5),

$$u(W-P) \le u\left(W-E\left[X\right]\right).$$

As u is an increasing function, it follows that $P \ge E[X]$. This result simply states that the maximum premium that the individual is prepared to pay is at least equal to the expected loss.

A similar line of argument applies from an insurer's viewpoint. Suppose that an insurer whose utility function is v and whose wealth is W is asked by an individual to provide complete insurance protection against a random loss, X. From the insurer's viewpoint, the minimum acceptable premium for this protection is Π, where

$$v(W) = E\left[v(W+\Pi-X)\right]. \tag{2.6}$$

This follows from the expected utility criterion, noting that the insurer is choosing between offering and not offering insurance. Also, as v is an increasing function, for any premium $\bar{\Pi} > \Pi$,

$$E\left[v(W+\bar{\Pi}-X)\right] > E\left[v(W+\Pi-X)\right].$$

Applying Jensen's inequality to the right-hand side of equation (2.6) we have

$$v(W) = E\left[v(W+\Pi-X)\right] \leq v\left(W+\Pi-E\left[X\right]\right),$$

and as v is an increasing function, $\Pi \geq E[X]$. Thus, the insurer requires a premium that is at least equal to the expected loss, and so an insurance contract is feasible when $P \geq \Pi$.

2.5 Types of Utility Function

It is possible to construct a utility function by assigning different values to different levels of wealth. For example, an individual might set $u(0) = 0$, $u(10) = 5$, $u(20) = 8$ and so on. Clearly it is more practical to assign values through a suitable mathematical function. Therefore, we now consider some mathematical functions which may be regarded as having suitable forms to be utility functions.

2.5.1 Exponential

A utility function of the form $u(x) = -\exp\{-\beta x\}$, where $\beta > 0$, is called an exponential utility function. An important feature of this utility function, which was in evidence in Example 2.1, is that decisions do not depend on the individual's wealth. To see this in general, consider the case of an individual with wealth W who has a choice between n courses of action. Suppose that the ith course of action will result in random wealth of $W + X_i$, for $i = 1, 2, \ldots, n$. Then, under the expected utility criterion, the individual would calculate $E[u(W + X_i)]$ for $i = 1, 2, \ldots, n$, and would choose course of action j if and only if

$$E[u(W+X_j)] > E[u(W+X_i)] \tag{2.7}$$

for $i = 1, 2, \ldots, n$, and $i \neq j$. Inserting for u in equation (2.7) this condition becomes

$$-E\left[\exp\{-\beta(W+X_j)\}\right] > -E\left[\exp\{-\beta(W+X_i)\}\right]$$

or, equivalently,

$$E\left[\exp\{-\beta X_j\}\right] < E[\exp\{-\beta X_i\}],$$

so that the individual's wealth, W, does not affect the decision. An appealing feature of decision making using an exponential utility function is that decisions are based on comparisons between moment generating functions. In a sense, these moment generating functions capture all the characteristics of the random outcomes being compared, so that comparisons are based on a range of features. This contrasts with other utility functions. For example, for the quadratic utility function discussed below, comparisons depend only on the first two moments of the random outcomes.

The maximum premium, P, that an individual with utility function $u(x) = -\exp\{-\beta x\}$ would be prepared to pay for insurance against a random loss, X, is

$$P = \beta^{-1} \log M_X(\beta), \tag{2.8}$$

a result that follows from equation (2.5).

Example 2.2 *Show that the maximum premium, P, that an individual with utility function $u(x) = -\exp\{-\beta x\}$ is prepared to pay for complete insurance cover against a random loss, X, where $X \sim N(\mu, \sigma^2)$, is an increasing function of β, and explain this result.*

Solution 2.2 *Since $X \sim N(\mu, \sigma^2)$, $M_X(\beta) = \exp\left\{\mu\beta + \frac{1}{2}\sigma^2\beta^2\right\}$, and hence by equation (2.8),*

$$P = \mu + \tfrac{1}{2}\sigma^2\beta,$$

so that P is an increasing function of β. To interpret this result, note that β is the coefficient of risk aversion under this exponential utility function, since

$$r(x) = -\frac{u''(x)}{u'(x)} = \beta,$$

independent of x. Thus, the more risk averse an individual is, i.e. the higher the value of β, the higher the value of P.

Example 2.3 *An individual is facing a random loss, X, where $X \sim \gamma(2, 0.01)$, and can obtain complete insurance cover against this loss for a premium of 208. The individual makes decisions on the basis of an exponential utility function with parameter 0.001. Is the individual prepared to insure for this premium?*

Solution 2.3 *The maximum premium the individual is prepared to pay is given by equation (2.8), with*

$$M_X(\beta) = \left(\frac{0.01}{0.01 - \beta}\right)^2$$

and $\beta = 0.001$. *Thus, the maximum premium is*

$$\frac{1}{0.001} \log\left(\frac{0.01}{0.009}\right)^2 = 210.72,$$

so that the individual would be prepared to pay a premium of 208.

2.5.2 Quadratic

A utility function of the form $u(x) = x - \beta x^2$, for $x < 1/(2\beta)$ and $\beta > 0$, is called a quadratic utility function. The use of this type of utility function is restricted by the constraint $x < 1/(2\beta)$, which is required to ensure that $u'(x) > 0$. Thus, we cannot apply the function to problems under which random outcomes are distributed on $(-\infty, \infty)$.

As indicated in the previous section, decisions made using a quadratic utility function depend only on the first two moments of the random outcomes, as illustrated in the following examples.

Example 2.4 *An individual whose wealth is* W *has a choice between Investments 1 and 2, which will result in wealth of* $W + X_1$ *and* $W + X_2$ *respectively, where* $E[X_1] = 10$, $V[X_1] = 2$ *and* $E[X_2] = 10.1$. *The individual makes decisions on the basis of a quadratic utility function with parameter* $\beta = 0.002$. *For what range of values for* $V[X_2]$ *will the individual choose Investment 1 when* $W = 200$? *Assume that* $\Pr(W + X_i < 250) = 1$ *for* $i = 1$ *and 2.*

Solution 2.4 *The individual will choose Investment 1 if and only if*

$$E\left[u(W + X_1)\right] > E\left[u(W + X_2)\right]$$

or, equivalently,

$$E\left[200 + X_1 - \beta\left(200 + X_1\right)^2\right] > E\left[200 + X_2 - \beta\left(200 + X_2\right)^2\right],$$

where $\beta = 0.002$. *After some straightforward algebra, this condition becomes*

$$E\left[X_1\right](1 - 400\beta) - \beta E\left[X_1^2\right] > E\left[X_2\right](1 - 400\beta) - \beta E\left[X_2^2\right]$$

or

$$E\left[X_2^2\right] > (E[X_2] - E[X_1])\left(\beta^{-1} - 400\right) + E\left[X_1^2\right] = 112,$$

which is equivalent to $V[X_2] > 9.99$.

Example 2.5 *An insurer is considering offering complete insurance cover against a random loss, X, where* $E[X] = V[X] = 100$ *and* $\Pr(X > 0) = 1$. *The insurer adopts the utility function* $u(x) = x - 0.001x^2$ *for decision making purposes. Calculate the minimum premium that the insurer would accept for this insurance cover when the insurer's wealth, W, is (a)* 100, *(b)* 200 *and (c)* 300.

Solution 2.5 *The minimum premium,* Π, *is given by*

$$u(W) = E[u(W + \Pi - X)],$$

so when $W = 100$, *we have*

$$\begin{aligned} u(100) &= 90 \\ &= E\left[100 + \Pi - X - 0.001\left((100+\Pi)^2 - 2(100+\Pi)X + X^2\right)\right] \\ &= 100 + \Pi - E[X] \\ &\quad -0.001\left((100+\Pi)^2 - 2(100+\Pi)E[X] + E\left[X^2\right]\right). \end{aligned}$$

This simplifies to

$$\Pi^2 - 1{,}000\Pi + 90{,}100 = 0,$$

which gives $\Pi = 100.13$. *Similarly, when* $W = 200$ *we find that* $\Pi = 100.17$, *and when* $W = 300$, $\Pi = 100.25$. *We note that* Π *increases as W increases, and that this is an undesirable property as we would expect that as the insurer's wealth increases, the insurer should be better placed to absorb random losses and hence should be able to reduce the minimum acceptable premium.*

2.5.3 Logarithmic

A utility function of the form $u(x) = \beta \log x$, for $x > 0$ and $\beta > 0$, is called a logarithmic utility function. As $u(x)$ is defined only for positive values of x, this utility function is unsuitable for use in situations where outcomes could lead to negative wealth.

Individuals who use a logarithmic utility function are risk averse since

$$u'(x) = \frac{\beta}{x} > 0 \quad \text{and} \quad u''(x) = \frac{-\beta}{x^2} < 0,$$

and the coefficient of risk aversion is thus

$$r(x) = \frac{1}{x},$$

so that risk aversion is a decreasing function of wealth.

Example 2.6 *An investor who makes decisions on the basis of a logarithmic utility function is considering investing in shares of one of n companies. The investor has wealth B, and investment in shares of company i will result in wealth BX_i, for $i = 1, 2, \ldots, n$. Show that the investment decision is independent of B.*

Solution 2.6 *The investor prefers the shares of company i to those of company j if and only if*

$$E\left[u(BX_i)\right] > E\left[u(BX_j)\right].$$

Now

$$E\left[u(BX_i)\right] = E\left[\beta \log\left(BX_i\right)\right] = \beta E\left[\log B\right] + \beta E\left[\log X_i\right],$$

so the investor prefers the shares of company i to those of company j if and only if

$$E\left[\log X_i\right] > E\left[\log X_j\right],$$

independent of B.

The solution to the above example highlights a major difficulty in using a logarithmic utility function, namely that, in general, it is difficult to find closed form expressions for quantities like $E[\log X]$. A notable exception is when X has a lognormal distribution.

2.5.4 Fractional Power

A utility function of the form $u(x) = x^\beta$, for $x > 0$ and $0 < \beta < 1$, is called a fractional power utility function. As with a logarithmic utility function, $u(x)$ is defined only for positive x, and so its applications are limited in the same way as for a logarithmic utility function.

Example 2.7 *An individual is facing a random loss, X, that is uniformly distributed on* $(0, 200)$. *The individual can buy partial insurance cover against this loss under which the individual would pay* $Y = \min(X, 100)$, *so that the individual would pay the loss in full if the loss was less than 100, and would pay 100 otherwise. The individual makes decisions using the utility function* $u(x) = x^{2/5}$. *Is the individual prepared to pay 80 for this partial insurance cover if the individual's wealth is 300?*

Solution 2.7 *The individual is prepared to pay 80 for this partial insurance cover if*

$$E[u(300 - X)] \le E[u(300 - 80 - Y)]$$

since the individual is choosing between not insuring (resulting in wealth of $300 - X$*) and insuring, in which case the resulting wealth is a random variable as the individual is buying partial insurance cover. Noting that the density function of* X *is* $1/200$*, we have*

$$\begin{aligned} E[u(300 - X)] &= \tfrac{1}{200} \int_0^{200} (300 - x)^{2/5}\, dx \\ &= \tfrac{-5}{200\times 7} (300 - x)^{7/5} \Big|_0^{200} \\ &= 8.237 \end{aligned}$$

and

$$\begin{aligned} E[u(300 - 80 - Y)] &= \tfrac{1}{200} \left(\int_0^{100} (220 - x)^{2/5}\, dx + \int_{100}^{200} 120^{2/5} dx \right) \\ &= \tfrac{1}{200} \left(\tfrac{-5}{7} (220 - x)^{7/5} \Big|_0^{100} + 100 \times 120^{2/5} \right) \\ &= 7.280. \end{aligned}$$

Hence the individual is not prepared to pay 80 for this partial insurance cover.

As with the logarithmic utility function, it is generally difficult to obtain closed form solutions in problems involving fractional power utility functions.

2.6 Notes and References

A comprehensive reference on utility theory is Gerber and Pafumi (1998), which discusses applications in both risk theory and finance. For a more general discussion of the economics of insurance, including applications of utility theory, see Borch (1990).

2.7 Exercises

1. An insurer, whose current wealth is W, uses the utility function

$$u(x) = x - \frac{x^2}{2\beta},$$

where $x < \beta$ and $\beta > 0$, for decision making purposes. Show that the insurer is risk averse, and that the insurer's coefficient of risk aversion, $r(x)$, is an increasing function of x.

2. An individual is facing a random loss, X, which is uniformly distributed on $(0, 200)$. The individual can purchase partial insurance cover under which the insurer will pay $\max(0, X - 20)$, and the premium for this cover is 85. The individual has wealth 250 and makes decisions on the basis of the utility function $u(x) = x^{2/3}$ for $x > 0$.

   (a) Show that the individual is risk averse.
   (b) Will the individual purchase insurance cover?

3. An insurer has been asked to provide complete insurance cover against a random loss, X, where $X \sim N(10^6, 10^8)$. Calculate the minimum premium that the insurer would accept if the insurer bases decisions on the utility function $u(x) = -\exp\{-0.002x\}$.
4. An investor makes decisions on the basis of the utility function $u(x) = \sqrt{x}$ where $x > 0$. The investor is considering investing in shares, and assumes that an investment of A in share i will accumulate to AX_i at the end of one year, where X_i has a lognormal distribution with parameters μ_i and σ_i. Suppose that the investor has a choice between Share 1 and Share 2.

   (a) Show that the decision whether to invest in Share 1 or in Share 2 is independent of A.
   (b) Suppose that for Share 1, $\mu_1 = 0.09$ and $\sigma_1 = 0.02$, and for Share 2, $\mu_2 = 0.08$. For what range of values for σ_2 will the investor choose to invest in Share 2?
   (c) Now suppose that the expected accumulation is the same under each share but the variance of the accumulation is smaller for Share 1. Show that the investor will choose Share 1 and give an interpretation of this result.

5. An insurer has offered an individual insurance cover against a random loss, X, where X has a mixed distribution with distribution function F given by

$$F(x) = \begin{cases} 0 & \text{for } x < 0 \\ 1 - 0.2e^{-0.01x} & \text{for } x \geq 0 \end{cases}.$$

   The insurance cover includes a policy excess of 20. Calculate the minimum premium that the insurer would accept if the insurer bases decisions on the utility function $u(x) = -\exp\{-0.005x\}$.
6. An individual is about to take a vacation in a very remote and exotic island which does not have a hospital, but does have a private air ambulance service to a mainland hospital. The individual models his potential

hospitalisation costs on this vacation as a mixed random variable, X, with $\Pr(X = 0) = 0.99$, and for $10,000 \le x \le 12,000$,

$$\Pr(X \le x) = 0.99 + \frac{x - 10,000}{200,000}.$$

The individual approaches an insurance company which offers him either

- complete insurance protection for a premium of 120 or
- partial insurance cover, under which the individual would have a policy excess of 1,000, for a premium of 115.

The individual has wealth 10^6 and uses the logarithmic utility function $u(x) = k \log x$ for decision making purposes. Assuming that hospitalisation would end the vacation, which, if either, of these insurance policies would the individual choose?

3

Principles of Premium Calculation

3.1 Introduction

Although we have previously used the term *premium*, we have not formally defined it. A premium is the payment that a policyholder makes for complete or partial insurance cover against a risk. In this chapter we describe and discuss some ways in which premiums may be calculated, but we consider premium calculation from a mathematical viewpoint only. In practice, insurers have to take account not only of the characteristics of risks they are insuring, but also of other factors such as the premiums charged by their competitors.

We denote by Π_X the premium that an insurer charges to cover a risk X. When we refer to a risk X, what we mean is that claims from this risk are distributed as the random variable X. The premium Π_X is some function of X, and a rule that assigns a numerical value to Π_X is referred to as a premium calculation principle. Thus, a premium principle is of the form $\Pi_X = \phi(X)$ where ϕ is some function. In this chapter we start by describing some desirable properties of premium calculation principles. We then list some principles and consider which of the desirable properties they satisfy.

3.2 Properties of Premium Principles

There are many desirable properties for premium calculation principles. The following list is not exhaustive, but it does include most of the basic properties for premium principles.

(1) *Non-negative loading*. This property requires that $\Pi_X \geq E[X]$, i.e. that the premium should not be less than the expected claims. In Chapter 7 we will see the importance of this property in the context of ruin theory.
(2) *Additivity*. This property requires that if X_1 and X_2 are independent risks, then the premium for the combined risk, denoted $\Pi_{X_1+X_2}$, should equal

$\Pi_{X_1} + \Pi_{X_2}$. If this property is satisfied, then there is no advantage, to either an individual or an insurer, in combining risks or splitting them, as the total premium does not alter under such courses of action.

(3) *Scale invariance*. This property requires that if $Z = aX$ where $a > 0$, then $\Pi_Z = a\Pi_X$. As an example of how this might apply, imagine that the currency of Great Britain changes from sterling to Euros with one pound sterling being converted to a Euros. Then, if a British insurer uses a scale invariant premium principle, a premium of 100 pounds sterling would change to $100a$ Euros.

(4) *Consistency*. This property requires that if $Y = X+c$ where $c > 0$, then we should have $\Pi_Y = \Pi_X + c$. Thus, if the distribution of Y is the distribution of X shifted by c units, then the premium for risk Y should be that for risk X increased by c.

(5) *No ripoff*. This property requires that if there is a (finite) maximum claim amount for the risk, say, x_m, then we should have $\Pi_X \leq x_m$. If this condition is not satisfied, then there is no incentive for an individual to effect insurance.

3.3 Examples of Premium Principles

3.3.1 The Pure Premium Principle

The pure premium principle sets

$$\Pi_X = E[X].$$

Thus, the pure premium is equal to the insurer's expected claims under the risk.

From an insurer's point of view, the pure premium principle is not a very attractive one. The premium covers the expected claims from the risk and contains no loading for profit or against an adverse claims experience. It is unlikely that an insurer who calculates premiums by this principle will remain in business very long. In the examples given below, the premium will exceed the pure premium, and the excess over the pure premium is referred to as the premium loading.

It is a straightforward exercise to show that the pure premium principle satisfies all five properties in Section 3.2.

3.3.2 The Expected Value Principle

The expected value principle sets

$$\Pi_X = (1+\theta)E[X],$$

where $\theta > 0$ is referred to as the premium loading factor. The loading in the premium is thus $\theta E[X]$.

The expected value principle is a very simple one. However, its major deficiency is that it assigns the same premium to all risks with the same mean. Intuitively, risks with identical means but different variances should have different premiums.

The expected value principle satisfies the non-negative loading property since $(1+\theta)E[X] \geq E[X]$. (Strictly this requires that $E[X] \geq 0$, but this is invariably the case in practice.) Similarly, the principle is additive since

$$(1+\theta)E[X_1+X_2] = (1+\theta)E[X_1] + (1+\theta)E[X_2]$$

and is scale invariant since for $Z = aX$,

$$\begin{aligned}\Pi_Z &= (1+\theta)E[Z] \\ &= a(1+\theta)E[X] \\ &= a\Pi_X.\end{aligned}$$

The expected value principle is not consistent, since for $Y = X + c$,

$$\Pi_Y = (1+\theta)(E[X]+c) > \Pi_X + c.$$

An alternative way of showing that a premium calculation principle does not satisfy a particular property is to construct a counter example. Thus, we can see that the no ripoff property is not satisfied by letting $\Pr(X = b) = 1$ where $b > 0$. Then as $\theta > 0$, $\Pi_X = (1+\theta)b > b$.

3.3.3 The Variance Principle

Motivated by the fact that the expected value principle takes account only of the expected claims, the variance principle sets

$$\Pi_X = E[X] + \alpha V[X],$$

where $\alpha > 0$. Thus, the loading in this premium is proportional to $V[X]$.

Since $\alpha > 0$, the variance principle clearly has a non-negative loading. The principle is additive since $V[X_1+X_2] = V[X_1] + V[X_2]$ when X_1 and X_2 are independent, so that

$$\begin{aligned}\Pi_{X_1+X_2} &= E[X_1+X_2] + \alpha V[X_1+X_2] \\ &= E[X_1] + E[X_2] + \alpha V[X_1] + \alpha V[X_2] \\ &= \Pi_{X_1} + \Pi_{X_2}.\end{aligned}$$

The principle is also consistent since for $Y = X + c$, $V[Y] = V[X]$, and so

$$\begin{aligned}\Pi_Y &= E[Y] + \alpha V[Y] \\ &= E[X] + c + \alpha V[X] \\ &= \Pi_X + c.\end{aligned}$$

However, the variance principle is not scale invariant since for $Z = aX$,

$$\begin{aligned}\Pi_Z &= E[Z] + \alpha V[Z] \\ &= aE[X] + \alpha a^2 V[X] \\ &\neq a\Pi_X,\end{aligned}$$

nor does it satisfy the no ripoff property. To see this, let

$$\Pr(X = 8) = \Pr(X = 12) = 0.5.$$

Then $E[X] = 10$ and $V[X] = 4$. Hence $\Pi_X = 10 + 4\alpha$, which exceeds 12 when $\alpha > 0.5$.

3.3.4 The Standard Deviation Principle

The standard deviation principle sets

$$\Pi_X = E[X] + \alpha V[X]^{1/2},$$

where $\alpha > 0$. Thus, under this premium principle, the loading is proportional to the standard deviation of X. Although the motivation for the standard deviation principle is the same as for the variance principle, these two principles have different properties.

As in the case of the variance principle, as $\alpha > 0$ the standard deviation principle clearly has a non-negative loading. The principle is consistent since for $Y = X + c$,

$$\begin{aligned}\Pi_Y &= E[Y] + \alpha V[Y]^{1/2} \\ &= E[X] + c + \alpha V[X]^{1/2} \\ &= \Pi_X + c,\end{aligned}$$

and is scale invariant since for $Z = aX$,

$$\begin{aligned}\Pi_Z &= E[Z] + \alpha V[Z]^{1/2} \\ &= aE[X] + \alpha a V[X]^{1/2} \\ &= a\Pi_X.\end{aligned}$$

The standard deviation principle is not additive since standard deviations are not additive, nor does it satisfy the no ripoff condition. This final point can be seen by considering the example at the end of the discussion on the variance principle.

3.3.5 The Principle of Zero Utility

Suppose that the insurer has utility function $u(x)$ such that $u'(x) > 0$ and $u''(x) < 0$. The principle of zero utility sets

$$u(W) = E[u(W + \Pi_X - X)], \tag{3.1}$$

where W is the insurer's surplus. Thus, the premium will in general depend on the insurer's surplus. An exception is when the utility function is exponential, i.e. $u(x) = -\exp\{-\beta x\}$, where $\beta > 0$. In this case equation (3.1) yields

$$\Pi_X = \beta^{-1} \log E[\exp\{\beta X\}], \tag{3.2}$$

and we refer to the premium principle as the exponential principle.

The exponential principle is an attractive one as it is based on the moment generating function of X and hence incorporates more information about X than any of the principles discussed so far.

The principle of zero utility satisfies the non-negative loading property since

$$u(W) = E[u(W + \Pi_X - X)] \le u(W + \Pi_X - E[X])$$

(by Jensen's inequality). Since $u'(x) > 0$, we have $\Pi_X \ge E[X]$. The principle is consistent since for $Y = X + c$, Π_Y is given by

$$u(W) = E[u(W + \Pi_Y - Y)]$$

and

$$E[u(W + \Pi_Y - Y)] = E[u(W + \Pi_Y - c - X)],$$

so that $\Pi_Y - c = \Pi_X$. The no ripoff property is also satisfied since

$$W + \Pi_X - X \ge W + \Pi_X - x_m,$$

and so

$$u(W) = E[u(W + \Pi_X - X)] \ge E[u(W + \Pi_X - x_m)] = u(W + \Pi_X - x_m).$$

As $u'(x) > 0$, we have $\Pi_X - x_m \le 0$.

In general, the principle of zero utility is not additive (see Exercise 3), but the exponential principle is. This latter statement follows by noting that equation (3.2) gives

$$\begin{aligned}\Pi_{X_1+X_2} &= \beta^{-1}\log E[\exp\{\beta\,(X_1+X_2)\}]\\ &= \beta^{-1}\log E\left[\exp\{\beta X_1\}\right]E\left[\exp\{\beta X_2\}\right]\\ &= \beta^{-1}\log E\left[\exp\{\beta X_1\}\right]+\beta^{-1}\log E\left[\exp\{\beta X_2\}\right]\\ &= \Pi_{X_1}+\Pi_{X_2},\end{aligned}$$

where the second line follows by the independence of X_1 and X_2.

The principle of zero utility is not scale invariant, as the following example illustrates. Suppose that $u(x) = -\exp\{-\beta x\}$, $X \sim N(\mu, \sigma^2)$, and $Y = \alpha X$ where $\alpha > 0$. Then

$$\Pi_X = \beta^{-1}\log E[\exp\{\beta X\}] = \mu + \tfrac{1}{2}\sigma^2\beta,$$

and so

$$\Pi_Y = \mu\alpha + \tfrac{1}{2}\sigma^2\beta\alpha^2 \neq \alpha\Pi_X.$$

3.3.6 The Esscher Premium Principle

The Esscher premium principle sets

$$\Pi_X = \frac{E[Xe^{hX}]}{E[e^{hX}]},$$

where $h > 0$.

We can interpret the Esscher premium as being the pure premium for a risk $\tilde{X}$ that is related to X as follows. Suppose that X is a continuous random variable on $(0, \infty)$ with density function f, and define the function g by

$$g(x) = \frac{e^{hx}f(x)}{\int_0^\infty e^{hy}f(y)dy}. \tag{3.3}$$

Then g is the density function of a random variable $\tilde{X}$ which has distribution function

$$G(x) = \frac{\int_0^x e^{hy}f(y)dy}{M_X(h)}.$$

The distribution function G is known as the Esscher transform of F with parameter h. As

$$M_{\tilde{X}}(t) = \int_0^\infty e^{tx}g\,(x)\,dx,$$

equation (3.3) yields

$$M_{\tilde{X}}(t) = \frac{M_X(t+h)}{M_X(h)}.$$

Example 3.1 *Let $F(x) = 1-\exp\{-\lambda x\}$, $x \geq 0$. What is the Esscher transform of F with parameter h, where $h < \lambda$?*

Solution 3.1 *When $X \sim F$, $M_X(t) = \lambda/(\lambda - t)$, and so*

$$M_{\tilde{X}}(t) = \frac{M_X(t+h)}{M_X(h)} = \frac{\lambda - h}{\lambda - h - t},$$

so that the Esscher transform of F is $G(x) = 1 - \exp\{-(\lambda - h)x\}$.

The density g is just a weighted version of the density f since we can write equation (3.3) as $g(x) = w(x)f(x)$ where $w(x) = e^{hx}/M_X(h)$. As $h > 0$, $w'(x) > 0$, and so increasing weight attaches as x increases. From Example 3.1, it follows that the Esscher transform with parameter $h = 0.2$ of the density $f(x) = e^{-x}$ is $g(x) = 0.8e^{-0.8x}$, and these functions are shown in Figure 3.1. Note that initially the density g is below the density f, but in the tail the opposite is true, so that the transform results in a density with a fatter tail.

In the context of premium calculation, the relationship

$$M_{\tilde{X}}(t) = \frac{M_X(t+h)}{M_X(h)}$$

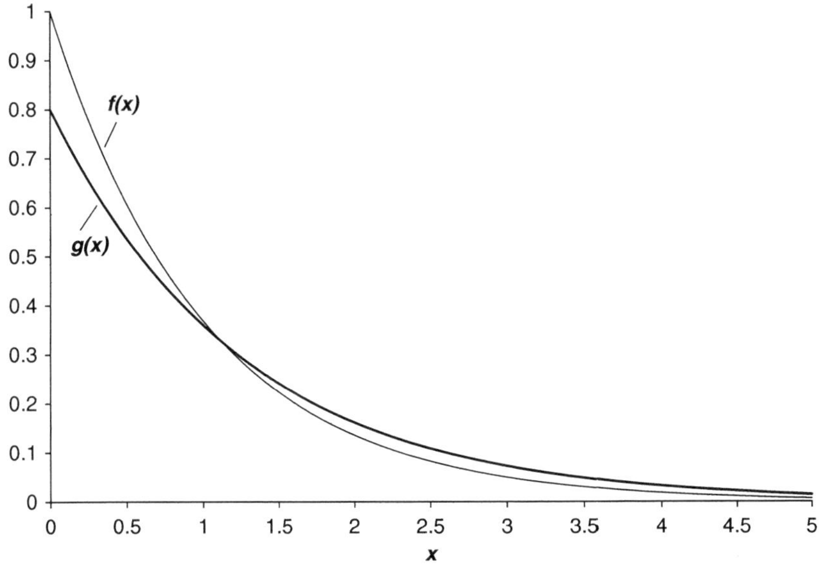

Figure 3.1 Exponential density, f, and its Esscher transform, g.

is important since

$$E[\tilde{X}] = \frac{\int_0^\infty xe^{hx}f(x)dx}{\int_0^\infty e^{hx}f(x)dx} = \frac{E[Xe^{hX}]}{E[e^{hX}]} = \Pi_X,$$

i.e. the mean of $\tilde{X}$ gives the Esscher premium Π_X.

Example 3.2 *Let X be exponentially distributed with mean 1. Find Π_X under the Esscher premium principle with parameter $h < 1$.*

Solution 3.2 *From Example 3.1, it follows that the Esscher transform of this exponential distribution is the exponential distribution with parameter $1 - h$, and the Esscher premium is the mean of this distribution, i.e.,*

$$\Pi_X = \frac{1}{1-h}.$$

The Esscher principle satisfies the non-negative loading property. This can be seen by first noting that when $h = 0$, $M_{\tilde{X}}(t) = M_X(t)$ and so $E[\tilde{X}] = \Pi_X = E[X]$. Next, for $h \geq 0$,

$$\begin{aligned} E[\tilde{X}^r] &= \frac{d^r}{dt^r} M_{\tilde{X}}(t)\Big|_{t=0} \\ &= \frac{d^r}{dt^r} \frac{M_X(t+h)}{M_X(h)}\Bigg|_{t=0} \\ &= \frac{M_X^{(r)}(h)}{M_X(h)}, \end{aligned}$$

and so

$$\begin{aligned} \frac{d}{dh}\Pi_X &= \frac{d}{dh}E[\tilde{X}] \\ &= \frac{d}{dh}\frac{M_X'(h)}{M_X(h)} \\ &= \frac{1}{M_X(h)^2}\left(M_X^{(2)}(h)M_X(h) - M_X'(h)^2\right) \\ &= E[\tilde{X}^2] - E[\tilde{X}]^2 \geq 0. \end{aligned}$$

Hence Π_X is a non-decreasing function of h and so $\Pi_X \geq E[X]$ for all $h \geq 0$. Note that Example 3.2 above gives an illustration of this.

The Esscher principle is consistent since for $Y = X + c$,

$$\begin{aligned} \Pi_Y &= \frac{E\left[Ye^{hY}\right]}{E\left[e^{hY}\right]} \\ &= \frac{E\left[(X+c)e^{h(X+c)}\right]}{E\left[e^{h(X+c)}\right]} \end{aligned}$$

$$= \frac{E\left[Xe^{hX}\right]e^{hc} + cE\left[e^{hX}\right]e^{hc}}{E\left[e^{hX}\right]e^{hc}}$$
$$= \frac{E\left[Xe^{hX}\right]}{E\left[e^{hX}\right]} + c$$
$$= \Pi_X + c.$$

The principle is also additive since

$$\Pi_{X_1+X_2} = \frac{E\left[(X_1+X_2)\,e^{h(X_1+X_2)}\right]}{E\left[e^{h(X_1+X_2)}\right]}$$
$$= \frac{E\left[X_1e^{hX_1}\right]E\left[e^{hX_2}\right] + E\left[e^{hX_1}\right]E\left[X_2e^{hX_2}\right]}{E\left[e^{hX_1}\right]E\left[e^{hX_2}\right]}$$
$$= \frac{E\left[X_1e^{hX_1}\right]}{E\left[e^{hX_1}\right]} + \frac{E\left[X_2e^{hX_2}\right]}{E\left[e^{hX_2}\right]}$$
$$= \Pi_{X_1} + \Pi_{X_2}.$$

The no ripoff condition is also satisfied since if x_m is the largest possible claim amount, so that $\Pr(X \le x_m) = 1$, then

$$Xe^{hX} \le x_m e^{hX},$$

and so

$$\Pi_X = \frac{E\left[Xe^{hX}\right]}{E\left[e^{hX}\right]} \le \frac{E\left[x_m e^{hX}\right]}{E\left[e^{hX}\right]} = x_m.$$

The Esscher principle is not, however, scale invariant. To see this, let us now denote the Esscher premium with parameter h for a risk X as $\Pi_X(h)$. Then if $Z = aX$, the Esscher premium for Z is $\Pi_Z(h)$ where

$$\Pi_Z(h) = \frac{E[Ze^{hZ}]}{E[e^{hZ}]} = \frac{aE[Xe^{ahX}]}{E[e^{ahX}]} = a\Pi_X(ah) \ne a\Pi_X(h).$$

Thus, $\Pi_Z(h) \ne a\Pi_X(h)$ unless $a = 1$.

3.3.7 The Risk Adjusted Premium Principle

Let X be a non-negative valued random variable with distribution function F. Then the risk adjusted premium principle sets

$$\Pi_X = \int_0^\infty [\Pr(X > x)]^{1/\rho} dx = \int_0^\infty [1 - F(x)]^{1/\rho} dx,$$

where $\rho \ge 1$ is known as the risk index.

The essence of this principle is similar to that of the Esscher principle. The Esscher transform weights the distribution of X, giving increasing weight to (right) tail probabilities. The risk adjusted premium is also based on a transform, as follows. Define the distribution function H of a non-negative random variable X^* by

$$1 - H(x) = [1 - F(x)]^{1/\rho}.$$

Since

$$E[X^*] = \int_0^\infty [1 - H(x)]dx,$$

it follows that $\Pi_X = E[X^*]$.

Example 3.3 *Let X be exponentially distributed with mean $1/\lambda$. Find the risk adjusted premium Π_X.*

Solution 3.3 *We have*

$$1 - F(x) = e^{-\lambda x},$$

and so

$$1 - H(x) = e^{-\lambda x/\rho}.$$

Thus, X^* has an exponential distribution with mean ρ/λ, and so $\Pi_X = \rho/\lambda$.

Example 3.4 *Let $X \sim Pa(\alpha, \lambda)$. Find the risk adjusted premium Π_X.*

Solution 3.4 *We have*

$$1 - F(x) = \left(\frac{\lambda}{\lambda + x}\right)^\alpha,$$

and so

$$1 - H(x) = \left(\frac{\lambda}{\lambda + x}\right)^{\alpha/\rho}.$$

Thus, $X^* \sim Pa(\alpha/\rho, \lambda)$, and hence $\Pi_X = \rho\lambda/(\alpha - \rho)$ provided that $\rho < \alpha$.

When X is a continuous random variable with density function f, the density function of X^* is h where

$$h(x) = \frac{1}{\rho}[1 - F(x)]^{(1/\rho)-1}f(x), \tag{3.4}$$

so that the density function of X^* is simply a weighted version of the density function of X. The weight attaching to f increases as x increases – see Exercise 7. Figure 3.2 shows the densities f and h from Example 3.4 when $\alpha = 2$, $\lambda = 1$ and $\rho = 1.5$. The density h is initially below the density f, but

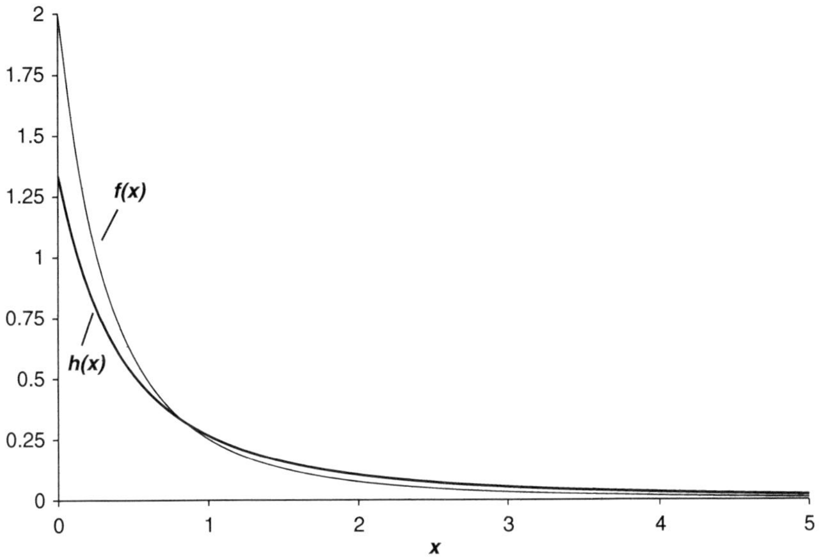

Figure 3.2 $Pa(2, 1)$ density, f, and its weighted version, h.

as x increases, this changes so that, as with the Esscher transform, the transformed density has a fatter tail.

The risk adjusted premium principle satisfies all properties listed in Section 3.2 except additivity. To see that $\Pi_X \geq E[X]$, note that since $\rho \geq 1$, we have

$$1 - F(x) \leq [1 - F(x)]^{1/\rho}$$

for all $x > 0$, and since

$$E[X] = \int_0^\infty [1 - F(x)]dx,$$

it follows that $\Pi_X \geq E[X]$. Consistency can be shown by noting that if Y is defined by $Y = X + c$, then

$$\Pr(Y > x) = \begin{cases} 1 & \text{for } x < c \\ 1 - F(x - c) & \text{for } x \geq c \end{cases} .$$

Then

$$\begin{aligned} \Pi_Y &= \int_0^\infty [\Pr(Y > x)]^{1/\rho}\, dx \\ &= \int_0^c dx + \int_c^\infty [1 - F(x - c)]^{1/\rho} dx \end{aligned}$$

$$= c + \int_0^\infty [1 - F(y)]^{1/\rho} dy$$
$$= c + \Pi_X.$$

The scale invariance of the principle follows by noting that if $Z = aX$, then

$$\Pr(Z > x) = \Pr(X > x/a),$$

so that

$$\begin{aligned}\Pi_Z &= \int_0^\infty [\Pr(Z > x)]^{1/\rho}\, dx \\ &= \int_0^\infty [\Pr(X > x/a)]^{1/\rho}\, dx \\ &= a\int_0^\infty [\Pr(X > y)]^{1/\rho}\, dy \\ &= a\Pi_X.\end{aligned}$$

The no ripoff property is satisfied since if x_m is such that $F(x_m) = 1$, then

$$\Pi_X = \int_0^{x_m} [1 - F(x)]^{1/\rho} dx \leq \int_0^{x_m} dx = x_m.$$

We can show that the additivity property does not hold by considering two independent and identically distributed risks, X_1 and X_2, with

$$\Pr(X_1 = 0) = \Pr(X_1 = 1) = 0.5.$$

Let the risk index be $\rho = 2$. Then $\Pi_{X_1} = \Pi_{X_2} = 0.5^{1/2}$ and $\Pi_{X_1+X_2} = 0.5$ $(1 + 3^{1/2})$, and a simple calculation shows that $\Pi_{X_1} + \Pi_{X_2} > \Pi_{X_1+X_2}$.

3.4 Notes and References

Which premium principle should an insurer use? We have so far avoided this question simply because there is no one correct answer. The discussion in the previous section shows that some premium principles have a greater number of desirable properties than others. Even though mathematical considerations alone are unlikely to determine the premium an insurer charges to cover a risk, it would be reasonable for an insurer to decide which properties are relevant for a given risk, and to select a principle which satisfies these properties.

Other examples of premium principles and desirable properties for premium principles can be found in the actuarial literature, in particular in Goovaerts et al. (1984). Bühlmann (1980) derives the Esscher principle using economic arguments, while Gerber (1979) discusses properties of the exponential principle in some detail. In particular, he shows that the principle of zero utility is additive if and only if it is the net premium principle or the exponential principle. Properties of the risk adjusted premium principle are discussed at length by Wang (1995).

3.5 Exercises

1. A premium principle is said to be sub-additive if for two risks X_1 and X_2 (which may be dependent), $\Pi_{X_1+X_2} \leq \Pi_{X_1} + \Pi_{X_2}$. Under what conditions is the variance principle sub-additive?
2. The mean value principle states that the premium, Π_X, for a risk X is given by

$$\Pi_X = v^{-1}\left(E[v(X)]\right),$$

where v is a function such that $v'(x) > 0$ and $v''(x) \geq 0$ for $x > 0$.

   (a) Calculate Π_X when $v(x) = x^2$ and $X \sim \gamma(2, 2)$.
   (b) Construct a counter example to show that this principle is not consistent.
3. Let X_1 have probability function

$$\Pr(X_1 = 80) = 0.5 = 1 - \Pr(X_1 = 120),$$

and let X_2 have probability function

$$\Pr(X_2 = 90) = 0.6 = 1 - \Pr(X_2 = 120).$$

An insurer has wealth 300 and calculates premiums using the principle of zero utility with utility function

$$u(x) = x - 0.001x^2$$

for $x < 500$. Calculate Π_{X_1}, Π_{X_2} and $\Pi_{X_1+X_2}$ and hence verify that the principle of zero utility is not additive in general.
4. Let F be the distribution function of a random variable distributed as $P(\lambda)$. What is the Esscher transform of F with parameter h?
5. Let $X \sim \gamma(2, 0.01)$. Given that $\Pi_X = 250$ and that Π_X has been calculated by the Esscher principle with parameter h, calculate h.
6. Let X be uniformly distributed on $(5, 15)$. Calculate Π_X using the risk adjusted premium principle with risk index 1.2.
7. Consider the risk adjusted premium principle and equation (3.4). Show that the weight attaching to f is an increasing function of x when $\rho > 1$.

8. Let Y have a shifted Pareto distribution with distribution function

$$F(x) = 1 - \frac{10^4}{x^2}$$

for $x > 100$. If the risk adjusted premium for this risk is 400, what is the value of ρ?

9. The premium for a risk X is calculated by the exponential principle with parameter β. Let $\Pi_X(\beta)$ denote this premium.
   (a) Show that $\lim_{\beta \to 0+} \Pi'_X(\beta) = \frac{1}{2}V[X]$ and
   (b) Show that $(\beta^2 \Pi'_X(\beta))' > 0$, and hence deduce that $\Pi_X(\beta)$ is an increasing function of β. (Hint: apply results about Esscher transforms.)

4
The Collective Risk Model

4.1 Introduction

In this chapter we consider the aggregate claims arising from a general insurance risk over a short period of time, typically one year. We use the term 'risk' to describe a collection of similar policies, although the term could also apply to an individual policy. As indicated in Chapter 1, at the start of a period of insurance cover the insurer does not know how many claims will occur and, if claims do occur, what the amounts of these claims will be. It is therefore necessary to construct a model that takes account of these two sources of variability. In the following, we consider claims arising over a one year time interval purely for ease of presentation, but any unit of time can be used.

We start by modelling aggregate claims in Section 4.2 as a random variable, S, and derive expressions for the distribution function and moments of S. We then consider the important special case when the distribution of S is compound Poisson, and we give an important result concerning the sum of independent compound Poisson random variables. In Section 4.4 we consider the effect of reinsurance on aggregate claims, from the point of view of both the insurer and the reinsurer.

The remainder of the chapter is devoted to the important practical question of calculating an aggregate claims distribution. In Section 4.5 we introduce certain classes of counting distribution for the number of claims from a risk. The importance of these classes is that if we assume that individual claims under the risk are modelled as discrete random variables, it is then possible to calculate the probability function for aggregate claims recursively. We conclude the chapter by describing two methods of approximating an aggregate claims distribution.

4.2 The Model

We define the random variable S to be the aggregate (i.e. total) amount of claims arising from a risk in one year. Let the random variable N denote the number of claims from the risk in this year, and let the random variable X_i denote the amount of the ith claim. The aggregate claim amount is just the sum of individual claim amounts, so we can write

$$S = \sum_{i=1}^{N} X_i$$

with the understanding that $S = 0$ when $N = 0$. (If there are no claims, the aggregate claim amount is trivially zero.) Throughout this chapter, we model individual claim amounts as non-negative random variables with a positive mean.

We now make two important assumptions. First, we assume that $\{X_i\}_{i=1}^{\infty}$ is a sequence of independent and identically distributed random variables, and, second, we assume that the random variable N is independent of $\{X_i\}_{i=1}^{\infty}$. These assumptions say that the amount of any claim does not depend on the amount of any other claim, and that the distribution of claim amounts does not change throughout the year. They also state that the number of claims has no effect on the amounts of claims.

Typically, our risk is a portfolio of insurance policies, and the name *collective risk model* arises from the fact that we consider the risk as a whole. In particular, we are counting the number of claims from the portfolio, and not from individual policies.

4.2.1 The Distribution of S

We start with some notation. Let $G(x) = \Pr(S \le x)$ denote the distribution function of aggregate claims, $F(x) = \Pr(X_1 \le x)$ denote the distribution function of individual claim amounts, and let $p_n = \Pr(N = n)$, so that $\{p_n\}_{n=0}^{\infty}$ is the probability function for the number of claims.

We can derive the distribution function of S by noting that the event $\{S \le x\}$ occurs if n claims occur, $n = 0, 1, 2, \ldots$, and if the sum of these n claims is no more than x. Thus, we can represent the event $\{S \le x\}$ as the union of the mutually exclusive events $\{S \le x \text{ and } N = n\}$, so that

$$\{S \le x\} = \bigcup_{n=0}^{\infty} \{S \le x \text{ and } N = n\},$$

so that

$$G(x) = \Pr(S \le x) = \sum_{n=0}^{\infty} \Pr(S \le x \text{ and } N = n).$$

Now

$$\Pr(S \le x \text{ and } N = n) = \Pr(S \le x \mid N = n) \Pr(N = n)$$

and

$$\Pr(S \le x \mid N = n) = \Pr\left(\sum_{i=1}^{n} X_i \le x\right) = F^{n*}(x).$$

Thus, for $x \ge 0$,

$$G(x) = \sum_{n=0}^{\infty} p_n F^{n*}(x), \tag{4.1}$$

recalling from Chapter 1 that $F^{0*}(x)$ is defined to be 1 for $x \ge 0$, and zero otherwise.

In principle, equation (4.1) provides a means of calculating the aggregate claims distribution. However, the convolution F^{n*} does not exist in a closed form for many individual claim amount distributions of practical interest such as Pareto and lognormal. Even in cases when a closed form does exist, the distribution function in equation (4.1) still has to be evaluated as an infinite sum.

By an analogous argument, in the case when individual claim amounts are distributed on the positive integers with probability function

$$f_j = F(j) - F(j-1)$$

for $j = 1, 2, 3, \ldots$, the probability function $\{g_x\}_{x=0}^{\infty}$ of S is given by $g_0 = p_0$, and for $x = 1, 2, 3, \ldots$,

$$g_x = \sum_{n=1}^{\infty} p_n f_x^{n*}, \tag{4.2}$$

where $f_x^{n*} = \Pr\left(\sum_{i=1}^{n} X_i = x\right)$. Formula (4.2) is not much more useful than formula (4.1). However, for certain distributions for N, g_x can be calculated recursively for $x = 1, 2, 3, \ldots$ using g_0 as the starting value for the recursive calculation, and this approach is discussed in detail in Sections 4.5 to 4.7.

4.2.2 The Moments of S

The moments and moment generating function of S can be calculated using conditional expectation arguments. The key results are that for any two random variables Y and Z for which the relevant moments exist,

$$E[Y] = E[E(Y|Z)] \tag{4.3}$$

and

$$V[Y] = E[V(Y|Z)] + V[E(Y|Z)]. \tag{4.4}$$

As an immediate application of equation (4.3) we have

$$E[S] = E[E(S \mid N)].$$

Now let $m_k = E\left[X_1^k\right]$ for $k = 1, 2, 3, \ldots$. Then

$$E[S|N=n] = E\left[\sum_{i=1}^{n} X_i\right] = \sum_{i=1}^{n} E[X_i] = nm_1,$$

and as this holds for $n = 0, 1, 2, \ldots$, $E[S|N] = Nm_1$, and hence

$$E[S] = E[Nm_1] = E[N]m_1. \tag{4.5}$$

This is a very appealing result as it states that the expected aggregate claim amount is the product of the expected number of claims and the expected amount of each claim.

Similarly, using the fact that $\{X_i\}_{i=1}^{\infty}$ are independent random variables,

$$V[S|N=n] = V\left[\sum_{i=1}^{n} X_i\right] = \sum_{i=1}^{n} V[X_i] = n\left(m_2 - m_1^2\right),$$

so that $V[S|N] = N\left(m_2 - m_1^2\right)$. Then, by applying equation (4.4) we get

$$\begin{aligned} V[S] &= E[V(S|N)] + V[E(S|N)] \\ &= E\left[N\left(m_2 - m_1^2\right)\right] + V[Nm_1] \\ &= E[N]\left(m_2 - m_1^2\right) + V[N]m_1^2. \end{aligned} \tag{4.6}$$

Formula (4.6) does not have the same type of natural interpretation as formula (4.5), but it does show that the variance of S is expressed in terms of the mean and variance of both the claim number distribution and the individual claim amount distribution.

The same technique can be used to obtain the moment generating function of S. We have

$$M_S(t) = E\left[e^{tS}\right] = E\left[E\left(e^{tS} \mid N\right)\right]$$

and

$$E\left[e^{tS} \mid N=n\right] = E\left[\exp\left\{t\sum_{i=1}^{n} X_i\right\}\right] = \prod_{i=1}^{n} E\left[\exp\{tX_i\}\right],$$

where we have again used the independence of $\{X_i\}_{i=1}^{\infty}$. Further, as $\{X_i\}_{i=1}^{\infty}$ are identically distributed,

$$E\left[e^{tS}|N=n\right] = M_X(t)^n,$$

where $M_X(t) = E\left[\exp\{tX_1\}\right]$. This leads to

$$\begin{aligned} M_S(t) &= E\left[M_X(t)^N\right] \\ &= E\left[\exp\left\{\log M_X(t)^N\right\}\right] \\ &= E\left[\exp\{N\log M_X(t)\}\right] \\ &= M_N\left[\log M_X(t)\right]. \end{aligned} \tag{4.7}$$

Thus, M_S is expressed in terms of M_N and M_X.

Similarly, when X_1 is a discrete random variable distributed on the non-negative integers with probability generating function P_X, the above arguments lead to

$$P_S(r) = P_N[P_X(r)],$$

where P_S and P_N are the probability generating functions of S and N respectively.

In the above development of results, it has been tacitly assumed that all relevant quantities exist. However, we have seen in Chapter 1 that moments and moment generating functions may exist only under certain conditions. Thus, for example, if the second moment of X_1 does not exist, then the second moment of S does not exist either.

4.3 The Compound Poisson Distribution

When N has a Poisson distribution with parameter λ, we say that S has a compound Poisson distribution with parameters λ and F, and similar terminology applies in the case of other claim number distributions. Since the mean and variance of the $P(\lambda)$ distribution are both λ, it follows from formulae (4.5) and (4.6) that when S has a compound Poisson distribution

$$E[S] = \lambda m_1$$

and

$$V[S] = \lambda m_2.$$

Further, the third central moment is

$$E\left[(S-\lambda m_1)^3\right] = \lambda m_3. \tag{4.8}$$

To derive formula (4.8), we can use the moment generating function of S, which by equation (1.1) and formula (4.7) is

$$M_S(t) = \exp\{\lambda\,(M_X(t) - 1)\}.$$

Differentiation with respect to t yields

$$M_S'(t) = \lambda M_X'(t) M_S(t),$$

$$M_S''(t) = \lambda M_X''(t) M_S(t) + \lambda M_X'(t) M_S'(t)$$

and

$$M_S'''(t) = \lambda M_X'''(t) M_S(t) + 2\lambda M_X''(t) M_S'(t) + \lambda M_X'(t) M_S''(t). \tag{4.9}$$

Setting $t = 0$ in formula (4.9) we get

$$\begin{aligned} E\left[S^3\right] &= \lambda m_3 + 2\lambda m_2 E[S] + \lambda m_1 E[S^2] \\ &= \lambda m_3 + 2V[S]E[S] + E[S]E[S^2] \\ &= \lambda m_3 + 3E[S]E[S^2] - 2E[S]^3, \end{aligned}$$

which yields formula (4.8).

An important point about the compound Poisson distribution that will be relevant in the context of approximation methods discussed in Section 4.8 is that the coefficient of skewness is positive under our assumptions that $\Pr(X_1 < 0) = 0$ and $m_1 > 0$ (which gives $m_k > 0$ for $k = 2, 3, 4, \ldots$), and hence

$$Sk[S] = \frac{E\left[(S - \lambda m_1)^3\right]}{V\,[S]^{3/2}} = \frac{\lambda m_3}{(\lambda m_2)^{3/2}} > 0.$$

Example 4.1 *Let S have a compound Poisson distribution with Poisson parameter 100, and let the individual claim amount distribution be $Pa(4, 1500)$. Calculate $E[S]$, $V[S]$ and $Sk[S]$.*

Solution 4.1 *From Chapter 1 (Section 1.3.3 and Exercise 5) we know that when $X \sim Pa(\alpha, \beta)$, $E[X] = \beta/(\alpha - 1)$, $E[X^2] = 2\beta^2/(\alpha - 1)(\alpha - 2)$ and $E[X^3] = 6\beta^3/(\alpha - 1)(\alpha - 2)(\alpha - 3)$. Thus,*

$$E[S] = 100 \times \frac{1,500}{3} = 50,000,$$

$$V[S] = 100 \times \frac{2 \times 1,500^2}{6} = 7.5 \times 10^7$$

and

$$E\left[(S - E[S])^3\right] = 100 \times 1,500^3 = 1.5^3 \times 10^{11},$$

so that

$$Sk[S] = \frac{1.5^3 \times 10^{11}}{\left(7.5 \times 10^7\right)^{3/2}} = 0.5196.$$

An important property of compound Poisson random variables is that the sum of independent, but not necessarily identically distributed, compound Poisson random variables is itself a compound Poisson random variable. Formally, let $\{S_i\}_{i=1}^n$ be independent compound Poisson random variables, with parameters λ_i and F_i, and let $\mathcal{S} = \sum_{i=1}^n S_i$. Then $\mathcal{S}$ has a compound Poisson distribution with parameters Λ and $\mathcal{F}$ where $\Lambda = \sum_{i=1}^n \lambda_i$ and

$$\mathcal{F}(x) = \frac{1}{\Lambda}\sum_{i=1}^{n} \lambda_i F_i(x). \tag{4.10}$$

To prove this, we use the moment generating function of $\mathcal{S}$, noting that

$$E\left[\exp\{t\mathcal{S}\}\right] = E\left[\exp\{t(S_1 + \cdots + S_n)\}\right] = \prod_{i=1}^{n} E\left[\exp\{tS_i\}\right]$$

since $\{S_i\}_{i=1}^n$ are independent. Now let M_i denote the moment generating function of a random variable whose distribution function is F_i. Then, as S_i has a compound Poisson distribution,

$$E\left[\exp\{tS_i\}\right] = \exp\{\lambda_i\left(M_i(t) - 1\right)\},$$

and hence

$$\begin{aligned} E\left[\exp\{t\mathcal{S}\}\right] &= \prod_{i=1}^{n} \exp\{\lambda_i\left(M_i(t) - 1\right)\} \\ &= \exp\left\{\sum_{i=1}^{n} \lambda_i\left(M_i(t) - 1\right)\right\} \\ &= \exp\left\{\Lambda\left(\sum_{i=1}^{n} \frac{\lambda_i M_i(t)}{\Lambda} - 1\right)\right\}. \end{aligned}$$

It then follows that $\mathcal{S}$ has a compound Poisson distribution by the uniqueness of a moment generating function and by the fact that a random variable whose distribution function is $\mathcal{F}$ has moment generating function

$$\int_0^\infty e^{tx} d\mathcal{F}(x) = \frac{1}{\Lambda}\sum_{i=1}^{n} \lambda_i \int_0^\infty e^{tx} dF_i(x) = \sum_{i=1}^{n} \frac{\lambda_i M_i(t)}{\Lambda}.$$

This is an important result that has applications not just in the collective risk model, but, as we shall see in Chapter 5, to the individual risk model too.

Example 4.2 *Let S_1 have a compound Poisson distribution with Poisson parameter $\lambda_1 = 10$, and distribution function F_1 for individual claim amounts where $F_1(x) = 1 - e^{-x}$, $x \geq 0$. Let S_2 have a compound Poisson distribution with Poisson parameter $\lambda_2 = 15$, and distribution function F_2 for individual claim amounts where $F_2(x) = 1 - e^{-x}(1 + x)$, $x \geq 0$. What is the distribution of $S_1 + S_2$ assuming S_1 and S_2 are independent?*

Solution 4.2 *The distribution of $S_1 + S_2$ is compound Poisson by the above result, and the Poisson parameter is $\lambda_1 + \lambda_2 = 25$. From equation (4.10), the individual claim amount distribution is*

$$\begin{aligned}\mathcal{F}(x) &= \frac{\lambda_1}{\lambda_1 + \lambda_2} F_1(x) + \frac{\lambda_2}{\lambda_1 + \lambda_2} F_2(x) \\ &= \tfrac{2}{5}\left(1 - e^{-x}\right) + \tfrac{3}{5}\left(1 - e^{-x}(1 + x)\right) \\ &= 1 - e^{-x}(1 + \tfrac{3}{5}x).\end{aligned}$$

4.4 The Effect of Reinsurance

In Chapter 1 we introduced both proportional and excess of loss reinsurance. We now consider the effect of such reinsurance arrangements on an aggregate claims distribution. Note that as the aggregate claim amount is shared by the insurer and the reinsurer regardless of the type of reinsurance arrangement, we can write S as $S_I + S_R$ where S_I denotes the insurer's aggregate claims, net of reinsurance, and S_R denotes the reinsurer's aggregate claim amount.

4.4.1 Proportional Reinsurance

Under a proportional reinsurance arrangement with proportion retained a, the insurer pays proportion a of each claim. Thus, the insurer's net aggregate claim amount is

$$S_I = \sum_{i=1}^{N} aX_i = aS$$

with $S_I = 0$ if $S = 0$. Similarly $S_R = (1 - a)S$.

Example 4.3 *Aggregate claims from a risk have a compound Poisson distribution with Poisson parameter 100 and an individual claim amount distribution which is exponential with mean 1,000. The insurer effects proportional reinsurance with proportion retained 0.8. Find the distribution of S_R.*

Solution 4.3 *As the reinsurer pays 20% of each claim, S_R has a compound Poisson distribution with Poisson parameter 100 and an individual claim amount distribution that is exponential with mean 200.*

Example 4.4 *Aggregate claims from a risk are distributed with mean μ and standard deviation σ. The insurer of the risk has effected proportional reinsurance with proportion retained a. Find $Cov(S_I, S_R)$.*

Solution 4.4 *By definition,*

$$Cov(S_I, S_R) = E\left[(S_I - a\mu)\,(S_R - (1-a)\mu)\right]$$

since $E[S_I] = a\mu$ and $E[S_R] = (1-a)\mu$. As $S_I = aS$ and $S_R = (1-a)S$,

$$\begin{aligned} Cov(S_I, S_R) &= E\left[a(S-\mu)(1-a)(S-\mu)\right] \\ &= a(1-a)E\left[(S-\mu)^2\right] \\ &= a(1-a)\sigma^2. \end{aligned}$$

4.4.2 Excess of Loss Reinsurance

Let us assume that the insurer of a risk, S, has effected excess of loss reinsurance with retention level M. Then we can write

$$S_I = \sum_{i=1}^{N} \min(X_i, M)$$

with $S_I = 0$ when $N = 0$, and

$$S_R = \sum_{i=1}^{N} \max(0, X_i - M) \qquad (4.11)$$

with $S_R = 0$ when $N = 0$.

An important point to note is that S_R can equal 0 even if N is greater than zero. This situation would arise if $n > 0$ claims occurred and each of these n claims was for an amount less than M, so that the insurer would pay each of these claims in full. Thus, there are two ways of considering the reinsurer's aggregate claim amount. The first is as specified by equation (4.11), in which case the interpretation is that each time a claim occurs for the insurer, a claim also occurs for the reinsurer, and we allow 0 to be a possible claim amount. The second approach is to count only claims (for the insurer) whose amount exceeds M as these claims give rise to non-zero claim payments by the reinsurer. Thus, an alternative way of writing S_R is

$$S_R = \sum_{i=1}^{N_R} \hat{X}_i$$

with $S_R = 0$ when $N_R = 0$. Here, N_R denotes the number of non-zero claims for the reinsurer, and $\hat{X}_i$ denotes the amount of the ith claim payment by the reinsurer with formula (1.13) giving

$$\Pr\left(\hat{X}_i \leq x\right) = \frac{F(x+M) - F(M)}{1 - F(M)}.$$

To find the distribution of N_R, we introduce the sequence of independent and identically distributed indicator random variables $\{I_j\}_{j=1}^{\infty}$, where I_j takes the value 1 if $X_j > M$, so that there is a non-zero claim payment by the reinsurer, and I_j takes the value 0 otherwise. Then

$$\Pr(I_j = 1) = \Pr(X_j > M) = 1 - F(M) \stackrel{def}{=} \pi_M$$

and

$$N_R = \sum_{i=1}^{N} I_j$$

with $N_R = 0$ when $N = 0$. As N_R has a compound distribution, its probability generating function is

$$P_{N_R}(r) = P_N\left[P_I(r)\right],$$

where P_I is the probability generating function of each indicator random variable, and

$$P_I(r) = 1 - \pi_M + \pi_M r.$$

Example 4.5 *Let $N \sim P(\lambda)$. What is the distribution of N_R?*

Solution 4.5 *As*

$$P_N(r) = \exp\left\{\lambda\left(r - 1\right)\right\},$$

we have

$$\begin{aligned} P_{N_R}(r) &= \exp\left\{\lambda\left(1 - \pi_M + \pi_M r - 1\right)\right\} \\ &= \exp\left\{\lambda \pi_M (r - 1)\right\}. \end{aligned}$$

Hence $N_R \sim P(\lambda \pi_M)$ by the uniqueness property of probability generating functions.

Example 4.6 *Let $N \sim NB(k, p)$. What is the distribution of N_R?*

Solution 4.6 *As*

$$P_N(r) = \left(\frac{p}{1 - qr}\right)^k,$$

where $q = 1 - p$, we have

$$\begin{aligned} P_{N_R}(r) &= \left(\frac{p}{1 - q(1 - \pi_M + \pi_M r)}\right)^k \\ &= \left(\frac{p}{p + q\pi_M - q\pi_M r}\right)^k. \end{aligned} \tag{4.12}$$

Now let $p^* = p/(p+q\pi_M)$ and $q^* = q\pi_M/(p+q\pi_M) = 1-p^*$. Then division of both the numerator and the denominator inside the brackets in formula (4.12) by $p + q\pi_M$ yields

$$P_{N_R}(r) = \left(\frac{p^*}{1 - q^* r}\right)^k,$$

so that $N_R \sim NB(k, p^*)$.

Example 4.7 *Aggregate claims from a risk have a compound Poisson distribution with Poisson parameter 200 and an individual claim amount distribution which is $Pa(3, 300)$ so that*

$$F(x) = 1 - \left(\frac{300}{300 + x}\right)^3$$

for $x \geq 0$. The insurer of this risk has effected excess of loss reinsurance with retention level 300. Calculate the mean and variance of the reinsurer's aggregate claims by two methods.

Solution 4.7 *The first approach is to say that S_R has a compound Poisson distribution where the Poisson parameter is 200 and the individual claim amounts are distributed as $\max(0, X - 300)$, where $X \sim F$. Then*

$$\begin{aligned} E[S_R] &= 200E[\max(0, X - 300)] \\ &= 200 \int_{300}^{\infty} (x - 300) \frac{3 \times 300^3}{(300 + x)^4} dx \\ &= 200 \int_0^{\infty} y \frac{3 \times 300^3}{(y + 600)^4} dy \\ &= \frac{200}{8} \int_0^{\infty} y \frac{3 \times 600^3}{(y + 600)^4} dy \\ &= 7,500 \end{aligned}$$

since the final integral is the mean of the Pa(3,600) distribution and hence equals 300. Similarly,

$$\begin{aligned} V[S_R] &= 200E\left[\max(0, X-300)^2\right] \\ &= 200\int_{300}^{\infty}(x-300)^2\frac{3\times 300^3}{(300+x)^4}dx \\ &= \frac{200}{8}\int_0^{\infty}y^2\frac{3\times 600^3}{(y+600)^4}dy \\ &= 9\times 10^6. \end{aligned}$$

The second approach is to say that S_R has a compound Poisson distribution with Poisson parameter

$$200\,(1-F(300)) = 200\left(\tfrac{1}{2}\right)^3 = 25,$$

and individual claim amounts are distributed as $\hat{X}$ where

$$\Pr(\hat{X}\le x) = \frac{F(x+300)-F(300)}{1-F(300)} = 1-\left(\frac{600}{600+x}\right)^3,$$

so that $\hat{X}\sim Pa(3,600)$. Then

$$E[S_R] = 25E\left[\hat{X}\right] = 25\times 300 = 7,500$$

and

$$V[S_R] = 25E\left[\hat{X}^2\right] = 25\times 600^2 = 9\times 10^6.$$

4.5 Recursive Calculation of Aggregate Claims Distributions

In this section we derive the Panjer recursion formula, which permits recursive calculation of the aggregate claims distribution when individual claim amounts are distributed on the non-negative integers and when the claim number distribution belongs to the $(a,b,0)$ class of distributions. We therefore start by defining this class of distributions.

4.5.1 The $(a,b,0)$ Class of Distributions

A counting distribution is said to belong to the $(a,b,0)$ class of distributions if its probability function $\{p_n\}_{n=0}^{\infty}$ can be calculated recursively from the formula

$$p_n = \left(a+\frac{b}{n}\right)p_{n-1} \tag{4.13}$$

for $n = 1, 2, 3, \ldots$, where a and b are constants. The starting value for the recursive calculation is p_0, which is assumed to be greater than 0, and the term '0' in $(a, b, 0)$ is used to indicate this fact.

There are exactly three non-trivial distributions in the $(a, b, 0)$ class, namely Poisson, binomial and negative binomial. To see this, we note that the recursion scheme given by formula (4.13) starts from

$$p_1 = (a + b)p_0.$$

Hence we require that $a + b \geq 0$ since we would otherwise obtain a negative value for p_1. Members of the $(a, b, 0)$ class can be identified by considering possible values for a and b, as follows.

Suppose, first, that $a + b = 0$. Then $p_n = 0$ for $n = 1, 2, 3, \ldots$, and as $\sum_{n=0}^{\infty} p_n = 1$, we see that p_0 must equal 1, so that the distribution is degenerate at 0.

Secondly, let us consider the situation when $a = 0$. This gives $p_n = (b/n)p_{n-1}$ for $n = 1, 2, 3, \ldots$, so that

$$p_n = \frac{b}{n}\frac{b}{n-1}\cdots\frac{b}{2}bp_0 = \frac{b^n}{n!}p_0,$$

and again using the fact that $\sum_{n=0}^{\infty} p_n = 1$, we have

$$\sum_{n=0}^{\infty} p_n = p_0 \sum_{n=0}^{\infty} \frac{b^n}{n!} = p_0 e^b,$$

giving $p_0 = e^{-b}$. Hence, when $a = 0$, we obtain the Poisson distribution with mean b.

Thirdly, we consider the situation when $a > 0$ and $a \neq -b$, so that $a+b > 0$. Then by repeated application of formula (4.13) we have

$$\begin{aligned}
p_n &= \left(a + \frac{b}{n}\right)\left(a + \frac{b}{n-1}\right)\cdots\left(a + \frac{b}{2}\right)(a + b)p_0 \\
&= \frac{(an + b)(a(n-1) + b)\cdots(2a + b)(a + b)}{n(n-1)\cdots 2}p_0 \\
&= \frac{a^n}{n!}\left(n + \frac{b}{a}\right)\left(n - 1 + \frac{b}{a}\right)\cdots\left(2 + \frac{b}{a}\right)\left(1 + \frac{b}{a}\right)p_0.
\end{aligned}$$

If we now write α for $1 + b/a$, then we have

$$\begin{aligned}
p_n &= \frac{a^n}{n!}(n - 1 + \alpha)(n - 2 + \alpha)\cdots(1 + \alpha)\alpha p_0 \qquad (4.14) \\
&= \binom{\alpha + n - 1}{n} a^n p_0.
\end{aligned}$$

To identify a distribution, note that as $p_0 > 0$, we require that $\sum_{n=1}^{\infty} p_n < 1$. By the ratio test, we have absolute convergence if

$$\lim_{n\to\infty} \left| \frac{p_n}{p_{n-1}} \right| < 1,$$

and as $p_n = (a + b/n)p_{n-1}$, we have absolute convergence if $|a| < 1$, and as we have assumed $a > 0$, this condition reduces to $a < 1$. Then

$$p_0 + p_0 \sum_{n=1}^{\infty} \binom{\alpha + n - 1}{n} a^n = 1,$$

and from formula (1.3) of Section 1.2.3, we know that for the $NB(k,p)$ probability function

$$p^k \sum_{n=1}^{\infty} \binom{k + n - 1}{n} q^n = 1 - p^k,$$

where $p + q = 1$. Hence $p_0 = (1 - a)^{\alpha}$, and the distribution of N is negative binomial with parameters $1 - a$, where $0 < a < 1$, and $\alpha = 1 + b/a$.

The final case to consider is when $a + b > 0$ and $a < 0$. As $a < 0$, there must exist some positive integer κ such that

$$a + \frac{b}{\kappa + 1} = 0,$$

so that $p_n = 0$ for $n = \kappa + 1, \kappa + 2, \ldots$. If this were not true, then as $a < 0$ and $b > 0$, we would find that there would be a first value of n such that $a + b/n$ would be less than 0, generating a negative value for p_n. Proceeding as in the third case above,

$$p_n = \frac{a^n}{n!} \left(n + \frac{b}{a}\right) \left(n - 1 + \frac{b}{a}\right) \cdots \left(2 + \frac{b}{a}\right) \left(1 + \frac{b}{a}\right) p_0,$$

and as $\kappa = -(1 + b/a)$, we can write this as

$$\begin{aligned}
p_n &= \frac{a^n}{n!} (-\kappa + n - 1)(-\kappa + n - 2) \cdots (-\kappa + 1)(-\kappa) p_0 \\
&= (-1)^n \frac{a^n}{n!} (\kappa - n + 1)(\kappa - n + 2) \cdots (\kappa - 1)\kappa p_0 \\
&= (-1)^n \frac{a^n}{n!} \frac{\kappa!}{(\kappa - n)!} p_0 \\
&= (-a)^n \binom{\kappa}{n} p_0.
\end{aligned}$$

Table 4.1 *Values of a and b for the Poisson, binomial and negative binomial distributions.*

	a	b
$P(\lambda)$	0	λ
$B(n,q)$	$-q/(1-q)$	$(n+1)q/(1-q)$
$NB(k,p)$	$1-p$	$(1-p)(k-1)$

We have assumed that $a < 0$, so let $A = -a > 0$. Then

$$p_0 + p_0 \sum_{n=1}^{\kappa} \binom{\kappa}{n} A^n = p_0 \sum_{n=0}^{\kappa} \binom{\kappa}{n} A^n = 1.$$

To find p_0 we can write $A = p/(1-p)$, which is equivalent to $p = A/(1+A) = a/(a-1)$, so that $0 < p < 1$. Then

$$p_0 \sum_{n=0}^{\kappa} \binom{\kappa}{n} p^n (1-p)^{-n} = 1$$

gives $p_0 = (1-p)^{\kappa}$, so that the distribution of N is binomial with parameters κ and $a/(a-1)$.

Table 4.1 shows the values of a and b for the parameterisations of distributions in Section 1.2.

We conclude our discussion of the $(a,b,0)$ class by considering the probability generating function of a distribution in this class, and deriving a result that will be applied in Section 4.5.2. Let

$$P_N(r) = p_0 + \sum_{n=1}^{\infty} r^n p_n.$$

Then

$$\begin{aligned} P'_N(r) &= \sum_{n=1}^{\infty} n r^{n-1} p_n \\ &= \sum_{n=1}^{\infty} n r^{n-1} \left(a + \frac{b}{n}\right) p_{n-1} \\ &= a \sum_{n=1}^{\infty} n r^{n-1} p_{n-1} + b \sum_{n=1}^{\infty} r^{n-1} p_{n-1} \\ &= a \sum_{n=1}^{\infty} n r^{n-1} p_{n-1} + b P_N(r). \end{aligned}$$

Using the trivial identity $n = n - 1 + 1$, we have

$$a\sum_{n=1}^{\infty} nr^{n-1}p_{n-1} = a\sum_{n=1}^{\infty}(n-1)\,r^{n-1}p_{n-1} + a\sum_{n=1}^{\infty} r^{n-1}p_{n-1}$$
$$= ar\sum_{n=2}^{\infty}(n-1)\,r^{n-2}p_{n-1} + aP_N(r)$$
$$= arP_N'(r) + aP_N(r).$$

Hence

$$P_N'(r) = arP_N'(r) + (a+b)\,P_N(r). \tag{4.15}$$

This differential equation can be solved, but the solution is not necessary in what follows, and so we omit the details.

4.5.2 The Panjer Recursion Formula

The Panjer recursion formula is one of the most important results in risk theory. Not only is it useful in the context of aggregate claims distributions, but, as we shall see in Chapter 7, it has applications in ruin theory. The recursion formula allows us to calculate the probability function of aggregate claims when the counting distribution belongs to the $(a, b, 0)$ class and when the individual claim amount distribution is discrete with probability function $\{f_j\}_{j=0}^{\infty}$. Until now we have tacitly assumed that individual claims follow some continuous distribution such as lognormal or Pareto. Indeed, we have not discussed discrete distributions as candidates to model individual claim amounts, and we defer a discussion of this until Section 4.7. Similarly, we simply note here that it is useful to allow $f_0 > 0$, even though in the context of individual claims, an individual claim amount of zero would not constitute a claim in practice. We shall see why this seemingly artificial condition is useful in Sections 4.7 and 7.9.1.

Since we are now assuming that individual claim amounts are distributed on the non-negative integers, it follows that S is also distributed on the non-negative integers. Further, as $S = \sum_{i=1}^{N} X_i$ it follows that $S = 0$ if $N = 0$ or if $N = n$ and $\sum_{i=1}^{n} X_i = 0$. As $\sum_{i=1}^{n} X_i = 0$ only if each $X_i = 0$, it follows by independence that

$$\Pr\left(\sum_{i=1}^{n} X_i = 0\right) = f_0^n,$$

and hence by the arguments in Section 4.2.1,

$$g_0 = p_0 + \sum_{n=1}^{\infty} p_n f_0^n = P_N(f_0). \tag{4.16}$$

From Section 4.2.2, the probability generating function of S is given by

$$P_S(r) = P_N\left[P_X(r)\right], \tag{4.17}$$

and so differentiation with respect to r gives

$$P_S'(r) = P_N'\left[P_X(r)\right] P_X'(r). \tag{4.18}$$

Applying formula (4.15) to the above identity by replacing the argument r by $P_X(r)$ gives

$$P_S'(r) = \left(aP_X(r)P_N'\left[P_X(r)\right] + (a+b)P_N\left[P_X(r)\right]\right) P_X'(r)$$

or, using formulae (4.17) and (4.18),

$$P_S'(r) = aP_X(r)P_S'(r) + (a+b)P_S(r)P_X'(r). \tag{4.19}$$

Now P_S and P_X are probability generating functions, and they are respectively given by

$$P_S(r) = \sum_{j=0}^{\infty} r^j g_j \quad \text{and} \quad P_X(r) = \sum_{k=0}^{\infty} r^k f_k,$$

so that

$$P_S'(r) = \sum_{j=0}^{\infty} j\, r^{j-1} g_j \quad \text{and} \quad P_X'(r) = \sum_{k=0}^{\infty} k\, r^{k-1} f_k.$$

Using these expressions in equation (4.19) we obtain

$$\sum_{j=0}^{\infty} j\, r^{j-1} g_j = a\left(\sum_{k=0}^{\infty} r^k f_k\right)\left(\sum_{j=0}^{\infty} j\, r^{j-1} g_j\right) + (a+b)\left(\sum_{j=0}^{\infty} r^j g_j\right)\left(\sum_{k=0}^{\infty} k\, r^{k-1} f_k\right)$$

or, on multiplying throughout by r,

$$\sum_{j=0}^{\infty} j\, r^j g_j = a\left(\sum_{k=0}^{\infty} r^k f_k\right)\left(\sum_{j=0}^{\infty} j\, r^j g_j\right) + (a+b)\left(\sum_{j=0}^{\infty} r^j g_j\right)\left(\sum_{k=0}^{\infty} k\, r^k f_k\right). \tag{4.20}$$

To obtain a formula for g_x, $x = 1, 2, 3, \ldots$, from equation (4.20), all that is required is that we identify coefficients of powers of r on each side of the equation. On the left-hand side, the coefficient of r^x is xg_x. In the first product of sums on the right-hand side we can obtain terms in r^x by multiplying together the term in r^k in the first sum with the term in r^{x-k} in the second sum, for $k = 0, 1, 2, \ldots, x$. Hence, the coefficient of r^x in the first product of sums is

$$a \sum_{k=0}^{x} f_k (x-k) g_{x-k}.$$

Similarly, the coefficient of r^x in the second product of sums is

$$(a+b) \sum_{k=0}^{x} k f_k g_{x-k}.$$

Thus,

$$\begin{aligned} x g_x &= a \sum_{k=0}^{x} f_k (x-k) g_{x-k} + (a+b) \sum_{k=0}^{x} k f_k g_{x-k} \\ &= a f_0 x g_x + a \sum_{k=1}^{x} f_k (x-k) g_{x-k} + (a+b) \sum_{k=1}^{x} k f_k g_{x-k}, \end{aligned}$$

so that

$$(1 - a f_0) x g_x = \sum_{k=1}^{x} (a(x-k) + (a+b)k) f_k g_{x-k}$$

or

$$g_x = \frac{1}{1 - a f_0} \sum_{k=1}^{x} \left(a + \frac{bk}{x} \right) f_k g_{x-k}. \tag{4.21}$$

Formula (4.21) is the Panjer recursion formula, with starting value g_0 given by formula (4.16). It shows that g_x is expressed in terms of $g_0, g_1, \ldots, g_{x-1}$, so that calculation of the probability function is recursive. In all practical applications of this formula, a computer is required to perform calculations. However, the advantage that the Panjer recursion formula has over formula (4.2) for g_x is that there is no need to calculate convolutions, and from a computational point of view this is much more efficient.

Example 4.8 *Let $N \sim P(2)$, and let $f_j = 0.6(0.4^{j-1})$ for $j = 1, 2, 3, \ldots$. Calculate g_x for $x = 0, 1, 2$ and 3.*

Solution 4.8 *As $f_0 = 0$, we have $g_0 = p_0$. Further, as $a = 0$ and $b = 2$,*

$$g_x = \frac{2}{x} \sum_{k=1}^{x} k f_k g_{x-k}.$$

Thus,

$$\begin{aligned}
g_0 &= e^{-2} = 0.1353, \\
g_1 &= 2f_1 g_0 = 0.1624, \\
g_2 &= f_1 g_1 + 2f_2 g_0 = 0.1624 \textit{ and} \\
g_3 &= \tfrac{2}{3}\left(f_1 g_2 + 2f_2 g_1 + 3f_3 g_0\right) = 0.1429.
\end{aligned}$$

In general, a recursion formula for the distribution function of S does not exist. An exception is when N has a geometric distribution with $p_n = pq^n$ for $n = 0, 1, 2, \ldots$. In this case, $a = q$ and $b = 0$, so that

$$g_x = \frac{q}{1 - qf_0} \sum_{k=1}^{x} f_k g_{x-k},$$

and for $y = 1, 2, 3, \ldots$,

$$\begin{aligned}
G(y) = \sum_{x=0}^{y} g_x &= g_0 + \sum_{x=1}^{y} \frac{q}{1 - qf_0} \sum_{k=1}^{x} f_k g_{x-k} \\
&= g_0 + \frac{q}{1 - qf_0} \sum_{k=1}^{y} f_k \sum_{x=k}^{y} g_{x-k} \\
&= g_0 + \frac{q}{1 - qf_0} \sum_{k=1}^{y} f_k G(y-k),
\end{aligned} \tag{4.22}$$

so that in this special case, the distribution function of S can also be calculated recursively. We shall see in Chapter 7 that this is a particularly useful result.

We can also find the moments of S recursively by using the Panjer recursion formula. For $r = 1, 2, 3, \ldots$, we have

$$\begin{aligned}
E\left[S^r\right] &= \sum_{x=0}^{\infty} x^r g_x \\
&= \frac{1}{1 - af_0} \sum_{x=1}^{\infty} x^r \sum_{k=1}^{x} \left(a + \frac{bk}{x}\right) f_k g_{x-k} \\
&= \frac{1}{1 - af_0} \sum_{k=1}^{\infty} \sum_{x=k}^{\infty} \left(ax^r + bkx^{r-1}\right) f_k g_{x-k} \\
&= \frac{1}{1 - af_0} \sum_{k=1}^{\infty} f_k \sum_{t=0}^{\infty} \left(a(t+k)^r + bk(t+k)^{r-1}\right) g_t.
\end{aligned}$$

Using the binomial expansion,

$$\begin{aligned}\sum_{t=0}^{\infty}(t+k)^r g_t &= \sum_{t=0}^{\infty}\sum_{i=0}^{r}\binom{r}{i}t^i k^{r-i}g_t\\ &= \sum_{i=0}^{r}\binom{r}{i}k^{r-i}\sum_{t=0}^{\infty}t^i g_t\\ &= \sum_{i=0}^{r}\binom{r}{i}k^{r-i}E\left[S^i\right],\end{aligned}$$

and so

$$\begin{aligned}E\left[S^r\right] &= \frac{1}{1-af_0}\sum_{k=1}^{\infty}f_k\left[a\sum_{i=0}^{r}\binom{r}{i}k^{r-i}E\left[S^i\right]+bk\sum_{i=0}^{r-1}\binom{r-1}{i}k^{r-1-i}E\left[S^i\right]\right]\\ &= \frac{1}{1-af_0}\left[a\sum_{i=0}^{r}\binom{r}{i}E\left[S^i\right]\sum_{k=1}^{\infty}k^{r-i}f_k+b\sum_{i=0}^{r-1}\binom{r-1}{i}E\left[S^i\right]\sum_{k=1}^{\infty}k^{r-i}f_k\right]\\ &= \frac{1}{1-af_0}\left[\sum_{i=0}^{r-1}\left[a\binom{r}{i}+b\binom{r-1}{i}\right]E\left[S^i\right]E\left[X_1^{r-i}\right]+aE\left[S^r\right]\sum_{k=1}^{\infty}f_k\right].\end{aligned}$$

As $\sum_{k=1}^{\infty}f_k = 1-f_0$, we can rearrange the above identity to yield

$$E\left[S^r\right] = \frac{1}{1-a}\sum_{i=0}^{r-1}\left[a\binom{r}{i}+b\binom{r-1}{i}\right]E\left[S^i\right]E\left[X_1^{r-i}\right]. \tag{4.23}$$

Example 4.9 *Use formula (4.23) to find the first three moments of a compound Poisson distribution when the Poisson parameter is λ and the individual claim amounts are distributed on the non-negative integers.*

Solution 4.9 *For the $P(\lambda)$ distribution, $a=0$ and $b=\lambda$, so formula (4.23) becomes*

$$E\left[S^r\right] = \lambda\sum_{i=0}^{r-1}\binom{r-1}{i}E\left[S^i\right]E\left[X_1^{r-i}\right].$$

Setting $r=1$ we get $E[S]=\lambda E[X_1]$, setting $r=2$ we get

$$\begin{aligned}E[S^2] &= \lambda\left(E[X_1^2]+E[S]E[X_1]\right)\\ &= \lambda E[X_1^2]+E[S]^2\end{aligned}$$

so that $V[S] = \lambda E[X_1^2]$, *and setting* $r = 3$ *we get*

$$\begin{aligned} E\left[S^3\right] &= \lambda\left(E\left[X_1^3\right] + 2E[S]E[X_1^2] + E[S^2]E[X_1]\right) \\ &= \lambda E\left[X_1^3\right] + 2E[S]V[S] + E[S^2]E[S] \\ &= \lambda E\left[X_1^3\right] + 3E[S]E[S^2] - 2E[S]^3. \end{aligned}$$

We remark that these results are consistent with results in Section 4.3, noting that the third result can be rearranged as

$$\begin{aligned} \lambda E\left[X_1^3\right] &= E\left[S^3\right] - 3E[S]E[S^2] + 2E[S]^3 \\ &= E\left[(S - E[S])^3\right]. \end{aligned}$$

4.6 Extensions of the Panjer Recursion Formula

4.6.1 The $(a, b, 1)$ Class of Distributions

A counting distribution is said to belong to the $(a, b, 1)$ class of distributions if its probability function $\{q_n\}_{n=0}^{\infty}$ can be calculated recursively from the formula

$$q_n = \left(a + \frac{b}{n}\right) q_{n-1} \tag{4.24}$$

for $n = 2, 3, 4, \ldots$, where a and b are constants. This class differs from the $(a, b, 0)$ class because the starting value for the recursive calculation is q_1, which is assumed to be greater than 0, and the term '1' in $(a, b, 1)$ is used to indicate the starting point for the recursion.

As the recursion formula is the same for the $(a, b, 1)$ class as for the $(a, b, 0)$ class, we can construct members of the $(a, b, 1)$ class by modifying the mass of probability at 0 in distributions in the $(a, b, 0)$ class, and there are two ways in which we can do this. The first method of modification is called zero-truncation. Let $\{p_n\}_{n=0}^{\infty}$ be a probability function in the $(a, b, 0)$ class. Its zero-truncated counterpart is given by

$$q_n = \frac{p_n}{1 - p_0}$$

for $n = 1, 2, 3, \ldots$. For example, the zero-truncated Poisson distribution with parameter λ has probability function

$$q_n = \frac{e^{-\lambda}}{1 - e^{-\lambda}} \frac{\lambda^n}{n!}$$

for $n = 1, 2, 3, \ldots$.

The second method of modification is called zero-modification. If $\{p_n\}_{n=0}^{\infty}$ is a probability function in the $(a,b,0)$ class, its zero-modified counterpart is given by $q_0 = \alpha$, where $0 < \alpha < 1$, and for $n = 1, 2, 3, \ldots$,

$$q_n = \frac{1-\alpha}{1-p_0} p_n.$$

Thus, the probability p_0 in the $(a,b,0)$ probability function is being replaced by the probability α, and the remaining probabilities, $\{p_n\}_{n=1}^{\infty}$, are being rescaled. For example, the zero-modified version of the geometric distribution with probability function $p_n = pq^n$ for $n = 0, 1, 2, \ldots$ is given by $q_0 = \alpha$, and for $n = 1, 2, 3, \ldots$,

$$q_n = \frac{1-\alpha}{1-p} pq^n = (1-\alpha)pq^{n-1}.$$

There are four other members of the $(a,b,1)$ class. Two of these are the logarithmic distribution, introduced in Exercise 1 of Chapter 1, and the extended truncated negative binomial distribution given by

$$q_n = \binom{-r}{n} \frac{(-\theta)^n}{(1-\theta)^{-r} - 1}$$

for $n = 1, 2, 3, \ldots$, where $r > -1$ and $0 < \theta < 1$. As each of these distributions is defined on the positive integers, we can create the other two distributions in the $(a,b,1)$ class from these two distributions by creating zero-modified versions of these distributions.

When the counting distribution belongs to the $(a,b,1)$ class and individual claim amounts are distributed on the non-negative integers, the techniques of the previous section can be used to derive a recursion formula for the probability function for aggregate claims. Let

$$Q_N(r) = \sum_{n=0}^{\infty} r^n q_n.$$

Then, using the arguments of Section 4.5.1,

$$Q_N'(r) = [q_1 - (a+b)q_0] + arQ_N'(r) + (a+b)Q_N(r).$$

Similarly, following the arguments in Section 4.5.2, $P_S(r) = Q_N[P_X(r)]$ yields

$$P_S'(r) = [q_1 - (a+b)q_0]\, P_X'(r) + aP_X(r)P_S'(r) + (a+b)P_S(r)P_X'(r),$$

from which we find

$$g_x = \frac{1}{1-af_0}\left(\sum_{j=1}^{x} \left(a + \frac{bj}{x}\right) f_j g_{x-j} + (q_1 - (a+b)q_0) f_x \right) \tag{4.25}$$

for $x = 1, 2, 3, \ldots$. The starting value for this recursion formula is

$$g_0 = \sum_{n=0}^{\infty} q_n f_0^n = Q_N(f_0) \tag{4.26}$$

when $f_0 > 0$. When $f_0 = 0$ and $q_0 > 0$, the starting value is simply $g_0 = q_0$, and when both q_0 and f_0 equal 0, the starting value is

$$g_1 = \Pr(N = 1)\Pr(X_1 = 1) = q_1 f_1.$$

Example 4.10 *Let N have a logarithmic distribution with parameter $\theta = 0.5$, and let $f_j = 0.2(0.8^j)$ for $j = 0, 1, 2, \ldots$. Calculate* $\Pr(S \leq 3)$.

Solution 4.10 *The logarithmic probability function is*

$$q_n = \frac{-1}{\log 0.5}\frac{0.5^n}{n}$$

for $n = 1, 2, 3, \ldots$, so that $q_1 = 0.7213$, and in formula (4.24), $a = 0.5$ and $b = -0.5$. From Exercise 1 of Chapter 1, it is easy to see that

$$Q_N(r) = \frac{\log(1 - 0.5r)}{\log(1 - 0.5)},$$

so that the starting value for the recursive calculation, calculated by formula (4.26), is $g_0 = Q_N(0.2) = 0.1520$. Applying formula (4.25), we have

$$g_x = \tfrac{10}{9}\left(\tfrac{1}{2}\sum_{j=1}^{x}\left(1 - \frac{j}{x}\right) f_j g_{x-j} + q_1 f_x\right),$$

giving

$$\begin{aligned} g_1 &= \tfrac{10}{9} q_1 f_1 = 0.1282, \\ g_2 &= \tfrac{10}{9}\left(\tfrac{1}{4} f_1 g_1 + q_1 f_2\right) = 0.1083, \\ g_3 &= \tfrac{10}{9}\left(\tfrac{1}{2}\left(\tfrac{2}{3} f_1 g_2 + \tfrac{1}{3} f_2 g_1\right) + q_1 f_3\right) = 0.0915, \end{aligned}$$

and hence $\Pr(S \leq 3) = 0.4801$. *(Rounded values are shown in this solution.)*

4.6.2 Other Classes of Distributions

A distribution is said to belong to Schröter's class of distributions if its probability function $\{p_n\}_{n=0}^{\infty}$ can be calculated recursively from the formula

$$p_n = \left(a + \frac{b}{n}\right) p_{n-1} + \frac{c}{n} p_{n-2} \tag{4.27}$$

for $n = 1, 2, 3, \ldots$, where a, b and c are constants and p_{-1} is defined to be zero.

When the counting distribution belongs to Schröter's class and individual claim amounts are distributed on the non-negative integers, we can again apply the techniques of the previous section to derive a recursion formula for the probability function of aggregate claims. By inserting formula (4.27) into

$$P_N(r) = \sum_{n=0}^{\infty} r^n p_n,$$

we find after some algebra that

$$P'_N(r) = arP'_N(r) + (a + b + cr)P_N(r), \tag{4.28}$$

and, proceeding as in previous derivations, differentiation of the identity $P_S(r) = P_N[P_X(r)]$ leads to

$$P'_S(r) = aP_X(r)P'_S(r) + (a + b + cP_X(r))\, P_S(r)P'_X(r). \tag{4.29}$$

In previous derivations of recursion formulae, this is the stage at which we have written probability generating functions and their derivatives in summation form. Instead of doing this immediately, we first note that if we define a random variable Y by $Y = X_1 + X_2$, then $P_Y(r) = P_X(r)^2$ and consequently

$$P'_Y(r) = 2P_X(r)P'_X(r).$$

Further, $\Pr(Y = j) = \Pr(X_1 + X_2 = j) = f_j^{2*}$ for $j = 0, 1, 2, \ldots$, so that

$$P'_Y(r) = \sum_{j=0}^{\infty} j r^{j-1} f_j^{2*}.$$

We can now write equation (4.29) as

$$P'_S(r) = aP_X(r)P'_S(r) + (a + b)P_S(r)P'_X(r) + \frac{c}{2}P_S(r)P'_Y(r)$$

or, in summation form,

$$\begin{aligned}\sum_{j=0}^{\infty} j\, r^{j-1} g_j = a &\left(\sum_{k=0}^{\infty} r^k f_k\right)\left(\sum_{j=0}^{\infty} j\, r^{j-1} g_j\right) \\ &+ (a + b)\left(\sum_{j=0}^{\infty} r^j g_j\right)\left(\sum_{k=0}^{\infty} k\, r^{k-1} f_k\right) \\ &+ \frac{c}{2}\left(\sum_{j=0}^{\infty} r^j g_j\right)\left(\sum_{k=0}^{\infty} k\, r^{k-1} f_k^{2*}\right).\end{aligned}$$

If we multiply this equation by r and then equate coefficients of powers of r, we obtain

$$g_x = \frac{1}{1 - af_0} \sum_{j=1}^{x} \left[\left(a + \frac{bj}{x} \right) f_j + \frac{cj}{2x} f_j^{2*} \right] g_{x-j} \tag{4.30}$$

for $x = 1, 2, 3, \ldots$, and the starting value for this recursion formula is $g_0 = P_N(f_0)$.

Formula (4.30) has one important drawback as a recursion formula, namely that in order to apply it to calculate g_x, we must first calculate $\{f_j^{2*}\}_{j=1}^{x}$. Thus, the need to calculate convolutions to find g_x is not eliminated as it is in the case when the claim number distribution belongs to one of the $(a, b, 0)$ and $(a, b, 1)$ classes.

It is beyond our scope to discuss ranges for the parameters a, b and c in formula (4.27). However, we note that if $N_3 = N_1 + N_2$ where N_1 and N_2 are independent, the distribution of N_1 is in the $(a, b, 0)$ class and the distribution of N_2 is Poisson, then the distribution of N_3 is in Schröter's class. This can be shown by noting that for a random variable N_1 in the $(a, b, 0)$ class with parameters $a = \alpha$ and $b = \beta$, equation (4.15) gives

$$\frac{P'_{N_1}(r)}{P_{N_1}(r)} = \frac{\alpha + \beta}{1 - \alpha r},$$

and note that

$$\frac{P'_{N_1}(r)}{P_{N_1}(r)} = \frac{d}{dr} \log P_{N_1}(r).$$

Similarly, for $N_2 \sim P(\lambda)$,

$$\frac{P'_{N_2}(r)}{P_{N_2}(r)} = \lambda = \frac{d}{dr} \log P_{N_2}(r).$$

Then for $N_3 = N_1 + N_2$,

$$P_{N_3}(r) = P_{N_1}(r) P_{N_2}(r)$$

gives

$$\log P_{N_3}(r) = \log P_{N_1}(r) + \log P_{N_2}(r),$$

so that

$$\frac{P'_{N_3}(r)}{P_{N_3}(r)} = \frac{P'_{N_1}(r)}{P_{N_1}(r)} + \frac{P'_{N_2}(r)}{P_{N_2}(r)}$$
$$= \frac{\alpha + \beta}{1 - \alpha r} + \lambda$$
$$= \frac{\alpha + \beta + \lambda - \lambda\alpha r}{1 - \alpha r}.$$

Now note that for a random variable N whose distribution belongs to Schröter's class, equation (4.28) can be written as

$$\frac{P'_N(r)}{P_N(r)} = \frac{a + b + cr}{1 - ar}.$$

Hence, the distribution of N_3 belongs to Schröter's class, and the parameters are $a = \alpha$, $b = \beta + \lambda$ and $c = -\lambda\alpha$.

Example 4.11 *Aggregate claims from Risk 1, denoted S_1, have a compound Poisson distribution with Poisson parameter $\lambda = 2$, and aggregate claims from Risk 2, denoted S_2, have a compound negative binomial distribution with negative binomial parameters $k = 2$ and $p = 0.5$. For each risk, individual claims have probability function f, where*

$$f_1 = 0.4, \quad f_2 = 0.35, \quad f_3 = 0.25.$$

Let $S = S_1 + S_2$. Calculate $\Pr(S = x)$ for $x = 0, 1, 2, 3$ by two methods, assuming S_1 and S_2 are independent.

Solution 4.11 *As $S = S_1 + S_2$, it follows that the probability function of S can be calculated as*

$$\Pr(S = x) = \sum_{y=0}^{x} \Pr(S_1 = y) \Pr(S_2 = x - y) \qquad (4.31)$$

for $x = 0, 1, 2, \ldots$. The probability functions of S_1 and S_2 can each be calculated by the Panjer recursion formula, and values are shown in Table 4.2, as is the probability function of S, calculated by formula (4.31).

The second approach is to note that as S represents aggregate claims from Risks 1 and 2, the distribution of the number of claims from these risks belongs to Schröter's class. To apply formula (4.30) we need

$$f_1^{2*} = 0, \quad f_2^{2*} = f_1^2 = 0.16, \quad f_3^{2*} = 2 f_1 f_2 = 0.28.$$

Table 4.2 *Probability functions for S_1, S_2 and S.*

x	$\Pr(S_1 = x)$	$\Pr(S_2 = x)$	$\Pr(S = x)$
0	0.1353	0.2500	0.0338
1	0.1083	0.1000	0.0406
2	0.1380	0.1175	0.0612
3	0.1550	0.1230	0.0819

We also require $a = 0.5$, $b = 2.5$ and $c = -1$. The starting value for the recursive calculation is $g_0 = 0.25e^{-2} = 0.0338$, and by formula (4.30),

$$g_1 = 3f_1 g_0 = 0.0406,$$

$$g_2 = \tfrac{7}{4} f_1 g_1 + \left(3f_2 - \tfrac{1}{2} f_2^{2*}\right) g_0 = 0.0612,$$

$$g_3 = \tfrac{4}{3} f_1 g_2 + \left(\tfrac{13}{6} f_2 - \tfrac{1}{3} f_2^{2*}\right) g_1 + \left(3f_3 - \tfrac{1}{2} f_3^{2*}\right) g_0 = 0.0819.$$

In the above solution, we have exploited the fact that we knew that the counting variable when the risks were combined was the sum of Poisson and negative binomial random variables. If, instead, all we had known was the values of a, b and c, we could have obtained g_0 by finding p_0 numerically. It follows from the recursive nature of formula (4.27) that each value p_n is some multiple of p_0. We can use this fact to set the starting value in formula (4.27) to 1 (a convenient, but arbitrary, choice), and using the values of $a = 0.5$, $b = 2.5$ and $c = -1$ from Example 4.11, a simple computer program gives

$$\sum_{n=0}^{10{,}000} p_n = 29.5562.$$

This tells us that setting $p_0 = 29.5562^{-1} = 0.0338$ in formula (4.27) would give $\sum_{n=0}^{10{,}000} p_n = 1$. Care must be exercised in applying such an approach, and the obvious test to apply is to increase the upper limit of summation.

Schröter's class of counting distributions belongs to a larger class of distributions known as the $\mathcal{R}_k$ class. A distribution is said to belong to this class if its probability function $\{p_n\}_{n=0}^{\infty}$ can be calculated recursively from the formula

$$p_n = \sum_{i=1}^{k} \left(a_i + \frac{b_i}{n}\right) p_{n-i},$$

where k is a positive integer, $\{a_i\}_{i=1}^{k}$ and $\{b_i\}_{i=1}^{k}$ are constants, and p_n is defined to be zero for $n < 0$. Thus, Schröter's class forms a subset of the $\mathcal{R}_2$ class. As the principles involved in dealing with the $\mathcal{R}_k$ class are not different from those involved in dealing with Schröter's class, they will not be discussed further here, but some details are given in Exercise 13.

4.7 The Application of Recursion Formulae

4.7.1 Discretisation Methods

In order to develop recursion formulae for the probability function of S we have assumed that individual claim amounts are distributed on the non-negative integers. In practice, however, continuous distributions such as Pareto or lognormal are used to model individual claim amounts. In order to apply a recursion formula in such a situation we must replace a continuous distribution by an appropriate discrete distribution on the non-negative integers, and we refer to this process as discretising a distribution.

There are a number of ways in which a continuous distribution, F, with $F(0) = 0$, might be discretised. One approach is through matching probabilities. A discrete distribution with probability function $\{h_j\}_{j=1}^{\infty}$ can be created by setting

$$h_j = F(j) - F(j-1). \tag{4.32}$$

The rationale behind this approximation is that for $x = 0, 1, 2, \ldots$ values of distribution functions are equal, i.e.

$$H(x) = \sum_{j=1}^{x} h_j = F(x).$$

Also, for non-integer $x > 0$, $H(x) < F(x)$ so that H is a lower bound for F.

In the same vein, we can create a discrete distribution $\tilde{H}$ that is an upper bound for F by defining the probability function $\{\tilde{h}_j\}_{j=0}^{\infty}$ by $\tilde{h}_0 = F(1)$ and

$$\tilde{h}_j = F(j+1) - F(j)$$

for $j = 1, 2, 3, \ldots$, so that

$$\tilde{H}(x) = \sum_{j=0}^{x} \tilde{h}_j = F(x+1)$$

for $x = 0, 1, 2, \ldots$. Thus, $H(x) \leq F(x) \leq \tilde{H}(x)$ for all $x \geq 0$, and an application of this result is given in Chapter 7.

An alternative approach is to match moments of the discrete and continuous distributions. For example, we can define a probability function $\{\hat{h}_j\}_{j=0}^{\infty}$, with distribution function $\hat{H}$ by

$$\hat{H}(x) = \sum_{j=0}^{x} \hat{h}_j = \int_x^{x+1} F(y)dy \tag{4.33}$$

for $x = 0, 1, 2, \ldots$. Then, if $X \sim F$ and $Y \sim \hat{H}$,

$$\begin{aligned} E[Y] &= \sum_{x=0}^{\infty} \left(1 - \hat{H}(x)\right) \\ &= \sum_{x=0}^{\infty} \int_x^{x+1} (1 - F(y))\, dy \\ &= \int_0^{\infty} (1 - F(y))\, dy \\ &= E[X]. \end{aligned}$$

Thus, the discretisation procedure is mean preserving.

Note that although we are discretising on the integers, this technique also applies to discretising on $0, z, 2z, \ldots$ for any positive z. To see this, suppose that X has an exponential distribution with mean 100, and let Y be a random variable whose distribution is a discretised version of this exponential distribution on $0, 1, 2, \ldots$. If we scale both X and Y by dividing by 100, then $X/100$ has an exponential distribution with mean 1, while $Y/100$ has a discrete distribution on $0, 1/100, 2/100, \ldots$ with $\Pr(Y/100 = j/100) = \Pr(Y = j)$. Thus, we can think of the quality of a discretisation process improving as the fraction of the mean on which the distribution is discretised decreases. Figures 4.1 and 4.2 show discretised versions of the exponential distribution with mean 1, calculated by formula (4.32), as well as the true exponential distribution. In Figure 4.1, discretisation is on 1/10ths of the mean, whereas in Figure 4.2 it is on 1/20ths of the mean. The better approximation is clearly in Figure 4.2, and if we were to plot the discretisation on 1/100ths of the mean, it would be difficult to distinguish the discretised distribution from the continuous one.

Turning now to the calculation of the aggregate claims distribution, suppose that we want to calculate $\Pr(S \leq x)$ when the individual claim amount distribution is continuous. In particular, suppose that S has a compound Poisson distribution with Poisson parameter λ and individual claim amounts are distributed as $Pa(\alpha, \alpha - 1)$ so that $m_1 = 1$. Then for any positive constant k, kS has a compound Poisson distribution with Poisson parameter λ and individual claim amounts are distributed as $Pa(\alpha, k(\alpha - 1))$ (for reasons given in Section 4.4.1). Now define a random variable S_d to have a compound Poisson distribution with Poisson parameter λ and an individual claim amount

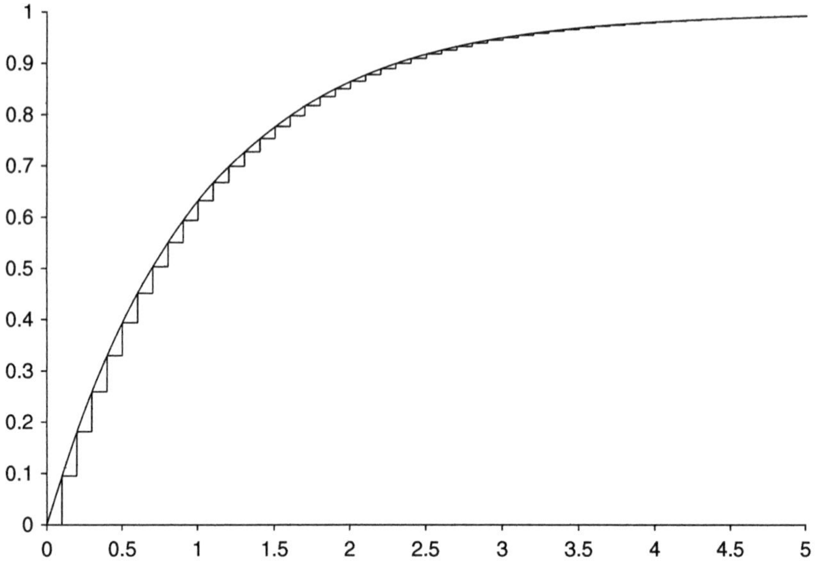

Figure 4.1 Exponential distribution with mean 1 discretised on 1/10ths.

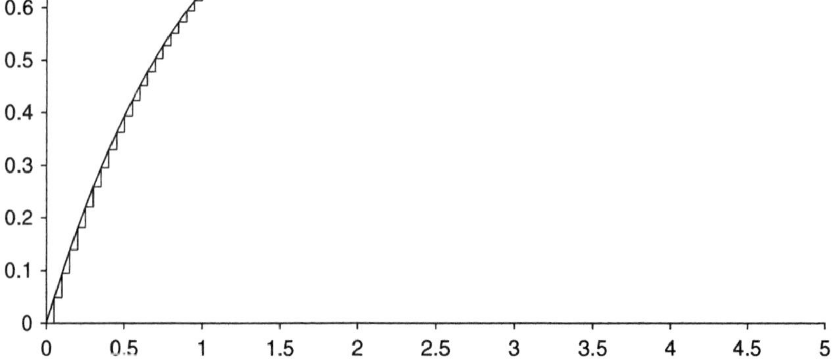

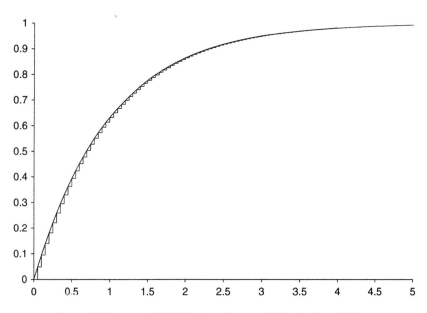

Figure 4.2 Exponential distribution with mean 1 discretised on 1/20ths.

distribution that is a discretised version of the $Pa(\alpha, k(\alpha-1))$ distribution. Then S_d is a discrete random variable whose probability function can be calculated by the Panjer recursion formula, and the distribution function of S can be found approximately since

$$\Pr(S \le x) = \Pr(kS \le kx) \approx \Pr(S_d \le kx).$$

The quality of this approximation depends on the value of the scaling factor k. In general, the larger the value of k, the better the approximation should be. In the examples in Section 4.8, the mean individual claim amount is 1 and a scaling factor of $k = 20$ has been used, so that discretisation is effectively on 1/20ths of the mean individual claim amount. This level of scaling should be appropriate for most practical purposes. It is important to appreciate that a larger scaling factor, say $k = 100$, would significantly increase computer run time.

Table 4.3 shows some approximations to $\Pr(S \le x)$ when S has a compound Poisson distribution with Poisson parameter 20 and a $Pa(2, 1)$ individual claim amount distribution. This Pareto distribution has been discretised using formula (4.33). Three scaling factors have been used, namely 20, 50 and 100. We can see from this table that an increase in the scaling factor does not have a great effect on the approximation, and this is particularly the case for larger probabilities.

Table 4.3 *Approximate values of* $\Pr(S \le x)$.

x	$\Pr(S \le x), k = 20$	$\Pr(S \le x), k = 50$	$\Pr(S \le x), k = 100$
5	0.0091	0.0090	0.0090
10	0.1322	0.1315	0.1313
15	0.3869	0.3861	0.3858
20	0.6258	0.6252	0.6250
25	0.7838	0.7834	0.7833
30	0.8741	0.8739	0.8739
35	0.9237	0.9236	0.9236
40	0.9513	0.9512	0.9512
45	0.9672	0.9671	0.9671
50	0.9768	0.9767	0.9767
55	0.9828	0.9828	0.9828
60	0.9869	0.9869	0.9869
65	0.9897	0.9897	0.9897
70	0.9917	0.9917	0.9917
75	0.9932	0.9932	0.9932
80	0.9943	0.9943	0.9943

4.7.2 Numerical Issues

We conclude our discussion of recursive methods with two warnings on computational issues. First, not all recursion schemes are stable. This means that a recursion formula may produce sensible answers initially, but will ultimately produce values that are clearly wrong. For example, when the claim number distribution is binomial, the Panjer recursion formula is unstable. Instability manifests itself in this case by producing values for the probability function of S that are outside the interval $[0, 1]$. The Panjer recursion formula is, however, stable when the claim number distribution is either Poisson or negative binomial. Instability does not mean that a recursion scheme is not useful. It simply means that we should be careful in analysing the output from our calculations.

A second issue is numerical underflow. This occurs when the initial value in a recursive calculation is so small that a computer stores it as zero. For example, if we were computing a compound Poisson probability function through the Panjer recursion formula and the Poisson parameter was so large that our computer stored g_0 as zero, then the recursion formula would give $g_1 = 0$, then $g_2 = 0$, and so on. One solution to the problem is to set g_0 to an arbitrary value such as 1, then proceed with the recursive calculation. Required values can be obtained from these values by appropriate scaling, for example by multiplying each calculated value n times by $g_0^{1/n}$. It may also be desirable to perform scaling at intermediate points in the calculation to prevent the possibility of numerical overflow.

4.8 Approximate Calculation of Aggregate Claims Distributions

In previous sections we have seen that exact calculation of aggregate claims distributions is possible in many situations. However, a problem with recursive methods is that they can be computationally intensive, even with modern computing power. Therefore, approximate calculation can still be very useful, particularly if it can be done quickly. We now describe two methods of approximating the aggregate claims distribution, each of which can be implemented easily with basic software such as a spreadsheet.

4.8.1 The Normal Approximation

The idea under the normal approximation is simple: if we know the mean and variance of S, we approximate the distribution of S by a normal distribution with the same mean and variance. A justification for this approach is that S is the sum of a (random) number of independent and identically distributed random variables. As the number of variables being summed increases, we would expect the distribution of this sum to tend to a normal distribution by the Central Limit Theorem. The problem with this argument is that we are dealing with a random sum, but if the expected number of claims is large, it is not unreasonable to expect that a normal distribution would give a reasonable approximation to the true distribution of S.

Example 4.12 *S has a compound Poisson distribution with Poisson parameter λ and individual claim amounts are lognormally distributed with mean 1 and variance 1.5. Using a normal approximation, find x such that* $\Pr(S \leq x) = 0.95$ *(a) when $\lambda = 10$, and (b) when $\lambda = 100$.*

Solution 4.12 *As $E[S] = \lambda$ and $V[S] = 2.5\lambda$, the approximate distribution of S is $N(\lambda, 2.5\lambda)$. Thus,*

$$\Pr(S \leq x) \approx \Pr\left(Z \leq \frac{x - \lambda}{\sqrt{2.5\lambda}}\right),$$

where $Z \sim N(0, 1)$, and we know from tables of the standard normal distribution that $\Pr(Z \leq 1.645) = 0.95$. *Thus,*

$$x = \lambda + 1.645\sqrt{2.5\lambda},$$

so that when $\lambda = 10$, $x = 18.23$, and when $\lambda = 100$, $x = 126.0$.

Figure 4.3 shows the exact and approximating densities from Example 4.12 when $\lambda = 10$, and Figure 4.4 shows the situation when $\lambda = 100$. In Figure 4.3, we see that the approximation is not particularly good. There are two features to note from this figure. First, the true distribution of S is positively skewed, whereas the normal distribution is symmetric. Second, under the true distribution, $\Pr(S < 0) = 0$, but this is clearly not the case under the normal approximation. The situation is different in Figure 4.4. The true distribution of S is still positively skewed, but the coefficient of skewness is now much smaller (0.395 compared with 1.25 in the case $\lambda = 10$). Also, under the normal approximation, the approximate value for $\Pr(S < 0)$ is now 0 (to many decimal places). A common feature of Figures 4.3 and 4.4 is that the normal approximation understates tail probabilities, i.e. quantities of the form $\Pr(S > x)$, and these are typically the probabilities of most interest to insurers. For example, using the Panjer recursion formula and a discretisation based on 20ths of the mean individual claim amount, the answers to the questions in Example 4.12 are $x = 19.15$ when $\lambda = 10$ and $x = 127.5$ when $\lambda = 100$.

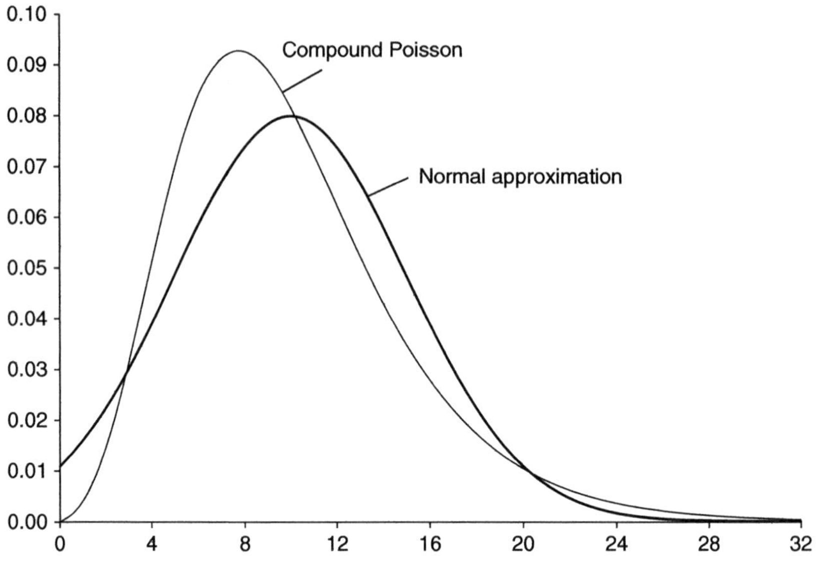

Figure 4.3 Normal approximation, $\lambda = 10$.

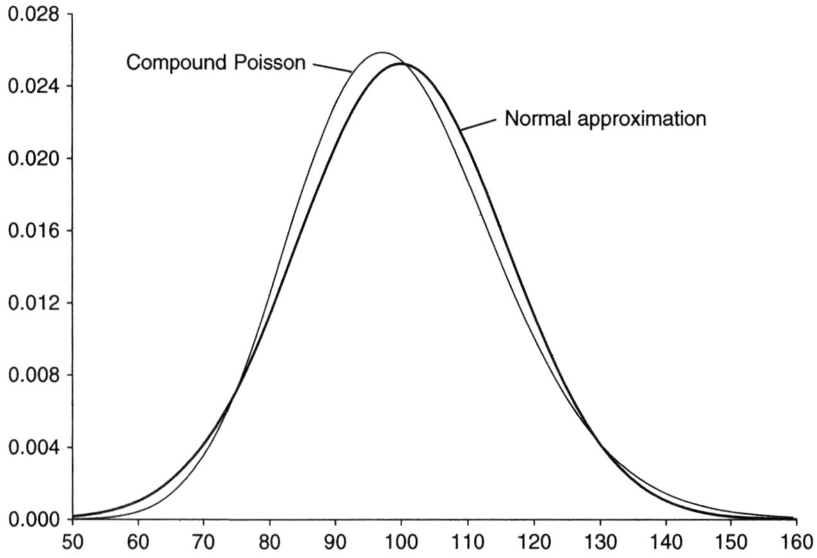

Figure 4.4 Normal approximation, $\lambda = 100$.

In each case the normal approximation has understated the 95th percentile of the distribution.

In summary, the advantages of the normal approximation are that we need little information to apply it (just the mean and variance of S), it is easy to apply, and it should give reasonable approximations if the expected number of claims is large. Its main disadvantages are that it can lead to non-zero approximations to $\Pr(S < 0)$, the approximating distribution is symmetric whereas the true distribution is usually skewed, and the approximation tends to understate tail probabilities.

4.8.2 The Translated Gamma Approximation

A failing of the normal approximation is that as it is based on the first two moments of S, the approximation cannot capture the skewness of the true distribution. The translated gamma approximation overcomes this failing by using the first three moments of S. The idea under the translated gamma approximation is that the distribution of S is approximated by that of $Y + k$, where $Y \sim \gamma(\alpha, \beta)$ and k is a constant. The parameters α, β and k of the approximating distribution are found by matching mean, variance and coefficient of skewness of the two distributions. There is no strong theoretical justification for the translated gamma approximation. However, as the approximating distribution has the same first three moments as S, we would expect this approximation to perform better than the normal approximation.

In Section 1.3.1 we saw that the coefficient of skewness of a $\gamma(\alpha, \beta)$ random variable is $2/\sqrt{\alpha}$, and translating any variable by k units does not change the coefficient of skewness. Thus, the parameters α, β and k are found from

$$Sk[S] = \frac{2}{\sqrt{\alpha}}, \tag{4.34}$$

$$V[S] = \frac{\alpha}{\beta^2}, \tag{4.35}$$

$$E[S] = \frac{\alpha}{\beta} + k. \tag{4.36}$$

Example 4.13 *S has the same compound Poisson distribution as in Example 4.12. Using a translated gamma approximation, find x such that* $\Pr(S \leq x) = 0.95$ *(a) when $\lambda = 10$, and (b) when $\lambda = 100$.*

Solution 4.13 *The first step is to calculate the parameters of the approximating distribution, for which we need the third moment of the lognormal distribution. As*

$$m_1 = 1 = \exp\{\mu + \sigma^2/2\}$$

and

$$m_2 = 2.5 = \exp\{2\mu + 2\sigma^2\},$$

we find that $\mu = -0.4581$ *and* $\sigma = 0.9572$, *so that*

$$m_3 = \exp\{3\mu + 9\sigma^2/2\} = 15.625.$$

By equation (4.34),

$$\frac{\lambda m_3}{(\lambda m_2)^{3/2}} = \frac{2}{\sqrt{\alpha}},$$

which gives

$$\alpha = \frac{4\lambda m_2^3}{m_3^2}.$$

Next, equation (4.35) gives

$$\lambda m_2 = \frac{\alpha}{\beta^2},$$

so that

$$\beta = \frac{2m_2}{m_3},$$

and finally equation (4.36) gives

$$\lambda m_1 = \frac{\alpha}{\beta} + k,$$

so that

$$k = \lambda m_1 - \alpha/\beta = \lambda\left(m_1 - \frac{2m_2^2}{m_3}\right).$$

Thus, when $\lambda = 10$, $\alpha = 2.560$, $\beta = 0.3200$ *and* $k = 2.000$. *Setting* $S = Y + k$ *where* $Y \sim \gamma(\alpha, \beta)$, *we have*

$$\Pr(S \leq x) \approx \Pr(Y \leq x - k),$$

and using software – for example, most spreadsheets have a supplied function to find the inverse of a gamma distribution – we find that

$$\Pr(Y \leq 17.59) = 0.95,$$

so that the required value of x is 19.59.

When $\lambda = 100$, *we get* $\alpha = 25.60$, $\beta = 0.3200$ *and* $k = 20.00$, *and in this case, when* $Y \sim (\alpha, \beta)$,

$$\Pr(Y \leq 107.7) = 0.95,$$

and so the required value of x is 127.7.

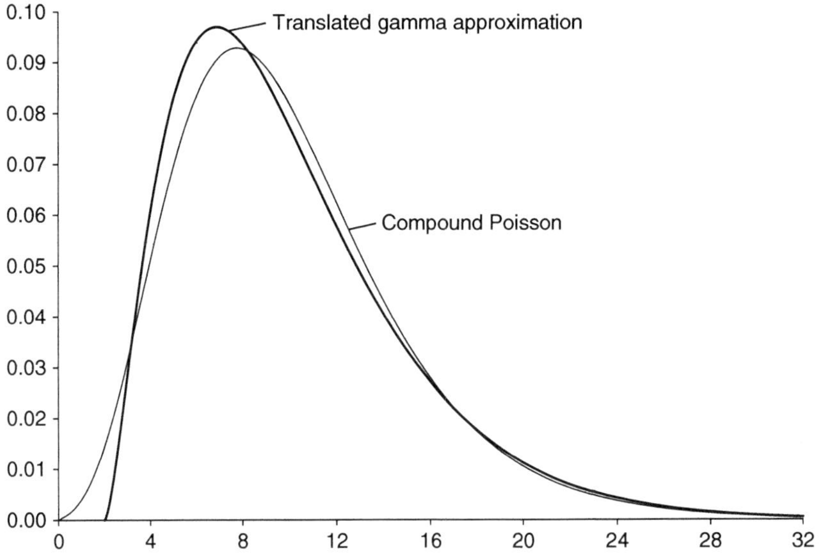

Figure 4.5 Translated gamma approximation, $\lambda = 10$.

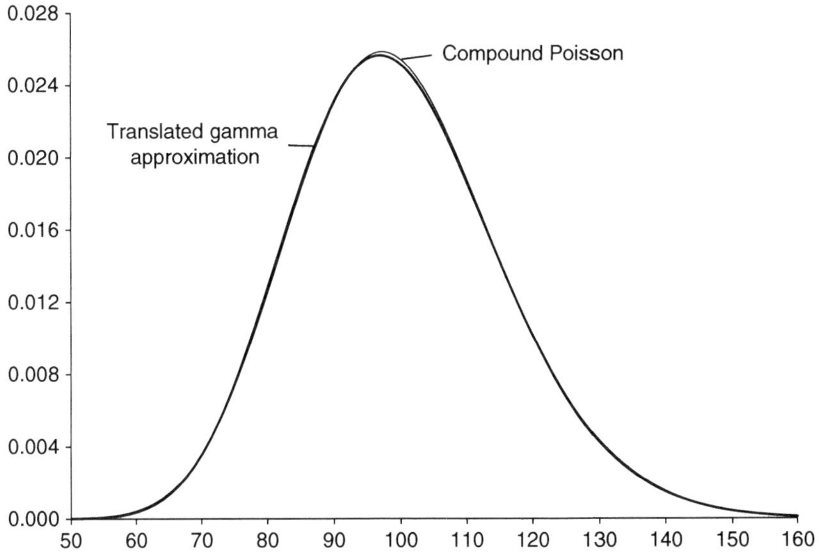

Figure 4.6 Translated gamma approximation, $\lambda = 100$.

Figure 4.5 shows the exact and approximating densities from Example 4.13 when $\lambda = 10$, and Figure 4.6 shows the situation when $\lambda = 100$. Note that in Figure 4.5 the approximating density has the same shape as the exact density and that the approximating density is above the exact density in the right-hand tail, in contrast to the normal approximation. In Figure 4.6 the approximation is excellent, and it is difficult to distinguish between the two densities in this figure. As noted in the discussion following Example 4.12, the answers to the questions in Example 4.13 are $x = 19.15$ when $\lambda = 10$, and $x = 127.5$ when $\lambda = 100$. Thus, the approximations in Example 4.13 are very good indeed.

The major advantage that the translated gamma approximation has over the normal approximation is that it takes account of the skewness of the distribution of S. However, we need one more piece of information in order to apply this approximation. In Example 4.13 the value of k is positive in each scenario, but this is not the case in general. Thus, the translated gamma approximation can give an approximation to $\Pr(S < 0)$ that is non-zero, even though this probability is zero. Nevertheless, the translated gamma approximation is a simple and easily implemented approach that can produce excellent approximations.

4.9 Notes and References

Further details on most of the topics covered in this chapter can be found in the comprehensive textbook by Klugman et al. (1998). Original references are Panjer (1981) for the Panjer recursion formula, Sundt and Jewell (1981) for the $(a, b, 1)$ class, Schröter (1991) for Schröter's class, and Sundt (1992) for the $\mathcal{R}_k$ class. Discretisation methods are discussed by Panjer and Lutek (1983), while the discretisation given by formula (4.33) is due to De Vylder and Goovaerts (1988). Numerical aspects of recursive calculations are discussed by Panjer and Willmot (1986) and Panjer and Wang (1993). These papers deal with underflow/overflow issues and stability of recursion formulae respectively.

4.10 Exercises

1. Aggregate claims, S, from a risk have a compound negative binomial distribution with negative binomial parameters $k = 80$ and $p = 0.4$. Individual claim amounts are lognormally distributed with mean 1 and variance 2. Calculate $E[S]$ and $V[S]$.

2. Aggregate claims from a risk have a compound Poisson distribution with Poisson parameter 100 and individual claim amounts are distributed as $\gamma(2, 0.001)$. Calculate the premium for this risk using the exponential premium principle with parameter 0.0001.
3. Aggregate claims from a risk have a compound Poisson distribution with Poisson parameter 200, and individual claim amounts are exponentially distributed with mean 100. Calculate the premium for this risk using the Esscher premium principle with parameter 0.001.
4. Aggregate claims from Risk 1, denoted S_1, have a compound Poisson distribution with Poisson parameter $\lambda_1 = 20$, and individual claim amounts are distributed as the random variable X where

$$\Pr(X = 10) = 0.25, \quad \Pr(X = 20) = 0.5, \quad \Pr(X = 30) = 0.25.$$

Aggregate claims from Risk 2, denoted S_2, have a compound Poisson distribution with Poisson parameter $\lambda_2 = 30$, and individual claim amounts are distributed as the random variable Y where

$$\Pr(Y = 20) = 0.3, \quad \Pr(Y = 30) = 0.4, \quad \Pr(Y = 40) = 0.3.$$

Find the distribution of $S_1 + S_2$, assuming the risks are independent.
5. Using the notation of Section 4.4.2, show that when the distribution of N is binomial, the distribution of N_R is also binomial.
6. Using the notation of Section 4.4.2, find the distribution of N_R when N has a logarithmic distribution with parameter θ.
7. Aggregate claims from a risk have a compound negative binomial distribution, with negative binomial parameters $k = 100$ and $p = 0.5$. The individual claim amount distribution is Pareto with parameters $\alpha = 3$ and $\lambda = 400$. The insurer of this risk effects excess of loss reinsurance with retention level 400 with Reinsurance Company A.

   (a) Show that the distribution of the number of (non-zero) claims for Reinsurance Company A is negative binomial with parameters 100 and $8/9$.
   (b) Show that the distribution of individual claim payments for Reinsurance Company A is Pareto with parameters 3 and 800.
   (c) Suppose that Reinsurance Company A effects a proportional reinsurance treaty with Reinsurance Company B, retaining 70% of each claim. Let S_A and S_B respectively denote aggregate claims for Reinsurance Companies A and B. Calculate $Cov(S_A, S_B)$.

8. Aggregate claims from a risk have a compound Poisson distribution with Poisson parameter 10, and the individual claim amount distribution is

exponential with mean 100. An insurer charges a premium of 1,100 to cover this risk, and arranges excess of loss reinsurance with retention level M. The random variable S_R denotes aggregate claims paid by the reinsurer, and the reinsurance premium is $E[S_R] + 0.001V[S_R]$.

(a) Find the reinsurance premium as a function of M.
(b) Let $g(M)$ denote the insurer's net profit for the year as a function of M. Show that $E[g(M)]$ is an increasing function of M. For which values of M is $E[g(M)]$ positive?
(c) Show that $V[g(M)]$ is an increasing function of M.

9. Let $X \sim F$, and let $Y \sim \hat{H}$, where $\hat{H}$ is the discrete distribution on the non-negative integers created from F by formula (4.33). Let M be a positive integer. Show that $E[\min(Y,M)] = E[\min(X,M)]$.
10. Aggregate claims, S, from a risk have a compound binomial distribution where the binomial parameters are $n = 10$ and $q = 0.6$. Individual claim amounts have probability function

$$f_1 = 0.4, \quad f_2 = 0.35, \quad f_3 = 0.25.$$

Calculate $\Pr(S \leq 5)$.
11. Aggregate claims from a risk have a compound negative binomial distribution. The distribution of the number of claims is $NB(10, 0.5)$ and individual claim amounts have probability function

$$f_x = 0.2(0.8)^{x-1}$$

for $x = 1, 2, 3, \ldots$. The insurer effects excess of loss reinsurance with retention level 4. Find the probability that the reinsurer's aggregate claim amount is less than 3.
12. The distribution of the number of claims, N, from a risk is zero-truncated geometric, with probability function $p_n = \alpha p_{n-1}$ for $n = 2, 3, 4, \ldots$, and individual claim amounts, X, have probability function $\{f_x\}_{x=0}^{\infty}$. Let $\{g_x\}_{x=0}^{\infty}$ denote the probability function of aggregate claims, S.

(a) Show that

$$P'_N(r) = 1 - \alpha + \alpha r P'_N(r) + \alpha P_N(r).$$

(b) Starting from $P_S(r) = P_N[P_X(r)]$, show that

$$P'_S(r) - (1 - \alpha) P'_X(r) + \alpha \left(P_X(r) P'_S(r) + P_S(r) P'_X(r) \right).$$

(c) Find a recursion formula for g_x, $x = 1, 2, 3, \ldots$, and show that $g_0 = (1 - \alpha) f_0 / (1 - \alpha f_0)$.

(d) Use your answer to (c) to show that

$$E\left[S^r\right] = E\left[X^r\right] + \frac{\alpha}{1-\alpha}\sum_{j=0}^{r-1}\binom{r}{j}E\left[S^j\right]E\left[X^{r-j}\right].$$

13. The probability function $\{p_n\}_{n=0}^{\infty}$ of the number of claims, N, from a risk satisfies the recursion formula

$$p_n = \sum_{i=1}^{k}\left(a_i + \frac{b_i}{n}\right)p_{n-i}, \tag{4.37}$$

where $p_n = 0$ for $n < 0$, and $\{a_i\}_{i=1}^{k}$ and $\{b_i\}_{i=1}^{k}$ are constants. Individual claim amounts $\{X_i\}_{i=1}^{\infty}$ have probability function $\{f_x\}_{x=0}^{\infty}$, and $\{g_x\}_{x=0}^{\infty}$ denotes the probability function of aggregate claims, S.

(a) Show that

$$P'_N(r) = \sum_{i=1}^{k}\left[a_i r^i P'_N(r) + (ia_i + b_i)r^{i-1}P_N(r)\right].$$

(b) Let $Y_i = \sum_{j=1}^{i} X_j$ for $i = 1, 2, \ldots, k$. Find an expression for $P'_{Y_i}(r)$ in terms of $P_{X_1}(r)$ and $P'_{X_1}(r)$.

(c) Show that

$$P'_S(r) = \sum_{i=1}^{k} a_i P_{Y_i}(r)P'_S(r) + \sum_{i=1}^{k}\left(a_i + \frac{b_i}{i}\right)P'_{Y_i}(r)P_S(r).$$

(d) Show that for $x = 1, 2, 3, \ldots$

$$g_x = \frac{1}{1 - \sum_{i=1}^{k} a_i f_0^i}\sum_{j=1}^{x} g_{x-j}\sum_{i=1}^{k}\left(a_i + \frac{b_i j}{ix}\right)f_j^{i*} \tag{4.38}$$

and that the starting value for this recursion formula is $g_0 = P_N(f_0)$.

(e) What is the main problem associated with the use of formula (4.38)?

14. Aggregate claims, S, from a risk have a compound Poisson distribution with Poisson parameter 50 and individual claim amounts are distributed according to the mixed exponential distribution

$$F(x) = 1 - 0.4e^{-0.01x} - 0.6e^{-0.02x}$$

for $x \geq 0$. Calculate approximate values of $\Pr(S \leq 4{,}500)$ using (a) a normal approximation and (b) a translated gamma approximation.

15. An insurer offers travel insurance policies. The probability that a policy produces a claim is q and the amount of a claim is an exponential random variable with mean $1,000$. The premium for such a policy is 100. This premium has been calculated on the following assumptions:

    (a) the insurer sells $10,000$ policies,
    (b) the distribution of the total claim amount from these policies can be approximated by a normal distribution and
    (c) the probability that the insurer makes a profit from this business is 0.95.

    Find the value of q.

5
The Individual Risk Model

5.1 Introduction

In the previous chapter we discussed the collective risk model, where we considered the number of claims arising from a portfolio, rather than from individual policies within that portfolio. An alternative approach is to consider the aggregate claim amount from a portfolio as the sum of the claim amounts from the individual policies that comprise the portfolio. This approach gives rise to the individual risk model, which we discuss in this chapter. In the next section we specify the model assumptions, and in subsequent sections we consider different approaches to evaluating the aggregate claims distribution. A numerical illustration of these methods is given in Section 5.6.

5.2 The Model

Consider a portfolio of n independent policies. We assume that the number of claims arising under the ith policy is either zero, with probability $1-q_i$, or one, with probability q_i, for $i = 1, 2, \ldots, n$. As in the previous chapter, we denote the aggregate claim amount by S, and write

$$S = \sum_{i=1}^{n} S_i,$$

where S_i denotes the amount paid out in claims under the ith policy. It is important to realise that the amount paid out under an individual policy can be zero (and often is in practice). We note that

$$E[S] = \sum_{i=1}^{n} E[S_i] \qquad \text{and} \qquad V[S] = \sum_{i=1}^{n} V[S_i], \tag{5.1}$$

where the second identity follows by independence.

We now introduce some further notation. Suppose that a claim occurs under the ith policy. This claim amount is modelled as a random variable with distribution function F_i such that $F_i(0) = 0$, mean μ_i and variance σ_i^2. Note that S_i has a compound binomial distribution since the distribution of the number of claims under the ith policy is $B(1, q_i)$, and so it immediately follows from formulae (4.5) and (4.6) in Section 4.2.2 that

$$E[S_i] = q_i\mu_i \qquad \text{and} \qquad V[S_i] = q_i\sigma_i^2 + q_i(1-q_i)\mu_i^2. \tag{5.2}$$

The assumption that the number of claims from a policy is either zero or one is inappropriate for most forms of general insurance. However, it represents perfectly the situation in life insurance. For the remainder of this chapter it is convenient to use the terminology of life insurance, so that q_i is the mortality rate of the holder of policy i. Further, the assumption of independence implies that there are n distinct individuals in the portfolio. We assume in the next two sections that the benefit under life insurance is fixed rather than random, so that μ_i represents the sum assured under the ith policy, and $\sigma_i^2 = 0$ for all i. We concentrate on developing formulae which can be used to calculate the aggregate claims distribution within this life insurance framework, which is the most important application for the individual risk model. It is worth noting, however, that the ideas presented in the next section can easily be extended to the case of random, rather than fixed, benefits. We consider the case $\sigma_i^2 > 0$ in Section 5.5 where we approximate the aggregate claims distribution.

Before considering the methods available to us, we remark that the distribution of S may be found by convoluting the distributions of $\{S_i\}_{i=1}^n$. In most practical applications n is large, and so this approach is not particularly attractive. Hence we seek alternative methods which involve fewer computations.

5.3 De Pril's Recursion Formula

De Pril's recursion formula provides a means of calculating the aggregate claims distribution for the individual risk model. In this section we derive the recursion formula and describe a variation of it. However, we defer application of these formulae until Section 5.6 where we compare the numerical results of different approaches to computing the aggregate claims distribution.

It is convenient to subdivide the portfolio according to mortality rate and sum assured. We assume that sums assured in the portfolio are integers, namely $1, 2, \ldots, I$, and that a policyholder is subject to one of J different mortality rates. Let n_{ij} denote the number of policyholders with mortality rate q_j and sum assured i, for $j = 1, 2, \ldots, J$ and $i = 1, 2, \ldots, I$, and let $g_x = \Pr(S = x)$ for $x = 0, 1, 2, \ldots$.

The probability generating function of the claim amount from a policyholder with mortality rate q_j and sum assured i is

$$P_{ij}(r) = 1 - q_j + q_j r^i.$$

Hence, by independence of the policyholders, the probability generating function of S is

$$P_S(r) = \prod_{i=1}^{I} \prod_{j=1}^{J} \left(1 - q_j + q_j r^i\right)^{n_{ij}} = \sum_{x=0}^{\infty} r^x g_x,$$

so that

$$\log P_S(r) = \sum_{i=1}^{I} \sum_{j=1}^{J} n_{ij} \log(1 - q_j + q_j r^i). \tag{5.3}$$

The idea now is to establish an identity in terms of the probability generating function P_S and its derivative, and to express this identity in terms of power series in r. Then by using the technique of equating coefficients of powers of r, we can establish a formula for g_x. Differentiating equation (5.3) we find that

$$\frac{d}{dr} \log P_S(r) = \frac{P'_S(r)}{P_S(r)} = \sum_{i=1}^{I} \sum_{j=1}^{J} n_{ij} \frac{q_j i r^{i-1}}{1 - q_j + q_j r^i},$$

so that

$$\begin{aligned} rP'_S(r) &= P_S(r) \sum_{i=1}^{I} \sum_{j=1}^{J} n_{ij} i \frac{q_j r^i}{1 - q_j + q_j r^i} \\ &= P_S(r) \sum_{i=1}^{I} \sum_{j=1}^{J} n_{ij} i \frac{q_j r^i}{1 - q_j} \left(1 + \frac{q_j r^i}{1 - q_j}\right)^{-1} \\ &= P_S(r) \sum_{i=1}^{I} \sum_{j=1}^{J} n_{ij} i \frac{q_j r^i}{1 - q_j} \sum_{k=1}^{\infty} (-1)^{k-1} \left(\frac{q_j r^i}{1 - q_j}\right)^{k-1}, \end{aligned}$$

where the final step holds provided that

$$\left| \frac{q_j r^i}{1 - q_j} \right| < 1$$

for all i and j. In most applications, values of q_j are small, so that this condition is usually satisfied in practice. Hence, we have

$$rP'_S(r) = P_S(r) \sum_{i=1}^{I} \sum_{j=1}^{J} n_{ij} i \sum_{k=1}^{\infty} (-1)^{k-1} \left(\frac{q_j}{1-q_j} \right)^k r^{ik}. \tag{5.4}$$

We now define

$$h(i,k) = \begin{cases} i(-1)^{k-1} \sum_{j=1}^{J} n_{ij} \left(\frac{q_j}{1-q_j} \right)^k & \text{for } i = 1, 2, \ldots, I, \\ 0 \quad \text{otherwise} & \end{cases}$$

so that equation (5.4) becomes

$$rP'_S(r) = P_S(r) \sum_{i=1}^{I} \sum_{k=1}^{\infty} r^{ik} h(i,k). \tag{5.5}$$

If we now write $P_S(r)$ and $P'_S(r)$ in summation form in equation (5.5), we get

$$\sum_{x=1}^{\infty} x r^x g_x = \sum_{x=0}^{\infty} r^x g_x \sum_{i=1}^{I} \sum_{k=1}^{\infty} r^{ik} h(i,k). \tag{5.6}$$

For $x = 1, 2, 3, \ldots$ the coefficient of r^x on the left-hand side of equation (5.6) is xg_x. The coefficient of r^x on the right-hand side is found by summing $g_{x-ik} h(i,k)$ over all i and k such that $1 \leq ik \leq x$. Letting $[x/i]$ denote the integer part of x/i we find that

$$xg_x = \sum_{i=1}^{x} \sum_{k=1}^{[x/i]} g_{x-ik} h(i,k),$$

and hence

$$g_x = \frac{1}{x} \sum_{i=1}^{x} \sum_{k=1}^{[x/i]} g_{x-ik} h(i,k)$$

for $x = 1, 2, 3, \ldots$. Finally, as $h(i,k)$ is defined to be zero for $i > I$, our recursion formula for g_x, known as De Pril's recursion formula, is

$$g_x = \frac{1}{x} \sum_{i=1}^{\min(x,I)} \sum_{k=1}^{[x/i]} g_{x-ik} h(i,k)$$

for $x = 1, 2, 3, \ldots$, and the starting value for the recursion formula is

$$g_0 = \prod_{i=1}^{I} \prod_{j=1}^{J} (1 - q_j)^{n_{ij}},$$

since $S = 0$ only if no claim occurs under each policy.

Values of q_j are small in practice, and this means that for large values of k, the terms which contribute to $h(i,k)$ are very small, and $h(i,k)$ itself is usually small. For large portfolios, it can be computationally intensive to compute the exact probability function of S through De Pril's recursion formula. One way of reducing computing time is to discard small values of $h(i,k)$, and we can do this in the following way. Let K be a positive integer, and define

$$g_0^K = g_0 \tag{5.7}$$

and

$$g_x^K = \frac{1}{x} \sum_{i=1}^{\min(x,I)} \sum_{k=1}^{\min(K,[x/i])} g_{x-ik}^K h(i,k) \tag{5.8}$$

for $x = 1, 2, 3, \ldots$. In practice, a value such as $K = 4$ is usually sufficient to give a very good approximation to the probability function of S. In fact, when each q_i is less than $1/2$,

$$\sum_{x=0}^{m^*} \left| g_x - g_x^K \right| \le \exp\{\delta(K)\} - 1,$$

where

$$m^* = \sum_{i=1}^{I} \sum_{j=1}^{J} i n_{ij}$$

is the maximum aggregate claim amount and

$$\delta(K) = \frac{1}{K+1} \sum_{i=1}^{I} \sum_{j=1}^{J} n_{ij} \frac{1-q_j}{1-2q_j} \left(\frac{q_j}{1-q_j} \right)^{K+1}. \tag{5.9}$$

A proof of this result can be found in the reference given in Section 5.7.

5.4 Kornya's Method

Kornya's method provides us with a means of approximating the distribution of S. We use ideas similar to those in the previous section to develop this method, and our set-up is identical to that in the previous section. It is now convenient to introduce the notation $p_j = 1 - q_j$, so that the probability generating function of S can be written as

$$P_S(r) = \prod_{i=1}^{I} \prod_{j=1}^{J} \left(p_j + q_j r^i\right)^{n_{ij}}.$$

We now write

$$p_j + q_j r^i = \left(1 + \frac{q_j}{p_j} r^i\right) \left(1 + \frac{q_j}{p_j}\right)^{-1}$$

using the fact that $p_j + q_j = 1$. Hence, we have

$$P_S(r) = \prod_{i=1}^{I} \prod_{j=1}^{J} \left(1 + \frac{q_j}{p_j} r^i\right)^{n_{ij}} \left(1 + \frac{q_j}{p_j}\right)^{-n_{ij}}.$$

For the remainder of this section we assume that $q_j < 1/2$ for all j. Then for $|q_j r^i / p_j| < 1$,

$$\begin{aligned}
\log P_S(r) &= \sum_{i=1}^{I} \sum_{j=1}^{J} n_{ij} \left[\log\left(1 + \frac{q_j}{p_j} r^i\right) - \log\left(1 + \frac{q_j}{p_j}\right)\right] \\
&= \sum_{i=1}^{I} \sum_{j=1}^{J} n_{ij} \sum_{k=1}^{\infty} \frac{(-1)^{k+1}}{k} \left[\left(\frac{q_j}{p_j} r^i\right)^k - \left(\frac{q_j}{p_j}\right)^k\right] \\
&= \sum_{k=1}^{\infty} \frac{(-1)^{k+1}}{k} \sum_{i=1}^{I} \sum_{j=1}^{J} n_{ij} \left[\left(\frac{q_j}{p_j} r^i\right)^k - \left(\frac{q_j}{p_j}\right)^k\right].
\end{aligned}$$

Now define $Q_S = \log P_S$, and define

$$S_k(r) = \sum_{i=1}^{I} \sum_{j=1}^{J} n_{ij} \left[\left(\frac{q_j}{p_j} r^i\right)^k - \left(\frac{q_j}{p_j}\right)^k\right],$$

so that

$$Q_S(r) = \sum_{k=1}^{\infty} \frac{(-1)^{k+1}}{k} S_k(r).$$

Next, define

$$Q_K(r) = \sum_{k=1}^{K} \frac{(-1)^{k+1}}{k} S_k(r),$$

so that Q_K contains the first K terms of Q_S.

The idea of Kornya's method is as follows. We know that

$$P_S(r) = \exp\{Q_S(r)\} = \sum_{x=0}^{\infty} r^x g_x.$$

Let us define

$$P_K(r) = \exp\{Q_K(r)\} = \sum_{x=0}^{\infty} r^x g_x^{(K)}. \tag{5.10}$$

The objective is to find values of $g_x^{(K)}$ and to use $\sum_{x=0}^{y} \left| g_x^{(K)} \right|$ as an approximation to $\sum_{x=0}^{y} g_x$. The reason for using absolute values is that our construction does not guarantee that each $g_x^{(K)}$ is positive. To find $g_x^{(K)}$ values, let us write $Q_K(r)$ as

$$\begin{aligned} Q_K(r) &= \sum_{x=0}^{\infty} r^x b_x^{(K)} \\ &= \sum_{k=1}^{K} \frac{(-1)^{k+1}}{k} \sum_{i=1}^{I} \sum_{j=1}^{J} n_{ij} \left[\left(\frac{q_j}{p_j} r^i \right)^k - \left(\frac{q_j}{p_j} \right)^k \right]. \end{aligned} \tag{5.11}$$

Then we can use equation (5.11) to find $b_x^{(K)}$ for $x = 0, 1, 2, \ldots$ by equating coefficients of powers of r.

Equating coefficients of r^0 immediately gives

$$b_0^{(K)} = \sum_{k=1}^{K} \frac{(-1)^k}{k} \sum_{i=1}^{I} \sum_{j=1}^{J} n_{ij} \left(\frac{q_j}{p_j} \right)^k.$$

To find the coefficient of r^x for $x = 1, 2, 3, \ldots$ in the second line of equation (5.11) we must consider how the product ik can equal x, as we must sum

$$\frac{(-1)^{k+1}}{k} \sum_{j=1}^{J} n_{ij} \left(\frac{q_j}{p_j} \right)^k$$

over certain values of k. The constraints on k are as follows.

(i) It is clear that k must be a divisor of x.

(ii) Recall that i represents the sum assured, and that I is the largest sum assured. Then, if $ki = x$ and $i \leq I$, we have $x \leq kI$ or $k \geq x/I$. This means that the lower limit of summation will be the least integer greater than or equal to x/I that is also a divisor of x. For example, if $x = 6$ and $I = 4$, then the only possible values for k would be 2, 3 and 6.

(iii) The upper limit of summation will be either x or K, whichever is smaller. Note that when the upper limit is K, there is a contribution at K only if K is a divisor of x. For example, in the illustration in condition (ii) above, if $K = 4$, then the upper limit of summation is 3, since 4 is not a divisor of 6.

Hence, we find that

$$b_x^{(K)} = \sum_{k=\{x/I\},k|x}^{\min(K,x)} \frac{(-1)^{k+1}}{k} \sum_{j=1}^{J} n_{x/k,j} \left(\frac{q_j}{p_j}\right)^k, \tag{5.12}$$

where $k|x$ means that k is a divisor of x, and $\{x/I\}$ denotes the least integer greater than or equal to x/I. Of course, when $x \leq I$, the lower limit of summation is 1.

Having established formulae from which we can calculate $b_x^{(K)}$ for $x = 0, 1, 2, \ldots$ we can use these values to calculate values of $g_x^{(K)}$ for $x = 0, 1, 2, \ldots$ from the following recursion formula:

$$g_x^{(K)} = \frac{1}{x} \sum_{j=1}^{x} j b_j^{(K)} g_{x-j}^{(K)} \tag{5.13}$$

for $x = 1, 2, 3, \ldots$, with $g_0^{(K)} = \exp\left\{b_0^{(K)}\right\}$. To see this, note from equation (5.10) that

$$P_K'(r) = Q_K'(r) P_K(r)$$

or, in summation form,

$$\sum_{x=1}^{\infty} x r^{x-1} g_x^{(K)} = \sum_{x=1}^{\infty} x r^{x-1} b_x^{(K)} \sum_{y=0}^{\infty} r^y g_y^{(K)}.$$

Equation (5.13) then follows by equating coefficients of powers of r, and the starting value for the recursion follows from

$$P_K(0) = g_0^{(K)} = \exp\left\{Q_K(0)\right\} = \exp\left\{b_0^{(K)}\right\}.$$

Finally, we note that when $x > IK$, the lower limit of summation in equation (5.12) is greater than the upper limit, and so $b_x^{(K)} = 0$ for $x > IK$. Hence, for $x = 1, 2, 3, \ldots$ we calculate $g_x^{(K)}$ as

$$g_x^{(K)} = \frac{1}{x} \sum_{j=1}^{\min(x,IK)} j b_j^{(K)} g_{x-j}^{(K)}.$$

Kornya's method gives an approximation to the distribution of S. The larger the value of K, the better we would expect this approximation to be, and in practice a value of $K = 4$ appears to give good results. Under the assumption that $q_j < 1/3$ for all j, it can be shown that

$$\sup_y \left| \sum_{x=0}^{y} g_x - \sum_{x=0}^{y} \left| g_x^{(K)} \right| \right| \leq \exp\{\sigma(K)\} - 1,$$

where

$$\sigma(K) = \frac{8}{3(K+1)} \sum_{i=1}^{I} \sum_{j=1}^{J} n_{ij} \left(\frac{q_j}{p_j} \right)^{K+1}. \tag{5.14}$$

A proof of this result can be found in the reference given in Section 5.7.

Kornya's method is an efficient computational tool which is easy to apply. As with other methods, we illustrate it numerically in Section 5.6.

5.5 Compound Poisson Approximation

In this section we illustrate how the aggregate claims distribution can be approximated by a compound Poisson distribution, and we give bounds for the error of this approximation. In presenting ideas, we revert to the general model described in Section 5.2. Thus, we drop the assumption of the previous two sections that the amount of a claim is fixed. Hence, we are no longer able to classify policyholders by mortality rate and sum assured as we did in those sections.

Let G_i be the distribution function of the amount paid out in claims under the ith policy. As noted in Section 5.2, G_i is a (very simple) compound binomial distribution. Assuming that all claim amounts are non-negative, and again letting $p_i = 1 - q_i$ we have

$$G_i(x) = p_i + q_i F_i(x)$$

for $x \geq 0$ and for $i = 1, 2, \ldots, n$, and G is given by

$$G(x) = G_1 * G_2 * \cdots * G_n(x) = \mathop{*}_{i=1}^{n} G_i(x).$$

There is no simple representation for the convolution of compound Binomial distributions. However, as shown in Section 4.3, there is one for the convolution of compound Poisson distributions. This motivates a simple idea. For $i = 1, 2, \ldots, n$, we can approximate G_i by P_i, where P_i is a compound Poisson distribution, and approximate G by P where

$$P(x) = \mathop{*}_{i=1}^{n} P_i(x).$$

Then P is a compound Poisson distribution.

Table 5.1 *Comparison of methods of choosing* λ_i.

	$\lambda_i = q_i$		$\exp\{-\lambda_i\} = p_i$	
q_i	λ_i	$\Pr(N_i > 1)$	λ_i	$\Pr(N_i > 1)$
0.1	0.1	0.0047	0.1054	0.0052
0.01	0.01	5×10^{-5}	0.0101	5×10^{-5}
0.001	0.001	5×10^{-7}	0.0010	5×10^{-7}
0.0001	0.0001	5×10^{-9}	0.0001	5×10^{-9}

We set

$$P_i(x) = \sum_{n=0}^{\infty} e^{-\lambda_i} \frac{\lambda_i^n}{n!} F_i^{n*}(x)$$

for $x \geq 0$ and for $i = 1, 2, \ldots, n$. Note that G_i and P_i are both compound distributions – they have different claim number distributions, but the same individual claim amount distribution.

There are two ways in which we can choose the parameter λ_i. First, we can set $\lambda_i = q_i$ so that the expected number of claims is the same under the exact binomial counting distribution and the approximating Poisson distribution. Second, we can set $\exp\{-\lambda_i\} = p_i$ so that the probability of no claims is the same under each counting distribution. In practice it matters little which method we choose if $\{q_i\}_{i=1}^n$ are small. Table 5.1 shows values of λ_i under each method for different values of q_i, as well as values of $\Pr(N_i > 1)$ where $N_i \sim P(\lambda_i)$. The message from Table 5.1 is very clear. If the value of q_i is small, then the two methods give virtually the same value of λ_i. Further, each method produces a very good approximation to the $B(1, q_i)$ distribution when q_i is small. The probability of more than one claim under each approximating Poisson distribution is non-zero, but is sufficiently close to zero not to cause concern.

The main result of this section is as follows:

$$\sum_{i=1}^{n} \left(p_i - e^{-\lambda_i}\right)^- \leq G(x) - P(x) \leq \sum_{i=1}^{n} \left(p_i - e^{-\lambda_i} + \left(q_i - \lambda_i e^{-\lambda_i}\right)^+\right) \quad (5.15)$$

for all x, where $z^+ = \max(0, z)$ and $z^- = \min(0, z)$. To prove this result we need the following two auxiliary results.

(i) Let F, G and H be distribution functions, and let a and b be constants such that

$$a \leq F(x) - G(x) \leq b$$

for all x. Then

$$a \leq F * H(x) - G * H(x) \leq b \tag{5.16}$$

for all x.

(ii) Let $\{F_i\}_{i=1}^n$ and $\{G_i\}_{i=1}^n$ be distribution functions satisfying

$$a_i \leq F_i(x) - G_i(x) \leq b_i$$

for all x and for $i = 1, 2, \ldots, n$. Then

$$\sum_{i=1}^n a_i \leq \mathop{*}_{i=1}^{n} F_i(x) - \mathop{*}_{i=1}^{n} G_i(x) \leq \sum_{i=1}^n b_i \,. \tag{5.17}$$

To prove equation (5.16), note that

$$F * H(x) = \int_{-\infty}^{\infty} F(x-y)dH(y),$$

and so

$$F * H(x) - G * H(x) = \int_{-\infty}^{\infty} [F(x-y) - G(x-y)]\, dH(y).$$

The bounds immediately follow since $a \leq F(x-y) - G(x-y) \leq b$.

The proof of equation (5.17) is by induction. By definition, equation (5.17) holds for $n = 1$. Now assume that it holds for $n = k-1$, so that

$$\sum_{i=1}^{k-1} a_i \leq \mathop{*}_{i=1}^{k-1} F_i(x) - \mathop{*}_{i=1}^{k-1} G_i(x) \leq \sum_{i=1}^{k-1} b_i \,. \tag{5.18}$$

As the convolutions in equation (5.18) are just distribution functions, we can apply the result in equation (5.16) to equation (5.18), giving

$$\sum_{i=1}^{k-1} a_i \leq \left(\mathop{*}_{i=1}^{k-1} F_i\right) * F_k(x) - \left(\mathop{*}_{i=1}^{k-1} G_i\right) * F_k(x) \leq \sum_{i=1}^{k-1} b_i \,. \tag{5.19}$$

Also

$$a_k \leq F_k(x) - G_k(x) \leq b_k,$$

and applying the result in equation (5.16) to this inequality gives

$$a_k \leq F_k * \left(\mathop{*}_{i=1}^{k-1} G_i\right)(x) - G_k * \left(\mathop{*}_{i=1}^{k-1} G_i\right)(x) \leq b_k \,. \tag{5.20}$$

By adding equations (5.19) and (5.20) we obtain equation (5.17).

We are now in a position to prove equation (5.15). Recall the definitions of G and P:

$$G(x) = \mathop{*}_{i=1}^{n} G_i(x) \qquad \text{and} \qquad P(x) = \mathop{*}_{i=1}^{n} P_i(x).$$

If equation (5.15) holds for $n = 1$, then by equation (5.17) we know that equation (5.15) holds for any value of n. Hence it is sufficient to prove equation (5.15) for $n = 1$. For $x \geq 0$ we have

$$G_i(x) = p_i + q_i F_i(x)$$

and

$$P_i(x) = \sum_{n=0}^{\infty} e^{-\lambda_i} \frac{\lambda_i^n}{n!} F_i^{n*}(x).$$

Hence

$$\begin{aligned}
G_i(x) - P_i(x) &= p_i + q_i F_i(x) - \sum_{n=0}^{\infty} e^{-\lambda_i} \frac{\lambda_i^n}{n!} F_i^{n*}(x) \\
&= (p_i - e^{-\lambda_i}) + (q_i - \lambda_i e^{-\lambda_i}) F_i(x) - \sum_{n=2}^{\infty} e^{-\lambda_i} \frac{\lambda_i^n}{n!} F_i^{n*}(x) \\
&\leq (p_i - e^{-\lambda_i}) + (q_i - \lambda_i e^{-\lambda_i}) F_i(x) \\
&\leq (p_i - e^{-\lambda_i}) + (q_i - \lambda_i e^{-\lambda_i})^+.
\end{aligned}$$

Note that the final step follows since either $q_i - \lambda_i e^{-\lambda_i} < 0$, in which case $(q_i - \lambda_i e^{-\lambda_i}) F_i(x) < 0 = (q_i - \lambda_i e^{-\lambda_i})^+$, or $q_i - \lambda_i e^{-\lambda_i} \geq 0$, in which case

$$(q_i - \lambda_i e^{-\lambda_i}) F_i(x) = (q_i - \lambda_i e^{-\lambda_i})^+ F_i(x) \leq (q_i - \lambda_i e^{-\lambda_i})^+.$$

To prove the lower bound, we make use of the fact that $F_i \geq F_i^{n*}$ for $n = 2, 3, 4, \ldots$. Then

$$\begin{aligned}
G_i(x) - P_i(x) &= p_i + q_i F_i(x) - \sum_{n=0}^{\infty} e^{-\lambda_i} \frac{\lambda_i^n}{n!} F_i^{n*}(x) \\
&\geq p_i + q_i F_i(x) - e^{-\lambda_i} - \sum_{n=1}^{\infty} e^{-\lambda_i} \frac{\lambda_i^n}{n!} F_i(x) \\
&= (p_i - e^{-\lambda_i}) + (q_i - (1 - e^{-\lambda_i})) F_i(x) \\
&= (p_i - e^{-\lambda_i}) + (e^{-\lambda_i} - p_i) F_i(x) \\
&\geq (p_i - e^{-\lambda_i}) + (e^{-\lambda_i} - p_i)^-.
\end{aligned}$$

To make the final step, we note that either $e^{-\lambda_i} - p_i \geq 0$, in which case $(e^{-\lambda_i} - p_i)^- = 0$, or $e^{-\lambda_i} - p_i < 0$, in which case

$$(e^{-\lambda_i} - p_i)F_i(x) = (e^{-\lambda_i} - p_i)^- F_i(x) \geq (e^{-\lambda_i} - p_i)^-.$$

Finally, since $z + (-z)^- = z^-$, we have

$$G_i(x) - P_i(x) \geq (p_i - e^{-\lambda_i})^-.$$

Thus, we have proved equation (5.15) for $x \geq 0$. Since we have assumed that $F_i(x) = 0$ for $x < 0$, we know that $G_i(x) - P_i(x) = 0$ for $x < 0$. Thus, for $x < 0$ the bounds are of no practical interest. It is nevertheless true that equation (5.15) holds for $x < 0$.

5.6 Numerical Illustration

Table 5.2 shows the number of policyholders, the death benefit and the mortality rate at each age for a hypothetical portfolio of life insurance policies. This is a fairly straightforward portfolio in the sense that for each possible death benefit, there is only one mortality rate. For this portfolio, formulae (5.1) and (5.2) give $E[S] = 107.03$ and $V[S] = 1{,}073.16$.

Table 5.3 shows exact and approximate values of $\Pr(S \leq x)$, calculated according to the methods described in previous sections. The legend for this table is as follows:

1. DP denotes the exact value, calculated by De Pril's recursion formula;
2. DPA denotes the approximation based on De Pril's recursion given by formulae (5.7) and (5.8) with $K = 2$;

Table 5.2 *Mortality rates and sums assured.*

Age	Death benefit	Mortality rate, $\times 10^3$	Number of policyholders
45	15	1.467	600
46	14	2.064	600
47	12	2.660	400
48	11	3.003	400
49	10	3.386	400
50	8	3.813	400
51	6	4.290	400
52	4	4.821	400
53	2	5.410	400
54	1	6.065	400

3. K2 denotes the approximation given by Kornya's method with parameter $K = 2$;
4. K3 denotes the approximation given by Kornya's method with parameter $K = 3$;
5. CP1 denotes the compound Poisson approximation when the Poisson parameter for each policy is the mortality rate;
6. CP2 denotes the compound Poisson approximation when the Poisson parameter for each policy is $-\log(1-q)$, where q is the policyholder's mortality rate;
7. N denotes the normal approximation, where the approximating normal distribution has mean 107.03 and variance 1,073.16. This is a natural approximation to apply when the number of policyholders is large, and its justification is the Central Limit Theorem.

We can see from Table 5.3 that the approximations in the columns DPA, K2 and K3 are all very good, while the compound Poisson approximations are poorer, but still good. The normal approximation is the poorest of all the approximations. However, Figure 5.1, which shows the exact probability function, suggests that as a simple approximation, a normal distribution might be reasonable.

In terms of computing time required, all approximations can be calculated almost instantaneously, whilst the exact calculation is much slower. For the approximations based on De Pril's method and Kornya's method, the value of K is small, but the error in each approximation is also small. In the case of the approximation based on De Pril's method, formula (5.9) gives $\delta(2) = 0.9934 \times 10^{-4}$, and hence

$$\sum_{x=0}^{m^*} \left| g_x - g_x^K \right| \leq \exp\{\delta(K)\} - 1 = 0.9934 \times 10^{-4},$$

Table 5.3 *Exact and approximate values of* $\Pr(S \leq x)$.

x	DP	DPA	K2	K3	CP1	CP2	N
25	0.0013	0.0013	0.0013	0.0013	0.0013	0.0013	0.0061
50	0.0298	0.0298	0.0298	0.0298	0.0299	0.0296	0.0408
75	0.1690	0.1690	0.1691	0.1690	0.1694	0.1681	0.1641
100	0.4437	0.4437	0.4437	0.4437	0.4439	0.4419	0.4150
125	0.7262	0.7261	0.7262	0.7262	0.7260	0.7243	0.7083
150	0.9015	0.9014	0.9015	0.9015	0.9012	0.9003	0.9052
175	0.9736	0.9735	0.9736	0.9736	0.9734	0.9731	0.9810
200	0.9946	0.9945	0.9946	0.9946	0.9945	0.9945	0.9977
225	0.9991	0.9990	0.9991	0.9991	0.9991	0.9991	0.9998
250	0.9999	0.9998	0.9999	0.9999	0.9999	0.9999	1.0000

Table 5.4 *Values of* $h(i, k)$.

i	$h(i,1)$	$h(i,2)$	$h(i,3)$	$h(i,4)$
1	2.441	−0.0149	9.088×10^{-5}	-5.546×10^{-7}
6	10.34	−0.0446	1.919×10^{-4}	-8.270×10^{-7}
10	13.59	−0.0462	1.569×10^{-4}	-5.330×10^{-7}
14	17.37	−0.0359	7.432×10^{-5}	-1.537×10^{-7}

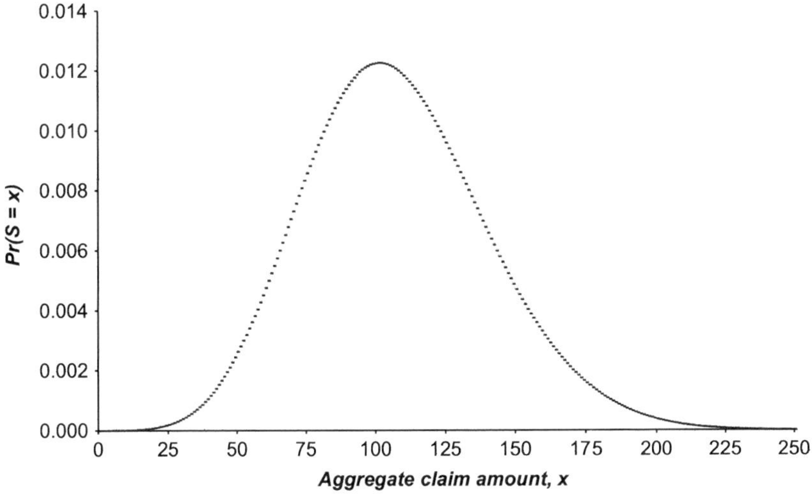

Figure 5.1 Probability function of aggregate claims.

where $m^* = 39{,}000$. Similarly, for Kornya's method with $K = 2$, formula (5.14) gives $\sigma(2) = 0.000264$ and hence

$$\sup_y \left| \sum_{x=0}^{y} g_x - \sum_{x=0}^{y} \left| g_x^{(K)} \right| \right| \leq 0.000264.$$

As an illustration of the point made in Section 5.3 about values of $h(i, k)$ being small for large values of k, Table 5.4 shows values of $h(i, k)$ for selected values of i and for $k = 1, 2, 3, 4$. We can see in this table that for each value of i, the values of $h(i, k)$ decrease in absolute value as k increases.

For the compound Poisson approximations, from equation (5.15) we find that the difference between the true distribution function and the approximation given by CP1 lies in the interval $(-0.0318, 0.0318)$, while the difference under approximation CP2 lies in the interval $(0, 0.0319)$. We note from Table 5.3 that the differences between the exact values and the compound

Poisson approximations lie comfortably within these intervals. We also note that a consequence of the choice of Poisson parameters in approximation CP2 is that the approximating distribution function always takes values less than the true distribution function.

We conclude by remarking that in practice sums assured in a portfolio can vary considerably, and it may be practical to round sums assured, perhaps to the nearest \$100. In such circumstances an 'exact' calculation would be both unnecessary and inappropriate.

5.7 Notes and References

De Pril (1986) proposed the recursion formula which bears his name, and he discussed error bounds for both his formula and Kornya's method in De Pril (1988). In De Pril (1989) he extended his recursion formula to the case when the claim amounts are random variables, rather than fixed amounts – see Exercise 3 for an illustration of this. Kornya's method is described in detail in Kornya (1983). The bounds in Section 5.5, and extensions of them, were derived by De Pril and Dhaene (1992). A practical overview of the different methods presented in this chapter is given by Kuon et al. (1987). Table 5.2 is based on Dickson and Waters (1999) who discuss a multi-period version of De Pril's recursion formula.

5.8 Exercises

1. The table below shows data for a life insurance portfolio in which the lives are independent with respect to mortality.

Mortality rate	Sum assured	Number of lives
0.001	1	100
0.002	1	300
0.002	2	200

   (a) Calculate the mean and variance of aggregate claims from this portfolio.
   (b) From first principles, calculate the probability that the aggregate claim amount from this portfolio is 2.

2. A group life insurance policy provides a death benefit on the death within one year of members of a national university superannuation scheme. For the purposes of insurance, members are classified as either Academic or General, and members are assumed to be independent with respect to

mortality. The table below shows the number of members, the death benefit and the mortality rate in each category at age 45.

Category	Number	Death benefit	Mortality rate
Academic	225	60	$0.95q$
General	300	45	q

(a) Find expressions in terms of q for the mean and variance of aggregate claims from these lives in a year.

(b) The aggregate claims distribution for this policy can be approximated by a compound Poisson distribution. Under the assumption that the number of claims by each individual has a Poisson distribution whose mean is that individual's mortality rate:

(i) fully specify the approximating compound Poisson distribution,

(ii) find expressions for the mean and variance of this compound Poisson distribution in terms of q and

(iii) explain why the expression for variance in (ii) exceeds that in part (a).

3. Consider a portfolio of n insurance policies. For $i = 1, 2, \ldots, n$, let S_i denote the amount of claims paid under policy i and let $\Pr(S_i = 0) = p_i$ and $\Pr(S_i = x) = q_i h_x$ for $x = 1, 2, 3, \ldots$, where $0 < p_i < 1$, $p_i + q_i = 1$, $q_i < 1/2$ and $\{h_x\}_{x=1}^{\infty}$ is a probability function.
Define the probability generating functions

$$B(r) = \sum_{x=1}^{\infty} r^x h_x$$

and

$$C(r, n) = \sum_{x=1}^{\infty} r^x h_x^{n*} = B(r)^n.$$

Now define $\{g_x\}_{x=0}^{\infty}$ to be the probability function of $S = \sum_{i=1}^{n} S_i$, and let $A(r) = E\left[r^S\right]$.

(a) Show that

$$\frac{d}{dr}A(r) = A(r)\sum_{i=1}^{n}\sum_{k=1}^{\infty}(-1)^{k-1}\left(\frac{q_i}{p_i}\right)^k \frac{1}{k}\frac{d}{dr}C(r,k)$$

provided that

$$\left|\frac{q_i}{p_i}B(r)\right| < 1.$$

(b) Define

$$f_x(i) = \sum_{k=1}^{\infty} \frac{(-1)^{k-1}}{k} \left(\frac{q_i}{p_i}\right)^k h_x^{k*}$$

and

$$\phi_x = \sum_{i=1}^{n} f_x(i).$$

By equating coefficients of powers of r in the expression in part (a), show that

$$g_x = \frac{1}{x} \sum_{i=1}^{x} i\phi_i g_{x-i}$$

for $x = 1, 2, 3, \ldots$, and write down an expression for g_0.

(c) Show that g_0 can also be written as

$$g_0 = \exp\left(-\sum_{i=1}^{n}\sum_{k=1}^{\infty} \frac{(-1)^{k-1}}{k} \left(\frac{q_i}{p_i}\right)^k\right).$$

(d) The mth order approximation to g_x is $g_x^{(m)}$ where

$$g_x^{(m)} = \frac{1}{x} \sum_{i=1}^{x} i\phi_i^{(m)} g_{x-i}^{(m)}$$

for $x = 1, 2, 3, \ldots$,

$$\phi_x^{(m)} = \sum_{i=1}^{n} f_x^{(m)}(i)$$

and

$$f_x^{(m)}(i) = \sum_{k=1}^{m} \frac{(-1)^{k-1}}{k} \left(\frac{q_i}{p_i}\right)^k h_x^{k*}.$$

The mth order approximation to g_0 is

$$g_0^{(m)} = \exp\left(-\sum_{i=1}^{n}\sum_{k=1}^{m} \frac{(-1)^{k-1}}{k} \left(\frac{q_i}{p_i}\right)^k\right).$$

Deduce that the first order approximation is a compound Poisson distribution.

4. In a life insurance portfolio the sums assured are $1, 2, \ldots, I$, and for a given sum assured a policyholder is subject to one of J mortality rates. Let n_{ij} denote the number of policyholders with sum assured i and mortality rate

$q_j, j = 1, 2, \ldots, J$, and let $p_j = 1 - q_j$. Claims from policies are assumed to be independent of each other. Let S denote the aggregate claim amount in one year from this portfolio, let $g_k = \Pr(S = k)$ for $k = 0, 1, 2, \ldots$, and let $P_S(r) = E[r^S]$.

(a) Show that

$$\log P_S(r) = \log g_0 + \sum_{k=1}^{\infty} \frac{(-1)^{k+1}}{k} \sum_{i=1}^{I} \sum_{j=1}^{J} n_{ij} \left(\frac{q_j r^i}{p_j} \right)^k .$$

(b) Define

$$S_k(r) = \sum_{i=1}^{I} \sum_{j=1}^{J} n_{ij} \left(\frac{q_j r^i}{p_j} \right)^k$$

and

$$Q_K(r) = \sum_{k=1}^{K} \frac{(-1)^{k+1}}{k} S_k(r) = \sum_{x=1}^{\infty} b_x^{(K)} r^x,$$

where $K \geq 1$. Find expressions for $b_x^{(2)}$ when x is even, and when x is odd. State the values of x for which these expressions are non-zero.

5. Write computer programs to verify the values given in Table 5.3.

6
Introduction to Ruin Theory

6.1 Introduction

Ruin theory is motivated by the practical issue of solvency. Solvency is a complicated topic, but in simple terms an insurance company could be described as being solvent if it has sufficient assets to meet its liabilities. This statement is somewhat vague, and in practice it is common for a level of solvency to be set by an insurance regulator. For example, a regulator might stipulate that with a suitably high probability, say 0.99, an insurance company can meet its liabilities over a specified time horizon.

Ruin theory is concerned with the level of an insurer's surplus for a portfolio of insurance policies. In Chapter 4 we considered the aggregate amount of claims paid out in a single time period. We now consider the evolution of an insurance fund over time, taking account of the times at which claims occur, as well as their amounts. To make our study mathematically tractable, we simplify a real life insurance operation by assuming that the insurer starts with some non-negative amount of money, collects premiums and pays claims as they occur. Our model of an insurance surplus process is thus deemed to have three components: initial surplus (or surplus at time zero), premiums received and claims paid. For the model discussed in this chapter, if the insurer's surplus falls to zero or below, we say that ruin occurs.

The aim of this chapter is to provide an introduction to the ideas of ruin theory, in particular probabilistic arguments. We use a discrete time model to introduce ideas that we apply in the next two chapters where we consider a continuous time model. Indeed, we will meet analogues of results given in this chapter in these two chapters. We start in the next section by describing our model, then in Section 6.3 we derive a general equation for the probability of ruin in an infinite time horizon, and consider situations in which it is possible to obtain an explicit solution for this probability. We then consider the probability of ruin in a finite time horizon in Section 6.4, while in Section 6.5 we prove Lundberg's inequality, which is one of the most famous results in risk theory.

6.2 A Discrete Time Risk Model

Throughout this chapter we consider a discrete time model for an insurer's surplus. The insurer's surplus at time n, $n = 1, 2, 3, \ldots$, is denoted $U_d(n)$ and is defined by

$$U_d(n) = u + n - \sum_{i=1}^{n} Z_i$$

for $n = 1, 2, 3, \ldots$, where

- $u = U_d(0)$ is the insurer's initial surplus, or surplus at time 0,
- Z_i denotes the insurer's aggregate claim amount in the ith time interval, and $\{Z_i\}_{i=1}^{\infty}$ is a sequence of independent and identically distributed random variables, each distributed on the non-negative integers, with $E[Z_1] < 1$, probability function $\{h_k\}_{k=0}^{\infty}$ and distribution function H and
- the insurer's premium income per unit time is 1, so that n is the total premium income up to time n.

The process $\{U_d(n)\}_{n=0}^{\infty}$ is called a surplus process, with the subscript d being used throughout this chapter to indicate that we are considering a discrete time surplus process. For the remainder of this chapter we assume that u is a non-negative integer so that the surplus process is always at an integer value (since the premium income per unit time is 1 and claim amounts are integer valued).

For this surplus process, we say that ultimate ruin occurs if the surplus ever falls to 0 or below. Formally, we define the improper random variable $T_{d,u}$ as

$$T_{d,u} = \min\{n \geq 1 \colon U_d(n) \leq 0\}$$

with $T_{d,u} = \infty$ if $U_d(n) > 0$ for $n = 1, 2, 3, \ldots$. The probability of ultimate ruin from initial surplus u, which we denote by $\psi_d(u)$, is defined by

$$\begin{aligned}\psi_d(u) &= \Pr(T_{d,u} < \infty)\\ &= \Pr\left(u + n - \sum_{i=1}^{n} Z_i \leq 0 \text{ for some } n,\ n = 1, 2, 3, \ldots\right).\end{aligned}$$

Note that under this definition, ruin does not occur at time 0 if $u = 0$.

Before proceeding to a mathematical analysis, let's first consider some features of our model. A premium income of 1 per unit time may appear rather unrealistic, although in practice we can always choose a time interval such that the insurer's premium income per unit time would be 1 (in some monetary unit, e.g. \$10,000). We will see in Chapter 7 that this is simply a very convenient modelling assumption. The assumption that $\{Z_i\}_{i=1}^{\infty}$ is a sequence of independent and identically distributed random variables implies that the distribution of the insurer's aggregate claims does not change over time, and in practice this is a realistic assumption over a short period. The assumption that $E[Z_1] < 1$ means that in each unit of time, the insurer's premium income exceeds the insurer's expected aggregate claim amount, so that we can write $1 = (1 + \theta)E[Z_1]$ where θ is the insurer's premium loading factor. In Chapter 4 we saw that appropriate use of scaling allowed us to apply a model in which individual claims were distributed on the integers, and as we will see in Chapter 7, scaling can similarly be applied to this discrete time model.

6.3 The Probability of Ultimate Ruin

In this section we derive a general equation which can be used to calculate ψ_d. We also find an explicit solution for $\psi_d(0)$ and show that explicit solutions for ψ_d can be found for certain forms of H.

Consider the aggregate claim amount, Z_1, in the first time period. If $Z_1 > u$, then $U_d(1) \leq 0$, and so ruin occurs at time 1. However, if $Z_1 = j$, $j = 0, 1, 2, \ldots, u$, then the surplus at time 1 is $u + 1 - j$, and the probability of ruin from this new surplus level is $\psi_d(u + 1 - j)$. This latter point follows because $\{Z_i\}_{i=1}^{\infty}$ is a sequence of independent and identically distributed random variables. Consequently, if the surplus level at time 1 is $U_d(1) > 0$, then the probability of ultimate ruin from this level is

$$\Pr\left(U_d(1) + n - 1 - \sum_{i=2}^{n} Z_i \leq 0 \text{ for some } n,\ n = 2, 3, 4, \ldots\right),$$

which is just $\psi_d(U_d(1))$.

Hence, we have

$$\psi_d(u) = \sum_{j=0}^{u} h_j \psi_d(u + 1 - j) + 1 - H(u)$$

for $u = 0, 1, 2, \ldots$, or, equivalently,

$$\psi_d(u) = \sum_{r=1}^{u+1} h_{u+1-r} \psi_d(r) + 1 - H(u), \tag{6.1}$$

from which it follows that for $w = 0, 1, 2, \ldots$,

$$\begin{aligned}\sum_{u=0}^{w} \psi_d(u) &= \sum_{u=0}^{w} \sum_{r=1}^{u+1} h_{u+1-r} \psi_d(r) + \sum_{u=0}^{w} [1 - H(u)] \\ &= \sum_{r=1}^{w+1} \psi_d(r) \sum_{u=r-1}^{w} h_{u+1-r} + \sum_{u=0}^{w} [1 - H(u)] \\ &= \sum_{r=1}^{w+1} \psi_d(r) H(w + 1 - r) + \sum_{u=0}^{w} [1 - H(u)] \\ &= \sum_{r=1}^{w} \psi_d(r) H(w + 1 - r) + \psi_d(w + 1) h_0 + \sum_{u=0}^{w} [1 - H(u)].\end{aligned}$$

Hence

$$\psi_d(w+1)h_0 = \psi_d(0) + \sum_{r=1}^{w} \psi_d(r)[1 - H(w+1-r)] - \sum_{r=0}^{w} [1 - H(r)]. \quad (6.2)$$

(Note that in equation (6.2) we have applied the convention that $\sum_{j=a}^{b} = 0$ if $b < a$ to the case $w = 0$, and we use this convention throughout.)

It also follows from equation (6.1) that

$$\psi_d(w + 1)h_0 = \psi_d(w) - \sum_{r=1}^{w} h_{w+1-r} \psi_d(r) - [1 - H(w)], \quad (6.3)$$

and so, equating the right-hand sides of equations (6.2) and (6.3), we have

$$\psi_d(w) = \psi_d(0) + \sum_{r=1}^{w} \psi_d(r)[1 - H(w - r)] - \sum_{r=0}^{w-1} [1 - H(r)] \quad (6.4)$$

for $w = 0, 1, 2, \ldots$.

We now show that $\psi_d(0) = E[Z_1]$. To do this, let $g_d(y)$ denote the probability that ruin occurs from initial surplus 0 and that the deficit at the time of ruin is y, $y = 0, 1, 2, \ldots$. (Note that a "deficit" of 0 is just a consequence of our definition of ψ_d. We refer to this as a deficit even though the insurer would not actually be in deficit under the usual meaning of the word.) To apply the function g_d it is important to note that it has an alternative interpretation. For $y = 1, 2, 3, \ldots$ and $u > 0$, $g_d(y)$ is the probability that the surplus falls below its initial level at some time in the future and that the resulting surplus when this occurs is $u - y$, with a similar interpretation applying when $y = 0$.

We can use the function g_d to write an expression for ψ_d using a probabilistic argument. If ruin occurs from initial surplus u, then either

(i) on the first occasion that the surplus falls below (or to) its initial level, the resulting surplus level is $u-y$, $y = 0, 1, 2, \ldots, u-1$, and ruin subsequently occurs from this surplus level, or
(ii) on the first occasion that the surplus falls below its initial level, the resulting surplus is 0 or less, so that ruin occurs.

Hence, for $u = 1, 2, 3, \ldots$,

$$\psi_d(u) = \sum_{y=0}^{u-1} g_d(y)\psi_d(u-y) + \sum_{y=u}^{\infty} g_d(y). \tag{6.5}$$

Also

$$\psi_d(0) = \sum_{y=0}^{\infty} g_d(y)$$

as the insurer's deficit at ruin must be one of $0, 1, 2, \ldots$ if ruin occurs. Hence equation (6.5) can be written as

$$\begin{aligned}\psi_d(u) &= \sum_{y=0}^{u-1} g_d(y)\psi_d(u-y) + \psi_d(0) - \sum_{y=0}^{u-1} g_d(y)\\ &= \psi_d(0) + \sum_{y=1}^{u} g_d(u-y)\psi_d(y) - \sum_{y=0}^{u-1} g_d(y).\end{aligned} \tag{6.6}$$

By equations (6.4) and (6.6) it follows that

$$g_d(y) = 1 - H(y)$$

for $y = 0, 1, 2, \ldots$, and so

$$\psi_d(0) = \sum_{y=0}^{\infty}[1 - H(y)] = E[Z_1].$$

Hence, we can write equation (6.5) as

$$\psi_d(u) = \sum_{y=0}^{u-1}[1 - H(y)]\psi_d(u-y) + \sum_{y=u}^{\infty}[1 - H(y)]. \tag{6.7}$$

Example 6.1 *Let* $\Pr(Z_1 = 0) = p = 1 - \Pr(Z_1 = 2)$ *where* $0.5 < p < 1$, *so that in each time period the insurer's surplus either increases by* 1 *or decreases by* 1. *Find an expression for* $\psi_d(u)$ *for* $u = 1, 2, 3, \ldots$.

Solution 6.1 *Setting $q = 1 - p$ we have $E[Z_1] = 2q$, giving $\psi_d(0) = 2q$. Next, as $H(0) = H(1) = p$, and $H(k) = 1$ for $k \geq 2$, equation (6.7) gives*

$$\psi_d(1) = q\psi_d(1) + q$$

or, equivalently,

$$\psi_d(1) = q/p.$$

Similarly, for $u = 2, 3, 4, \ldots$ equation (6.7) gives

$$\psi_d(u) = q\psi_d(u) + q\psi_d(u-1),$$

so that

$$\begin{aligned}\psi_d(u) &= (q/p)\psi_d(u-1)\\ &= (q/p)^u.\end{aligned}$$

Example 6.2 *Let $\Pr(Z_1 = 0) = p$ and*

$$\Pr(Z_1 = k) = q(1-\alpha)\alpha^{k-1}$$

for $k = 1, 2, 3, \ldots$, where $0 < p < 1$, $p + q = 1$ and α is such that $E[Z_1] < 1$. Find an expression for $\psi_d(u)$ for $u = 0, 1, 2, \ldots$.

Solution 6.2 *First, note that for $k = 0, 1, 2, \ldots$,*

$$H(k) = 1 - q\alpha^k,$$

so that

$$E[Z_1] = \sum_{k=0}^{\infty} [1 - H(k)] = \frac{q}{1-\alpha},$$

and hence $\psi_d(0) = q/(1-\alpha)$. If we now insert for H in equation (6.7) we get

$$\psi_d(u) = \sum_{y=0}^{u-1} q\alpha^y \psi_d(u-y) + \sum_{y=u}^{\infty} q\alpha^y$$

or, equivalently,

$$\psi_d(u) = \sum_{y=1}^{u} q\alpha^{u-y}\psi_d(y) + \sum_{y=u}^{\infty} q\alpha^y. \tag{6.8}$$

Increasing the initial surplus by 1, we have

$$\psi_d(u+1) = \sum_{y=1}^{u+1} q\alpha^{u+1-y}\psi_d(y) + \sum_{y=u+1}^{\infty} q\alpha^y. \tag{6.9}$$

Multiplication of equation (6.8) by α gives

$$\alpha\psi_d(u) = \sum_{y=1}^{u} q\alpha^{u+1-y}\psi_d(y) + \sum_{y=u+1}^{\infty} q\alpha^y, \tag{6.10}$$

and subtraction of equation (6.10) from equation (6.9) gives

$$\psi_d(u+1) - \alpha\psi_d(u) = q\psi_d(u+1)$$

or

$$\psi_d(u+1) = \frac{\alpha}{p}\psi_d(u)$$

for $u = 0, 1, 2, \ldots$. Hence

$$\psi_d(u) = \psi_d(0)\left(\frac{\alpha}{p}\right)^u = \frac{q}{1-\alpha}\left(\frac{\alpha}{p}\right)^u.$$

6.4 The Probability of Ruin in Finite Time

For an integer value of t, we define the finite time ruin probability as

$$\psi_d(u,t) = \Pr(T_{d,u} \le t).$$

Thus, $\psi_d(u,t)$ gives the probability that ruin occurs from initial surplus u at or before the fixed point in time t.

Explicit solutions for $\psi_d(u,t)$ are generally not available, but recursive calculation of this probability is possible. Consider first the case $t = 1$. Ruin occurs at time 1 if $Z_1 > u$. Hence,

$$\psi_d(u,1) = \sum_{k=u+1}^{\infty} h_k = 1 - H(u). \tag{6.11}$$

For any integer value of t greater than 1 we have

$$\psi_d(u,t) = \psi_d(u,1) + \sum_{k=0}^{u} h_k\psi_d(u+1-k, t-1). \tag{6.12}$$

This identity follows by considering what happens in the first time period. If ruin occurs at or before time t, then either

(i) $Z_1 > u$ so that ruin occurs at time 1 or
(ii) $Z_1 = k$, $k = 0, 1, 2, \ldots, u$, and ruin occurs in the next $t-1$ time periods, from surplus level $u+1-k$ at time 1.

Provided we can calculate the probability function $\{h_k\}_{k=0}^{\infty}$ we can use these formulae to calculate finite time ruin probabilities recursively. Suppose we wish to calculate $\psi_d(u,t)$ for fixed integer values of u and t. The first step is to calculate $\psi_d(\omega,1)$ for $\omega = 1,2,3,\ldots,u+t-1$ from equation (6.11). We next calculate $\psi_d(\omega,2)$ for $\omega = 1,2,3,\ldots,u+t-2$ from equation (6.12). We continue in this manner, using equation (6.12) to calculate values of $\psi_d(\omega,\tau)$ for $\omega = 1,2,3,\ldots,u+t-\tau$, having previously calculated values of $\psi_d(\omega,\tau-1)$ for $\omega = 1,2,3,\ldots,u+t-\tau+1$, until we calculate values of $\psi_d(\omega,t-1)$ for $\omega = 1,2,3,\ldots,u+1$. This final set of values can then by applied to calculate $\psi_d(u,t)$.

If the values of u and t are large, it can be time consuming (even for a computer) to apply the above procedure to calculate $\psi_d(u,t)$. Since many of the probabilities used in the calculations will be very small, we can reduce the number of calculations involved by ignoring small probabilities. For a (small) fixed value $\epsilon > 0$, define k_1 to be the least integer such that $H(k_1) \geq 1-\epsilon$, and define

$$h_k^{\epsilon} = \begin{cases} h_k & \text{for } k = 0,1,2,\ldots,k_1 \\ 0 & \text{for } k = k_1+1, k_1+2,\ldots \end{cases}$$

and define

$$\psi_d^{\epsilon}(u,1) = \begin{cases} 1-H(u) & \text{for } u = 0,1,2,\ldots,k_1 \\ 0 & \text{for } u = k_1+1, k_1+2,\ldots \end{cases}.$$

Thus, we are setting values less than ϵ to be zero.

For $t = 2,3,4,\ldots$, let

$$\psi_d^{\epsilon}(u,t) = \psi_d^{\epsilon}(u,1) + \sum_{k=0}^{u} h_k^{\epsilon}\psi_d^{\epsilon}(u+1-k,t-1) \tag{6.13}$$

for $u = 0,1,2,\ldots,k_t$, where k_t is the integer such that

$$\psi_d(k_t-1,t) > \epsilon \geq \psi_d(k_t,t).$$

The definition of $\psi_d^{\epsilon}(u,t)$ is completed by setting $\psi_d^{\epsilon}(u,t) = 0$ for $u = k_t + 1, k_t+2,\ldots$.

We can calculate $\psi_d^{\epsilon}(u,t)$ instead of $\psi_d(u,t)$, and the difference between the two values is given by

$$\psi_d^{\epsilon}(u,t) \leq \psi_d(u,t) \leq \psi_d^{\epsilon}(u,t) + 3t\epsilon \tag{6.14}$$

for $t = 1,2,3,\ldots$. We will not prove this result, but simply indicate the advantage of calculating $\psi_d^{\epsilon}(u,t)$ instead of $\psi_d(u,t)$. First, by a suitable choice of ϵ, we can control the error in our calculation. For example, if we set

$\epsilon = 10^{-3}/(3t)$, then the difference between $\psi_d^\epsilon(u,t)$ and $\psi_d(u,t)$ will be at most 10^{-3}. Second, the upper limit of summation in equation (6.13) is in fact $\min(u,k_1)$ since $h_k^\epsilon = 0$ for $k > k_1$ and the lower limit of summation is $\max(0, u+1-k_{t-1})$ since $\psi_d^\epsilon(j,t-1) = 0$ for $j > k_{t-1}$. Thus, the number of computations involved in calculating $\psi_d^\epsilon(u,t)$ may be considerably less than the number required to calculate $\psi_d(u,t)$.

We illustrate an application of this algorithm in Chapter 8.

6.5 Lundberg's Inequality

In each of the examples in Section 6.3, $\psi_d(u)$ is an exponential function for $u > 0$. In this section, we derive a famous result known as Lundberg's inequality, which shows that ψ_d is bounded above by an exponential function whenever the moment generating function of Z_1 exists. To do this we need to introduce a new quantity known as the adjustment coefficient.

For our surplus process, the adjustment coefficient, which we denote by R_d, is defined to be the unique positive root of

$$E\left[\exp\{r(Z_1 - 1)\}\right] = 1,$$

so that R_d is given by

$$E\left[\exp\{R_d(Z_1 - 1)\}\right] = 1.$$

We have provided no motivation for this definition, but it will be apparent from the proof below of Lundberg's inequality why R_d is defined in this way. To show that the adjustment coefficient exists, we consider the function

$$g(r) = E\left[\exp\{r(Z_1 - 1)\}\right].$$

First, we note that $g(r) > 0$ for $r > 0$ so the function is positive. Also, $g(0) = 1$ and

$$g'(r) = E\left[(Z_1 - 1)\exp\{r(Z_1 - 1)\}\right],$$

so that $g'(0) = E[Z_1] - 1 < 0$. Thus, the function is decreasing at 0. Further, any turning point of the function is a minimum since

$$g''(r) = E\left[(Z_1 - 1)^2\exp\{r(Z_1 - 1)\}\right] > 0,$$

and there is exactly one turning point since $\lim_{r\to\infty} g(r) = \infty$. This final point can be seen by noting that

$$g(r) = \sum_{k=0}^{\infty} e^{r(k-1)}h_k > \sum_{k=2}^{\infty} e^{r(k-1)}h_k > e^r\sum_{k=2}^{\infty} h_k = e^r(1 - H(1)).$$

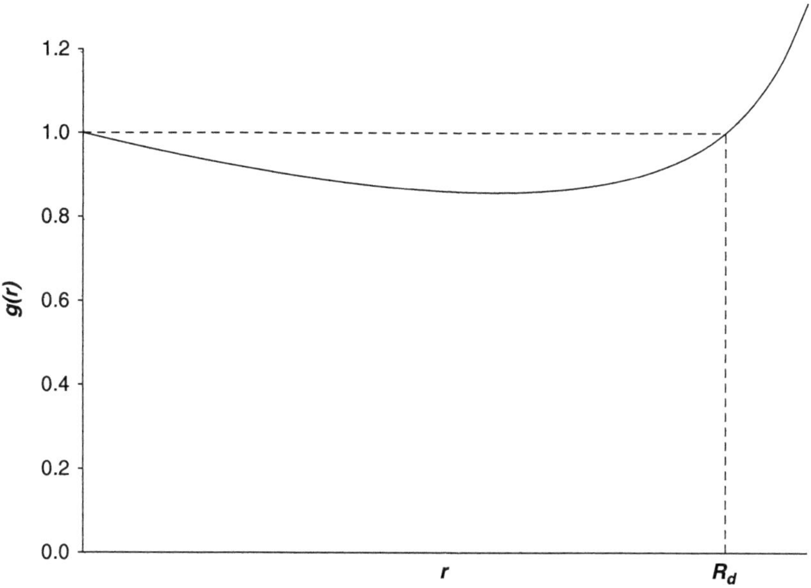

Figure 6.1 The function g.

Thus, $g(r)$ decreases with r from the value 1 when $r = 0$ to a turning point, then increases. Hence there is a unique positive number R_d such that $g(R_d) = 1$, as illustrated in Figure 6.1.

Example 6.3 *Let* $\Pr(Z_1 = 0) = p = 1 - \Pr(Z_1 = 2)$ *where* $0.5 < p < 1$ *(as in Example 6.1). Find* R_d.

Solution 6.3 *Again writing* $q = 1 - p$*, we have*

$$E\left[\exp\{R_d(Z_1 - 1)\}\right] = p\exp\{-R_d\} + q\exp\{R_d\}, \tag{6.15}$$

and setting this equal to 1 gives

$$q\exp\{2R_d\} - \exp\{R_d\} + p = 0.$$

The solutions to this quadratic are $\exp\{R_d\} = 1$ *and* $\exp\{R_d\} = p/q$*, from which we deduce that* $R_d = \log(p/q)$ *since* R_d *is the positive number satisfying equation (6.15).*

Lundberg's inequality states that

$$\psi_d(u) \leq e^{-R_d u},$$

and we can prove this by proving that

$$\psi_d(u,t) \le e^{-R_d u}$$

for $t = 1, 2, 3, \ldots$ since

$$\psi_d(u) = \lim_{t\to\infty} \psi_d(u,t).$$

We use induction on t to prove the result. As

$$\psi_d(u,1) = \sum_{k=u+1}^{\infty} h_k$$

and $\exp\{-R_d(u+1-k)\} \ge 1$ for $k = u+1, u+2, u+3, \ldots$, since the exponent is non-negative, we have

$$\begin{aligned}\psi_d(u,1) &\le \sum_{k=u+1}^{\infty} e^{-R_d(u+1-k)} h_k \\ &\le \sum_{k=0}^{\infty} e^{-R_d(u+1-k)} h_k \\ &\le e^{-R_d u} \sum_{k=0}^{\infty} e^{R_d(k-1)} h_k \\ &= e^{-R_d u},\end{aligned}$$

where we have used the fact that

$$\sum_{k=0}^{\infty} e^{R_d(k-1)} h_k = E\left[\exp\{R_d(Z_1 - 1)\}\right] = 1.$$

Now assume that $\psi_d(u,t) \le e^{-R_d u}$ for a fixed integer value of t, where $t \ge 1$. As

$$\psi_d(u,t+1) = \psi_d(u,1) + \sum_{k=0}^{u} h_k \psi_d(u+1-k,t),$$

our inductive hypothesis gives

$$\psi_d(u,t+1) \le \sum_{k=u+1}^{\infty} h_k + \sum_{k=0}^{u} h_k e^{-R_d(u+1-k)},$$

and as

$$\sum_{k=u+1}^{\infty} h_k \le \sum_{k=u+1}^{\infty} e^{-R_d(u+1-k)} h_k,$$

it follows that

$$\psi_d(u, t+1) \leq \sum_{k=0}^{\infty} e^{-R_d(u+1-k)} h_k = e^{-R_d u},$$

and this completes the proof.

Example 6.4 *Let* $\Pr(Z_1 = 0) = 0.8 = 1 - \Pr(Z_1 = 3)$. *Calculate an upper bound for* $\psi_d(5)$.

Solution 6.4 *The equation defining* R_d *is*

$$0.2\exp\{3R_d\} - \exp\{R_d\} + 0.8 = 0.$$

Solving numerically, for example by the Newton-Raphson method, gives $R_d = 0.4457$, *and so*

$$\psi_d(5) \leq \exp\{-5 \times 0.4457\} = 0.1077.$$

6.6 Notes and References

The model discussed in this chapter can be described as a compound binomial model. The reason for this is that the probability function $\{h_k\}_{k=0}^{\infty}$ is the same as a compound binomial probability function whose counting distribution is $B(1, 1 - h_0)$ and whose individual claim amount distribution has probability function $\{h_k/(1 - h_0)\}_{k=1}^{\infty}$.

Example 6.1 is a well-known problem from probability theory, known as the gambler's ruin problem. See, for example, Grimmett and Welsh (1986).

The truncation procedure in the recursive algorithm to calculate $\psi_d(u, t)$ was proposed by De Vylder and Goovaerts (1988), and this paper also contains the method of proof of equation (6.14).

Readers who are familiar with martingales will recognise that the process $\{\exp\{-R_d U(n)\}\}_{n=0}^{\infty}$ is a martingale, and that Lundberg's inequality can be proved by martingale arguments – see, for example, Gerber (1979) or Rolski et al. (1999). Under this approach, the equation defining R_d appears natural, and this comment equally applies to the equation defining the adjustment coefficient for the model discussed in Chapter 7. However, martingale arguments are not required to prove results discussed in Chapters 7 and 8 and so will not be discussed further.

6.7 Exercises

1. Let $\Pr(Z_1 = 0) = p = 1 - \Pr(Z_1 = 3) = 1 - q$, where $E[Z_1] < 1$.
   (a) Find expressions for $\psi_d(u)$ for $u = 0, 1$ and 2 and prove that
   $$\psi_d(u) = \frac{q}{p}\left(\psi_d(u-1) + \psi_d(u-2)\right)$$
   for $u = 3, 4, 5, \ldots$.
   (b) Find the least value of u such that $\psi_d(u) < 0.01$ when $p = 0.8$.
2. Let $\Pr(Z_1 = 0) = p$ and for $k = 1, 2, 3, \ldots$ let
   $$\Pr(Z_1 = k) = q(1-\alpha)\alpha^{k-1},$$
   where $0 < p < 1, p + q = 1$ and $E[Z_1] < 1$. Prove that $R_d = \log(p/\alpha)$.
3. Define
   $$G_d(u, y) = \Pr(T_{d,u} < \infty \quad \text{and} \quad U_d(T_{d,u}) > -y)$$
   for $u = 0, 1, 2, \ldots$ and $y = 1, 2, 3, \ldots$, so that $G_d(u, y)$ is the probability that ruin occurs from initial surplus u and that the insurer's deficit at the time of ruin is less than y.
   (a) Verify that
   $$G_d(0, y) = \sum_{j=0}^{y-1}[1 - H(j)].$$
   (b) Explain why
   $$G_d(u, y) = \sum_{j=0}^{u-1}[1 - H(j)]G_d(u-j, y) + \sum_{j=u}^{u+y-1}[1 - H(j)].$$
   (c) Let Z_1 have the same distribution as in Exercise 2. Show that
   $$G_d(u, y) = (1 - \alpha^y)\frac{q}{1-\alpha}\left(\frac{\alpha}{p}\right)^u$$
   for $u = 0, 1, 2, \ldots$ and $y = 0, 1, 2, \ldots$.
   (d) Let Z_1 have the same distribution as in Exercise 1. Show that if ruin occurs from initial surplus 0, the insurer's deficit at ruin is uniformly distributed on 0, 1, 2.
4. Let $\Pr(Z_1 = 0) = 0.7$, $\Pr(Z_1 = 1) = 0.2$ and $\Pr(Z_1 = 2) = 0.1$. Calculate $\psi_d(0, 3)$.

7
Classical Ruin Theory

7.1 Introduction

In Chapter 6 we considered a discrete time model for a surplus process. We now consider a continuous time risk process known as the classical risk process, and for most of the chapter we consider the probability of ruin in infinite time. We do this for two reasons. First, it is easier to consider an infinite time horizon compared with a finite time horizon. Second, ideas introduced in this chapter can be applied to more complex problems, as illustrated in Chapter 8.

Our main objective is to be able to calculate ruin probabilities, and we take two approaches to this. First, we show how explicit solutions for the probability of ruin in infinite time can be found. Second, we discuss numerical approaches to finding ruin probabilities which are applicable in situations when we cannot obtain an explicit formula for a ruin probability.

We start with a description of the classical risk process, then derive Lundberg's inequality for this risk process before considering ruin probabilities.

7.2 The Classical Risk Process

In the classical risk process, an insurer's surplus at a fixed time $t > 0$ is determined by three quantities: the amount of surplus at time 0, the amount of premium income received up to time t and the amount paid out in claims up to time t. The only one of these three which is random is claims outgo, so we start by describing the aggregate claims process, which we denote by $\{S(t)\}_{t\geq 0}$.

Let $\{N(t)\}_{t\geq 0}$ be a counting process for the number of claims, so that for a fixed value $t > 0$, the random variable $N(t)$ denotes the number of claims that occur in the fixed time interval $[0, t]$. In the classical risk process it is assumed that $\{N(t)\}_{t\geq 0}$ is a Poisson process, a process which we briefly review in the next section.

Individual claim amounts are modelled as a sequence of independent and identically distributed random variables $\{X_i\}_{i=1}^{\infty}$, so that X_i denotes the amount of the ith claim. We can then say that the aggregate claim amount up to time t, denoted $S(t)$, is

$$S(t) = \sum_{i=1}^{N(t)} X_i$$

with the understanding that $S(t) = 0$ when $N(t) = 0$. The aggregate claims process $\{S(t)\}_{t\geq 0}$ is then a compound Poisson process, and we describe some properties of this process in the next section.

We can now describe the surplus process, denoted by $\{U(t)\}_{t\geq 0}$, as

$$U(t) = u + ct - S(t),$$

where u is the insurer's surplus at time 0 and c is the insurer's rate of premium income per unit time, which we assume to be received continuously. Figure 7.1 shows a realisation of a surplus process.

Throughout this chapter we denote the distribution function of X_1 by F, and we assume that $F(0) = 0$, so that all claim amounts are positive. For simplicity, we assume that this distribution is continuous with density function f, and keeping the notation of Chapter 4, the kth moment of X_1 is denoted by m_k. Whenever the moment generating function of X_1 exists, we denote

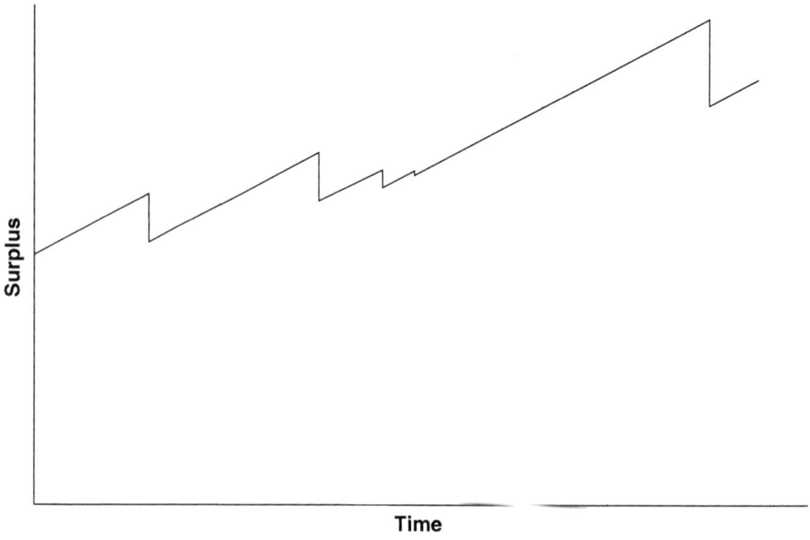

Figure 7.1 A realisation of a surplus process.

it by M_X, and we assume that when it exists, there exists some quantity γ, $0 < \gamma \leq \infty$, such that $M_X(r)$ is finite for all $r < \gamma$ with

$$\lim_{r \to \gamma^-} M_X(r) = \infty.$$

This is a technical condition which we require in Section 7.5. As an illustration, suppose that $X_1 \sim \gamma(3, 3)$. Then $M_X(r) = 27/(3 - r)^3$ for $r < 3$ and

$$\lim_{r \to 3^-} M_X(r) = \infty,$$

so that in this case, the value of γ is 3.

This model is, of course, a simplification of reality. Some of the more important simplifications are that we assume claims are settled in full as soon as they occur, there is no allowance for interest on the insurer's surplus and there is no mention of expenses that an insurer would incur. Nevertheless, this is a useful model which can give us some insight into the characteristics of an insurance operation.

7.3 Poisson and Compound Poisson Processes

In the literature on probability theory, Poisson processes are defined in different ways. For our purposes, it is sufficient to define a Poisson process in the following way. A counting process is a Poisson process with parameter λ if the distribution of times between events is exponential with mean $1/\lambda$. In our context, an event is the occurrence of a claim. Thus, if we define A_i to be the time between the $(i - 1)$th and ith events, with A_1 being the time to the first event, then $\{A_i\}_{i=1}^{\infty}$ is a sequence of independent, exponentially distributed random variables, each with mean $1/\lambda$.

If a counting process is a Poisson process, then the distribution of the number of events up to a fixed time t is Poisson with parameter λt. This can be seen from our definition, as follows. For fixed $t > 0$, let $N(t)$ be the number of events up to time t. Then for $n = 0, 1, 2, \ldots$,

$$N(t) \geq n + 1 \Leftrightarrow \sum_{i=1}^{n+1} A_i \leq t.$$

Since each of $A_1, A_2, \ldots, A_{n+1}$ is exponentially distributed with mean $1/\lambda$ it follows that $\sum_{i=1}^{n+1} A_i$ is distributed as $\gamma(n + 1, \lambda)$. Hence

$$\Pr(N(t) \geq n + 1) = \Pr\left(\sum_{i=1}^{n+1} A_i \leq t\right) = 1 - \sum_{j=0}^{n} e^{-\lambda t} \frac{(\lambda t)^j}{j!}$$

or, equivalently,

$$\Pr(N(t) \le n) = \sum_{j=0}^{n} e^{-\lambda t} \frac{(\lambda t)^j}{j!},$$

giving

$$\Pr(N(t) = n) = e^{-\lambda t} \frac{(\lambda t)^n}{n!}$$

for $n = 0, 1, 2, \ldots$. Thus, the distribution of $N(t)$ is Poisson with parameter λt.

Now let $\{N(t)\}_{t\ge 0}$ be a Poisson process with parameter λ, and let $\{X_i\}_{i=1}^{\infty}$ be a sequence of independent and identically distributed random variables, each with distribution function F, independent of $N(t)$ for all $t > 0$. We define the process $\{S(t)\}_{t\ge 0}$ by

$$S(t) = \sum_{i=1}^{N(t)} X_i$$

with $S(t) = 0$ when $N(t) = 0$. $\{S(t)\}_{t\ge 0}$ is said to be a compound Poisson process with Poisson parameter λ. For a fixed value of $t > 0$, the random variable $S(t)$ has a compound Poisson distribution with Poisson parameter λt.

An important property of compound Poisson processes is that they have stationary and independent increments. In general, a stochastic process $\{Y(t)\}_{t\ge 0}$ is said to have stationary increments if for $0 < s < t$, the distribution of $Y(t) - Y(s)$, i.e. the increment of the process over the time interval from s to t, depends only on $t - s$ and not on the values of s and t.

A stochastic process $\{Y(t)\}_{t\ge 0}$ is said to have independent increments if for $0 < s < t \le u < v$, $Y(t) - Y(s)$ is independent of $Y(v) - Y(u)$. Thus, if a process has independent increments, the increments over non-overlapping time intervals are independent. A process with stationary and independent increments can be thought of as 'starting over' in a probabilistic sense at any point in time.

In particular, the idea of 'starting over' holds for a compound Poisson process because of the memoryless property of the exponential distribution. To see this, consider the distribution of the time until the next event from a fixed time t. Define τ to be the time of the last event prior to time t, letting $\tau = 0$ if no events occur prior to t. Now define A_τ and A_t to be the time until the next event from times τ and t respectively. By definition, A_τ has an exponential distribution with parameter λ. Hence

$$\begin{aligned}
\Pr(A_t > s) &= \Pr(A_\tau > t - \tau + s \mid A_\tau > t - \tau) \\
&= \Pr(A_\tau > t - \tau + s) / \Pr(A_\tau > t - \tau) \\
&= \exp\{-\lambda(t - \tau + s)\} / \exp\{-\lambda(t - \tau)\} \\
&= \exp\{-\lambda s\}.
\end{aligned}$$

In the context of a compound Poisson process representing an aggregate claims process, from any fixed time $t > 0$, the distribution of the time until the next claim is exponential with parameter λ and the distribution function of the next claim amount is F. This is exactly the same situation as at time 0. A consequence of this that we apply in the next chapter is that for a given time t, the probability of one claim occurring in the infinitesimal time interval $(t, t + dt)$ is approximately λdt. This follows since

$$\Pr(N(dt) = 1) = \lambda dt\, e^{-\lambda dt} \approx \lambda dt(1 - \lambda dt) \approx \lambda dt.$$

7.4 Definitions of Ruin Probability

The probability of ruin in infinite time, also known as the ultimate ruin probability, is defined as

$$\psi(u) = \Pr(U(t) < 0 \quad \text{for some } t > 0).$$

In words, $\psi(u)$ is the probability that the insurer's surplus falls below zero at some time in the future, i.e. that claims outgo exceeds the initial surplus plus premium income. This is a probability of ruin in continuous time, and we can also define a discrete time ultimate ruin probability as

$$\psi_r(u) = \Pr(U(t) < 0 \quad \text{for some } t,\, t = r, 2r, 3r, \ldots).$$

Thus, under this definition, ruin occurs only if the surplus is less than zero at one of the time points $r, 2r, 3r, \ldots$. If ruin occurs under the discrete time definition, it must also occur under the continuous time definition. However, the opposite is not true. To see this, we consider a realisation of a surplus process which, for some integer n, has $U(nr) > 0$ and $U((n + 1)r) > 0$ with $U(\tau) < 0$ for some $\tau \in (nr, (n + 1)r)$. If $U(t) > 0$ for all t outside the interval $(nr, (n + 1)r)$, then ruin occurs under the continuous time definition, but not under the discrete time definition. Thus, $\psi_r(u) < \psi(u)$. However, as r becomes small, so that we are 'checking' the surplus level very frequently, then $\psi_r(u)$ should be a good approximation to $\psi(u)$.

We define the finite time ruin probability $\psi(u, t)$ by

$$\psi(u, t) = \Pr(U(s) < 0 \text{ for some } s,\, 0 < s \leq t).$$

Thus, $\psi(u, t)$ is the probability that the insurer's surplus falls below zero in the finite time interval $(0, t]$. We can also define a discrete time ruin probability in finite time as

$$\psi_r(u, t) = \Pr(U(s) < 0 \quad \text{for some } s,\, s = r, 2r, 3r, \ldots, t),$$

where t is an integer multiple of r. The arguments used above to explain why $\psi_r(u) < \psi(u)$ also apply in finite time to give $\psi_r(u,t) < \psi(u,t)$, and if r is small, then $\psi_r(u,t)$ should be a good approximation to $\psi(u,t)$.

In this chapter we concentrate mostly on the ultimate ruin probability. In Sections 7.7 and 7.8 we illustrate how some explicit solutions for $\psi(u)$ can be found, before describing numerical techniques for calculating $\psi(u)$ and $\psi(u,t)$ in Section 7.9. However, we start with an upper bound for $\psi(u)$, Lundberg's inequality, which is described in the next two sections.

Throughout this chapter we assume that $c > \lambda m_1$, so that, per unit of time, the premium income exceeds the expected aggregate claim amount. It can be shown that if this condition, known as the net profit condition, does not hold, then $\psi(u) = 1$ for all $u \geq 0$. It is often convenient to write $c = (1+\theta)\lambda m_1$, so that θ is the premium loading factor.

7.5 The Adjustment Coefficient

The adjustment coefficient, which we denote by R, gives a measure of risk for a surplus process. It takes account of two factors in the surplus process: aggregate claims and premium income. For the classical risk process, the adjustment coefficient is defined to be the unique positive root of

$$\lambda M_X(r) - \lambda - cr = 0, \tag{7.1}$$

so that R is given by

$$\lambda + cR = \lambda M_X(R). \tag{7.2}$$

We remark that by writing c as $(1+\theta)\lambda m_1$, we can see that R is independent of the Poisson parameter λ, and we discuss this point further in Section 7.7. To see that there is a unique positive root of equation (7.1) we consider the function

$$g(r) = \lambda M_X(r) - \lambda - cr,$$

and show that it has the shape given in Figure 7.2. To see this, first note that $g(0) = 0$. Second,

$$\frac{d}{dr}g(r) = \lambda \frac{d}{dr}M_X(r) - c,$$

so that

$$\left.\frac{d}{dr}g(r)\right|_{r=0} = \lambda m_1 - c,$$

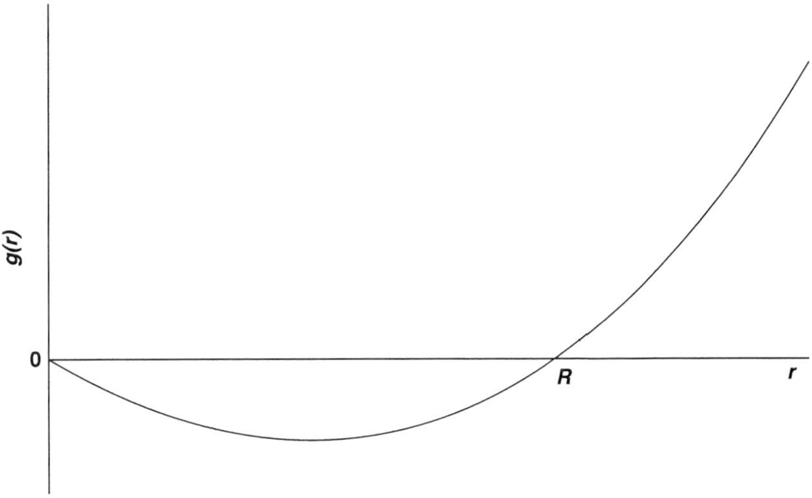

Figure 7.2 The function g.

and hence g is a decreasing function at zero as we have assumed that $c > \lambda m_1$. Next, we note that

$$\frac{d^2}{dr^2}g(r) = \lambda \frac{d^2}{dr^2}M_X(r) = \lambda \int_0^\infty x^2 e^{rx} f(x)dx > 0,$$

so that if g has a turning point, then the function attains its minimum at that turning point. Finally, we note that

$$\lim_{r \to \gamma^-} g(r) = \infty \tag{7.3}$$

(where γ is as defined in Section 7.2) so that as g is decreasing at zero, the function must have a unique turning point, and hence there is a unique positive number R such that $g(R) = 0$. To see that equation (7.3) is true, consider separately the cases $\gamma < \infty$ and $\gamma = \infty$. In the former case, equation (7.3) clearly holds. In the latter case, we note that since all claim amounts are positive, there exists a positive number ε and a probability p such that

$$\Pr(X_1 > \varepsilon) = p > 0,$$

so that

$$M_X(r) = \int_0^\infty e^{rx} f(x)dx \geq \int_\varepsilon^\infty e^{rx} f(x)dx \geq e^{r\varepsilon} p,$$

and hence

$$\lim_{r \to \infty} g(r) \geq \lim_{r \to \infty} (\lambda e^{r\varepsilon} p - \lambda - cr) = \infty.$$

Example 7.1 *Let $F(x) = 1 - \exp\{-\alpha x\}$, $x \geq 0$. Find an expression for R.*

Solution 7.1 *As $M_X(r) = \alpha/(\alpha - r)$ equation (7.2) becomes*

$$\lambda + cR = \lambda\alpha/(\alpha - R),$$

which gives

$$R^2 - (\alpha - \lambda/c)R = 0,$$

and so $R = \alpha - \lambda/c$ since R is the positive root of equation (7.1).

Example 7.2 *Let the individual claim amount distribution be $\gamma(2, 2)$, and let the premium loading factor be 10%. Calculate R.*

Solution 7.2 *As the mean individual claim amount is 1 and $M_X(r) = 4/(2 - r)^2$ for $r < 2$, equation (7.2) becomes*

$$1 + 1.1R = 4/(2 - R)^2,$$

which gives

$$1.1R^3 - 3.4R^2 + 0.4R = 0.$$

The three solutions to this equation are $R = 0$, $R = 0.1225$ and $R = 2.968$, and the solution we require is $R = 0.1225$ since the adjustment coefficient must be positive and $M_X(r)$ exists when $r < 2$.

In the two examples above, we have exact solutions for the adjustment coefficient, but in other cases we must solve numerically. For example, when $X_1 \sim \gamma(2.5, 2.5)$, the adjustment coefficient is the unique positive root of

$$\lambda \left(\frac{2.5}{2.5 - r} \right)^{2.5} - cr - \lambda = 0.$$

Given values of λ and c, such a root can easily be found using a mathematical software package. However, we can often approximate the adjustment coefficient by calculating an upper bound, as follows. Since

$$e^{Rx} \geq 1 + Rx + \tfrac{1}{2}(Rx)^2$$

for $x \geq 0$, equation (7.2) yields the inequality

$$\lambda + cR \geq \lambda \int_0^\infty \left(1 + Rx + \tfrac{1}{2}(Rx)^2\right) f(x)dx,$$

and as

$$\int_0^\infty \left(1 + Rx + \tfrac{1}{2}(Rx)^2\right) f(x)dx = 1 + Rm_1 + \tfrac{1}{2}R^2 m_2\,,$$

Table 7.1 *Values of r_n.*

n	r_n
1	0.06862
2	0.06850
3	0.06850
4	0.06850

we obtain

$$R \leq \frac{2(c - \lambda m_1)}{\lambda m_2},$$

and this upper bound often provides a good approximation to R.

Example 7.3 *Let the individual claim amount distribution be $\gamma(2.5, 2.5)$, and let the premium loading factor be 5%. Calculate an upper bound for R, and use a numerical method to find the value of R to four decimal places.*

Solution 7.3 *As $m_1 = 1$ and $m_2 = 7/5$, we have*

$$R \leq \frac{2\,(1.05\lambda - \lambda)}{7\lambda/5} = \frac{1}{14} = 0.0714.$$

We can solve numerically for R using the Newton-Raphson method with a starting value of 0.0714. Writing

$$g(r) = \left(\frac{5}{5-2r}\right)^{5/2} - 1.05r - 1,$$

so that

$$g'(r) = \left(\frac{5}{5-2r}\right)^{7/2} - 1.05,$$

we apply the Newton-Raphson method by calculating the sequence $\{r_n\}$ where $r_0 = 0.0714$ and $r_{n+1} = r_n - g(r_n)/g'(r_n)$. Table 7.1 shows values of r_n for $n = 1, 2, 3$ and 4, and we deduce from this that to four decimal places $R = 0.0685$, so that the upper bound is a reasonable approximation here.

7.6 Lundberg's Inequality

In the previous chapter we proved Lundberg's inequality for the risk process discussed there. For the classical risk process, Lundberg's inequality states that

$$\psi(u) \leq \exp\{-Ru\},$$

where R is the adjustment coefficient.

As in the previous chapter, we can prove this result by an inductive argument. We define $\psi_n(u)$ to be the probability of ruin at or before the nth claim. It is then sufficient to show that

$$\psi_n(u) \leq \exp\{-Ru\}$$

for $n = 1, 2, 3, \ldots$, since

$$\psi(u) = \lim_{n\to\infty} \psi_n(u).$$

Therefore, we assume that for a fixed value of n, where $n \geq 1$, $\psi_n(u) \leq \exp\{-Ru\}$. Next, we establish an expression for $\psi_{n+1}(u)$ by considering the time and the amount of the first claim, as follows.

Suppose that the first claim occurs at time $t > 0$ and that the amount of this claim is x. If ruin occurs at or before the $(n+1)$th claim, then either

(i) ruin occurs at the first claim, so that $x > u + ct$ or
(ii) ruin does not occur at the first claim, so that the surplus after payment of this claim, $u + ct - x$, is non-negative, and ruin occurs from this surplus level at one of the next n claims.

Since claims occur as a Poisson process (with parameter λ), the distribution of the time until the first claim is exponential with parameter λ. Hence, integrating over all possible times and amounts for the first claim we have

$$\psi_{n+1}(u) = \int_0^\infty \lambda e^{-\lambda t} \int_{u+ct}^\infty f(x)dxdt + \int_0^\infty \lambda e^{-\lambda t} \int_0^{u+ct} f(x)\psi_n(u+ct-x)dxdt.$$

Note that the first integral represents the probability of ruin at the first claim, and the second represents the probability that ruin does not occur at the first claim but does occur at one of the next n claims. Note also, that in probabilistic terms, the surplus process 'starts over' again after payment of the first claim, and so the probability of ruin within n claims after payment of the first claim is just $\psi_n(u + ct - x)$.

We now apply our inductive hypothesis to write

$$\psi_{n+1}(u) \leq \int_0^\infty \lambda e^{-\lambda t} \int_{u+ct}^\infty f(x)dxdt + \int_0^\infty \lambda e^{-\lambda t} \int_0^{u+ct} f(x)e^{-R(u+ct-x)}dxdt.$$

Next, we use the fact that $\exp\{-R(u+ct-x)\} \geq 1$ for $x \geq u+ct$, so that

$$\int_{u+ct}^{\infty} f(x)dx \leq \int_{u+ct}^{\infty} e^{-R(u+ct-x)} f(x)dx,$$

and hence

$$\begin{aligned}
\psi_{n+1}(u) &\leq \int_0^{\infty} \lambda e^{-\lambda t} \int_0^{\infty} f(x) e^{-R(u+ct-x)} dxdt \\
&= e^{-Ru} \int_0^{\infty} \lambda e^{-(\lambda+cR)t} \int_0^{\infty} e^{Rx} f(x)dxdt \\
&= e^{-Ru} \int_0^{\infty} \lambda e^{-(\lambda+cR)t} M_X(R)dt.
\end{aligned}$$

Since $\lambda + cR = \lambda M_X(R)$, the integral equals 1, and hence

$$\psi_{n+1}(u) \leq \exp\{-Ru\}.$$

Finally, we must show that the result is true when $n = 1$. Following the above arguments we have

$$\begin{aligned}
\psi_1(u) &= \int_0^{\infty} \lambda e^{-\lambda t} \int_{u+ct}^{\infty} f(x)dxdt \\
&\leq \int_0^{\infty} \lambda e^{-\lambda t} \int_{u+ct}^{\infty} f(x) e^{-R(u+ct-x)} dxdt \\
&\leq \int_0^{\infty} \lambda e^{-\lambda t} \int_0^{\infty} f(x) e^{-R(u+ct-x)} dxdt \\
&= e^{-Ru},
\end{aligned}$$

and the proof is complete.

7.7 Survival Probability

Define $\phi(u) = 1 - \psi(u)$ to be the probability that ruin never occurs starting from initial surplus u, a probability also known as the survival probability. An equation for ϕ can be established by adapting the reasoning used to prove Lundberg's inequality. By considering the time and the amount of the first claim, we have

$$\phi(u) = \int_0^{\infty} \lambda e^{-\lambda t} \int_0^{u+ct} f(x)\phi(u+ct-x)dxdt, \tag{7.4}$$

noting that if the first claim occurs at time t, its amount must not exceed $u+ct$, since ruin otherwise occurs. Substituting $s = u + ct$ in equation (7.4) we get

$$\begin{aligned}\phi(u) &= \frac{1}{c}\int_u^\infty \lambda e^{-\lambda(s-u)/c}\int_0^s f(x)\phi(s-x)dxds \\ &= \frac{\lambda}{c}e^{\lambda u/c}\int_u^\infty e^{-\lambda s/c}\int_0^s f(x)\phi(s-x)dxds. \qquad (7.5)\end{aligned}$$

We can establish an equation for ϕ, known as an integro-differential equation, by differentiating equation (7.5), and the resulting equation can be used to derive explicit solutions for ϕ. Differentiation gives

$$\begin{aligned}\frac{d}{du}\phi(u) &= \frac{\lambda^2}{c^2}e^{\lambda u/c}\int_u^\infty e^{-\lambda s/c}\int_0^s f(x)\phi(s-x)dxds - \frac{\lambda}{c}\int_0^u f(x)\phi(u-x)dx \\ &= \frac{\lambda}{c}\phi(u) - \frac{\lambda}{c}\int_0^u f(x)\phi(u-x)dx. \qquad (7.6)\end{aligned}$$

At first sight equation (7.6) does not appear a very promising route, since the function ϕ appears in three different places in this equation. However, by eliminating the integral term, a differential equation can be created, and solved.

To see how such an approach works, let us consider the situation when $F(x) = 1 - e^{-\alpha x}$, $x \geq 0$. Then we have

$$\begin{aligned}\frac{d}{du}\phi(u) &= \frac{\lambda}{c}\phi(u) - \frac{\lambda}{c}\int_0^u \alpha e^{-\alpha x}\phi(u-x)dx \\ &= \frac{\lambda}{c}\phi(u) - \frac{\alpha\lambda}{c}\int_0^u e^{-\alpha(u-x)}\phi(x)dx \\ &= \frac{\lambda}{c}\phi(u) - \frac{\alpha\lambda}{c}e^{-\alpha u}\int_0^u e^{\alpha x}\phi(x)dx. \qquad (7.7)\end{aligned}$$

Differentiation of equation (7.7) yields

$$\frac{d^2}{du^2}\phi(u) = \frac{\lambda}{c}\frac{d}{du}\phi(u) + \frac{\alpha^2\lambda}{c}e^{-\alpha u}\int_0^u e^{\alpha x}\phi(x)dx - \frac{\alpha\lambda}{c}\phi(u). \qquad (7.8)$$

The integral term in equation (7.8) is simply the integral term in equation (7.7) multiplied by $-\alpha$. Hence, if we multiply equation (7.7) by α and add the resulting equation to equation (7.8), we find that

$$\frac{d^2}{du^2}\phi(u) + \alpha\frac{d}{du}\phi(u) = \frac{\lambda}{c}\frac{d}{du}\phi(u)$$

or

$$\frac{d^2}{du^2}\phi(u) + \left(\alpha - \frac{\lambda}{c}\right)\frac{d}{du}\phi(u) = 0.$$

This is a second order differential equation whose general solution is

$$\phi(u) = a_0 + a_1 e^{-(\alpha-\lambda/c)u},$$

where a_0 and a_1 are constants. Since Lundberg's inequality applies, we know that $\lim_{u\to\infty} \phi(u) = 1$, which gives $a_0 = 1$. It then follows that $\phi(0) = 1+a_1$, i.e. $a_1 = -\psi(0)$, so that

$$\phi(u) = 1 - \psi(0)e^{-(\alpha-\lambda/c)u}.$$

All that remains is to solve for $\psi(0)$, and this can be done generally on the assumption that Lundberg's inequality applies. Writing $\phi = 1 - \psi$ in equation (7.6) it follows that

$$\frac{d}{du}\psi(u) = \frac{\lambda}{c}\psi(u) - \frac{\lambda}{c}\int_0^u f(x)\psi(u-x)dx - \frac{\lambda}{c}(1-F(u)),$$

and integrating this equation over $(0,\infty)$ we find that

$$\begin{aligned} -\psi(0) = {} & \frac{\lambda}{c}\int_0^\infty \psi(u)du - \frac{\lambda}{c}\int_0^\infty\int_0^u f(x)\psi(u-x)dxdu \\ & -\frac{\lambda}{c}\int_0^\infty (1-F(u))\,du. \end{aligned} \tag{7.9}$$

Changing the order of integration in the double integral in equation (7.9), we have

$$\begin{aligned} \int_0^\infty\int_0^u f(x)\psi(u-x)dxdu &= \int_0^\infty\int_x^\infty \psi(u-x)duf(x)dx \\ &= \int_0^\infty\int_0^\infty \psi(y)dyf(x)dx \\ &= \int_0^\infty \psi(y)dy. \end{aligned}$$

Thus, the first two terms on the right-hand side of equation (7.9) cancel, and we find that

$$\psi(0) = \frac{\lambda}{c}\int_0^\infty (1-F(u))\,du = \frac{\lambda m_1}{c}. \tag{7.10}$$

We did not have to specify the form of F to prove this result, but we did assume that Lundberg's inequality applies. However, formula (7.10) holds generally, and in Section 7.9 we derive it without assuming Lundberg's inequality applies.

Thus, the complete solution for ϕ when $F(x) = 1 - e^{-\alpha x}$, $x \geq 0$, is

$$\phi(u) = 1 - \frac{\lambda}{\alpha c}\exp\{-(\alpha - \lambda/c)u\}. \tag{7.11}$$

We remark that as $R = \alpha - \lambda/c$, $\psi(u) = \psi(0)\exp\{-Ru\}$, and this is the analogue in the classical risk model of the result given in Example 6.2. Although this method of solution can be used for other forms of F, we do not pursue it further. In the next section we show how equation (7.6) can be used in a different way to solve for ϕ.

In Section 7.5 we saw that if the premium is written as $c = (1+\theta)\lambda m_1$, then the adjustment coefficient is independent of λ. If we write c in this way in equation (7.11), then

$$\phi(u) = 1 - \frac{1}{1+\theta}\exp\{-\alpha\theta u/(1+\theta)\},$$

independent of λ. This independence holds for any individual claim amount distribution, not just the exponential distribution. To see why this is the case, consider the following two risks:

Risk I: The aggregate claims process is a compound Poisson process with Poisson parameter 120, and individual claim amounts are exponentially distributed with mean 1. The premium income per unit time is 132.

Risk II: The aggregate claims process is a compound Poisson process with Poisson parameter 10, and individual claim amounts are exponentially distributed with mean 1. The premium income per unit time is 11.

If we take the unit of time for Risk II to be one month, and the unit of time for Risk I to be one year, we can see that the risks are identical. There is thus no difference in the probability of ultimate ruin for these two risks. However, if the unit of time for Risk II were one year, there would be a difference in the time of ruin, which is discussed in Chapter 8.

7.8 The Laplace Transform of ϕ

The Laplace transform is an important tool that can be used to solve both differential and integro-differential equations. For completeness, we start this section by defining the Laplace transform and listing some basic properties. We then find a general expression for the Laplace transform of ϕ, and explain how ϕ can be found from this expression.

Let $h(y)$ be a function defined for all $y \geq 0$. Then the Laplace transform of h is defined as

$$h^*(s) = \int_0^\infty e^{-sy}h(y)dy.$$

There are some technical conditions for the existence of h^*, but as these hold in our subsequent applications, we do not discuss them here.

An important property of a Laplace transform is that it uniquely identifies a function, in the same way that a moment generating function uniquely identifies a distribution. The process of going from h^* to h is known as inverting the transform.

In this and the next chapter, we apply the following properties of Laplace transforms:

(1) Let h_1 and h_2 be functions whose Laplace transforms exist, and let α_1 and α_2 be constants. Then

$$\int_0^\infty e^{-sy} (\alpha_1 h_1(y) + \alpha_2 h_2(y))\, dy = \alpha_1 h_1^*(s) + \alpha_2 h_2^*(s).$$

(2) Laplace transform of an integral: let h be a function whose Laplace transform exists, and let

$$H(x) = \int_0^x h(y) dy.$$

Then $H^*(s) = h^*(s)/s$.

(3) Laplace transform of a derivative: let h be a differentiable function whose Laplace transform exists. Then

$$\int_0^\infty e^{-sy} \left(\frac{d}{dy} h(y) \right) dy = sh^*(s) - h(0).$$

(4) Laplace transform of a convolution: let h_1 and h_2 be as in Result (1) above, and define

$$h(x) = \int_0^x h_1(y) h_2(x-y) dy.$$

Then $h^*(s) = h_1^*(s) h_2^*(s)$.

(5) Laplace transform of a non-negative valued random variable: let $X \sim H$. Then

$$E[e^{-sX}] = \int_0^\infty e^{-sy} dH(y).$$

When the distribution is continuous with density function h,

$$E[e^{-sX}] = h^*(s).$$

Example 7.4 *Let $h(y) = 1$ for $y \geq 0$. Find $h^*(s)$.*

Solution 7.4 *From the definition of a Laplace transform,*

$$h^*(s) = \int_0^\infty e^{-sy} dy = \frac{1}{s}.$$

Example 7.5 *Let $h(y) = \exp\{-\alpha y\}$, $y \geq 0$. Find $h^*(s)$.*

Solution 7.5 *We have*

$$h^*(s) = \int_0^\infty e^{-sy}e^{-\alpha y}dy = \frac{1}{s+\alpha}.$$

Example 7.6 *Let* $F(x) = 1 - pe^{-\alpha x} - qe^{-\beta x}$, $x \geq 0$, *be a mixed exponential distribution. Find* $F^*(s)$.

Solution 7.6 *Applying the results of the previous two examples,*

$$F^*(s) = \frac{1}{s} - \frac{p}{\alpha + s} - \frac{q}{\beta + s}.$$

We can apply these general results about Laplace transforms to find the Laplace transform of ϕ. Recall equation (7.6):

$$\frac{d}{du}\phi(u) = \frac{\lambda}{c}\phi(u) - \frac{\lambda}{c}\int_0^u f(x)\phi(u-x)dx.$$

From Result (3), the Laplace transform of the left-hand side is $s\phi^*(s) - \phi(0)$, and from Results (1) and (4) the Laplace transform of the second term on the right-hand side is $-(\lambda/c)f^*(s)\phi^*(s)$. Hence we have

$$s\phi^*(s) - \phi(0) = \frac{\lambda}{c}\phi^*(s) - \frac{\lambda}{c}f^*(s)\phi^*(s)$$

or

$$\phi^*(s) = \frac{c\phi(0)}{cs - \lambda(1 - f^*(s))}. \tag{7.12}$$

When f^* is a rational function we can invert ϕ^* to find ϕ, as illustrated in the following example.

Example 7.7 *Let* $f(x) = 4xe^{-2x}$, $x > 0$, *and let* $c = 1.2\lambda$. *Find a formula for* $\phi(u)$.

Solution 7.7 *We first note that* $m_1 = 1$ *so that* $\phi(0) = 1/6$. *Next,*

$$f^*(s) = 4\int_0^\infty xe^{-(2+s)x}dx = \frac{4}{(2+s)^2},$$

giving

$$\begin{aligned}\phi^*(s) &= \frac{0.2\lambda}{1.2\lambda s - \lambda\left(1 - 4(2+s)^{-2}\right)} \\ &= \frac{0.2(2+s)^2}{1.2s(2+s)^2 - (2+s)^2 + 4} \\ &= \frac{0.2(2+s)^2}{1.2s^3 + 3.8s^2 + 0.8s} \\ &= \frac{0.2(2+s)^2}{1.2s(s+R_1)(s+R_2)} \\ &= \frac{(1/6)(2+s)^2}{s(s+R_1)(s+R_2)},\end{aligned} \tag{7.13}$$

where $R_1 = 0.2268$ *and* $R_2 = 2.9399$. *Using partial fractions we can write*

$$\phi^*(s) = \frac{a_0}{s} + \frac{a_1}{s+R_1} + \frac{a_2}{s+R_2}, \tag{7.14}$$

where a_0, a_1 *and* a_2 *are constants. From equations (7.13) and (7.14) we have*

$$a_0(s+R_1)(s+R_2) + a_1 s(s+R_2) + a_2 s(s+R_1) = \tfrac{1}{6}(2+s)^2. \tag{7.15}$$

Equating coefficients of powers of s^2 *in equation (7.15) we obtain*

$$a_0 + a_1 + a_2 = \tfrac{1}{6}.$$

Similarly, equating powers of s, we obtain

$$a_0(R_1+R_2) + a_1R_2 + a_2R_1 = \tfrac{2}{3},$$

and equating constants we obtain

$$a_0R_1R_2 = \tfrac{2}{3}.$$

We can thus solve for a_0, a_1 *and* a_2, *giving*

$$\phi^*(s) = \frac{1}{s} - \frac{0.8518}{s+R_1} + \frac{0.0185}{s+R_2}.$$

Finally, we invert this Laplace transform to get

$$\phi(u) = 1 - 0.8518e^{-R_1u} + 0.0185e^{-R_2u}.$$

This is a very powerful method of solving for ϕ, although it can be somewhat tedious to apply by hand. However, it is usually a straightforward exercise to use this approach with mathematical software which has the capacity to invert Laplace transforms.

7.9 Recursive Calculation

In this section we describe two recursive methods which lead to (numerical) bounds and approximations to ruin/survival probabilities. We describe each method in turn, then conclude with numerical illustrations of each method.

7.9.1 The Distribution of the Maximum Aggregate Loss

We first show that ϕ is the distribution function of a compound geometric random variable. This allows the use of the recursion formula (4.22) in the calculation of bounds for, and approximations to, ϕ.

We start by considering a new process $\{L(t)\}_{t\geq 0}$, known as the aggregate loss process, defined by $L(t) = S(t) - ct$ for all $t \geq 0$, so that $U(t) = u - L(t)$. Next, we define the random variable L as the maximum of the aggregate loss process, and we can relate L to ϕ as follows:

$$\begin{aligned}\phi(u) &= \Pr(U(t) \geq 0 \quad \text{for all } t > 0) \\ &= \Pr(L(t) \leq u \quad \text{for all } t > 0) \\ &= \Pr(L \leq u).\end{aligned}$$

Thus, ϕ is the distribution function of L, and as $L(0) = 0$, L is a non-negative valued random variable. Further, since $\phi(0) = \Pr(L = 0)$, L has a mixed distribution with a mass of probability at zero.

In Section 7.7 we derived a formula for $\psi(0)$ under the assumption that Lundberg's inequality applied. We now show that this formula is generally true. Define L^* to be the Laplace transform of the random variable L, so that

$$\begin{aligned}L^*(s) = E\left[e^{-sL}\right] &= \int_0^\infty e^{-su} d\phi(u) \\ &= \phi(0) + \int_0^\infty e^{-su}\left(\frac{d}{du}\phi(u)\right) du.\end{aligned}$$

As the integral term is just the Laplace transform of the derivative of ϕ,

$$\begin{aligned}L^*(s) &= \phi(0) + s\phi^*(s) - \phi(0) \\ &= s\phi^*(s) \\ &= \frac{cs\phi(0)}{cs - \lambda(1 - f^*(s))},\end{aligned} \tag{7.16}$$

where the final step follows from equation (7.12). We know that

$$L^*(s)\big|_{s=0} = E\left[e^{-sL}\right]\big|_{s=0} = 1,$$

and we can also find $L^*(s)|_{s=0}$ from equation (7.16) as

$$L^*(s)\Big|_{s=0} = \frac{c\phi(0)}{c + \lambda\,(d/ds)f^*(s)|_{s=0}}$$

by l'Hôpital's rule. Further, as

$$\frac{d}{ds}f^*(s)\Bigg|_{s=0} = -\int_0^\infty ye^{-sy}f(y)dy\Bigg|_{s=0} = -m_1,$$

we find that

$$1 = \frac{c\phi(0)}{c - \lambda m_1},$$

and hence

$$\phi(0) = 1 - \frac{\lambda m_1}{c}.$$

We now turn our attention to the distribution of L. We proceed by noting that the maximum of the aggregate loss process will be greater than zero only if the surplus ever falls below its initial level, and the probability of this is $\psi(0)$. Suppose that this happens and the surplus falls to level $u - l_1$. Then the aggregate loss process attains a new record high at this point in time, namely l_1. The probability that the aggregate loss process attains another record high is again $\psi(0)$ because all that is required for this to happen is that the surplus falls below the level $u - l_1$ at some stage in the future. Here we are making use of the fact that the compound Poisson process has stationary and independent increments. If the fall below $u - l_1$ is by amount l_2, then the new record high of the aggregate loss process is $l_1 + l_2$ and the increase in the record high of the aggregate loss process is l_2. Continuing in this way, we see that the probability of n increases in the record high of the aggregate loss process is

$$\psi(0)^n\phi(0) \tag{7.17}$$

for $n = 0, 1, 2, \ldots$, and this is a geometric probability function. Further, the maximum of the aggregate loss process is simply the sum of the increases in the record high of the process. Thus, we can write L as a compound geometric random variable:

$$L = \sum_{i=1}^{N} L_i,$$

where N is the number of increases in the record high of the aggregate loss process, with probability function given by (7.17), and L_i denotes the amount of the ith increase in the record high of the aggregate loss process. As the aggregate loss process 'starts over' each time there is a new record high of

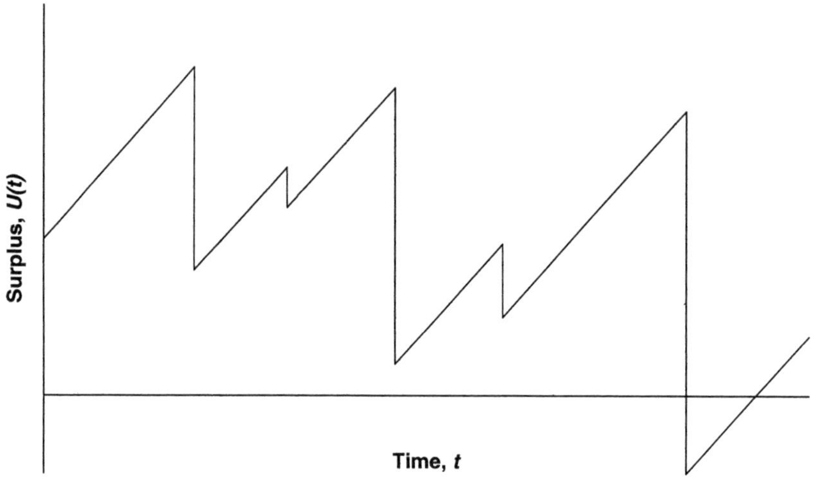

Figure 7.3 A realisation of a surplus process.

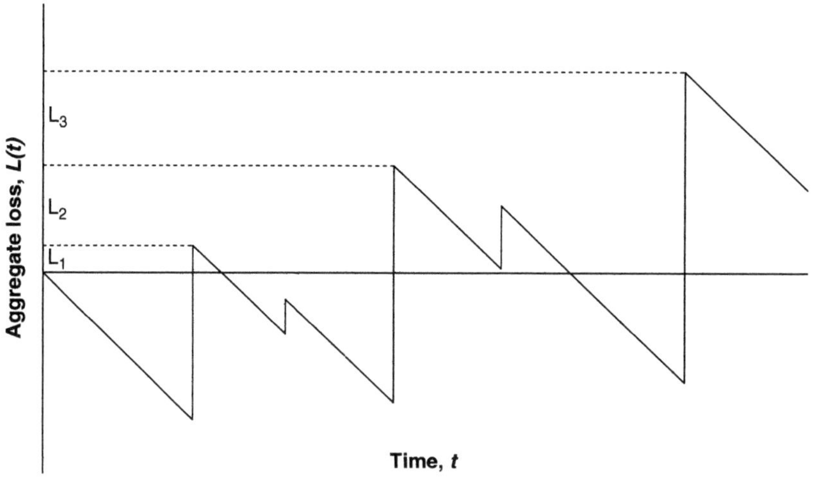

Figure 7.4 The realisation of the aggregate loss process corresponding to the surplus process in Figure 7.3.

the process, $\{L_i\}_{i=1}^{\infty}$ is a sequence of independent and identically distributed random variables. Figure 7.3 shows a realisation of a surplus process, and Figure 7.4 shows the corresponding realisation of the aggregate loss process, with three new record highs of the aggregate loss process occurring.

We need the distribution of L_1, a distribution known in the theory of stochastic processes as a ladder height distribution, and we can use Laplace transforms to find this distribution. Let $K(x) = \Pr(L_1 \le x)$, and let k be the associated density function. Then by applying techniques from Section 4.2.2,

$$E\left[e^{-sL}\right] = E\left[E\left(e^{-sL}|N\right)\right] = E\left[k^*(s)^N\right],$$

where $k^*(s) = E[\exp\{-sL_1\}]$. Further, as N has a geometric distribution, L has a compound geometric distribution with

$$E\left[e^{-sL}\right] = \frac{\phi(0)}{1-\psi(0)k^*(s)}. \tag{7.18}$$

We have already seen that

$$E\left[e^{-sL}\right] = \frac{cs\phi(0)}{cs-\lambda(1-f^*(s))},$$

and so equating these two expressions we have

$$\frac{cs\phi(0)}{cs-\lambda(1-f^*(s))} = \frac{\phi(0)}{1-\psi(0)k^*(s)},$$

which, on inserting $\psi(0) = \lambda m_1/c$, gives

$$k^*(s) = \frac{1}{m_1 s}\left(1-f^*(s)\right).$$

Using results from the previous section, we can invert this Laplace transform, obtaining

$$k(x) = \frac{1}{m_1}\left(1-F(x)\right).$$

Note that the distribution of L_1 is a continuous one. Hence, if we wish to apply formula (4.22) to compute (approximate) values of ϕ, we have to discretise this distribution. Although this approach does lead to reasonable approximations to ϕ, a better approach is to find bounds for ϕ. The numerical illustrations later in this section show that this approach gives us the correct value of ϕ, at least to a certain number of decimal places. To obtain bounds we define the random variable

$$L_\alpha = \sum_{i=1}^{N} L_{\alpha,i},$$

where N is as above, and $\left\{L_{\alpha,i}\right\}_{i=1}^{\infty}$ is a sequence of independent and identically distributed random variables, each with distribution function K_α and probability function

$$k_{\alpha,x} = K(x+1) - K(x)$$

for $x = 0, 1, 2, \ldots$. Thus, for $x \geq 0$, $K_\alpha(x) \geq K(x)$. Similarly, we define the random variable

$$L_\beta = \sum_{i=1}^{N} L_{\beta,i},$$

where N is as above, and $\{L_{\beta,i}\}_{i=1}^{\infty}$ is a sequence of independent and identically distributed random variables, each with distribution function K_β and probability function

$$k_{\beta,x} = K(x) - K(x-1)$$

for $x = 1, 2, 3, \ldots$. Thus, for $x \geq 0$, $K_\beta(x) \leq K(x)$ with equality occurring only when x is an integer. Thus,

$$K_\alpha(u) \geq K(u) \geq K_\beta(u),$$

and from Section 5.5 we know that this ordering is preserved under convolution, so that

$$K_\alpha^{n*}(u) \geq K^{n*}(u) \geq K_\beta^{n*}(u).$$

As

$$\phi(u) = \phi(0) + \sum_{n=1}^{\infty} \psi(0)^n \phi(0) K^{n*}(u), \tag{7.19}$$

it follows that

$$\Pr(L_\alpha \leq u) \geq \Pr(L \leq u) \geq \Pr(L_\beta \leq u) \tag{7.20}$$

and

$$\Pr(L_\alpha < u) \geq \Pr(L < u) \geq \Pr(L_\beta < u). \tag{7.21}$$

The key point in inequalities (7.20) and (7.21) is that for $u > 0$ the middle term in each is $\phi(u)$, but because L_α and L_β are discrete random variables,

$$\Pr(L_\alpha < u) < \Pr(L_\alpha \leq u) \quad \text{and} \quad \Pr(L_\beta < u) < \Pr(L_\beta \leq u).$$

We can therefore bound $\phi(u)$ for $u > 0$ by

$$\Pr(L_\beta \leq u) \leq \phi(u) \leq \Pr(L_\alpha < u).$$

These bounds apply only for $u > 0$, and they can be calculated from formula (4.22) since $L_{\alpha,1}$ and $L_{\beta,1}$ are discrete random variables. Specifically, let $\phi_\alpha(u) = \Pr(L_\alpha \leq u)$ and $\phi_\beta(u) = \Pr(L_\beta \leq u)$. Then

$$\phi_\alpha(0) = \frac{\phi(0)}{1 - \psi(0) k_{\alpha,0}},$$

and for $u = 1, 2, 3, \ldots$

$$\phi_\alpha(u) = \frac{1}{1 - \psi(0)k_{\alpha,0}} \left(\phi(0) + \psi(0) \sum_{j=1}^{u} k_{\alpha,j}\phi_\alpha(u-j) \right).$$

Similarly, $\phi_\beta(0) = \phi(0)$, and for $u = 1, 2, 3, \ldots$

$$\phi_\beta(u) = \phi(0) + \psi(0) \sum_{j=1}^{u} k_{\beta,j}\phi_\beta(u-j).$$

To calculate these bounds we apply the procedure described in Section 4.7, and, as illustrated in Section 7.9.3, tight bounds can be obtained by using high values of the scaling factor introduced in Section 4.7.

7.9.2 Recursive Calculation in a Discrete Time Model

In the previous chapter we described a discrete time risk model and gave formulae for both ultimate and finite time ruin probabilities. In this section, we explain how ruin probabilities from this model can be used to approximate both ultimate and finite time ruin probabilities in the classical risk model.

In the classical risk model we define the finite time ruin probability as

$$\psi(u,t) = \Pr\left(u + cs - \sum_{i=1}^{N(s)} X_i < 0 \quad \text{for some } s,\ 0 < s \le t \right),$$

where, for a fixed value of s, $N(s) \sim P(\lambda s)$. We now write c as $(1+\theta)\lambda m_1$, and set $\lambda = m_1 = 1$ so that we are working in monetary units equal to the mean individual claim amount and time units in which one claim is expected. This is a convenient scaling of parameters that does not affect principles.

Our approximating procedure is constructed on the basis of this scaled process, and there are three steps involved in the construction.

Step 1: For $i = 1, 2, 3, \ldots$, replace X_i by $X_{1,i}$ where $X_{1,i}$ is a discrete random variable distributed on $0, 1/\beta, 2/\beta, \ldots$ where $\beta > 0$. The distribution of $X_{1,i}$ should be chosen such that it is a good approximation to the distribution of X_i (and we have seen in Chapter 4 how this can be done). Define

$${}_1\psi(u,t) = \Pr\left(u + (1+\theta)s - \sum_{i=1}^{N(s)} X_{1,i} < 0 \quad \text{for some } s,\ 0 < s \le t \right).$$

Then ${}_1\psi(u,t)$ should be a good approximation to $\psi(u,t)$.

Step 2: For $i = 1, 2, 3, \ldots$, define $X_{2,i} = \beta X_{1,i}$ and define

$$_2\psi(w,t) = \Pr\left(w + (1+\theta)\beta s - \sum_{i=1}^{N(s)} X_{2,i} < 0 \quad \text{for some } s, 0 < s \le t\right).$$

Then we have $_2\psi(\beta u, t) = {}_1\psi(u,t)$.

Step 3: Now let us change the time scale. In particular, let us change the Poisson parameter to $1/(1+\theta)\beta$, which means that our premium income per unit time is 1, and so we can write

$$_3\psi(w,t) = \Pr\left(w + s - \sum_{i=1}^{N^*(s)} X_{2,i} < 0 \quad \text{for some } s, 0 < s \le t\right), \qquad (7.22)$$

where, for a fixed value of s, $N^*(s)$ has a Poisson distribution with mean $s/(1+\theta)\beta$. Then $_3\psi(w,(1+\theta)\beta t) = {}_2\psi(w,t)$, and so

$$\psi(u,t) \approx {}_3\psi(u\beta,(1+\theta)\beta t).$$

We remark that $_3\psi(u,t)$ gives the probability of ruin in continuous time (with discrete individual claim amounts). We can now approximate this by a probability of ruin in discrete time. To do this, we start by rewriting the definition of $\psi_d(u,t)$ from the previous chapter as

$$\psi_d(u,t) = \Pr\left(u + n - \sum_{i=1}^{n} Z_i \le 0 \quad \text{for some } n,\ n = 1,2,3,\ldots,t\right), \quad (7.23)$$

where Z_i represents the aggregate claim amount in the ith time period. Thus, when Z_i has a compound Poisson distribution with Poisson parameter $1/(1+\theta)\beta$ and with individual claim amounts distributed as $X_{2,i}$, equation (7.23) gives the discrete time ruin probability corresponding to equation (7.22). Hence, our approximation to $\psi(u,t)$ is $\psi_d(u\beta,(1+\theta)\beta t)$, and similarly our approximation to $\psi(u)$ is $\psi_d(u\beta)$. Intuitively, if we approximate a continuous time ruin probability by a discrete time one, we would expect the approximation to be good if the interval between the time points at which we 'check' the surplus is small. In our approximation, we can achieve this by choosing a large value of β.

In our numerical illustrations in the next section we consider only the ultimate ruin probability, while numerical illustrations relating to finite time ruin are given in Chapter 8. Thus, in Section 7.9.3 we use equation (6.3) in our approximation, i.e.

$$\psi_d(u+1) = h_0^{-1}\left(\psi_d(u) - \sum_{r=1}^{u} h_{u+1-r}\psi_d(r) - [1 - H(u)]\right).$$

From this formula we can calculate the function ψ_d recursively, starting from

$$\psi_d(0) = E[Z_1] = 1/(1+\theta).$$

Further, as Z_1 has a compound Poisson distribution with a discrete individual claim amount distribution, we can calculate the probability function of Z_1 by Panjer's recursion formula, and hence obtain values of H.

7.9.3 Numerical Illustrations

As a first illustration we consider the situation when $F(x) = 1 - e^{-x}$, $x \geq 0$. Then we know from Section 7.7 that for $u \geq 0$,

$$\psi(u) = \frac{1}{1+\theta} \exp\{-\theta u/(1+\theta)\},$$

so that this solution provides a benchmark against which we can compare the numerical solutions produced by each of the methods described in the preceding two sections.

To apply the method of bounds from Section 7.9.1 we first note that as $m_1 = 1$, $k(x) = f(x) = e^{-x}$, a result which we discuss in Chapter 8. We then rescale this distribution by a factor which we denote by κ. Table 7.2 shows values of bounds for $\psi(u)$ for a range of values of u and for three different values of κ when $\theta = 0.1$, while Table 7.3 shows approximations calculated by averaging the bounds. Each table also shows the exact value of $\psi(u)$.

In Table 7.2 the bounds become tighter as the value of κ increases. In particular, the lower bounds increase and the upper bounds decrease. We also note that for each value of u, the average of the bounds gives an excellent approximation to $\psi(u)$, particularly when $\kappa = 100$. We remark that from Table 7.2, to two decimal places the upper and lower bounds for $\psi(30)$ are both 0.06, so that to two decimal places $\psi(30) = 0.06$. By increasing the

Table 7.2 *Bounds for $\psi(u)$, exponential claims.*

	Lower Bounds for $\psi(u)$				Upper Bounds for $\psi(u)$		
u	$\kappa = 20$	$\kappa = 50$	$\kappa = 100$	$\psi(u)$	$\kappa = 100$	$\kappa = 50$	$\kappa = 20$
5	0.57102	0.57464	0.57584	0.57703	0.57822	0.57941	0.58294
10	0.35867	0.36323	0.36475	0.36626	0.36778	0.36929	0.37381
15	0.22529	0.22960	0.23104	0.23248	0.23392	0.23537	0.23970
20	0.14151	0.14513	0.14635	0.14756	0.14879	0.15001	0.15370
25	0.08889	0.09174	0.09270	0.09366	0.09463	0.09561	0.09856
30	0.05583	0.05799	0.05872	0.05945	0.06019	0.06094	0.06320

Table 7.3 *Approximations to $\psi(u)$ by averaging bounds, exponential claims.*

u	$\kappa = 20$	$\kappa = 50$	$\kappa = 100$	$\psi(u)$
5	0.57698	0.57703	0.57703	0.57703
10	0.36624	0.36626	0.36626	0.36626
15	0.23250	0.23249	0.23248	0.23248
20	0.14761	0.14757	0.14757	0.14756
25	0.09373	0.09368	0.09367	0.09366
30	0.05952	0.05947	0.05946	0.05945

Table 7.4 *Approximations to $\psi(u)$, exponential claims.*

u	$\beta = 20$	$\beta = 50$	$\beta = 100$	$\psi(u)$
5	0.57709	0.57704	0.57704	0.57703
10	0.36633	0.36628	0.36627	0.36626
15	0.23255	0.23249	0.23248	0.23248
20	0.14762	0.14757	0.14757	0.14756
25	0.09371	0.09367	0.09367	0.09366
30	0.05948	0.05946	0.05945	0.05945

value of κ it is possible to obtain ruin probabilities to more decimal places by using lower and upper bounds in this way.

Table 7.4 shows approximations to $\psi(u)$ for the same values of u as in Table 7.3 using the recursion formula of Section 7.9.2, together with exact values, using three different values for the scaling factor β (which can be thought of as corresponding to the above values of κ). In applying this method, the (scaled) exponential distribution was replaced by the discrete distribution given by formula (4.33). We see from this table that this method also gives very good approximations, and for this individual claim amount distribution there is little difference between the methods in terms of approximations.

As a second illustration we consider the situation when the individual claim amount distribution is $Pa(4, 3)$. In this case there is no explicit solution for ψ, but each of our numerical procedures can be used to provide excellent approximations. Table 7.5 shows approximations calculated by the method of Section 7.9.2 for the same three values of β and the same value of θ as in Table 7.4, again using the discretisation procedure given by formula (4.33). We can see that the pattern in this table is as in Table 7.4, and based on the accuracy in that table we expect the values calculated using $\beta = 100$ to be very close to the true values. For this situation, calculation by the method of Section 7.9.1 is discussed in Exercise 13.

Table 7.5 *Approximations to $\psi(u)$, $Pa(4,3)$ claims.*

u	$\beta = 20$	$\beta = 50$	$\beta = 100$
10	0.47524	0.47520	0.47519
20	0.26617	0.26614	0.26613
30	0.15136	0.15134	0.15133
40	0.08689	0.08687	0.08687
50	0.05027	0.05026	0.05026
60	0.02930	0.02929	0.02929

7.10 Approximate Calculation of Ruin Probabilities

There are many ways in which the ultimate ruin probability can be approximated. However, the need for approximations has diminished in recent years as numerical methods such as those described in the previous section can now be implemented easily with modern computing power. In this section we describe one simple approximation, known as De Vylder's method. The main reason for considering this approximation ahead of others is that it can be applied to problems other than finding the ultimate ruin probability, as illustrated in the next two chapters. Two further approximation methods are described in Exercises 9 and 10.

The idea underlying De Vylder's method is a simple one. Suppose we have a classical risk process $\{U(t)\}_{t\geq 0}$ for which we wish to calculate the probability of ultimate ruin. We can approximate this risk process by a classical risk process $\{\tilde{U}(t)\}_{t\geq 0}$, which has the following characteristics:

- $\tilde{U}(0) = u$,
- the Poisson parameter is $\tilde{\lambda}$,
- the premium income per unit time is $\tilde{c}$ and
- the individual claim amount distribution is $\tilde{F}(x) = 1 - \exp\{-\tilde{\alpha}x\}$, $x \geq 0$.

Since the individual claim amount distribution in the approximating risk process is exponential with parameter $\tilde{\alpha}$, it immediately follows by equation (7.11) that the probability of ultimate ruin for the risk process $\{\tilde{U}(t)\}_{t\geq 0}$ is

$$\frac{\tilde{\lambda}}{\tilde{\alpha}\tilde{c}} \exp\left\{-\left(\tilde{\alpha} - \tilde{\lambda}/\tilde{c}\right) u\right\},$$

and this is De Vylder's approximation to the ultimate ruin probability for the risk process $\{U(t)\}_{t\geq 0}$. The parameters $\tilde{\lambda}$, $\tilde{c}$ and $\tilde{\alpha}$ are chosen by matching moments of the two surplus processes. First, we set

$$E[U(t)] = E\left[\tilde{U}(t)\right],$$

which gives

$$u + ct - \lambda m_1 t = u + \tilde{c}t - \tilde{\lambda}t/\tilde{\alpha}$$

or

$$\tilde{c} = c - \lambda m_1 + \tilde{\lambda}/\tilde{\alpha}. \tag{7.24}$$

Next, we set

$$E\left[(U(t) - E\left[U(t)\right])^2\right] = E\left[\left(\tilde{U}(t) - E\left[\tilde{U}(t)\right]\right)^2\right],$$

and as

$$U(t) - E\left[U(t)\right] = -S(t) + \lambda m_1 t,$$

this is equivalent to setting

$$V\left[S(t)\right] = V\left[\tilde{S}(t)\right]$$

(where $\{\tilde{S}(t)\}_{t\geq 0}$ denotes the aggregate claims process in the approximating process $\{\tilde{U}(t)\}_{t\geq 0}$), which results in

$$\lambda m_2 = 2\tilde{\lambda}/\tilde{\alpha}^2. \tag{7.25}$$

Thirdly, we set

$$E\left[(U(t) - E\left[U(t)\right])^3\right] = E\left[\left(\tilde{U}(t) - E\left[\tilde{U}(t)\right]\right)^3\right],$$

which is equivalent to setting

$$Sk\left[S(t)\right] = Sk\left[\tilde{S}(t)\right],$$

which leads to

$$\lambda m_3 = 6\tilde{\lambda}/\tilde{\alpha}^3. \tag{7.26}$$

Equations (7.25) and (7.26) give

$$\tilde{\alpha} = 3m_2/m_3, \tag{7.27}$$

and substituting for $\tilde{\alpha}$ in equation (7.25) gives

$$\tilde{\lambda} = \frac{9\lambda m_2^3}{2m_3^2}. \tag{7.28}$$

The final step is to obtain $\tilde{c}$ by inserting expressions (7.27) and (7.28) for $\tilde{\alpha}$ and $\tilde{\lambda}$ into equation (7.24).

All that is required to apply De Vylder's approximation is that the first three moments of the individual claim amount distribution exist. In situations when the adjustment coefficient exists, the method usually provides good approximations when ruin probabilities are small, say below 5%. The approximation is, however, inaccurate for small values of u, especially $u = 0$, but such values are of little practical interest as the ruin probability is large. Generally, the method is not particularly accurate when the adjustment coefficient does not exist.

Example 7.8 *Let* $f(x) = 4xe^{-2x}$, $x > 0$, *and let* $c = 1.2\lambda$. *Calculate De Vylder's approximation to* $\psi(u)$ *for* $u = 0, 3, 6, \ldots, 18$ *and compare these approximations with the exact values.*

Solution 7.8 *For this individual claim amount distribution,* $m_1 = 1$, $m_2 = 3/2$ *and* $m_3 = 3$. *Then by equation (7.28),*

$$\tilde{\lambda} = \frac{9\lambda \times 1.5^3}{2 \times 9} = \frac{27\lambda}{16},$$

by equation (7.27), $\tilde{\alpha} = 3/2$, *and hence by equation (7.24),*

$$\tilde{c} = 1.2\lambda - \lambda + \frac{9\lambda}{8} = \frac{53\lambda}{40}.$$

The approximation to $\psi(u)$ *is thus*

$$\tfrac{45}{53} \exp\{-12u/53\}.$$

Table 7.6 shows exact and approximate values of $\psi(u)$, *where the exact values can be calculated from the solution to Example 7.7, and we can see from this table that the approximation is very good in this case.*

Table 7.6 *Exact and approximate values of* $\psi(u)$, $\gamma(2, 2)$ *claims.*

u	Exact	Approximate
0	0.8333	0.8491
3	0.4314	0.4305
6	0.2185	0.2182
9	0.1107	0.1107
12	0.0560	0.0561
15	0.0284	0.0284
18	0.0144	0.0144

7.11 Notes and References

Most of the material covered in both the early part of this chapter and the exercises below is also covered in standard texts such as Gerber (1979) and Klugman et al. (1998). The original reference for the recursive calculation of ϕ in Section 7.9.1 is Panjer (1986), and the method presented is due to Dufresne and Gerber (1989). The recursive procedure in Section 7.9.2 is based on Dickson and Waters (1991). Although there is no evidence in the examples presented in Section 7.9.3, this recursive procedure is unstable. An alternative, stable, algorithm is discussed in Dickson et al. (1995). De Vylder (1978) derived the approximation which bears his name.

7.12 Exercises

1. An aggregate claims process $\{S(t)\}_{t\geq 0}$ is a compound Poisson process with Poisson parameter 100, and the individual claim amount distribution is $Pa(4, 300)$.
   (a) Calculate the mean and variance of $S(1)$.
   (b) Calculate the mean and variance of $S(2)$.
   (c) Calculate the mean and variance of $S(2) - S(1)$.
2. The aggregate claims process for a risk is a compound Poisson process with Poisson parameter λ, and the individual claim amount distribution is $\gamma(2, 0.02)$. Calculate the adjustment coefficient when the premium income per unit time is 130λ.
3. Using the approximation
$$\exp\{Rx\} \approx 1 + Rx + \tfrac{1}{2}R^2x^2 + \tfrac{1}{6}R^3x^3,$$
   find an approximation to R when the individual claim amount distribution is $\gamma(2.5, 2.5)$ and $c = 1.05\lambda$.
4. Let the premium for $S(1)$ be calculated according to the exponential principle with parameter β. Show that $\beta = R$.
5. Consider a classical risk process with Poisson parameter $\lambda = 100$, an individual claim amount distribution that is exponential with mean 1, and a premium of 125 per unit time. Let $\psi_n(u)$ denote the probability of ruin at or before the nth claim, $n = 1, 2, \ldots$, for this risk, given an initial surplus u.
   (a) Show that
$$\psi_1(u) = \tfrac{4}{9}\exp\{-u\}.$$
   (b) Derive an expression for $\psi_2(u)$.

6. Consider a classical risk process with an individual claim amount distribution that is mixed exponential with density function

$$f(x) = \tfrac{1}{2}\left(2\exp\{-2x\} + \tfrac{2}{3}\exp\{-2x/3\}\right)$$

for $x > 0$. The premium for this risk is calculated with a loading factor of 10%.

   (a) Find the adjustment coefficient.
   (b) Use the method of Laplace transforms to find an expression for $\phi(u)$.
   (c) Find De Vylder's approximation to $\psi(u)$, and calculate exact and approximate values of $\psi(u)$ for $u = 0, 10, 20, \ldots, 50$. Comment on the quality of the approximation.

7. Cramer's asymptotic formula is

$$\psi(u) \sim Ce^{-Ru},$$

where R is the adjustment coefficient and

$$C = \frac{c/\lambda - m_1}{E[Xe^{RX}] - c/\lambda}.$$

   (a) Show that when $F(x) = 1 - e^{-\alpha x}$, $x \geq 0$, the asymptotic formula is exact.
   (b) Repeat question 6(c), but now use Ce^{-Ru} as an approximation to $\psi(u)$.

8. (a) Assuming that the required moments exist, show that

$$E[L_1^r] = \frac{m_{r+1}}{(r+1)m_1}.$$

   (b) Find expressions for $E[L]$ and $E[L^2]$ in terms of θ and m_k, $k = 1, 2, 3$, when $c = (1+\theta)\lambda m_1$.

9. Tijms' approximation to $\psi(u)$ is

$$Ce^{-Ru} + Ae^{-Su},$$

where C and R are as in Cramer's asymptotic formula, A is such that the approximation gives the exact value of $\psi(0)$, and S is such that

$$\int_0^\infty \psi(u)du = \int_0^\infty \left(Ce^{-Ru} + Ae^{-Su}\right) du. \tag{7.29}$$

   (a) What is the rationale underlying identity (7.29)?
   (b) Let the individual claim amount distribution be

$$f(x) = \tfrac{1}{6}e^{-x/2} + \tfrac{1}{3}e^{-x} + \tfrac{2}{3}e^{-2x}$$

   for $x > 0$, and let the premium loading factor be 5%. Calculate Tijms' approximation to $\psi(20)$.

10. Let the random variable Y have distribution function G where

$$G(x) = \phi(0) + \psi(0) \int_0^x \frac{\beta^\alpha y^{\alpha-1} e^{-\beta y}}{\Gamma(\alpha)} dy.$$

The Beekman-Bowers' approximation uses $G(u)$ as an approximation to $\phi(u)$, where the parameters α and β are chosen such that $E[Y^r] = E[L^r]$ for $r = 1, 2$.

(a) Show that when $F(x) = 1 - e^{-\mu x}$, $x \geq 0$, $G(u) = \phi(u)$.

(b) Repeat question 6(c), but now use the Beekman-Bowers' approximation to $\psi(u)$.

11. In the so-called dual model of risk theory, the surplus process of a company is modelled as

$$U(t) = u - ct + S(t),$$

where u is the surplus at time 0, c is the rate of expense outgo per unit time, and $\{S(t)\}_{t \geq 0}$ is a compound Poisson process with Poisson parameter λ and with jumps (representing income) distributed as a random variable X. (Thus, under the dual model, the surplus decreases at rate c per unit time, and is increased by random amounts. Such a model might be appropriate for a research and development company which has continuous expenses and which gains income from discoveries.) Assume that X has density function $f(x)$ for $x > 0$, and that $c < \lambda E[X]$.

The probability of ultimate ruin from initial surplus u for this process is denoted $\psi(u)$ and is given by

$$\psi(u) = \Pr(U(t) \leq 0 \text{ for some } t > 0).$$

(a) For this process, the adjustment coefficient is the unique positive solution of the equation

$$h(r) = \lambda - cr - \lambda E[e^{-rX}] = 0.$$

By considering the properties of $h(r)$ for $r \geq 0$, show that there is a unique positive number R such that $h(R) = 0$.

(b) Find an expression for R when $F(x) = 1 - \exp\{-\alpha x\}$, $x \geq 0$.

(c) For this process,

$$\psi(u) = e^{-\lambda u/c} + \int_0^{u/c} \lambda e^{-\lambda t} \int_0^\infty \psi(u - ct + x) f(x)\, dx\, dt. \quad (7.30)$$

Give an interpretation of this equation.

(d) By insertion in the right-hand side of equation (7.30), verify that $\psi(u) = \exp\{-Ru\}$, where R is as defined part (a).

(e) Suppose that $\lambda = 1$ and $F(x) = 1 - \exp\{-x\}$, $x \geq 0$. Find the maximum rate of expense outgo per unit time if the company requires that $\psi(40) \leq 0.01$.

12. Let the individual claim amount distribution be exponential with mean $1/\alpha$, and let $c = (1+\theta)\lambda/\alpha$. Use formula (7.19) to show that

$$\phi(u) = 1 - \frac{1}{1+\theta} \exp\{-\alpha\theta u/(1+\theta)\}.$$

13. Let the individual claim amount distribution be $Pa(4,3)$.

(a) What is the distribution of L_1?

(b) Using the method of Section 7.9.1, compute upper and lower bounds for $\psi(u)$ when $\theta = 0.1$ for the values of u in Table 7.5. Calculate approximations to ψ by averaging these bounds, and compare your answers with the approximations in Table 7.5.

8
Advanced Ruin Theory

8.1 Introduction

In this chapter we continue our study of the classical risk model. We start with a useful result concerning the probability that ruin occurs without the surplus process first attaining a specified level. This result will be applied in Sections 8.4 and 8.5 and Exercise 10. We then consider the insurer's deficit when ruin occurs and provide a means of finding the distribution of this deficit. We extend this study by considering the insurer's largest deficit before the surplus process recovers to level 0. Following this, we consider the distribution of the insurer's surplus immediately prior to ruin.

We then study in some detail finite time ruin problems. In particular, we consider the distribution of the time of ruin, introduce and apply Gerber-Shiu functions, and find moments of the time of ruin. We conclude this chapter with a discussion of a problem which involves modifying the surplus process through the payment of dividends.

In this chapter we use the same assumptions and notation as in Chapter 7.

8.2 A Barrier Problem

Let us consider the following question: What is the probability that ruin occurs from initial surplus u without the surplus process reaching level $b > u$ prior to ruin? An alternative way of expressing this question is to ask: What is the probability that ruin occurs in the presence of an absorbing barrier at b? We denote this probability by $\xi(u, b)$, and let $\chi(u, b)$ denote the probability that the surplus process attains the level b from initial surplus u without first falling below zero. To find expressions for $\xi(u, b)$ and $\chi(u, b)$, we consider the probabilities of ultimate ruin and survival respectively in an unrestricted surplus process.

First, note that if survival occurs from initial surplus u, then the surplus process must pass through the level $b > u$ at some point in time, as the condition $c > \lambda m_1$ guarantees that $U(t) \to \infty$ as $t \to \infty$. Also, as the distribution of the time to the next claim from the time the surplus attains b is exponential, the probabilistic behaviour of the surplus process once it attains level b is independent of its behaviour prior to attaining b. Hence $\phi(u) = \chi(u,b)\phi(b)$, or, equivalently,

$$\chi(u,b) = \frac{1-\psi(u)}{1-\psi(b)}.$$

Similarly, if ruin occurs from initial surplus u, then either the surplus process does or does not attain level b prior to ruin. Hence

$$\psi(u) = \xi(u,b) + \chi(u,b)\psi(b),$$

so that

$$\xi(u,b) = \psi(u) - \frac{1-\psi(u)}{1-\psi(b)}\psi(b) = \frac{\psi(u)-\psi(b)}{1-\psi(b)}.$$

Note that $\xi(u,b) + \chi(u,b) = 1$, so that eventually either ruin occurs without the surplus process attaining b or the surplus process attains level b.

8.3 The Severity of Ruin

In this section we are interested not just in the probability of ruin, but also in the amount of the insurer's deficit at the time of ruin should ruin occur.

Given an initial surplus u, we denote the time of ruin by T_u and define it by

$$T_u = \inf\{t\colon U(t) < 0\}$$

with $T_u = \infty$ if $U(t) \geq 0$ for all $t > 0$. Thus, $\psi(u) = \Pr(T_u < \infty)$. Now define

$$G(u,y) = \Pr(T_u < \infty \quad \text{and} \quad U(T_u) \geq -y)$$

to be the probability that ruin occurs and that the insurer's deficit at ruin, or severity of ruin, is at most y. Note that

$$\lim_{y\to\infty} G(u,y) = \psi(u),$$

so that

$$\frac{G(u,y)}{\psi(u)} = \Pr(|U(T_u)| \leq y \mid T_u < \infty)$$

is a proper distribution function. Hence, for a given initial surplus u, $G(u, \cdot)$ is a defective distribution with (defective) density

$$g(u, y) = \frac{\partial}{\partial y} G(u, y).$$

We can solve for G using Laplace transforms, but to do so we first need an expression for $g(0, y)$. This can be obtained from Section 7.9.1, where we saw that the amount of the first record high of the aggregate loss process (given that such a record high occurs) has density function

$$k(x) = \frac{1}{m_1} (1 - F(x)) . \tag{8.1}$$

We also saw that the probability of a first record high of the aggregate loss process is $\psi(0)$. It immediately follows that $k(y) = g(0, y)/\psi(0)$ so that

$$g(0, y) = \frac{\lambda}{c} (1 - F(y)) .$$

We can now write an expression for $G(u, y)$ by noting that if ruin occurs with a deficit of at most y, then on the first occasion on which the surplus falls below its initial level u either

(i) the surplus falls to $u - x(\geq 0)$, so that ruin subsequently occurs from this surplus level with a deficit of at most y, or
(ii) ruin occurs at this fall with a deficit of at most y.

Hence we find that

$$G(u, y) = \int_0^u g(0, x) G(u - x, y) dx + \int_u^{u+y} g(0, x) dx \tag{8.2}$$

$$= \psi(0) \int_0^u k(x) G(u - x, y) dx + \psi(0) \eta(u, y), \tag{8.3}$$

where

$$\eta(u, y) = \int_u^{u+y} k(x) dx = K(u + y) - K(u).$$

Now let

$$G^*(s, y) = \int_0^\infty e^{-su} G(u, y) du$$

and

$$\eta^*(s, y) = \int_0^\infty e^{-su} \eta(u, y) du.$$

Then by taking the Laplace transform of equation (8.3) we find that

$$G^*(s,y) = \frac{\psi(0)\eta^*(s,y)}{1-\psi(0)k^*(s)}.$$

Example 8.1 *Let $f(x) = \alpha e^{-\alpha x}$, $x > 0$. Show that $G(u,y) = \psi(u)(1-e^{-\alpha y})$.*

Solution 8.1 *As $k(x) = f(x)$,*

$$\eta(u,y) = e^{-\alpha u}(1-e^{-\alpha y})$$

and

$$\eta^*(s,y) = \frac{1-e^{-\alpha y}}{s+\alpha}.$$

Hence

$$G^*(s,y) = \frac{\psi(0)(1-e^{-\alpha y})}{s+\alpha-\psi(0)\alpha},$$

and as $\psi(0) = \lambda/(\alpha c)$,

$$G^*(s,y) = \frac{\lambda}{\alpha c}\frac{1-e^{-\alpha y}}{s+\alpha-\lambda/c},$$

giving

$$G(u,y) = \frac{\lambda}{\alpha c}e^{-(\alpha-\lambda/c)u}(1-e^{-\alpha y}) = \psi(u)(1-e^{-\alpha y}).$$

The result in the above example is interesting as it says that if ruin occurs, the distribution of the deficit at ruin is the same as the individual claim amount distribution. For the classical risk model, this occurs only in the case of an exponential distribution for individual claims, and the reason for this is the memoryless property of the exponential distribution. Suppose that the surplus at time T_u^- (i.e. immediately prior to T_u) is x. Then

$$\Pr\left(|U(T_u)| > y \mid U(T_u^-) = x\right)$$

is just the probability that the claim which occurs at time T_u exceeds $x+y$ given that it exceeds x, and this probability is

$$\frac{e^{-\alpha(x+y)}}{e^{-\alpha x}} = e^{-\alpha y},$$

so that

$$\Pr\left(|U(T_u)| \le y \mid U(T_u^-) = x\right) = 1-e^{-\alpha y}$$

independent of x. In Exercise 3 of Chapter 6 we saw the analogue of this result for the discrete model discussed in that chapter.

Example 8.2 *As in Example 7.7, let* $f(x) = 4xe^{-2x}$, $x > 0$, *and let* $c = 1.2\lambda$. *Find an expression for* $G(u, y)$.

Solution 8.2 *First, we note that* $m_1 = 1$, *and so*

$$\begin{aligned} k(x) &= 1 - F(x) = e^{-2x}(1 + 2x) \\ &= \tfrac{1}{2}\left(2e^{-2x} + 4xe^{-2x}\right) \end{aligned}$$

and $K(x) = 1 - e^{-2x}(1 + x)$. *Further,*

$$\begin{aligned} \eta(u, y) &= e^{-2u}(1 + u) - e^{-2(u+y)}(1 + u + y) \\ &= e^{-2u}(1 + u)(1 - e^{-2y}) - e^{-2(u+y)}y, \end{aligned}$$

and so

$$\eta^*(s, y) = (1 - e^{-2y})\left(\frac{1}{s+2} + \frac{1}{(s+2)^2}\right) - \frac{ye^{-2y}}{s+2}.$$

As $\psi(0) = 5/6$,

$$\begin{aligned} G^*(s, y) &= \frac{\frac{5}{6}\left(\left((1 - e^{-2y})\,(s+3)\,/(s+2)^2\right) - \left(ye^{-2y}/(s+2)\right)\right)}{1 - \frac{5}{12}\left((2/(s+2)) + \left(4/(s+2)^2\right)\right)} \\ &= \frac{\frac{5}{6}\left((1 - e^{-2y})(s+3) - ye^{-2y}(s+2)\right)}{(s+2)^2 - \frac{5}{6}(s+4)} \\ &= \frac{\frac{5}{6}\left((1 - e^{-2y})(s+3) - ye^{-2y}(s+2)\right)}{(s+R_1)(s+R_2)}, \end{aligned}$$

where $R_1 = 0.2268$ *and* $R_2 = 2.9399$ *as in Example 7.7. Thus,*

$$G^*(s, y) = \frac{a_1(y)}{s+R_1} + \frac{a_2(y)}{s+R_2},$$

where

$$a_1(y)(s+R_2) + a_2(y)(s+R_1) = \tfrac{5}{6}\left((1 - e^{-2y})(s+3) - ye^{-2y}(s+2)\right).$$

Setting $s = -R_1$ *yields*

$$a_1(y) = 0.8518(1 - e^{-2y}) - 0.5446ye^{-2y},$$

and setting $s = -R_2$ *yields*

$$a_2(y) = -0.0185(1 - e^{-2y}) - 0.2887ye^{-2y},$$

and inversion of $G^*(s,y)$ *gives*

$$\begin{aligned} G(u,y) &= a_1(y)e^{-R_1u} + a_2(y)e^{-R_2u} \\ &= 0.8518e^{-R_1u}(1-e^{-2y}) - 0.5446ye^{-R_1u-2y} \\ &\quad -0.0185e^{-R_2u}(1-e^{-2y}) - 0.2887ye^{-R_2u-2y}. \end{aligned}$$

As a check on the solution, note that

$$\lim_{y\to\infty} G(u,y) = 0.8518e^{-R_1u} - 0.0185e^{-R_2u},$$

which, from Example 7.7, is the solution for $\psi(u)$*. We explore this example further in Exercise 4.*

We recall from formula (7.18) that

$$L^*(s) = E\left[e^{-sL}\right] = \frac{\phi(0)}{1-\psi(0)k^*(s)},$$

and hence

$$G^*(s,y) = \frac{\psi(0)}{\phi(0)}\eta^*(s,y)L^*(s). \tag{8.4}$$

Since the right-hand side of equation (8.4) is the product of two Laplace transforms it is the transform of a convolution, and hence we can invert $G^*(s,y)$ to obtain

$$\begin{aligned} G(u,y) &= \frac{\psi(0)}{\phi(0)}\int_0^u \eta(u-x,y)d\phi(x) \\ &= \frac{\psi(0)}{\phi(0)}\int_0^u \left(K(u-x+y)-K(u-x)\right)d\phi(x). \end{aligned}$$

Note that since the distribution function ϕ has a mass of probability of amount $\phi(0)$ at 0, we have

$$\begin{aligned} G(u,y) &= \psi(0)\left(K(u+y)-K(u)\right) \\ &\quad + \frac{\psi(0)}{\phi(0)}\int_0^u \left(K(u-x+y)-K(u-x)\right)\phi'(x)dx. \end{aligned} \tag{8.5}$$

We can use this result to find an alternative way of expressing $G(u,y)$, which is not practical in terms of deriving explicit solutions, but which proves to be useful in Section 8.5. Recall from Chapter 7 that

$$\phi(u) = \phi(0) + \sum_{n=1}^{\infty}\psi(0)^n\phi(0)K^{n*}(u),$$

so that for $u > 0$,

$$\frac{d}{du}\phi(u) = \sum_{n=1}^{\infty} \psi(0)^n \phi(0) k^{n*}(u).$$

Then, noting that

$$K(u-x+y) - K(u-x) = \int_{u-x}^{u-x+y} k(z)dz,$$

we can write equation (8.5) as

$$G(u,y) = \psi(0)\left(K(u+y) - K(u)\right) + \sum_{n=1}^{\infty} \psi(0)^{n+1} \int_0^u k^{n*}(x) \int_{u-x}^{u-x+y} k(z)dzdx. \quad (8.6)$$

The interpretation of this result is that in the expression

$$\psi(0)^{n+1} k^{n*}(x) \int_{u-x}^{u-x+y} k(z)dzdx$$

$\psi(0)^n k^{n*}(x)dx$ represents the probability that the nth record low of the surplus process results in a surplus between $u-x$ and $u-x+dx$, and

$$\psi(0) \int_{u-x}^{u-x+y} k(z)dz$$

represents the probability that the next record low results in ruin with a deficit of at most y.

8.4 The Maximum Severity of Ruin

We now extend the analysis of the previous section. We allow the surplus process to continue if ruin occurs, and we consider the insurer's maximum severity of ruin from the time of ruin until the time that the surplus process next attains level 0. As we are assuming that $c > \lambda m_1$, it is certain that the surplus process will attain this level.

We define T'_u to be the time of the first upcrossing of the surplus process through level 0 after ruin occurs and define the random variable M_u by

$$M_u = \sup\left\{|U(t)|, T_u \le t \le T'_u\right\},$$

so that M_u denotes the maximum severity of ruin. Let

$$J_u(z) = \Pr(M_u \le z \mid T_u < \infty)$$

be the distribution function of M_u given that ruin occurs. The maximum severity of ruin will be no more than z if ruin occurs with a deficit $y \le z$

and if the surplus does not fall below $-z$ from the level $-y$. In the notation of Section 8.2, the probability of this latter event is $\chi(z-y,z)$ since attaining level 0 from level $-y$ without falling below $-z$ is equivalent to attaining level z from level $z-y$ without falling below 0. Thus,

$$\begin{aligned} J_u(z) &= \int_0^z \frac{g(u,y)}{\psi(u)}\chi(z-y,z)dy \\ &= \frac{1}{\psi(u)\phi(z)}\int_0^z g(u,y)\phi(z-y)dy. \end{aligned}$$

We can evaluate this expression by noting that

$$\psi(u+z) = \int_z^\infty g(u,y)dy + \int_0^z g(u,y)\psi(z-y)dy. \tag{8.7}$$

This follows by noting that if ruin occurs from initial surplus $u+z$, then the surplus process must fall below z at some time in the future. By partitioning this event according to whether ruin occurs at the time of this fall, the probability of which is given by the first integral, or at a subsequent time, the probability of which is given by the second integral, we obtain equation (8.7) for $\psi(u+z)$. Noting that $\psi = 1-\phi$, we can write equation (8.7) as

$$\begin{aligned} \int_0^z g(u,y)\phi(z-y)dy &= \int_z^\infty g(u,y)dy + \int_0^z g(u,y)dy - \psi(u+z) \\ &= \psi(u) - \psi(u+z). \end{aligned}$$

Thus,

$$J_u(z) = \frac{\psi(u)-\psi(u+z)}{\psi(u)\left(1-\psi(z)\right)}.$$

Example 8.3 *Let $f(x)=e^{-x}$, $x>0$, and let $c=(1+\theta)\lambda$. Show that J_u can be represented as an infinite mixture of exponential distributions.*

Solution 8.3 *From Section 7.7 we know that $\psi(u) = (1-R)e^{-Ru}$ where $R=\theta/(1+\theta)$. Hence*

$$\begin{aligned} J_u(z) &= \frac{1-e^{-Rz}}{1-(1-R)e^{-Rz}} \\ &= \left(1-e^{-Rz}\right)\sum_{j=0}^\infty (1-R)^j e^{-Rjz} \\ &= \sum_{j=0}^\infty (1-R)^j e^{-Rjz} - \sum_{j=0}^\infty (1-R)^j e^{-R(j+1)z} \\ &= 1-\sum_{j=1}^\infty R(1-R)^{j-1}e^{-Rjz}. \end{aligned}$$

As

$$\sum_{j=1}^{\infty} R(1-R)^{j-1} = 1,$$

we have

$$J_u(z) = \sum_{j=1}^{\infty} v_j \left(1 - e^{-Rjz}\right),$$

where $v_j = R(1-R)^{j-1}$ *so that* J_u *is an infinite mixture of exponential distributions.*

Note that in Example 8.3 $J_u(z)$ is independent of u. This is because the distribution of the deficit at ruin, given that ruin occurs, is independent of u in the case of exponentially distributed individual claim amounts – see Example 8.1. For other individual claim amount distributions, $J_u(z)$ will not be independent of u.

8.5 The Surplus Prior to Ruin

In this section we consider the distribution of the surplus immediately prior to ruin. In Section 8.3 we introduced the notation T_u^- to denote the time immediately prior to ruin. Now let $U(T_u^-)$ denote the level of the surplus process immediately prior to payment of the claim that causes ruin. Then the probability that ruin occurs from initial surplus u and that the surplus immediately prior to ruin is less than x is

$$W(u,x) = \Pr\left(T_u < \infty \quad \text{and} \quad U(T_u^-) < x\right).$$

We note that W is a defective distribution function for the same reason that G is in Section 8.3, namely that $\Pr(T_u < \infty) < 1$.

A key point in obtaining expressions for W is that for $0 \le u < x$, ruin may or may not occur with a surplus prior to ruin less than x on the first occasion that the surplus falls below its initial level, but for $u \ge x$ it may not. Thus, the two cases $0 \le u < x$ and $u \ge x$ must be treated separately.

Consider first the situation when $0 \le u < x$. Note that if the surplus process never reaches x, then ruin must occur with a surplus prior to ruin less than x. Hence, by considering whether the surplus process attains the level x prior to ruin or not, we can write

$$W(u,x) = \xi(u,x) + \chi(u,x)W(x,x), \tag{8.8}$$

where the functions ξ and χ are as defined in Section 8.2.

Next, consider the situation when $u = x$. Note that if the surplus prior to ruin is less than x, then on the first occasion that the surplus falls below its initial level, it must fall to some level between 0 and x. (Otherwise ruin occurs at the time of the first fall below the initial level, so that the surplus prior to ruin is at least x.) By conditioning on the amount of the first fall below the initial level we find that

$$W(x,x) = \int_0^x g(0,y)W(x-y,x)dy. \tag{8.9}$$

As we know the form of $W(u,x)$ for $u < x$, we can insert this in equation (8.9), giving

$$W(x,x) = \int_0^x g(0,y)\left(\xi(x-y,x) + \chi(x-y,x)W(x,x)\right)dy,$$

and rearranging this identity we get

$$W(x,x) = \frac{\int_0^x g(0,y)\xi(x-y,x)dy}{1 - \int_0^x g(0,y)\chi(x-y,x)dy}. \tag{8.10}$$

To simplify equation (8.10) note that as $y \to \infty$ in equation (8.2) we get

$$\begin{aligned}\psi(u) &= \int_0^u g(0,y)\psi(u-y)dy + \int_u^\infty g(0,y)dy \qquad (8.11)\\ &= \int_0^u g(0,y)\psi(u-y)dy + \psi(0) - G(0,u),\end{aligned}$$

so that

$$\int_0^u g(0,y)\psi(u-y)dy = \psi(u) - \psi(0) + G(0,u).$$

Hence, the numerator on the right-hand side of equation (8.10) can be written as

$$\begin{aligned}\int_0^x g(0,y)\xi(x-y,x)dy &= \int_0^x g(0,y)\frac{\psi(x-y)-\psi(x)}{1-\psi(x)}dy\\ &= \frac{\psi(x)-\psi(0)+G(0,x)-\psi(x)G(0,x)}{1-\psi(x)}\end{aligned}$$

and the integral in the denominator as

$$\begin{aligned}\int_0^x g(0,y)\chi(x-y,x)dy &= \int_0^x g(0,y)\frac{1-\psi(x-y)}{1-\psi(x)}dy\\ &= \frac{G(0,x)-\psi(x)+\psi(0)-G(0,x)}{1-\psi(x)}.\end{aligned}$$

Thus, we obtain

$$W(x,x) = \frac{\psi(x) - \psi(0) + G(0,x) - \psi(x)G(0,x)}{1 - \psi(0)}. \tag{8.12}$$

We can now use equations (8.8) and (8.12) to obtain

$$W(u,x) = \frac{1 - G(0,x)}{1 - \psi(0)}\psi(u) - \frac{\psi(0) - G(0,x)}{1 - \psi(0)} \tag{8.13}$$

for $0 \leq u < x$. In particular, note that when $u = 0$ we obtain the remarkable identity $W(0,x) = G(0,x)$, and we discuss this result at the end of this section.

We can now consider the situation when $u > x$. The argument applied to the case $u = x$ can be modified by noting that if the surplus prior to ruin is less than x, then there must be a first occasion on which the surplus falls below x, and the amount of this fall below x cannot exceed x. The probability that the surplus falls from u to a level between x and 0 is the same as the probability that ruin occurs from an initial surplus of $u - x$ with a deficit at ruin of at most x. Hence we can write

$$W(u,x) = \int_0^x g(u - x, y) W(x - y, x) dy. \tag{8.14}$$

As in the case $u = x$, we can insert for $W(x - y, x)$ in equation (8.14), but now using equation (8.13), and we obtain

$$\begin{aligned} W(u,x) = {} & \frac{1 - G(0,x)}{1 - \psi(0)} \int_0^x g(u - x, y)\psi(x - y) dy \\ & - \frac{\psi(0) - G(0,x)}{1 - \psi(0)} G(u - x, x). \end{aligned} \tag{8.15}$$

To evaluate the integral term in (8.15), we note that for any $x < u$ the ultimate ruin probability $\psi(u)$ can be written as

$$\psi(u) = \int_0^x g(u - x, y)\psi(x - y) dy + \int_x^\infty g(u - x, y) dy.$$

We can write this because ruin can occur in one of the two following ways. Either the surplus can fall below x for the first time (but by no more than x) to level $x - y$ and ruin can subsequently occur from this level, or the surplus can fall below x for the first time by an amount greater than x, causing ruin to occur. Thus,

$$\begin{aligned} \int_0^x g(u - x, y)\psi(x - y) dy &= \psi(u) - \int_x^\infty g(u - x, y) dy \\ &= \psi(u) - \psi(u - x) + G(u - x, x). \end{aligned}$$

Inserting this expression into equation (8.15) we obtain after a little algebra

$$W(u,x) = G(u-x,x) - \frac{1-G(0,x)}{1-\psi(0)}\left(\psi(u-x) - \psi(u)\right) \tag{8.16}$$

for $u > x$.

As equation (8.12) satisfies both (8.13) and (8.16), we can summarise the above results as

$$W(u,x) = \frac{1-G(0,x)}{1-\psi(0)}\psi(u) - \frac{\psi(0)-G(0,x)}{1-\psi(0)} \tag{8.17}$$

for $0 \le u \le x$ and

$$W(u,x) = G(u-x,x) - \frac{1-G(0,x)}{1-\psi(0)}\left(\psi(u-x) - \psi(u)\right) \tag{8.18}$$

for $u \ge x$. Thus, the defective distribution function of the surplus prior to ruin is expressed in terms of the ultimate ruin probability and the defective distribution function of the deficit at ruin. Although these results are relatively simple to apply when both ψ and G are known, it turns out that it is easier to deal with the defective density function w, which we define as

$$w(u,x) = \frac{\partial}{\partial x}W(u,x).$$

We note that although the function W is continuous at $u=x$ it is not differentiable, and so in considering w we must consider the two cases $u < x$ and $u > x$.

When $u<x$, it is straightforward to find $w(u,x)$ by differentiating equation (8.17). We get

$$w(u,x) = g(0,x)\frac{1-\psi(u)}{1-\psi(0)},$$

and as $W(0,x) = G(0,x)$, $w(0,x) = g(0,x) = (\lambda/c)(1-F(x))$, giving

$$w(u,x) = \frac{\lambda}{c}\left(1-F(x)\right)\frac{1-\psi(u)}{1-\psi(0)}.$$

When $u > x$, differentiation of equation (8.18) yields

$$w(u,x) = \frac{\partial}{\partial x}G(u-x,x) + g(0,x)\frac{\psi(u-x)-\psi(u)}{1-\psi(0)} - \frac{1-G(0,x)}{1-\psi(0)}\frac{\partial}{\partial x}\psi(u-x). \tag{8.19}$$

This equation simplifies considerably, and the key to it is the rather unattractive expression for G derived as formula (8.6). From this expression, we can write $G(u-x,x)$ as

$$G(u-x,x) = \psi(0)\,(K(u)-K(u-x)) + \sum_{n=1}^{\infty}\psi(0)^{n+1}\int_0^{u-x} k^{n*}(s)\int_{u-x-s}^{u-s} k(z)dzds,$$

and hence

$$\begin{aligned}\frac{\partial}{\partial x}G(u-x,x) &= \psi(0)k(u-x) - \sum_{n=1}^{\infty}\psi(0)^{n+1}k^{n*}(u-x)\int_0^x k(z)dz \\ &\quad + \sum_{n=1}^{\infty}\psi(0)^{n+1}\int_0^{u-x} k^{n*}(s)k(u-x-s)ds \\ &= \psi(0)k(u-x) - \sum_{n=1}^{\infty}\psi(0)^{n+1}k^{n*}(u-x)K(x) \\ &\quad + \sum_{n=1}^{\infty}\psi(0)^{n+1}k^{(n+1)*}(u-x) \\ &= \sum_{n=1}^{\infty}\psi(0)^n k^{n*}(u-x) - \sum_{n=1}^{\infty}\psi(0)^{n+1}k^{n*}(u-x)K(x) \\ &= \sum_{n=1}^{\infty}\psi(0)^n k^{n*}(u-x)\,[1-\psi(0)K(x)]\,.\end{aligned}$$

Similarly, letting $y \to \infty$ in formula (8.6), we can write

$$\psi(u-x) = \psi(0)\,(1-K(u-x)) + \sum_{n=1}^{\infty}\psi(0)^{n+1}\int_0^{u-x} k^{n*}(s)\int_{u-x-s}^{\infty} k(z)dzds,$$

so that

$$\begin{aligned}\frac{\partial}{\partial x}\psi(u-x) &= \psi(0)k(u-x) - \sum_{n=1}^{\infty}\psi(0)^{n+1}k^{n*}(u-x) \\ &\quad + \sum_{n=1}^{\infty}\psi(0)^{n+1}\int_0^{u-x} k^{n*}(s)k(u-x-s)ds \\ &= \sum_{n=1}^{\infty}\psi(0)^n k^{n*}(u-x) - \sum_{n=1}^{\infty}\psi(0)^{n+1}k^{n*}(u-x) \\ &= \sum_{n=1}^{\infty}\psi(0)^n k^{n*}(u-x)\,[1-\psi(0)]\,.\end{aligned}$$

Thus,

$$\frac{\partial}{\partial x}G(u-x,x) = \frac{1-\psi(0)K(x)}{1-\psi(0)}\frac{\partial}{\partial x}\psi(u-x),$$

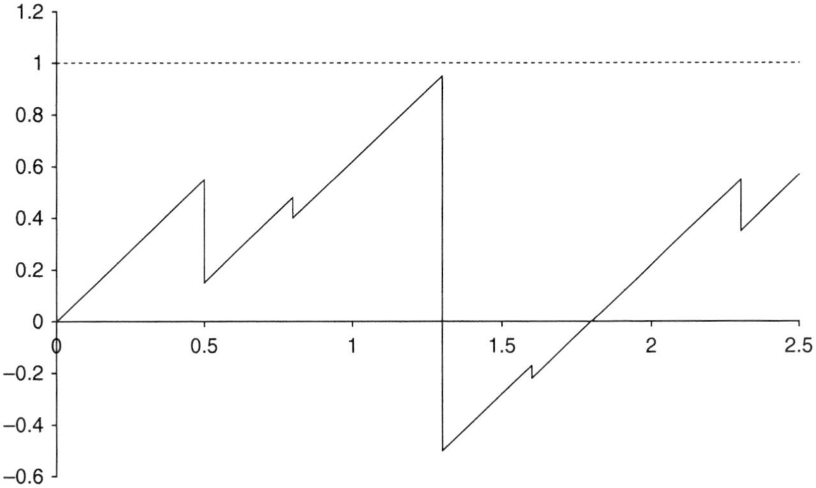

Figure 8.1 A realisation of a surplus process starting at $u = 0$ for which the surplus prior to ruin is less than 1.

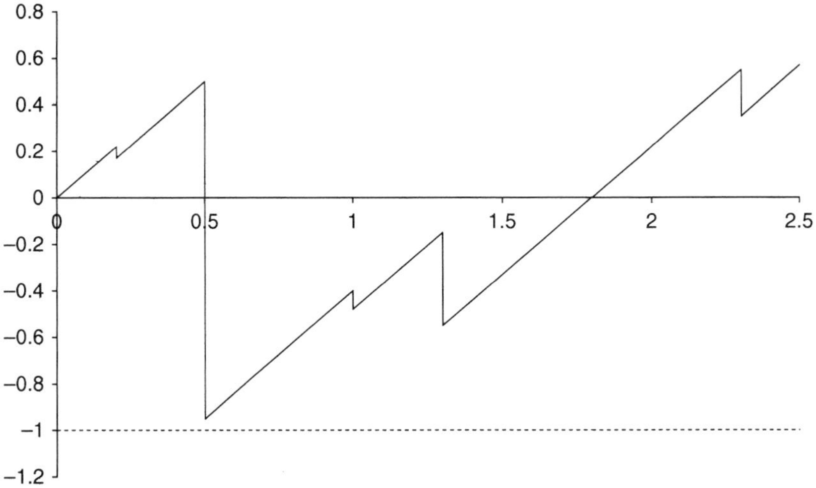

Figure 8.2 The dual of the realisation in Figure 8.1.

and as $G(0,x) = \psi(0)K(x)$, equation (8.19) gives

$$\begin{aligned} w(u,x) &= g(0,x)\frac{\psi(u-x)-\psi(u)}{1-\psi(0)} \\ &= \frac{\lambda}{c}\,(1-F(x))\,\frac{\psi(u-x)-\psi(u)}{1-\psi(0)} \end{aligned}$$

for $u > x$.

These results show that if we know both F and ψ, then we also know w, and it is indeed remarkable that so little information is required to find w. It is also clear from these results that for $u > 0$ the density $w(u,x)$ has a discontinuity at $x = u$.

We conclude this section by noting that the identity $W(0,x) = G(0,x)$ can be explained by dual events. Consider a realisation of a surplus process which starts at $u = 0$ for which ruin occurs with a surplus prior to ruin less than x. For this realisation, there is a unique realisation of a dual process $\{\hat{U}(t)\}_{t\geq 0}$ such that ruin occurs in the dual realisation with a deficit less than x. The dual process is constructed by defining

$$\begin{aligned} \hat{U}(t) &= -U(T_0' - t) && \text{for } 0 \leq t \leq T_0' \\ \hat{U}(t) &= U(t) && \text{for } t > T_0' \end{aligned},$$

where T_0' is the time of the first upcrossing of the surplus process through surplus level 0. Figure 8.1 shows a realisation of a surplus process for which ruin occurs from initial surplus 0 with a surplus less than 1 prior to ruin, while Figure 8.2 shows the dual realisation in which the deficit at ruin is less than 1. We can see in Figure 8.1 that four claims of amounts $x_1, \ldots, x_4$ (say) occur between time 0 and time T_0', at times $t_1, \ldots, t_4$ (say). In Figure 8.2 claims of amounts $x_4, \ldots, x_1$ occur at times $T_0' - t_4, \ldots, T_0' - t_1$, and so the likelihoods of these realisations are identical.

8.6 The Time of Ruin

In Section 8.3 we introduced the random variable T_u denoting the time of ruin. The distribution of T_u is important since $\Pr(T_u \leq t)$ gives the probability that ruin occurs at or before time t, a probability that we denoted by $\psi(u,t)$ in the previous chapter. In this and the following sections we consider finite time ruin problems. We start with some notation and basic relationships.

Let $\omega(u,\cdot)$ denote the density of T_u. Then we have

$$\Pr(T_u \leq t) = \psi(u,t) = \int_0^t \omega(u,s)\,ds$$

and

$$\omega(u,t) = \frac{\partial}{\partial t}\psi(u,t).$$

Further,

$$\lim_{t\to\infty} \psi(u,t) = \psi(u) = \int_0^\infty \omega(u,s)\,ds,$$

which is less than 1 under our assumption that $c > \lambda m_1$, meaning that $\omega(u, \cdot)$ is a defective density.

Next, we define the proper random variable $T_{u,c}$ as the time of ruin given that ruin occurs, so

$$T_{u,c} = T_u \mid T_u < \infty,$$

and the density of $T_{u,c}$ is $\omega_c(u, \cdot) = \omega(u, \cdot)/\psi(u)$. Finally, we define $\phi(u,t) = 1 - \psi(u,t)$ to be the finite time survival probability over the time interval $(0,t)$.

8.6.1 Prabhu's Formula

We now state a very important formula for $\phi(u,t)$, known as Prabhu's formula. The result is

$$\phi(u,t) = \mathcal{G}(u+ct,t) - c\int_0^t g(u+cs,s)\,\phi(0,t-s)\,ds, \tag{8.20}$$

where

$$\mathcal{G}(x,t) = \Pr(S(t) \le x) = e^{-\lambda t} + \sum_{n=1}^{\infty} e^{-\lambda t}\frac{(\lambda t)^n}{n!}F^{n*}(x)$$

and $g(x,t) = \frac{\partial}{\partial x}\mathcal{G}(x,t)$ for $x > 0$. Further,

$$\phi(0,t) = \frac{1}{ct}\int_0^{ct}\mathcal{G}(x,t)\,dx = e^{-\lambda t} + \int_0^{ct}\left(1 - \frac{x}{ct}\right)g(x,t)\,dx. \tag{8.21}$$

Formula (8.20) can be derived by establishing a partial integro-differential equation for $\phi(u,t)$ and solving this equation using Laplace transform techniques. We will not provide a mathematical proof of formula (8.20) but do provide one for formula (8.21) in Section 8.6.2. Formula (8.20) has a very simple interpretation, which is useful in addressing more complicated problems. We can write this formula as

$$\mathcal{G}(u+ct,t) = \phi(u,t) + c\int_0^t g(u+cs,s)\,\phi(0,t-s)\,ds.$$

The left-hand side gives $\Pr(S(t) \le u+ct)$, which is the same as $\Pr(U(t) \ge 0)$. If the surplus at time t is non-negative, one of two things could have happened, as illustrated in Figures 8.3 and 8.4. First, we could have the situation illustrated in Figure 8.3 where the surplus is non-negative throughout the interval $(0,t)$, the probability of which is $\phi(u,t)$. Second, we could have the situation

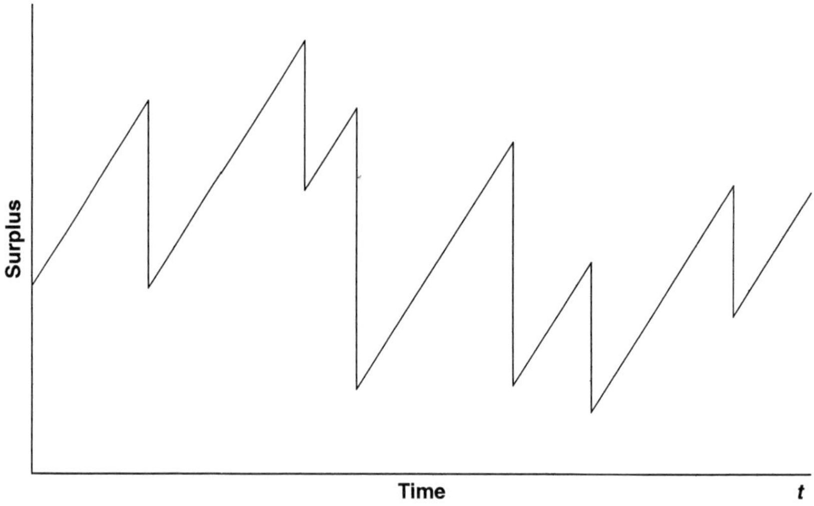

Figure 8.3 A realisation of the surplus process for which ruin does not occur by time t.

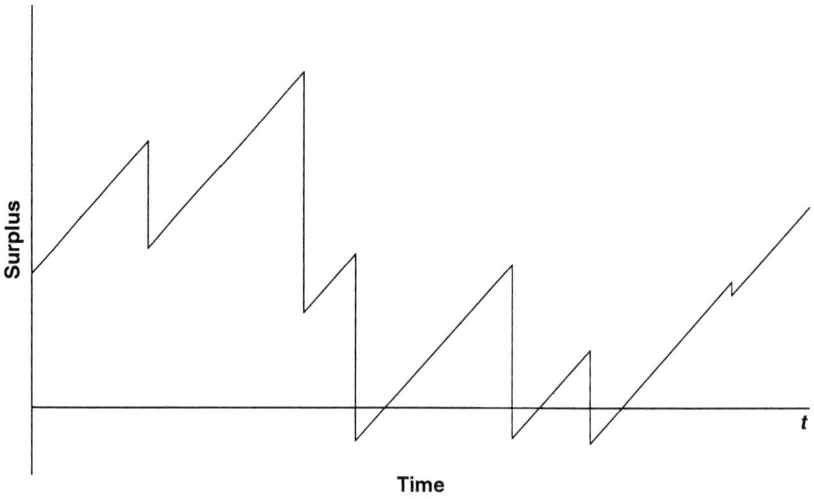

Figure 8.4 A realisation of the surplus process for which ruin does occur by time t.

illustrated in Figure 8.4 where the surplus falls below 0 before time t but has recovered to a non-negative level at time t. Let $s < t$ be the time of the last upcrossing of the surplus process through level 0. Then the aggregate claim amount at time s is $u + cs$, and, integrating over all possible times s, the probability that the surplus falls below zero before time t and is non-negative at time t is

$$c\int_0^t g(u+cs,s)\,\phi(0,t-s)\,ds.$$

Here $\phi(0,t-s)$ is the probability of survival from initial surplus 0 over a time interval of length $t-s$ (and note that when the surplus process upcrosses through 0 it is restarting in a probabilistic sense – the same argument as in Section 8.2). Further $c\,g(u+cs,s)$ is the density associated with an aggregate claim amount of $u+cs$ at time s with

$$c\,g(u+cs,s)=\sum_{n=1}^{\infty}e^{-\lambda s}\frac{(\lambda s)^n}{n!}\frac{\partial}{\partial s}F^{n*}(u+cs).$$

We now show that this type of interpretation extends to other results. It is possible to differentiate formula (8.20) to obtain

$$\begin{aligned}\omega(u,t)&=\lambda e^{-\lambda t}(1-F(u+ct))+\lambda\int_0^{u+ct}g(u+ct-x,t)\,(1-F(x))\,dx\\&\quad-c\int_0^t g(u+cs,s)\,\omega(0,t-s)\,ds.\end{aligned}\tag{8.22}$$

However, we can more easily obtain this formula by interpreting $\omega(u,t)dt$ as the probability that ruin occurs in the infinitesimal time interval $(t,t+dt)$. First, note that for ruin to occur in $(t,t+dt)$, we require a claim to occur in this time interval. Consider first the term $\lambda e^{-\lambda t}(1-F(u+ct))dt$. We interpret this to be the product of the probabilities of

- no claims up to time t $(e^{-\lambda t})$,
- a claim in the time interval $(t,t+dt)$ (λdt) and
- the claim amount exceeding $u+ct$ and hence causing the surplus to fall below 0 $(1-F(u+ct))$.

Next, we interpret $\lambda g(u+ct-x,t)(1-F(x))dxdt$ as the product of the probabilities of

- the aggregate claim amount at time t being $u+ct-x$ so that the surplus at time t is x $(g(u+ct-x,t)dx)$,
- a claim in the time interval $(t,t+dt)$ (λdt) and
- the claim amount exceeding x and hence causing the surplus to fall below 0 $(1-F(x))$.

As the second term in our formula for $\omega(u,t)$ does not take account of whether the surplus has been below 0 before time t we need to adjust for this. The term

$$c\int_0^t g(u+cs,s)\,\omega(0,t-s)\,ds$$

has exactly the same interpretation as the integral term in formula (8.20) except that the term $\phi(0,t-s)$ is replaced by the density $\omega(0,t-s)$ because we require the surplus to drop below 0 at time t.

Now suppose we extend the problem and define the defective density of the time of ruin and the deficit at ruin as

$$\omega(u,y,t)=\frac{\partial^2}{\partial y\,\partial t}\Pr(Y_u\le y,\ T_u\le t).$$

We can write down a formula for $\omega(u,y,t)$ by noting that in the first two terms in formula (8.22) instead of the claim amount at time t being above a certain amount, it should be a fixed amount, so $1-F(u+ct)$ becomes $f(u+ct+y)$ and $1-F(x)$ becomes $f(x+y)$, and in the second integral term $\omega(0,t-s)$ is replaced by $\omega(0,y,t-s)$ as we require ruin with a deficit of y. Hence

$$\omega(u,y,t)=\lambda e^{-\lambda t}f(u+ct+y)+\lambda\int_0^{u+ct}g(u+ct-x,t)f(x+y)\,dx$$
$$-c\int_0^t g(u+cs,s)\,\omega(0,y,t-s)\,ds. \tag{8.23}$$

We show this result formally in Section 8.6.3 and give expressions for $\omega(0,t)$ and $\omega(0,y,t)$ in the next section.

8.6.2 Gerber-Shiu Functions

We now introduce a function commonly known as a Gerber-Shiu function and sometimes called a discounted penalty function. The importance of this function is that it allows us to analyse ruin-related quantities in a unified approach.

The function is defined as

$$\varphi(u)=E\left[a(X_u,Y_u)\,e^{-\delta T_u}\,I(T_u<\infty)\right],$$

where

- $a(x,y)$ is a non-negative function of $x>0$ and $y>0$, which is referred to as the penalty function (even though no penalty in the formal sense of the word applies),
- $X_u=U(T_u^-)$ is the surplus immediately prior to ruin,
- $Y_u=|U(T_u)|$ is the deficit at ruin,

- $\delta \geq 0$ is a parameter which can be viewed either as the force of interest or as the parameter of a Laplace transform and
- I is the indicator function, so that $I(A) = 1$ if the event A occurs and equals 0 otherwise.

To illustrate the versatility of this function, we provide the following examples.

(i) Setting $a(x, y) = 1$ gives

$$\varphi(u) = E\left[e^{-\delta T_u} I(T_u < \infty)\right],$$

which is the Laplace transform of the time of ruin, T_u, from which we can find quantities such as moments of T_u.

(ii) Setting $a(x, y) = 1$ and $\delta = 0$ gives

$$\varphi(u) = E\left[I(T_u < \infty)\right],$$

which is the ultimate ruin probability $\psi(u)$.

(iii) Setting $a(x, y) = x^m y^n$ and $\delta = 0$ gives

$$\varphi(u) = E\left[X_u^m\, Y_u^n\, I(T_u < \infty)\right],$$

from which we can calculate quantities such as moments of X_u and Y_u and the covariance between X_u and Y_u.

(iv) Setting $a(x, y) = e^{-sx}$ and $\delta = 0$ gives

$$\varphi(u) = E\left[e^{-sX_u} I(T_u < \infty)\right],$$

which is the Laplace transform of the surplus immediately prior to ruin, from which we can find the distribution of X_u.

We can establish an integro-differential equation for $\varphi(u)$ by applying the usual argument of conditioning on the time and the amount of the first claim. However, we must now take account of the 'discount factor' in the definition of φ. We get

$$\begin{aligned}\varphi(u) = &\int_0^\infty \lambda e^{-\lambda t}\, e^{-\delta t} \int_0^{u+ct} f(x)\, \varphi(u + ct - x)\, dx\, dt \\ &+ \int_0^\infty \lambda e^{-\lambda t}\, e^{-\delta t} \int_{u+ct}^\infty f(x)\, a(u + ct, x - u - ct)\, dx\, dt,\end{aligned}$$

and the standard substitution $s = u + ct$ leads to

$$\frac{d}{du}\varphi(u) - \frac{\delta + \lambda}{c}\varphi(u) + \frac{\lambda}{c}\int_0^u f(u - x)\, \varphi(x) dx + \frac{\lambda}{c}\alpha(u) = 0, \tag{8.24}$$

where

$$\alpha(u) = \int_0^\infty f(u+y)\, a(u,y)\, dy.$$

Taking the Laplace transform of equation (8.24) we obtain

$$\varphi^*(s) = \frac{c\,\varphi(0) - \lambda\,\alpha^*(s)}{cs - \delta - \lambda + \lambda f^*(s)}. \tag{8.25}$$

The denominator in equation (8.25) plays a crucial role. We call the equation

$$\delta + \lambda - cs = \lambda f^*(s)$$

Lundberg's fundamental equation, and we now show that this equation has a unique non-negative solution, which we denote by ρ. Consider $l(s) = \delta + \lambda - cs$. Then

$$l(0) = \delta + \lambda \geq \lambda f^*(0) = \lambda.$$

Further, $f^*(s)$ is a decreasing convex function since

$$\frac{d}{ds} f^*(s) = -\int_0^\infty x\, e^{-sx} f(x)\, dx < 0$$

and

$$\frac{d^2}{ds^2} f^*(s) = \int_0^\infty x^2\, e^{-sx} f(x)\, dx > 0.$$

Figure 8.5 illustrates the situation in the case $\delta = 0$ where $l(s)$ is plotted as a dotted line and in the case $\delta > 0$ where $l(s)$ is plotted as a solid line. In the case $\delta = 0$, the solution to Lundberg's fundamental equation is $\rho = 0$. In the case $\delta > 0$, we can see that there is a unique positive value of s such that $l(s) = \lambda f^*(s)$, and that value is ρ. As illustrated in Figure 8.5, Lundberg's fundamental equation may also have a unique negative solution (for both $\delta > 0$ and $\delta = 0$ in this illustration). When considering Lundberg's fundamental equation it is important to remember that ρ depends on δ, so strictly we should write ρ_δ, but for brevity we simply write ρ.

The fact that Lundberg's fundamental equation has a unique positive solution allows us to find $\varphi(0)$. We can write equation (8.25) as

$$(cs - \delta - \lambda + \lambda f^*(s))\, \varphi^*(s) = c\,\varphi(0) - \lambda\,\alpha^*(s),$$

and if we set $s = \rho$ in this equation we see that the left-hand side is zero, meaning that

$$\varphi(0) = \frac{\lambda}{c}\alpha^*(\rho) = \frac{\lambda}{c}\int_0^\infty e^{-\rho z}\,\alpha(z)\, dz. \tag{8.26}$$

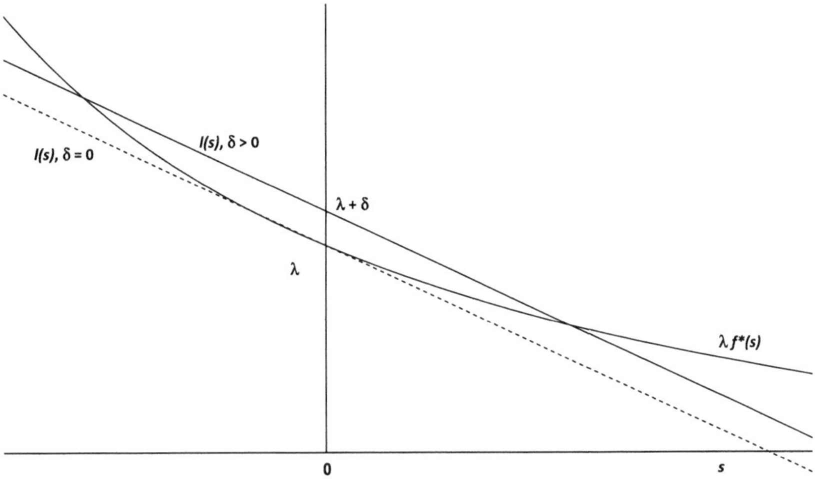

Figure 8.5 $l(s)$ for $\delta = 0$ and $\delta > 0$, and $\lambda f^*(s)$.

So $\varphi(0)$ is a multiple of the Laplace transform of α, where the transform parameter is ρ. However, we have already noted that in the definition of φ, we can think of δ as the parameter of a Laplace transform, but in equation (8.26) it is ρ that is the transform parameter. For example, consider the case $a(x, y) = e^{-sy}$. Then

$$\varphi(0) = E[e^{-sY_0-\delta T_0} I(T_0 < \infty)]$$

$$= \int_0^\infty \int_0^\infty e^{-sy-\delta t}\omega(0, y, t)\, dy\, dt, \tag{8.27}$$

so that $\varphi(0)$ is a bivariate Laplace transform with transform parameters s and δ. Further,

$$\alpha(z) = \int_0^\infty e^{-sy} f(z + y)\, dy,$$

so that equation (8.26) gives

$$\varphi(0) = \frac{\lambda}{c} \int_0^\infty \int_0^\infty e^{-\rho z-sy} f(z + y)\, dy\, dz, \tag{8.28}$$

which is a bivariate Laplace transform with transform parameters s and ρ. We remark that the bivariate Laplace transform is a straightforward extension of the Laplace transform introduced in the previous chapter. For example, to obtain the bivariate transform of $\omega(0, y, t)$ we could first take the transform with respect to y as

$$\int_0^\infty e^{-sy}\,\omega(0,y,t)\,dy,$$

which is a function of t. We then take the Laplace transform of this function of t as

$$\int_0^\infty e^{-\delta t}\int_0^\infty e^{-sy}\,\omega(0,y,t)\,dy\,dt,$$

which is the same as (8.27). Inversion is similarly a two-step process; we invert first with respect to one transform parameter, then the other.

We now state without proof a very useful result that allows us to invert Laplace transforms like (8.28) which have transform parameter ρ. For an arbitrary function b,

$$b^*(\rho) = \int_0^\infty e^{-\rho t}\,b(t)\,dt = h^*(\delta) = \int_0^\infty e^{-\delta t}\,h(t)\,dt, \qquad (8.29)$$

where

$$h(t) = ce^{-\lambda t}\,b(ct) + \sum_{n=1}^{\infty}\frac{\lambda^n t^{n-1}}{n!}e^{-\lambda t}\int_0^{ct} yf^{n*}(ct-y)\,b(y)\,dy. \qquad (8.30)$$

This result is explained in the Appendix.

In order to apply this result to invert equation (8.28) with respect to δ and s to obtain an expression for $\omega(0,y,t)$ (by equation (8.27)) it is convenient to write the equation as

$$\varphi(0) = \frac{\lambda}{c}\int_0^\infty e^{-\rho z}\int_z^\infty e^{-s(x-z)}f(x)\,dx\,dz, \qquad (8.31)$$

so that the function b in equation (8.29) is given by

$$b(t) = \frac{\lambda}{c}\int_t^\infty e^{-s(x-t)}f(x)\,dx.$$

Thus, inverting equation (8.31) for $\varphi(0)$ with respect to δ we get

$$\begin{aligned}
&ce^{-\lambda t}\frac{\lambda}{c}\int_{ct}^\infty e^{-s(y-ct)}f(y)\,dy \\
&+\sum_{n=1}^{\infty}\frac{\lambda^n t^{n-1}}{n!}e^{-\lambda t}\int_0^{ct} xf^{n*}(ct-x)\,\frac{\lambda}{c}\int_x^\infty e^{-s(r-x)}f(r)\,dr\,dx \\
&= \lambda e^{-\lambda t}\int_0^\infty e^{-sr}f(r+ct)\,dr \\
&+\sum_{n=1}^{\infty}\frac{\lambda^n t^{n-1}}{n!}e^{-\lambda t}\int_0^{ct} xf^{n*}(ct-x)\,\frac{\lambda}{c}\int_0^\infty e^{-sr}f(r+x)\,dr\,dx
\end{aligned}$$

$$= \lambda e^{-\lambda t} \int_0^\infty e^{-sr} f(r+ct)\, dr$$

$$+ \sum_{n=1}^{\infty} \frac{\lambda^n t^{n-1}}{n!} e^{-\lambda t} \frac{\lambda}{c} \int_0^\infty e^{-sr} \int_0^{ct} x f^{n*}(ct-x) f(r+x)\, dx\, dr,$$

and inverting with respect to s we get

$$\omega(0,y,t) = \lambda e^{-\lambda t} f(y+ct)$$

$$+ \sum_{n=1}^{\infty} \frac{\lambda^n t^{n-1}}{n!} e^{-\lambda t} \frac{\lambda}{c} \int_0^{ct} x f^{n*}(ct-x) f(y+x)\, dx$$

$$= \lambda e^{-\lambda t} f(y+ct)$$

$$+ \frac{\lambda}{c} \int_0^{ct} \frac{x}{t} \sum_{n=1}^{\infty} e^{-\lambda t} \frac{(\lambda t)^n}{n!} f^{n*}(ct-x) f(y+x)\, dx$$

$$= \lambda e^{-\lambda t} f(y+ct) + \frac{\lambda}{c} \int_0^{ct} \frac{x}{t} g(ct-x,t) f(y+x)\, dx. \quad (8.32)$$

If we integrate this expression with respect to y over $(0,\infty)$ we obtain the density of T_0 as

$$\omega(0,t) = \lambda e^{-\lambda t}(1-F(ct)) + \frac{\lambda}{c} \int_0^{ct} \frac{x}{t} g(ct-x,t)\,(1-F(x))\, dx. \quad (8.33)$$

The transform identity also allows us to find the survival probability $\phi(0,t)$ from the previous section. For the remainder of this section let $a(x,y) = 1$ for all x and y, so that $\alpha(u) = 1 - F(u)$. Then

$$\begin{aligned} \varphi(0) &= E\left[e^{-\delta T_0} I(T_0 < \infty)\right] \\ &= \frac{\lambda}{c} \int_0^\infty e^{-\rho x}\,(1-F(x))\, dx \\ &= \frac{\lambda}{c\rho} \left(1 - f^*(\rho)\right). \end{aligned}$$

As $\lambda + \delta - c\rho = \lambda f^*(\rho)$ we have

$$\frac{\lambda}{c}\left(1 - f^*(\rho)\right) = \rho - \frac{\delta}{c},$$

giving

$$\varphi(0) = 1 - \frac{\delta}{c\rho}.$$

Further,

$$\varphi(0) = \int_0^\infty e^{-\delta t}\,\omega(0,t)\,dt,$$

and as $\omega(0,t) = \frac{d}{dt}\psi(0,t)$, we get

$$\int_0^\infty e^{-\delta t}\,\psi(0,t)\,dt = \frac{1}{\delta} - \frac{1}{c\rho}$$

and hence

$$\int_0^\infty e^{-\delta t}\,\phi(0,t)\,dt = \frac{1}{c\rho}.$$

Thus, inversion with respect to ρ gives $1/c$ and hence with respect to δ yields

$$\begin{aligned}\phi(0,t) &= e^{-\lambda t} + \frac{1}{c}\sum_{n=1}^{\infty}\frac{\lambda^n t^{n-1}}{n!}e^{-\lambda t}\int_0^{ct} x f^{n*}(ct-x)\,dx \\ &= e^{-\lambda t} + \frac{1}{ct}\sum_{n=1}^{\infty}\frac{\lambda^n t^n}{n!}e^{-\lambda t}\int_0^{ct}(ct-x)\,f^{n*}(x)\,dx \\ &= e^{-\lambda t} + \int_0^{ct}\left(1-\frac{x}{ct}\right)g(x,t)\,dx,\end{aligned}$$

which is the second expression in formula (8.21). The first expression in formula (8.21) is simply found by integrating the second.

8.6.3 The Joint Density of the Time of Ruin and the Deficit at Ruin

Our main objective in this section is to derive formula (8.23) for the joint density of the time of ruin and the deficit at ruin when $u > 0$. We do this by constructing the Gerber-Shiu function to be the bivariate Laplace transform of the time of ruin, T_u, and the deficit at ruin, Y_u.

Before doing this, we obtain an important result. Consider the compound Poisson density $g(x,t)$ given by

$$g(x,t) = \sum_{n=1}^{\infty} e^{-\lambda t}\frac{(\lambda t)^n}{n!}f^{n*}(x).$$

If we take the Laplace transform with respect to x, with transform parameter s, we obtain

$$g^*(s,t) = \int_0^\infty e^{-sx}g(x,t)\,dx$$

$$= \sum_{n=1}^{\infty} e^{-\lambda t} \frac{(\lambda t)^n}{n!} f^*(s)^n$$
$$= \exp\{\lambda t(f^*(s) - 1)\} - \exp\{-\lambda t\}.$$

Similarly, the compound Poisson aggregate claims random variable $S(t)$ has Laplace transform

$$\begin{aligned} E[e^{-sS(t)}] &= \int_0^\infty e^{-sx}\, dG(x, t) \\ &= \exp\{-\lambda t\} + \int_0^\infty e^{-sx} g(x, t)\, dx \\ &= \exp\{\lambda t(f^*(s) - 1)\}, \end{aligned}$$

and if we then take the Laplace transform with respect to t, with transform parameter δ, we obtain

$$\int_0^\infty e^{-\delta t} \int_0^\infty e^{-sx}\, dG(x, t)\, dt = \frac{1}{\delta - \lambda(f^*(s) - 1)}. \tag{8.34}$$

Returning to the question of the joint density of T_u and Y_u, we set the penalty function as $a(x, y) = e^{-ry}$, giving

$$\begin{aligned} \varphi(u) &= E[e^{-rY_u - \delta T_u} I(T_u < \infty)] \\ &= \int_0^\infty \int_0^\infty e^{-ry-\delta t}\, \omega(u, y, t)\, dy\, dt, \end{aligned}$$

and its Laplace transform with respect to u is

$$\varphi^*(s) = \int_0^\infty \int_0^\infty \int_0^\infty e^{-su-ry-\delta t}\, \omega(u, y, t)\, dy\, dt\, du.$$

Our approach is to invert this function, first with respect to δ, then with respect to r, and finally with respect to s.

We write equation (8.25) as

$$\varphi^*(s) = \frac{\lambda \alpha^*(s) - c\,\varphi(0)}{\delta + \lambda - \lambda f^*(s) - cs}, \tag{8.35}$$

and it is convenient to write

$$\varphi(0) = \int_0^\infty e^{-\delta t} \gamma(r, t)\, dt,$$

where

$$\gamma(r, t) = \int_0^\infty e^{-ry}\, \omega(0, y, t)\, dy.$$

As the penalty function is $a(x, y) = e^{-ry}$, we have

$$\alpha(u) = \int_0^\infty e^{-ry} f(u+y)\, dy.$$

To emphasise the dependence on r we write α as α_r and its Laplace transform is

$$\alpha_r^*(s) = \int_0^\infty e^{-su}\, \alpha_r(u)\, du = \int_0^\infty e^{-su} \int_0^\infty e^{-ry} f(u+y)\, dy\, du.$$

The first step is to invert $\varphi^*(s)$ with respect to δ. Looking at equations (8.34) and (8.35) we see that

$$1/(\delta + \lambda - \lambda f^*(s) - c\, s)$$

inverts to

$$\begin{aligned}\exp\{\lambda t(f^*(s) - 1) + sct\} &= e^{sct} \int_0^\infty e^{-su}\, d\, G(u, t) \\ &= e^{sct}\left(e^{-\lambda t} + g^*(s, t)\right).\end{aligned}$$

So inversion of the right-hand side of equation (8.35) with respect to δ gives

$$\lambda\, \alpha_r^*(s)\, e^{sct} \int_0^\infty e^{-su}\, d\, G(u, t) - c \int_0^t \gamma(r, \tau)\, \exp\{\lambda(t-\tau)(f^*(s)-1) + sc(t-\tau)\}\, d\tau.$$

Thus, inverting equation (8.35) with respect to δ, then multiplying throughout by e^{-sct}, we get

$$\begin{aligned}&e^{-sct} \int_0^\infty \int_0^\infty e^{-su-ry}\, \omega(u, y, t)\, dy\, du \\ &= \lambda\, \alpha_r^*(s) \int_0^\infty e^{-su}\, dG(u, t) - c \int_0^t \gamma(r, \tau)\, \exp\{\lambda(t-\tau)(f^*(s) - 1) - sc\tau\} d\tau.\end{aligned}$$

Next, we invert with respect to r to get

$$\begin{aligned}e^{-sct} \int_0^\infty e^{-su}\, \omega(u, y, t)\, du &= \lambda \int_0^\infty e^{-su} f(u+y)\, du \int_0^\infty e^{-su}\, dG(u, t) \\ &\quad - c \int_0^t \omega(0, y, \tau)\, \exp\{\lambda(t-\tau)(f^*(s) - 1) - sc\tau\}\, d\tau \\ &= \lambda \int_0^\infty e^{-su} f(u+y)\, du \left(e^{-\lambda t} + g^*(s, t)\right) \\ &\quad - c \int_0^t \omega(0, y, \tau)\, \exp\{\lambda(t-\tau)(f^*(s) - 1) - sc\tau\}\, d\tau \\ &= \lambda e^{-\lambda t} \int_0^\infty e^{-su} f(u+y)\, du \\ &\quad + \lambda \int_0^\infty e^{-su} \int_0^u f(x+y)\, g(u-x, t)\, dx\, du \\ &\quad - c \int_0^t \omega(0, y, \tau)\, \exp\{\lambda(t-\tau)(f^*(s) - 1) - sc\tau\}\, d\tau.\end{aligned} \tag{8.36}$$

Last, we invert with respect to s. To do this, we write the left-hand side of equation (8.36) as

$$\int_{ct}^{\infty} e^{-su}\,\omega(u-ct,y,t)\,du,$$

and we note that the final integral expression in equation (8.36) can be written as

$$\begin{aligned}
& c\int_0^t \omega(0,y,\tau)\,\exp\{\lambda(t-\tau)(f^*(s)-1)-sc\tau\}\,d\tau \\
&= c\int_0^t \omega(0,y,\tau)\left(g^*(s,t-\tau)+e^{-\lambda(t-\tau)}\right)\,e^{-sc\tau}\,d\tau \\
&= c\int_0^t \omega(0,y,\tau)\int_0^{\infty} e^{-s(x+c\tau)}g(x,t-\tau)\,dx\,d\tau \\
&\quad +c\int_0^t \omega(0,y,\tau)\,e^{-sc\tau}\,e^{-\lambda(t-\tau)}\,d\tau \\
&= c\int_0^t \omega(0,y,\tau)\int_0^{\infty} e^{-s(x+c\tau)}g(x,t-\tau)\,dx\,d\tau \\
&\quad +\int_0^{ct} e^{-su}\,\omega(0,y,u/c)\,e^{-\lambda(t-u/c)}\,du.
\end{aligned}$$

We now write

$$\begin{aligned}
& c\int_0^t \omega(0,y,\tau)\int_0^{\infty} e^{-s(x+c\tau)}g(x,t-\tau)\,dx\,d\tau \\
&= c\int_0^t \omega(0,y,\tau)\int_{c\tau}^{\infty} e^{-su}g(u-c\tau,t-\tau)\,du\,d\tau \\
&= c\int_0^{ct} e^{-su}\int_0^{u/c} \omega(0,y,\tau)\,g(u-c\tau,t-\tau)\,d\tau\,du \\
&\quad +c\int_{ct}^{\infty} e^{-su}\int_0^{t} \omega(0,y,\tau)\,g(u-c\tau,t-\tau)\,d\tau\,du,
\end{aligned}$$

where the final step is simply a change in the order of integration. Combining everything we have

$$\begin{aligned}
\int_{ct}^{\infty} e^{-su}\,\omega(u-ct,y,t)\,du &= \lambda e^{-\lambda t}\int_0^{\infty} e^{-su}f(u+y)\,du \\
&\quad +\lambda\int_0^{\infty} e^{-su}\int_0^{u} f(x+y)\,g(u-x,t)\,dx\,du \\
&\quad -c\int_0^{ct} e^{-su}\int_0^{u/c} \omega(0,y,\tau)\,g(u-c\tau,t-\tau)\,d\tau\,du \\
&\quad -c\int_{ct}^{\infty} e^{-su}\int_0^{t} \omega(0,y,\tau)\,g(u-c\tau,t-\tau)\,d\tau\,du \\
&\quad -\int_0^{ct} e^{-su}\,\omega(0,y,u/c)\,e^{-\lambda(t-u/c)}\,du. \qquad (8.37)
\end{aligned}$$

Now the left-hand side is just the Laplace transform of a function of u that is 0 for $0 < u \le ct$ and $\omega(u-ct,y,t)$ for $u > ct$. By equating the coefficients of e^{-su} for $u > ct$ we obtain

$$\omega(u-ct,y,t) = \lambda\, e^{-\lambda t} f(u+y) + \lambda \int_0^u f(x+y)\,g(u-x,t)\,dx \\ -c \int_0^t \omega(0,y,\tau)\,g(u-c\tau,t-\tau)\,d\tau,$$

and so by replacing $u-ct$ with u we obtain the joint density of T_u and Y_u as

$$\omega(u,y,t) = \lambda\, e^{-\lambda t} f(u+ct+y) + \lambda \int_0^{u+ct} f(x+y)\,g(u+ct-x,t)\,dx \\ -c \int_0^t \omega(0,y,\tau)\,g(u+c(t-\tau),t-\tau)\,d\tau.$$

Integrating this expression with respect to y over $(0,\infty)$ we obtain the density of T_u as

$$\omega(u,t) = \lambda\, e^{-\lambda t}\,(1-F(u+ct)) + \lambda \int_0^{u+ct} (1-F(x))\,g(u+ct-x,t)\,dx \\ -c \int_0^t \omega(0,\tau)\,g(u+c(t-\tau),t-\tau)\,d\tau.$$

We remark that when we equate coefficients of e^{-su} for $u \le ct$ in equation (8.37) we obtain a further identity which is not of any patricular use, namely

$$0 = \lambda\, e^{-\lambda t} f(u+y) + \lambda \int_0^u f(x+y)\,g(u-x,t)\,dx \\ -c \int_0^{u/c} \omega(0,y,\tau)\,g(u-c\tau,t-\tau)\,d\tau - \omega(0,y,u/c)\,e^{-\lambda(t-u/c)}. \tag{8.38}$$

See Exercise 7 for an interpretation of this equation.

We conclude this section by considering the case when the individual claim amount distribution is Erlang with parameters n and β. Denoting the individual claim amount density f as γ_n, we showed in Exercise 4 in Chapter 1 that

$$f(x+y) \equiv \gamma_n(x+y) = \frac{1}{\beta} \sum_{j=1}^{n} \gamma_{n-j+1}(x)\gamma_j(y).$$

We now show that there is a similar type of factorisation for the joint density $\omega(u,y,t)$. Recalling from formula (8.32) that

$$\omega(0, y, t) = \lambda e^{-\lambda t} f(ct + y) + \lambda \int_0^{ct} \frac{x}{ct} g(ct - x, t) f(x + y)\, dx,$$

we get

$$\omega(0, y, t) = \frac{\lambda e^{-\lambda t}}{\beta} \sum_{j=1}^{n} \gamma_{n-j+1}(ct)\, \gamma_j(y) + \frac{\lambda}{\beta} \int_0^{ct} \frac{x}{ct} g(ct - x, t) \sum_{j=1}^{n} \gamma_{n-j+1}(x)\, \gamma_j(y)\, dx.$$

Thus,

$$\omega(0, y, t) = \sum_{j=1}^{n} \omega_j(0, t)\, \gamma_j(y),$$

where

$$\omega_j(0, t) = \frac{\lambda e^{-\lambda t}}{\beta} \gamma_{n-j+1}(ct) + \frac{\lambda}{\beta} \int_0^{ct} \frac{x}{ct} g(ct - x, t)\, \gamma_{n-j+1}(x)\, dx.$$

Similarly, from

$$\omega(u, y, t) = \lambda e^{-\lambda t} f(u + ct + y) + \lambda \int_0^{u+ct} f(x + y)\, g(u + ct - x, t)\, dx - c \int_0^t \omega(0, y, \tau)\, g(u + c(t - \tau), t - \tau)\, d\tau,$$

we get

$$\omega(u, y, t) = \sum_{j=1}^{n} \omega_j(u, t)\, \gamma_j(y), \tag{8.39}$$

where

$$\omega_j(u, t) = \frac{\lambda e^{-\lambda t}}{\beta} \gamma_{n-j+1}(u + ct) + \frac{\lambda}{\beta} \int_0^{u+ct} \gamma_{n-j+1}(x)\, g(u + ct - x, t)\, dx - c \int_0^t \omega_j(0, \tau)\, g(u + c(t - \tau), t - \tau)\, d\tau.$$

Formula (8.39) shows that $\omega(u, y, t)$ is a (defective) mixture of Erlang densities, and if we integrate with respect to t over $(0, \infty)$, we see that the (defective) density of the deficit at ruin, $g(u, y)$, is a similar mixture.

8.6.4 Exponential Claims

In this section we derive a formula for the density of the time of ruin when the individual claim amount distribution is exponential. The approach here differs from the approaches in the previous two sections, and the main point of interest in this approach is that it does not rely on claims occurring as a Poisson process when the claim size distribution is exponential. The ideas in this section can be extended to other individual claim amount distributions, but we do not discuss these as our main purpose here is to derive a formula we can use for numerical comparisons in Section 8.6.7.

When $F(x) = 1 - e^{-\alpha x}$, $x \geq 0$, we have

$$f(x+y) = \alpha e^{-\alpha(x+y)} = \alpha e^{-\alpha y}\,(1 - F(x)).$$

Thus, equation (8.32) becomes

$$\begin{aligned}\omega(0,y,t) &= \alpha e^{-\alpha y}\left(\lambda e^{-\lambda t}(1-F(ct)) + \frac{\lambda}{c}\int_0^{ct}\frac{x}{t}g(ct-x,t)\,(1-F(x))\,dx\right)\\ &= \alpha e^{-\alpha y}\,\omega(0,t),\end{aligned}$$

showing that Y_0 is independent of T_0.

To obtain our expression for $\omega(u,t)$ we extend the logic from earlier sections in this chapter to include a finite time horizon. Consider the finite time survival probability $\phi(u,t)$. If survival occurs over the time interval $(0,t)$, then either

(i) the surplus does not drop below its initial level, with probability $\phi(0,t)$ or
(ii) the surplus drops below its initial level for the first time by amount $y < u$ at time $\tau < t$, and survival occurs from surplus level $u - y$ in the subsequent time interval of length $t - \tau$.

Thus,

$$\phi(u,t) = \phi(0,t) + \int_0^t\int_0^u \omega(0,y,\tau)\,\phi(u-y,t-\tau)\,dy\,d\tau,$$

and differentiation with respect to t yields

$$\begin{aligned}-\omega(u,t) = -\omega(0,t) &+ \int_0^u \omega(0,y,t)\,dy\\ &- \int_0^t\int_0^u \omega(0,y,\tau)\,\omega(u-y,t-\tau)\,dy\,d\tau.\end{aligned}$$

Thus,

$$\omega(u,t) = \int_u^\infty \omega(0,y,t)\,dy + \int_0^t\int_0^u \omega(0,y,\tau)\,\omega(u-y,t-\tau)\,dy\,d\tau$$

since $\omega(0,t) = \int_0^\infty \omega(0,y,t)\,dy$. Next, we use the fact that $\omega(0,y,t) = \omega(0,t)\,\alpha e^{-\alpha y}$ to write this equation as

$$\omega(u,t) = \omega(0,t)\,e^{-\alpha u} + \int_0^t \omega(0,\tau) \int_0^u \alpha\, e^{-\alpha y}\, \omega(u-y, t-\tau)\,dy\,d\tau. \quad (8.40)$$

Now define the Laplace transforms

$$\omega^*(0,\delta) = \int_0^\infty e^{-\delta t}\,\omega(0,t)\,dt,$$

$$\omega^*(s,t) = \int_0^\infty e^{-su}\,\omega(u,t)\,du,$$

$$\omega^{**}(s,\delta) = \int_0^\infty \int_0^\infty e^{-su-\delta t}\,\omega(u,t)\,dt\,du.$$

Taking the Laplace transform of equation (8.40) with respect to u we obtain

$$\omega^*(s,t) = \frac{\omega(0,t)}{\alpha+s} + \int_0^t \omega(0,\tau)\,\frac{\alpha}{\alpha+s}\,\omega^*(s,t-\tau)\,d\tau,$$

and taking the Laplace transform of this with respect to t we get

$$\omega^{**}(s,\delta) = \frac{\omega^*(0,\delta)}{\alpha+s} + \omega^*(0,\delta)\,\frac{\alpha}{\alpha+s}\,\omega^{**}(s,\delta),$$

so that

$$\omega^{**}(s,\delta) = \frac{\omega^*(0,\delta)\frac{1}{\alpha+s}}{1-\omega^*(0,\delta)\frac{\alpha}{\alpha+s}} = \frac{1}{\alpha}\sum_{n=1}^{\infty} \omega^*(0,\delta)^n \left(\frac{\alpha}{\alpha+s}\right)^n,$$

and this inverts with respect to s as

$$\sum_{n=1}^{\infty} \omega^*(0,\delta)^n \frac{(\alpha u)^{n-1} e^{-\alpha u}}{\Gamma(n)}. \quad (8.41)$$

To invert with respect to δ we note that $\omega^*(0,\delta)$ is the same as the Gerber-Shiu function when $u = 0$ and $a(x,y) = 1$ for all x and y. Thus,

$$\omega^*(0,\delta) = \frac{\lambda}{c}\int_0^\infty e^{-\rho x}(1-F(x))\,dx = \frac{\lambda}{c}\int_0^\infty e^{-\rho x} e^{-\alpha x}\,dx = \frac{\lambda}{c\,(\alpha+\rho)},$$

and so

$$\omega^*(0,\delta)^n = \left(\frac{\lambda}{c\,(\alpha+\rho)}\right)^n.$$

The inverse of this with respect to ρ is

$$\frac{\lambda^n\, t^{n-1}\, e^{-\alpha t}}{c^n\,\Gamma(n)},$$

and so the inverse with respect to δ is found using equations (8.29) and (8.30) as

$$
\begin{aligned}
w^{n*}(0,t) &= ce^{-\lambda t}\frac{\lambda^n (ct)^{n-1} e^{-\alpha ct}}{c^n \Gamma(n)} \\
&\quad + \sum_{m=1}^{\infty} e^{-\lambda t}\frac{\lambda^m t^{m-1}}{m!}\int_0^{ct} y \frac{\alpha^m (ct-y)^{m-1} e^{-\alpha(ct-y)}}{\Gamma(m)} \frac{\lambda^n y^{n-1} e^{-\alpha y}}{c^n \Gamma(n)} dy \\
&= e^{-(\lambda+\alpha c)t}\frac{\lambda^n t^{n-1}}{\Gamma(n)} \\
&\quad + e^{-(\lambda+\alpha c)t}\frac{\lambda^n}{c^n \Gamma(n)}\sum_{m=1}^{\infty}\frac{(\alpha\lambda)^m t^{m-1}}{m!\,\Gamma(m)}\int_0^{ct} y^n (ct-y)^{m-1} dy \\
&= e^{-(\lambda+\alpha c)t}\frac{\lambda^n t^{n-1}}{\Gamma(n)} \\
&\quad + e^{-(\lambda+\alpha c)t}\frac{\lambda^n}{c^n \Gamma(n)}\sum_{m=1}^{\infty}\frac{(\alpha\lambda)^m t^{m-1}}{m!\,\Gamma(m)}\frac{\Gamma(n+1)\,\Gamma(m)}{\Gamma(n+m+1)}(ct)^{n+m} \\
&= e^{-(\lambda+\alpha c)t} n\,\lambda^n t^{n-1}\sum_{m=0}^{\infty}\frac{(\alpha\lambda ct^2)^m}{m!\,(n+m)!}.
\end{aligned}
\tag{8.42}
$$

In particular, when $n = 1$ we have

$$
\omega(0,t) = \lambda e^{-(\lambda+\alpha c)t}\sum_{m=0}^{\infty}\frac{\left(\alpha\lambda ct^2\right)^m}{m!\,(m+1)!}.
$$

For ease of computation of formula (8.42) we write

$$
\sum_{m=0}^{\infty}\frac{(\alpha\lambda ct^2)^m}{m!\,(n+m)!} = \frac{1}{n!}\,{}_0F_1(n+1;\alpha\lambda ct^2),
$$

where

$$
{}_0F_1(C;Z) = \sum_{m=0}^{\infty}\frac{\Gamma(C)}{\Gamma(C+m)}\frac{Z^m}{m!}
$$

is a generalised hypergeometric function.

Thus, the inversion of (8.41) yields

$$
\omega(u,t) = e^{-\alpha u-(\lambda+\alpha c)t}\sum_{n=1}^{\infty}\frac{(\alpha u)^{n-1}}{\Gamma(n)}\frac{\lambda^n t^{n-1}}{\Gamma(n)}\,{}_0F_1(n+1;\alpha\lambda ct^2). \tag{8.43}
$$

We remark that it is straightforward to implement this formula with mathematical software. In particular many packages have in-built routines to calculate generalised hypergeometric functions.

From formula (8.41) we see that

$$\omega(u,t) = \sum_{n=1}^{\infty} \frac{(\alpha u)^{n-1} e^{-\alpha u}}{\Gamma(n)} \omega^{n*}(0,t). \tag{8.44}$$

If we multiply and divide the nth term in the sum by $\psi(0)^n$ we obtain

$$\omega(u,t) = \psi(0) \sum_{n=1}^{\infty} \frac{(\psi(0)\alpha u)^{n-1} e^{-\alpha u}}{\Gamma(n)} \omega_c^{n*}(0,t). \tag{8.45}$$

Noting that ω_c is a proper density, we can integrate this expression over $(0,\infty)$ to obtain

$$\begin{aligned}\psi(u) &= \psi(0) \sum_{n=1}^{\infty} \frac{(\psi(0)\alpha u)^{n-1} e^{-\alpha u}}{\Gamma(n)} \\ &= \psi(0)\, e^{-\alpha u(1-\psi(0))},\end{aligned}$$

and writing $\psi(0) = \lambda/(\alpha c)$ gives the familiar form for $\psi(u)$ – see formula (7.11). If we divide equation (8.45) by this expression, we obtain

$$\omega_c(u,t) = \sum_{n=1}^{\infty} \frac{(\psi(0)\alpha u)^{n-1} e^{-\psi(0)\alpha u}}{\Gamma(n)} \omega_c^{n*}(0,t), \tag{8.46}$$

so that the distribution of $T_{u,c}$ is a compound distribution whose counting distribution is a Poisson distribution shifted one to the right. Further the moments of $T_{u,c}$ are expressed in terms of the moments of $T_{0,c}$. For example,

$$E[T_{u,c}] = (1 + \psi(0)\alpha u)E[T_{0,c}]. \tag{8.47}$$

In the next section we discuss how moments can be found more generally.

Although the approach in this section can be applied to a few other individual claim amount distributions, we will not pursue this approach further. The significance of formula (8.43) is that it offers a means of approximating the density of T_u for other individual claim amount distributions. The reason for this is that we can approximate a classical risk process using De Vylder's method, and for the approximating risk process the density of the time of ruin is of the form given by formula (8.43). This idea is explored further in Section 8.6.7.

We conclude this section by remarking that equation (8.46) is a general one. It holds when claims are exponentially distributed and occur as any ordinary renewal process, not just a Poisson process. The only place in this section where we made use of the fact that claims occur as a Poisson process to obtain equation (8.46) was in showing that $\omega(0,y,t) = \alpha\, e^{-\alpha y}\, \omega(0,t)$, and this result also holds more generally.

8.6.5 Moments of the Time of Ruin

In this section we derive a recursion formula from which moments of the time of ruin can be calculated. We start with some notation. Let

$$ {}_n\psi(u) = E\left[T_u^n I(T_u < \infty)\right], $$

so that ${}_0\psi(u) = \psi(u)$. Then the nth moment of the time of ruin, given that ruin occurs, is given by

$$ E\left[T_u^n \mid T_u < \infty\right] = E[T_{u,c}] = \frac{{}_n\psi(u)}{\psi(u)}. $$

To find moments of T_u we consider the Gerber-Shiu function with $a(x, y) = 1$ for all x and y, so that the Gerber-Shiu function is the Laplace transform of T_u. Thus,

$$ \varphi(u) = \int_0^\infty e^{-\delta t}\, \omega(u,t)\, dt, $$

so that

$$ \frac{d^n}{d\delta^n}\varphi(u) = (-1)^n \int_0^\infty t^n\, e^{-\delta t}\, \omega(u,t)\, dt. $$

Hence

$$ (-1)^n \left.\frac{d^n}{d\delta^n}\varphi(u)\right|_{\delta=0} = \int_0^\infty t^n\, \omega(u,t)\, dt = {}_n\psi(u). $$

Our starting point is equation (8.25),

$$ \varphi^*(s) = \frac{c\,\varphi(0) - \lambda\,\alpha^*(s)}{cs - \delta - \lambda + \lambda f^*(s)}, $$

which we can rearrange as

$$ (cs - \lambda + \lambda f^*(s))\varphi^*(s) - \delta\,\varphi^*(s) = c\,\varphi(0) - \lambda\,\alpha^*(s). \tag{8.48} $$

The idea is to differentiate equation (8.48) n times with respect to δ, then set $\delta = 0$. As α is not a function of δ, $\alpha^*(s)$ will disappear when we differentiate. It is straightforward to show by induction that

$$ \frac{d^n}{d\delta^n}\left(\delta\,\varphi^*(s)\right) = n\,\frac{d^{n-1}}{d\delta^{n-1}}\varphi^*(s) + \delta\,\frac{d^n}{d\delta^n}\varphi^*(s). $$

Next, it is convenient to define

$$ h_n(s) = \left.\frac{d^n}{d\delta^n}\varphi^*(s)\right|_{\delta=0}. $$

This function represents the Laplace transform of $(-1)^n\,{}_n\psi(u)$ since

$$\varphi^*(s) = \int_0^\infty e^{-su}\,\varphi(u)\,du = \int_0^\infty e^{-su} \int_0^\infty e^{-\delta t}\,\omega(u,t)\,dt\,du,$$

so that

$$\frac{d^n}{d\delta^n}\varphi^*(s) = \int_0^\infty e^{-su}(-1)^n \int_0^\infty t^n\,e^{-\delta t}\,\omega(u,t)\,dt\,du,$$

and hence

$$h_n(s) = \left.\frac{d^n}{d\delta^n}\varphi^*(s)\right|_{\delta=0} = \int_0^\infty e^{-su}\,(-1)^n\,{}_n\psi(u)\,du. \tag{8.49}$$

Now differentiate equation (8.48) n times with respect to δ, then set $\delta = 0$. This yields

$$(cs - \lambda + \lambda f^*(s))\,h_n(s) - n\,h_{n-1}(s) = (-1)^n\,c\,{}_n\psi(0)\,,$$

giving

$$h_n(s) = \frac{(-1)^n\,c\,{}_n\psi(0) + n\,h_{n-1}(s)}{cs - \lambda + \lambda f^*(s)}\,. \tag{8.50}$$

Recall from formula (7.12) that the Laplace transform of the (infinite time) survival probability $\phi(u)$ is

$$\phi^*(s) = \frac{c\,\phi(0)}{cs - \lambda + \lambda f^*(s)},$$

so that

$$h_n(s) = \frac{\phi^*(s)}{c\,\phi(0)}\left((-1)^n\,c\,{}_n\psi(0) + n\,h_{n-1}(s)\right). \tag{8.51}$$

Inversion of equation (8.51) gives

$${}_n\psi(u) = \frac{{}_n\psi(0)}{\phi(0)}\phi(u) - \frac{n}{c\,\phi(0)}\int_0^u {}_{n-1}\psi(x)\,\phi(u-x)\,dx\,. \tag{8.52}$$

Finally, we obtain ${}_n\psi(0)$ by noting that we can write equation (8.50) as

$$(cs - \lambda + \lambda f^*(s))\,h_n(s) = (-1)^n\,c\,{}_n\psi(0) + n\,h_{n-1}(s).$$

As the left-hand side is 0 when $s = 0$, the right-hand side must equal 0 too, meaning that

$$c\,{}_n\psi(0) = (-1)^{n+1}\,n\,h_{n-1}(0) = n\int_0^\infty {}_{n-1}\psi(u)\,du,$$

where we have used equation (8.49) in the final step. Thus, equation (8.52) becomes

$$ {}_n\psi(u) = \frac{n}{c\,\phi(0)}\left(\phi(u)\int_0^\infty {}_{n-1}\psi(u)\,du - \int_0^u {}_{n-1}\psi(x)\,\phi(u-x)\,dx\right), $$

which is our recursion formula, with ${}_n\psi$ expressed in terms of ${}_{n-1}\psi$.

Example 8.4 *Let $F(x) = 1 - e^{-\alpha x}$, $x \geq 0$, so that $\psi(u) = \psi(0)e^{-Ru}$ where $\psi(0) = \lambda/(\alpha c)$ and $R = \alpha - \lambda/c$. Find $E[T_{u,c}]$.*

Solution 8.4 *As $E[T_{u,c}] = {}_1\psi(u)/\psi(u)$ we start by finding ${}_1\psi(u)$ as*

$$ \frac{1}{c\,\phi(0)}\left(\phi(u)\int_0^\infty \psi(u)\,du - \int_0^u \psi(x)\,\phi(u-x)\,dx\right). $$

First,

$$ \int_0^\infty \psi(u)\,du = \psi(0)/R, $$

then

$$ \begin{aligned} \int_0^u \psi(x)\,\phi(u-x)\,dx &= \int_0^u \psi(0)e^{-Rx}\,(1-\psi(0)e^{-R(u-x)})\,dx \\ &= \frac{\psi(0)}{R}\left(1-e^{-Ru}\right) - \psi(0)^2\,u\,e^{-Ru}, \end{aligned} $$

so that

$$ {}_1\psi(u) = \frac{\psi(0)}{cR\,\phi(0)}\left(1-\psi(u)-(1-e^{-Ru})+Ru\psi(u)\right), $$

and hence

$$ E[T_{u,c}] = \frac{\psi(0)}{cR\,\phi(0)}\left(-1+\frac{1}{\psi(0)}+Ru\right). $$

A little algebra gives the final result as

$$ E[T_{u,c}] = \frac{c+\lambda u}{c(\alpha c-\lambda)}. \tag{8.53} $$

It is also possible to find explicit expressions for the moments of T_0. Recall that with $a(x, y) = 1$ for all x and y we have $\alpha(u) = 1 - F(u)$ and

$$ \varphi(0) = \frac{\lambda}{c}\alpha^*(\rho) = \frac{\lambda}{c}\int_0^\infty e^{-\rho u}\,(1-F(u))\,du\,. $$

We can find the first moment of T_0 from

$$ \begin{aligned} E\left[T_0\,I(T_0<\infty)\right] &= -\frac{d}{d\delta}\,\varphi(0)\bigg|_{\delta=0} \\ &= \frac{-\lambda}{c}\int_0^\infty\left(-\frac{d}{d\delta}\rho\right)u\,e^{-\rho u}\,(1-F(u))\,du\bigg|_{\delta=0}. \end{aligned} $$

If we now write ρ as ρ_δ to emphasise that ρ is a function of δ, Lundberg's fundamental equation gives

$$\delta + \lambda - c\,\rho_\delta = \lambda \int_0^\infty e^{-\rho_\delta x} f(x)\,dx\,.$$

Differentiating with respect to δ we get

$$1 - c\frac{d}{d\delta}\rho_\delta = \lambda \int_0^\infty \left(-\frac{d}{d\delta}\rho_\delta\right) x\,e^{-\rho_\delta x} f(x)\,dx\,,$$

and setting $\delta = 0$ and recalling that $\rho_0 = 0$, we get

$$1 - c\,\rho_0' = -\rho_0'\,\lambda \int_0^\infty x f(x)\,dx = -\rho_0'\,\lambda\,m_1\,.$$

Thus,

$$\rho_0' = \frac{1}{c - \lambda\,m_1}\,.$$

Then

$$\begin{aligned} E\,[T_0\,I(T_0 < \infty)] &= \frac{-\lambda}{c} \int_0^\infty \left(-\frac{d}{d\delta}\rho_\delta\right) u\,e^{-\rho_\delta u}\,(1 - F(u))\,du\,\Big|_{\delta=0} \\ &= \frac{\lambda}{c}\frac{1}{c - \lambda\,m_1} \int_0^\infty u\,(1 - F(u))\,du \\ &= \frac{\lambda m_1}{c}\,\frac{1}{c - \lambda\,m_1} \int_0^\infty u\,k(u)\,du \\ &= \psi(0)\,\frac{m_2/(2\,m_1)}{c - \lambda\,m_1}, \end{aligned}$$

where k is as in Section 7.9.1. Hence

$$E[T_{0,c}] = \frac{m_2}{2\,m_1\,(c - \lambda\,m_1)}.$$

Higher moments can be found in a similar manner (see Exercise 9).

Example 8.5 *Find $E[T_{0,c}]$ when $F(x) = 1 - e^{-\alpha x}$, $x \geq 0$.*

Solution 8.5 *We have $m_k = k!\,/\alpha^k$, so*

$$E[T_{0,c}] = \frac{2/\alpha^2}{(2/\alpha)(c - \lambda/\alpha)} = \frac{1}{\alpha c - \lambda},$$

in agreement with formulae (8.47) and (8.53).

Table 8.1 *Exact and approximate values of the density of $T_{u,c}$, exponential claims.*

t	Exact	Approximate
100	0.001859	0.001860
200	0.002415	0.002416
300	0.001827	0.001829
400	0.001257	0.001258
500	0.000850	0.000850
600	0.000576	0.000576
700	0.000393	0.000394
800	0.000271	0.000271
900	0.000189	0.000189
1,000	0.000132	0.000133

8.6.6 Application of a Discrete Time Model

Suppose that for some (small) $h > 0$ we can calculate $\psi(u, jh)$ for $j = 1, 2, 3, \ldots$, and that we can also calculate $\psi(u)$. Then a simple approximation to the density of $T_{u,c}$ at jh is

$$\frac{\psi(u, jh) - \psi(u, (j-1)h)}{h\psi(u)}. \tag{8.54}$$

Using the methods described in Section 7.9.2 we can approximate both finite and infinite time ruin probabilities, and hence we can apply this approximation with $j = 1/[(1+\theta)\beta]$.

Table 8.1 shows some exact and approximate values of the density of $T_{u,c}$ when $u = 40$, $\lambda = 1$, the individual claim amount distribution is exponential with mean 1, and $c = 1.1$. The exact values have been calculated from formula (8.43), while the approximate values have been calculated using formula (8.54) using the methods described in Section 7.9.2, with $\beta = 20$. The accuracy of this method could be improved by choosing a larger value of β, but the numbers in Table 8.1 indicate that this method of calculating the density of $T_{u,c}$ is reliable, and in the numerical examples that follow in Section 8.6.7, we refer to the density calculated by this method as the exact density.

8.6.7 Numerical Illustrations

We now illustrate the extension of De Vylder's method, as described at the end of Section 8.6.4, by considering two examples. In each case we plot the density of $T_{u,c}$ calculated by the approach of the previous section with $\beta = 20$, along with the density of $T_{u,c}$ in De Vylder's approximating surplus process.

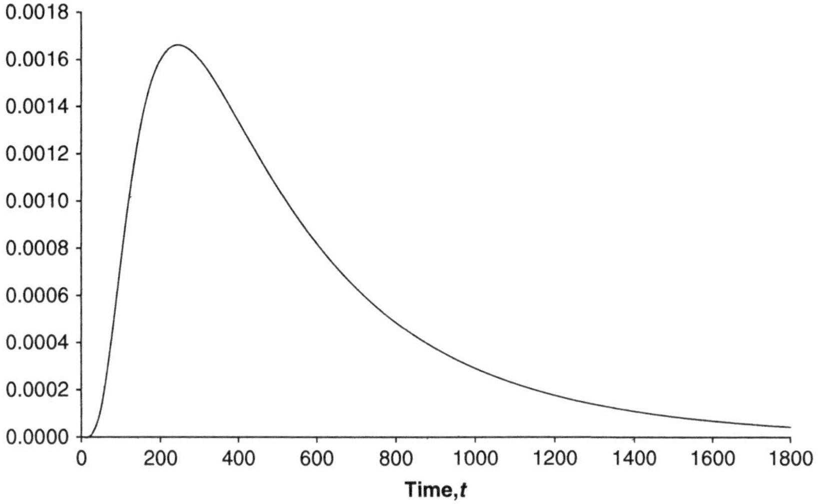

Figure 8.6 Exact and approximate density of $T_{u,c}$ when F is a mixture of two exponentials.

The advantage of De Vylder's method is that the density can be calculated very quickly, in contrast to the numerical approach, which is computationally intensive but accurate.

As a first illustration we consider the case when the individual claim amount distribution is a mixed exponential distribution with

$$F(x) = 1 - \tfrac{2}{3}e^{-2x} - \tfrac{1}{3}e^{-x/2}$$

for $x \geq 0$, so that the distribution has mean 1 and variance 2. Let $u = 60$, $\lambda = 1$ and $\theta = 0.1$, so that $\psi(60) = 0.025$. (This value was calculated by the method of Section 7.9.2 with $\beta = 20$.) Figure 8.6 shows the exact and approximate density functions, but they are virtually indistinguishable, showing that the De Vylder approximation is excellent in this case.

As a second illustration we consider another mixed exponential distribution as the individual claim amount distribution with

$$F(x) = 1 - 0.0040e^{-0.0146x} - 0.1078e^{-0.1902x} - 0.8882e^{-5.5146x}$$

for $x \geq 0$. This distribution has mean 1 and variance 42.2. Let $u = 400$, $\lambda = 1$ and $\theta = 0.25$, so that $\psi(400) = 0.039$. Figure 8.7 shows the exact and approximate density functions, and in this case we can see that the two density functions are very close together, but not as close as in Figure 8.6. In this figure values of the exact density are greater than those of the approximation for smaller values of t.

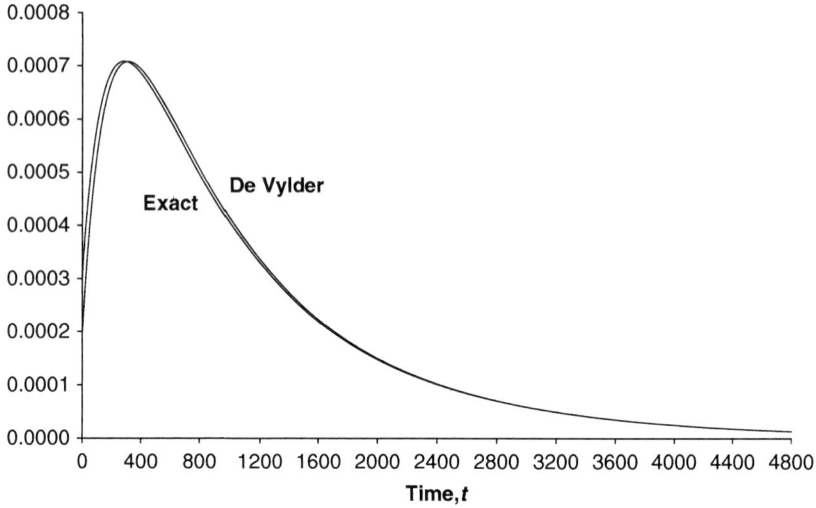

Figure 8.7 Exact and approximate density of $T_{u,c}$ when F is a mixture of three exponentials.

It is interesting that the approximation based on De Vylder's method performs so well, particularly when De Vylder's original intention was to approximate a much more straightforward function, namely the ultimate ruin probability. The approximation does not work well in all circumstances, but if the ruin probability is small (perhaps in the range 1% to 5%) and the moment generating function of the individual claim amount distribution exists, the method appears to give good approximations to the density of $T_{u,c}$.

8.7 Dividends

A criticism of the classical risk model is that $U(t) \to \infty$ as $t \to \infty$, which would be unrealistic in insurance practice. One way that an insurance company can restrict the growth of a surplus process is by paying dividends to its shareholders once the surplus reaches a certain level. We now assume that an insurance portfolio is used to provide dividend income for that insurance company's shareholders. Specifically, let u denote the initial surplus, and let $b \geq u$ be a dividend barrier. Whenever the surplus attains the level b, the premium income is paid to shareholders as dividends until the next claim occurs, so that in this modified surplus process, the surplus never attains a level greater than b. Figure 8.8 shows a realisation of a surplus process, and Figure 8.9 shows how this realisation would be modified by the introduction

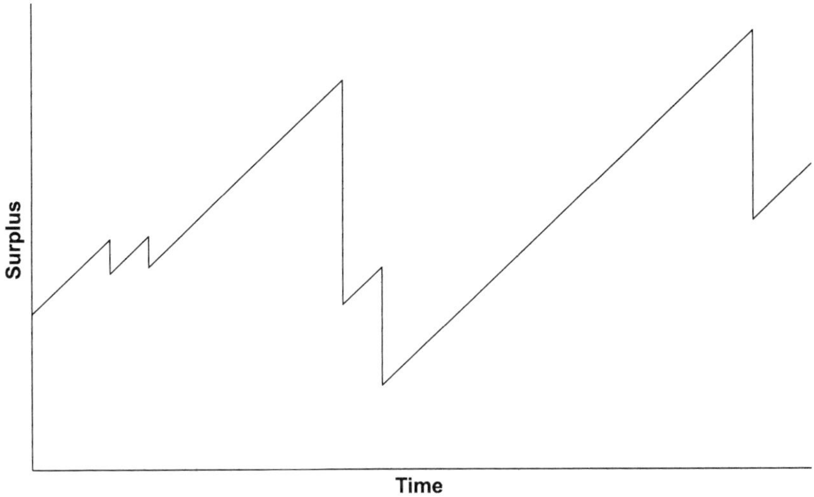

Figure 8.8 A realisation of a surplus process.

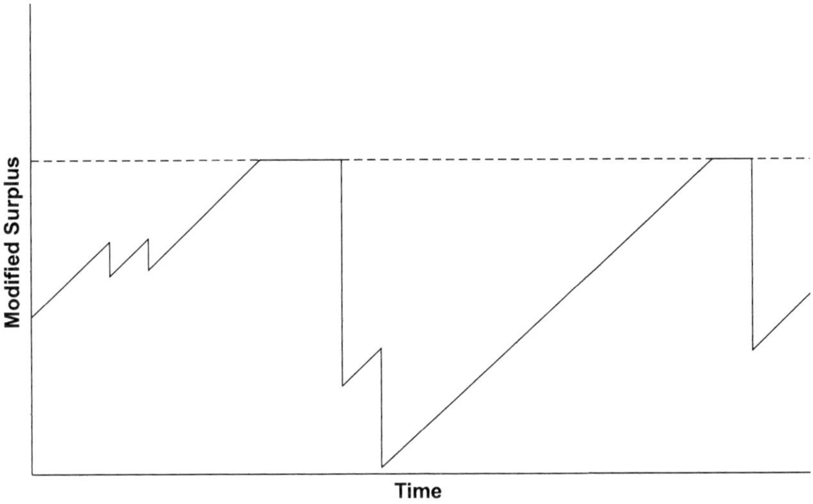

Figure 8.9 The realisation of the surplus process in Figure 8.8 modified by the introduction of a dividend barrier.

of a dividend barrier. It is straightforward to show (see Exercise 1) that it is certain that ruin will eventually occur for the modified surplus process.

Let us assume that the shareholders provide the initial surplus u and pay the deficit at ruin. A question of interest is how should the level of the barrier

b be chosen to maximise the expected present value of net income to the shareholders, assuming that there is no further business after the time of ruin. We define $V(u,b)$ to be the expected present value at force of interest δ of dividends payable to shareholders prior to ruin, $Y_{u,b}$ to be the deficit at ruin and $T_{u,b}$ to be the time of ruin, so that $E\left[Y_{u,b}\exp\{-\delta T_{u,b}\}\right]$ gives the expected present value of the deficit at ruin. Then we want to choose b such that

$$L(u,b) = V(u,b) - E\left[Y_{u,b}\exp\{-\delta T_{u,b}\}\right] - u$$

is maximised, and to address this question we must consider the components of $L(u,b)$.

We can find an expression for $V(u,b)$ by the standard technique of conditioning on the time and the amount of the first claim. We note that for $u < b$, if no claim occurs before time $\tau = (b-u)/c$, then the surplus process attains level b at time τ. Thus, for $0 \leq u < b$,

$$V(u,b) = e^{-(\lambda+\delta)\tau}V(b,b) + \int_0^\tau \lambda e^{-(\lambda+\delta)t} \int_0^{u+ct} f(x)\,V(u+ct-x,b)\,dx\,dt.$$

Substituting $s = u + ct$ we obtain

$$V(u,b) = e^{-(\lambda+\delta)(b-u)/c}V(b,b) + \frac{\lambda}{c}\int_u^b e^{-(\lambda+\delta)(s-u)/c}\int_0^s f(x)\,V(s-x,b)\,dx\,ds,$$

and differentiating with respect to u we get

$$\frac{\partial}{\partial u}V(u,b) = \frac{\lambda+\delta}{c}V(u,b) - \frac{\lambda}{c}\int_0^u f(x)V(u-x,b)\,dx. \tag{8.55}$$

Similarly, by considering dividend payments before and after the first claim, we have

$$V(b,b) = \int_0^\infty \lambda e^{-(\lambda+\delta)t} c\bar{s}_{\overline{t|}}\,dt + \int_0^\infty \lambda e^{-(\lambda+\delta)t}\int_0^b f(x)V(b-x,b)\,dx\,dt, \tag{8.56}$$

where $\bar{s}_{\overline{t|}} = (e^{\delta t}-1)/\delta$ is the accumulated amount at time t at force of interest δ of payments at rate 1 per unit time over $(0,t)$. Integrating out in equation (8.56) we obtain

$$V(b,b) = \frac{c}{\lambda+\delta} + \frac{\lambda}{\lambda+\delta}\int_0^b f(x)V(b-x,b)\,dx. \tag{8.57}$$

From equation (8.55) we find that

$$\frac{c}{\lambda+\delta}\,\frac{\partial}{\partial u}V(u,b)\bigg|_{u=b} = V(b,b) - \frac{\lambda}{\lambda+\delta}\int_0^b f(x)V(b-x,b)\,dx,$$

which, together with equation (8.57), gives the boundary condition

$$\left.\frac{\partial}{\partial u}V(u,b)\right|_{u=b} = 1.$$

Example 8.6 *Let $F(x) = 1 - e^{-\alpha x}$, $x \geq 0$. Find an expression for $V(u,b)$.*

Solution 8.6 *Writing equation (8.55) as*

$$\frac{\partial}{\partial u}V(u,b) = \frac{\lambda+\delta}{c}V(u,b) - \frac{\lambda}{c}\int_0^u \alpha e^{-\alpha(u-x)}V(x,b)\,dx, \tag{8.58}$$

we can follow the technique used in Section 7.7 to obtain the second order differential equation

$$\frac{\partial^2}{\partial u^2}V(u,b) + \left(\alpha - \frac{\lambda+\delta}{c}\right)\frac{\partial}{\partial u}V(u,b) - \frac{\alpha\delta}{c}V(u,b) = 0.$$

The general solution of this differential equation is

$$V(u,b) = \gamma_1 e^{\rho_\delta u} + \gamma_2 e^{-R_\delta u}, \tag{8.59}$$

where $\rho_\delta > 0$ and $-R_\delta < 0$ are the roots of the characteristic equation

$$s^2 + \left(\alpha - \frac{\lambda+\delta}{c}\right)s - \frac{\alpha\delta}{c} = 0, \tag{8.60}$$

and γ_1 and γ_2 depend on both δ and b. Further, the boundary condition gives

$$\gamma_1\rho_\delta e^{\rho_\delta b} - \gamma_2 R_\delta e^{-R_\delta b} = 1.$$

We now insert the functional form (8.59) of $V(u,b)$ into equation (8.58). This yields

$$\begin{aligned}\gamma_1\rho_\delta e^{\rho_\delta u} - \gamma_2 R_\delta e^{-R_\delta u} &= \frac{\lambda+\delta}{c}\left(\gamma_1 e^{\rho_\delta u} + \gamma_2 e^{-R_\delta u}\right)\\ &\quad - \frac{\lambda\alpha}{c}e^{-\alpha u}\int_0^u\left(\gamma_1 e^{(\alpha+\rho_\delta)x} + \gamma_2 e^{(\alpha-R_\delta)x}\right)dx\\ &= \frac{\lambda+\delta}{c}\left(\gamma_1 e^{\rho_\delta u} + \gamma_2 e^{-R_\delta u}\right)\\ &\quad - \frac{\lambda}{c}\left(\frac{\alpha\gamma_1}{\alpha+\rho_\delta}\left(e^{\rho_\delta u} - e^{-\alpha u}\right) + \frac{\alpha\gamma_2}{\alpha-R_\delta}\left(e^{-R_\delta u} - e^{-\alpha u}\right)\right),\end{aligned}$$

which can be written as

$$\begin{aligned}&\left(\rho_\delta - \frac{\lambda+\delta}{c} + \frac{\lambda\alpha}{c(\alpha+\rho_\delta)}\right)\gamma_1 e^{\rho_\delta u} - \left(R_\delta + \frac{\lambda+\delta}{c} - \frac{\lambda\alpha}{c(\alpha-R_\delta)}\right)\gamma_2 e^{-R_\delta u}\\ &= \frac{\lambda}{c}e^{-\alpha u}\left(\frac{\alpha\gamma_1}{\alpha+\rho_\delta} + \frac{\alpha\gamma_2}{\alpha-R_\delta}\right).\end{aligned} \tag{8.61}$$

Now

$$\rho_\delta - \frac{\lambda+\delta}{c} + \frac{\lambda\alpha}{c(\alpha+\rho_\delta)} = \frac{1}{\alpha+\rho_\delta}\left(\rho_\delta^2 + \left(\alpha - \frac{\lambda+\delta}{c}\right)\rho_\delta - \frac{\alpha\delta}{c}\right) = 0$$

since ρ_δ is a root of (8.60), and similarly the coefficient of $e^{-R_\delta u}$ in equation (8.61) is 0. The right-hand side of equation (8.61) then yields

$$\frac{\gamma_1}{\gamma_2} = -\frac{\alpha+\rho_\delta}{\alpha-R_\delta},$$

and so

$$V(u,b) = \frac{(\alpha+\rho_\delta)e^{\rho_\delta u} - (\alpha-R_\delta)e^{-R_\delta u}}{(\alpha+\rho_\delta)\rho_\delta e^{\rho_\delta b} + (\alpha-R_\delta)R_\delta e^{-R_\delta b}}.$$

Now let $\varphi_b(u) = E\left[Y_{u,b}\exp\{-\delta T_{u,b}\}\right]$. Then, by again considering the time and the amount of the first claim, and whether or not the first claim occurs before time τ, we obtain

$$\begin{aligned}\varphi_b(u) = &\int_0^\tau \lambda e^{-(\lambda+\delta)t}\int_{u+ct}^\infty (y-u-ct)f(y)dydt\\ &+\int_\tau^\infty \lambda e^{-(\lambda+\delta)t}\int_b^\infty (y-b)f(y)dydt\\ &+\int_0^\tau \lambda e^{-(\lambda+\delta)t}\int_0^{u+ct} f(y)\varphi_b(u+ct-y)dydt\\ &+\int_\tau^\infty \lambda e^{-(\lambda+\delta)t}\int_0^b f(y)\varphi_b(b-y)dydt,\end{aligned}$$

which leads to

$$\begin{aligned}ce^{-(\lambda+\delta)u/c}\varphi_b(u) = &\int_u^b \lambda e^{-(\lambda+\delta)s/c}\int_s^\infty (y-s)f(y)dyds\\ &+\int_b^\infty \lambda e^{-(\lambda+\delta)s/c}\int_b^\infty (y-b)f(y)dyds\\ &+\int_u^b \lambda e^{-(\lambda+\delta)s/c}\int_0^s f(y)\varphi_b(s-y)dyds\\ &+\int_b^\infty \lambda e^{-(\lambda+\delta)s/c}\int_0^b f(y)\varphi_b(b-y)dyds\end{aligned}$$

after making the standard substitution $s = u + ct$. Differentiation then leads to

$$\frac{\partial}{\partial u}\varphi_b(u) = \frac{\delta+\lambda}{c}\varphi_b(u) - \frac{\lambda}{c}\int_u^\infty (y-u)f(y)dy - \frac{\lambda}{c}\int_0^u f(y)\varphi_b(u-y)dy. \quad (8.62)$$

Further,

$$\varphi_b(b) = \int_0^\infty \lambda e^{-(\lambda+\delta)t} \left[\int_b^\infty (y-b)f(y)dy + \int_0^b f(y)\varphi_b(b-y)dy \right] dt$$

$$= \frac{\lambda}{\lambda+\delta} \left[\int_b^\infty (y-b)f(y)dy + \int_0^b f(y)\varphi_b(b-y)dy \right],$$

and as equation (8.62) yields

$$\varphi_b(b) = \frac{c}{\delta+\lambda} \frac{\partial}{\partial u}\varphi_b(u)\bigg|_{u=b} + \frac{\lambda}{\delta+\lambda} \left[\int_b^\infty (y-b)f(y)dy + \int_0^b f(y)\varphi_b(b-y)dy \right],$$

we obtain the boundary condition

$$\frac{\partial}{\partial u}\varphi_b(u)\bigg|_{u=b} = 0.$$

Example 8.7 *Let $F(x) = 1 - e^{-\alpha x}$, $x \geq 0$. Find an expression for $\varphi_b(u)$.*

Solution 8.7 *Proceeding as in the solution to Example 8.6, we obtain*

$$\frac{\partial}{\partial u}\varphi_b(u) = \frac{\delta+\lambda}{c}\varphi_b(u) - \frac{\lambda}{c}\int_u^\infty (y-u)\alpha e^{-\alpha y}dy - \frac{\lambda}{c}\int_0^u \alpha e^{-\alpha(u-y)}\varphi_b(y)dy, \tag{8.63}$$

and hence

$$\frac{\partial^2}{\partial u^2}\varphi_b(u) + \left(\alpha - \frac{\lambda+\delta}{c}\right)\frac{\partial}{\partial u}\varphi_b(u) - \frac{\alpha\delta}{c}\varphi_b(u) = 0.$$

It therefore follows that

$$\varphi_b(u) = \eta_1 e^{\rho_\delta u} + \eta_2 e^{-R_\delta u}, \tag{8.64}$$

where once again ρ_δ and $-R_\delta$ are the roots of equation (8.60), and η_1 and η_2 depend on both δ and b. Continuing as in the solution to Example 8.6, insertion of the functional form (8.64) of $\varphi_b(u)$ into equation (8.63) yields

$$\frac{1}{\alpha} = \frac{\eta_1\alpha}{\alpha+\rho_\delta} + \frac{\eta_2\alpha}{\alpha-R_\delta}, \tag{8.65}$$

and the boundary condition gives

$$\eta_1\rho_\delta e^{\rho_\delta b} - \eta_2 R_\delta e^{-R_\delta b} = 0,$$

so that

$$\frac{\eta_1}{\eta_2} = \frac{R_\delta e^{-R_\delta b}}{\rho_\delta e^{\rho_\delta b}}.$$

Division of equation (8.65) by η_2 *leads to*

$$\eta_2 = \frac{1}{\alpha^2}\frac{(\alpha+\rho_\delta)(\alpha-R_\delta)\rho_\delta e^{\rho_\delta b}}{(\alpha+\rho_\delta)\rho_\delta e^{\rho_\delta b}+(\alpha-R_\delta)R_\delta e^{-R_\delta b}},$$

and as

$$\frac{1}{\alpha}(\alpha+\rho_\delta)(\alpha-R_\delta)=\frac{\lambda}{c}$$

(since $\rho_\delta R_\delta=\alpha\delta/c$ *and* $R_\delta-\rho_\delta=\alpha-(\lambda+\delta)/c$*), we have*

$$\varphi_b(u)=\frac{\lambda}{\alpha c}\frac{\rho_\delta e^{\rho_\delta b-R_\delta u}+R_\delta e^{-R_\delta b+\rho_\delta u}}{(\alpha+\rho_\delta)\rho_\delta e^{\rho_\delta b}+(\alpha-R_\delta)R_\delta e^{-R_\delta b}}.$$

For the remainder of this section let us assume that the individual claim amount distribution is exponential with mean $1/\alpha$, so that we have an explicit solution for $L(u,b)$. Taking the derivative of $L(u,b)$ with respect to b we find after some simplification that

$$\begin{aligned}&\frac{\partial}{\partial b}L(u,b)\\&=\frac{-(\alpha+\rho_\delta)e^{\rho_\delta u}+(\alpha-R_\delta)e^{-R_\delta u}}{\left((\alpha+\rho_\delta)\rho_\delta e^{\rho_\delta b}+(\alpha-R_\delta)R_\delta e^{-R_\delta b}\right)^2}\left((\alpha+\rho_\delta)\rho_\delta^2 e^{\rho_\delta b}-(\alpha-R_\delta)R_\delta^2 e^{-R_\delta b}\right)\\&\quad+\frac{\lambda}{\alpha c}\frac{\rho_\delta R_\delta\,(\rho_\delta+R_\delta)\,e^{(\rho_\delta-R_\delta)b}\left((\alpha+\rho_\delta)e^{\rho_\delta u}-(\alpha-R_\delta)e^{-R_\delta u}\right)}{\left((\alpha+\rho_\delta)\rho_\delta e^{\rho_\delta b}+(\alpha-R_\delta)R_\delta e^{-R_\delta b}\right)^2},\end{aligned}$$

and it is straightforward to show that this partial derivative is zero when

$$(\alpha+\rho_\delta)\rho_\delta^2 e^{\rho_\delta b}-(\alpha-R_\delta)R_\delta^2 e^{-R_\delta b}=\frac{\lambda}{\alpha c}\left(\rho_\delta R_\delta\,(\rho_\delta+R_\delta)\,e^{(\rho_\delta-R_\delta)b}\right). \quad (8.66)$$

The solution to equation (8.66) is the optimal barrier level under our criterion of maximising the expected present value of net income to the shareholders. Strictly, we have not proved this, and we should consider the second derivative of $L(u,b)$. Figure 8.10 illustrates $L(u,b)$ for a range of values of b when $\alpha=1$, $\lambda=100$, $c=110$ and $\delta=0.1$, resulting in $\rho_\delta=0.00917$ and $R_\delta=0.09917$. As is clear from equation (8.66), the optimal barrier level is independent of u, and as equation (8.66) becomes

$$0.0088e^{\rho_\delta b}-0.88589e^{-R_\delta b}=0.00895e^{(\rho_\delta-R_\delta)b},$$

the optimal barrier is 43.049.

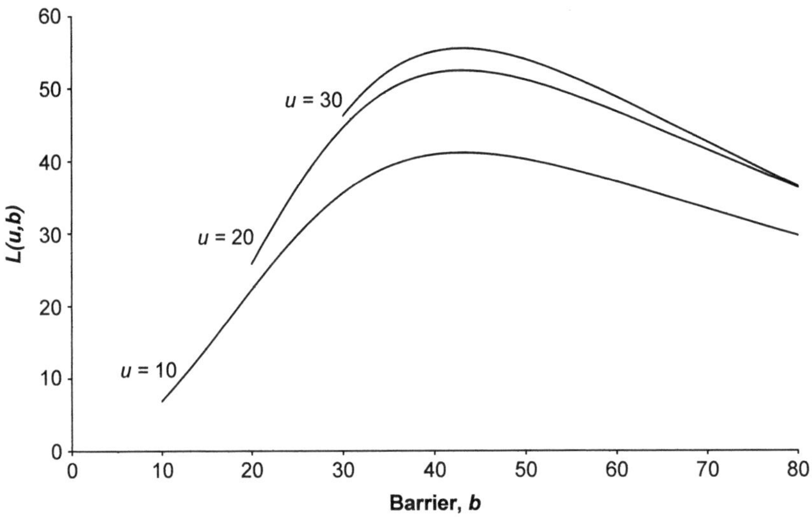

Figure 8.10 $L(u, b)$ for different values of u.

8.8 Notes and References

Section 8.3 is based on Gerber et al. (1987) and Willmot and Lin (1998). The maximum severity of ruin is discussed in Picard (1994), and Section 8.5 is based on Dickson (1992). Prabhu's formula comes from Prabhu (1961), and the dual risk model is also discussed in this paper (see Exercise 8). Gerber-Shiu functions first appeared in Gerber and Shiu (1998), while the transform inversion technique in Section 8.6.3 is based on Panjer and Willmot (1992) who find $\phi(u, t)$ by inverting its bivariate Laplace transform. The transform identity in equations (8.29) and (8.30) comes from Dickson and Willmot (2005). The moments of the time of ruin were first obtained by Lin and Willmot (2000), but our approach follows Albrecher and Boxma (2005). Results in Section 8.6.4 are based on Dickson and Li (2010). An alternative approach to finding formula (8.43) can be found in Drekic and Willmot (2003), while an alternative to formula (8.43) can be found in Dickson et al. (2005). The numerical approach to finding the density of the time of ruin is discussed by Dickson and Waters (2002). Section 8.7 is based on ideas discussed in Gerber (1979) and extended in Dickson and Waters (2004). We can also consider dividends problems for which the ultimate ruin probability is less than one; see, for example, Lin and Pavlova (2006). For a discussion of other advanced topics in ruin theory, see Asmussen and Albrecher (2010) or Rolski et al. (1999). The concept of dual events is discussed by Feller (1966).

8.9 Exercises

1. Let $\xi_r(u,b)$ denote the probability of ultimate ruin from initial surplus u when there is a reflecting barrier at $b \geq u$ (so that when the surplus process reaches level b, it remains there until a claim occurs). Show that

$$\xi_r(b,b) = \int_0^b \xi_r(b-x,b)f(x)dx + 1 - F(b)$$

and use the fact that $\xi_r(u,b) \geq \xi_r(b,b)$ to show that $\xi_r(u,b) = 1$ for $0 \leq u \leq b$.

2. An aggregate claims process is a compound Poisson process with Poisson parameter λ, and the individual claim amount density is $f(x) = \exp\{-x\}$ for $x > 0$. The insurer initially calculates its premium with a loading factor of 0.2. However, when the insurer's surplus reaches level $b > u$, the loading factor will reduce to 0.1 and will remain at that level thereafter. Calculate the probability of ultimate ruin when $u = 10$ and $b = 20$.

3. By conditioning on the time and the amount of the first claim show that

$$\frac{\partial}{\partial u}G(u,y) = \frac{\lambda}{c}G(u,y) - \frac{\lambda}{c}\int_0^u G(u-x,y)f(x)dx - \frac{\lambda}{c}\int_u^{u+y} f(x)dx.$$

By integrating this equation over $(0,w)$ show that

$$G(w,y) = \frac{\lambda}{c}\int_0^w G(w-x,y)\,(1-F(x))\,dx + \frac{\lambda}{c}\int_w^{w+y}(1-F(x))\,dx.$$

4. Show that the density of $|U(T_u)| \mid T_u < \infty$, i.e. $g(u,y)/\psi(u)$, in Example 8.2 can be written as a weighted average of an exponential density and an Erlang(2) density, where the weights depend on u. Calculate the value of these weights for $u = 0, 1, 2, \ldots, 5$. What conclusion can be drawn from these calculations?

5. Let the individual claim amount distribution be exponential with mean $1/\alpha$. Given that ruin occurs, find an expression for the probability that the maximum severity of ruin occurs at the time of ruin.

6. Consider the Gerber-Shiu function $\varphi(u)$ when $\delta = 0$.

   (a) Show that

$$\varphi(u) = \varphi(0)\frac{\phi(u)}{\phi(0)} - \frac{\lambda}{c\,\phi(0)}\int_0^u \alpha(x)\phi(u-x)\,dx.$$

   (b) Let $a(x,y) = \exp\{-sx\}$ for all x and y. Use Laplace transform inversion to obtain the density of $U(T_u^-)$.

7. (a) Show that equation (8.38) can be written as

$$\lambda e^{-\lambda t} f(u+y) + \lambda \int_0^u f(x+y)\, g(u-x,t)\, dx$$
$$= \omega(0,y,u/c)\, e^{-\lambda(t-u/c)} + \int_0^u \omega\left(0, y, \frac{u-x}{c}\right) g\left(x, t - \frac{u-x}{c}\right) dx.$$

(b) By considering how a surplus process can start at 0 at time 0 and be at level $ct - u - y$ at time t as a result of a claim at time t, explain why this identity holds.

8. Consider the dual risk model from Exercise 11 in Chapter 7, and again assume that $c < \lambda E[X]$. Let T_u denote the time of ruin from initial surplus u, and define $\varphi(u) = E[e^{-\delta T_u} I(T_u < \infty)]$.

(a) Use an argument similar to that in Section 8.2 to show that $\varphi(u)$ is of the form $e^{-\rho u}$ for some constant ρ.

(b) By establishing an equation satisfied by $\varphi(u)$ show that ρ is such that

$$\lambda + \delta - c\rho = \lambda f^*(\rho).$$

(c) Explain why $\Pr(T_u = u/c) = e^{-\lambda u/c}$.

(d) By expressing $e^{-\rho u}$ in terms of δ, find the mixed distribution of T_u.

(e) Find an expression for $E[T_u \mid T_u < \infty]$ when $F(x) = 1 - e^{-\alpha x}$, $x \geq 0$. (Hint: Unlike in the classical risk model, $\rho \neq 0$ when $\delta = 0$.)

9. (a) Starting from Lundberg's fundamental equation, show that

$$\rho_0'' = \frac{-\lambda m_2}{(c - \lambda m_1)^3}.$$

(b) Find an expression for $E[T_{0,c}^2]$.

(c) Consider the case when $F(x) = 1 - e^{-\alpha x}$, $x \geq 0$. By applying the ideas that gave formula (8.47), find an expression for $V[T_{u,c}]$.

10. Consider the dividends problem of Section 8.7 and let the initial surplus be b, so that dividends are payable immediately and this dividend stream ceases at the time of the first claim.

(a) What is the distribution of the amount of dividends in the first dividend stream?

(b) Let N denote the number of dividend streams. Show that

$$\Pr(N = r) = p(b)^{r-1}\,(1 - p(b))$$

for $r = 1, 2, 3, \ldots$ where

$$p(b) = \int_0^b f(x)\chi(b-x, b)dx.$$

(c) Find the moment generating function of the total amount of dividends payable until ruin, and hence deduce that the distribution of the total amount of dividends payable until ruin is exponential with mean

$$\frac{c}{\lambda(1 - p(b))}.$$

(d) Suppose instead that the initial surplus is $u < b$. Show that the distribution of the number of dividend streams is zero-modified geometric and that the distribution of the total amount of dividends payable until ruin is a mixture of a degenerate distribution at zero and the exponential distribution in part (c).

9
Reinsurance

9.1 Introduction

In this chapter we consider optimal reinsurance from an insurer's point of view and illustrate two different approaches to the problem. First, in Section 9.2 we illustrate how utility theory can be applied to determine the optimal retention level under both proportional and excess of loss reinsurance. Second, in Section 9.3 we apply ideas from ruin theory to find not only optimal retention levels, but also the optimal type of reinsurance under certain conditions.

9.2 Application of Utility Theory

In this section we consider two results relating to optimal retention levels given a particular type of reinsurance arrangement. Throughout this section we assume that an insurer makes decisions on the basis of the exponential utility function $u(x) = -\exp\{-\beta x\}$ where $\beta > 0$. We consider a (reinsured) risk over a one year period, so that the insurer's wealth at the end of the year is

$$W + P - P_R - S_I,$$

where W is the insurer's wealth at the start of the year, P is the premium the insurer receives to cover the risk, P_R is the amount of the reinsurance premium and S_I denotes the amount of claims paid by the insurer net of reinsurance. Our objective is to find the retention level that maximises the insurer's expected utility of year end wealth. As neither W nor P depends on the retention level, and as we are applying an exponential utility function, our objective is to maximise

$$-\exp\{\beta P_R\}E\left[\exp\{\beta S_I\}\right].$$

Finally, we assume that aggregate claims from the risk (before reinsurance) have a compound Poisson distribution with Poisson parameter λ and continuous individual claim amount distribution F such that $F(0) = 0$.

9.2.1 Proportional Reinsurance

Let us assume that the insurer effects proportional reinsurance and pays proportion a of each claim, and that the reinsurance premium is calculated by the exponential principle with parameter A. From Section 4.4.1, aggregate claims for the reinsurer have a compound Poisson distribution with Poisson parameter λ and with individual claim amounts distributed as $(1-a)X$ where $X \sim F$. Thus, by formula (3.2), the reinsurance premium is

$$P_R = \frac{\lambda}{A}\left(\int_0^\infty e^{(1-a)Ax} f(x)dx - 1\right).$$

Similarly, as S_I has a compound Poisson distribution with Poisson parameter λ and with individual claim amounts distributed as aX,

$$E\left[\exp\{\beta S_I\}\right] = \exp\left\{\lambda\left(\int_0^\infty e^{a\beta x} f(x)dx - 1\right)\right\},$$

and hence

$$\begin{aligned} &-\exp\{\beta P_R\}E\left[\exp\{\beta S_I\}\right] \\ &= -\exp\left\{\frac{\lambda\beta}{A}\left(\int_0^\infty e^{(1-a)Ax} f(x)dx - 1\right) + \lambda\left(\int_0^\infty e^{a\beta x} f(x)dx - 1\right)\right\}. \end{aligned}$$

Finding a to maximise this expression is the same as finding a to minimise $h(a)$ where

$$\begin{aligned} h(a) &= \frac{\lambda\beta}{A}\int_0^\infty e^{(1-a)Ax} f(x)dx + \lambda\int_0^\infty e^{a\beta x} f(x)dx \\ &= \lambda\int_0^\infty \left(A^{-1}\beta e^{(1-a)Ax} + e^{a\beta x}\right) f(x)dx. \end{aligned}$$

Differentiation gives

$$\frac{d}{da}h(a) = \lambda\int_0^\infty \left(-x\beta e^{(1-a)Ax} + \beta x e^{a\beta x}\right) f(x)dx,$$

and this equals 0 when

$$(1-a)A = a\beta$$

or

$$a = \frac{A}{A+\beta}.$$

Further, as

$$\frac{d^2}{da^2}h(a) = \lambda \int_0^\infty \left(Ax^2 \beta e^{(1-a)Ax} + \beta^2 x^2 e^{a\beta x} \right) f(x)dx > 0,$$

$h(a)$ has a minimum when $a = A/(A + \beta)$, and hence the insurer's expected utility of year end wealth is maximised by this value of a.

An interesting feature of this result is that the optimal retention level is independent of the individual claim amount distribution and depends only on the parameter of the insurer's utility function and the parameter of the reinsurance premium principle. If we consider a as a function of A, we see that a is an increasing function of A. As A is the reinsurer's coefficient of risk aversion, the more risk averse the reinsurer is, the greater the reinsurance premium is, and as the cost of reinsurance increases it is natural for the insurer to retain a greater part of the risk. Similarly, if we consider a as a function of β, we see that a is a decreasing function of β. This also makes sense intuitively as β is the insurer's coefficient of risk aversion. Thus, the result says that as the insurer's risk aversion increases, the insurer's share of each claim decreases.

9.2.2 Excess of Loss Reinsurance

Let us now assume that the insurer effects excess of loss reinsurance with retention level M and that the reinsurance premium is calculated by the expected value principle with loading θ, so that

$$P_R = (1 + \theta)\lambda \int_M^\infty (x - M) f(x)dx.$$

From Section 4.4.2 it follows that S_I has a compound Poisson distribution with Poisson parameter λ and with individual claim amounts distributed as $\min(X, M)$ where $X \sim F$. Thus,

$$E\left[\exp\{\beta S_I\}\right] = \exp\left\{\lambda \left(\int_0^M e^{\beta x} f(x)dx + e^{\beta M}\left(1 - F(M)\right) - 1 \right)\right\},$$

and so

$$\begin{aligned} &-\exp\{\beta P_R\} E\left[\exp\{\beta S_I\}\right] \\ &= -\exp\left\{(1+\theta)\lambda\beta \int_M^\infty (x - M) f(x)dx\right\} \\ &\quad \times \exp\left\{\lambda \left(\int_0^M e^{\beta x} f(x)dx + e^{\beta M}\left(1 - F(M)\right) - 1 \right)\right\}. \end{aligned}$$

Proceeding as in the previous section, finding M to maximise this expression is equivalent to finding M to minimise $g(M)$ where

$$g(M) = (1+\theta)\lambda\beta \int_M^\infty (x - M) f(x)dx + \lambda \left(\int_0^M e^{\beta x} f(x)dx + e^{\beta M} (1 - F(M)) \right).$$

Differentiation gives

$$\begin{aligned} \frac{d}{dM} g(M) &= -(1+\theta)\lambda\beta \int_M^\infty f(x)dx + \lambda\beta e^{\beta M} (1 - F(M)) \\ &= \lambda\beta (1 - F(M)) \left(e^{\beta M} - 1 - \theta \right), \end{aligned}$$

and this equals 0 when

$$M = \frac{1}{\beta} \log(1+\theta). \tag{9.1}$$

Further,

$$\frac{d^2}{dM^2} g(M) = -\lambda\beta f(M) \left(e^{\beta M} - 1 - \theta \right) + \lambda\beta^2 (1 - F(M)) e^{\beta M},$$

and this second derivative is positive when $M = \beta^{-1} \log(1+\theta)$, so that this value of M minimises $g(M)$ and hence maximises the insurer's expected utility of year end wealth.

As in the previous section, we find that the optimal retention level depends on the parameter of the insurer's utility function and on the parameter of the reinsurer's premium calculation principle, but does not depend on the individual claim amount distribution. If we consider the optimal retention level as a function of θ, then we see that M is an increasing function of θ. This simply states that as the price of reinsurance increases, the insurer should retain a greater share of each claim. Similarly, if we consider the optimal retention level as a function of β, we see that M is a decreasing function of β, and the intuitive explanation of this is the same as in the case of proportional reinsurance.

9.2.3 Comments on the Application of Utility Theory

The above results for optimal retention levels are based on a single period analysis. Although they are intuitively appealing, they also have limitations. As the analysis is based on an exponential utility function, the premium that the insurer receives to cover the risk does not affect the decision. However, if we assume that the reinsurance premium is paid from the premium income that the insurer receives, then it seems unreasonable that the premium income does not affect the decision. This point is addressed in the next section where we consider the effect of reinsurance on a surplus process.

We remark that in Sections 9.2.1 and 9.2.2 the reinsurance premiums are calculated by different premium principles. These principles provide solutions for optimal retention levels that are expressed in simple forms in terms of the parameter of the utility function and the parameter of the (reinsurance) premium principle, and are thus suitable to illustrate points. However, other premium principles can equally be used for the reinsurance premium, and some of these are illustrated in the exercises at the end of this chapter.

9.3 Reinsurance and Ruin

Under the classical risk model, the surplus process $\{U(t)\}_{t\geq 0}$ is given by

$$U(t) = u + ct - \sum_{i=1}^{N(t)} X_i.$$

If the insurer effects reinsurance by paying a reinsurance premium continuously at a constant rate, then this process becomes a net of reinsurance surplus process $\{U^*(t)\}_{t\geq 0}$ given by

$$U^*(t) = u + c^*t - \sum_{i=1}^{N(t)} X_i^*,$$

where c^* denotes the insurer's premium income per unit time net of reinsurance, and X_i^* denotes the amount the insurer pays on the ith claim, net of reinsurance. For this risk process, the net of reinsurance adjustment coefficient exists provided that $c^* > \lambda E\left[X_1^*\right]$ and $M_{X_1^*}$ exists and is the unique positive number R^* such that

$$\lambda + c^*R^* = \lambda E\left[\exp\{R^*X_1^*\}\right].$$

Further, the insurer's ultimate ruin probability is bounded above by $\exp\{-R^*u\}$.

In general, it is difficult to obtain analytic solutions for the probability of ultimate ruin when there is reinsurance. However, it is usually possible to solve for the net of reinsurance adjustment coefficient. In the following sections we therefore consider maximising the net of reinsurance adjustment coefficient, since by doing this we minimise Lundberg's upper bound for the ultimate ruin probability. First, we consider the optimal type of reinsurance arrangement in terms of maximising the net of reinsurance adjustment coefficient. Then we consider the situation under both proportional and excess of loss reinsurance.

9.3.1 The Optimal Type of Reinsurance

In this section we show that under certain assumptions the optimal type of reinsurance is excess of loss. In what follows, let X denote the amount of an individual claim, with $X \sim F$ and $F(0) = 0$, and let h denote a reinsurance arrangement, so that when a claim of amount x occurs, the insurer pays $h(x)$ where $0 \leq h(x) \leq x$. So, for example, under proportional reinsurance $h(x) = ax$ where $0 \leq a \leq 1$. Our objective is to compare excess of loss reinsurance with retention level M, under which the insurer pays $\min(X, M)$ when a claim occurs, with any reinsurance arrangement given by a rule h.

In order to make the comparison valid, we first assume that

$$E\left[\min(X, M)\right] = E\left[h(X)\right]. \tag{9.2}$$

This assumption says that given a reinsurance arrangement h, it is possible to arrange excess of loss reinsurance such that the mean individual claim amount, net of reinsurance, is the same under each reinsurance arrangement. Our second assumption is that the insurer's premium income per unit time, net of reinsurance, is given by

$$c^* = (1+\theta)\lambda E\left[X\right] - (1+\theta_R)\lambda E\left[X - h(X)\right], \tag{9.3}$$

with

$$c^* > \lambda E[h(X)]. \tag{9.4}$$

Note that c^* is just the difference between the premium the insurer receives to cover the risk and the reinsurance premium, and that each of these premiums is calculated by the expected value principle. In the following we assume that $\theta_R \geq \theta > 0$. In the case when $\theta_R = \theta$, it is clear that $c^* > \lambda E[h(X)]$. When $\theta_R > \theta$, the condition (9.4) ensures that the net adjustment coefficient exists, provided, of course, that the relevant moment generating function exists. An important point to note about equation (9.3) is that the cost of reinsurance is the same, regardless of the type of reinsurance effected, which follows by equality (9.2) and because h represents any reinsurance arrangement.

Now let R_h denote the net adjustment coefficient under a reinsurance arrangement given by a rule h, so that

$$\lambda + c^* R_h = \lambda E\left[\exp\{R_h h(X)\}\right] = \lambda \int_0^\infty \exp\{R_h h(x)\} f(x)dx,$$

and let R_e denote the net adjustment coefficient under an excess of loss reinsurance arrangement with retention level M, so that

$$\lambda + c^* R_e = \lambda E\left[\exp\{R_e \min(X, M)\}\right]$$
$$= \lambda \left(\int_0^M \exp\{R_e x\} f(x) dx + \exp\{R_e M\} (1 - F(M)) \right). \quad (9.5)$$

Then, under the assumptions of this section, excess of loss reinsurance is optimal in the sense that under this form of reinsurance the net adjustment coefficient is maximised, i.e. $R_e \geq R_h$.

To prove that $R_e \geq R_h$ it is sufficient to consider functions g_1 and g_2 defined as

$$g_1(r) = \lambda \int_0^\infty \exp\{rh(x)\} f(x) dx - \lambda - c^* r$$

and

$$g_2(r) = \lambda \left(\int_0^M \exp\{rx\} f(x) dx + \exp\{rM\} (1 - F(M)) \right) - \lambda - c^* r.$$

Thus, as shown in Figure 9.1, if $g_1(r) \geq g_2(r)$ for all $r \geq 0$, then $R_e \geq R_h$.

Now let

$$\varepsilon(y) = \begin{cases} y & \text{if } 0 \leq y \leq M \\ M & \text{if } y > M \end{cases},$$

so that ε gives the insurer's payment, net of reinsurance, on a claim under excess of loss reinsurance with retention level M.

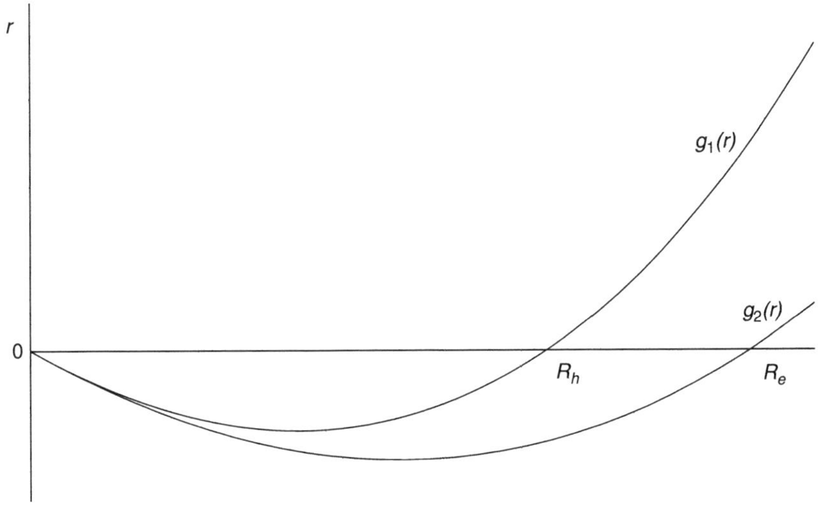

Figure 9.1 Functions g_1 and g_2 giving $R_e \geq R_h$.

A key step in proving that $R_e \geq R_h$ is that $e^z \geq 1 + z$ for all z. This implies that

$$\exp\{r(h(x) - \varepsilon(x))\} \geq 1 + r(h(x) - \varepsilon(x)),$$

or, alternatively,

$$\exp\{rh(x)\} \geq \exp\{r\varepsilon(x)\} + r\exp\{r\varepsilon(x)\}(h(x) - \varepsilon(x)).$$

Consequently, we have

$$\begin{aligned}\int_0^\infty \exp\{rh(x)\}f(x)dx \geq & \int_0^\infty \exp\{r\varepsilon(x)\}f(x)dx \\ & + r\int_0^\infty \exp\{r\varepsilon(x)\}(h(x) - \varepsilon(x))f(x)dx.\end{aligned}$$

It then follows that $R_e \geq R_h$ if

$$\int_0^\infty \exp\{r\varepsilon(x)\}(h(x) - \varepsilon(x))f(x)dx \geq 0. \tag{9.6}$$

To see that (9.6) is indeed true, note that

$$\begin{aligned}\int_0^\infty \exp\{r\varepsilon(x)\}(h(x) - \varepsilon(x))f(x)dx = & \int_0^M \exp\{r\varepsilon(x)\}(h(x) - \varepsilon(x))f(x)dx \\ & + \int_M^\infty \exp\{r\varepsilon(x)\}(h(x) - \varepsilon(x))f(x)dx.\end{aligned}$$

Further,

$$\int_0^M \exp\{r\varepsilon(x)\}(h(x) - \varepsilon(x))f(x)dx \geq \int_0^M \exp\{rM\}(h(x) - \varepsilon(x))f(x)dx.$$

This follows since for $x \in [0, M]$, $h(x) \leq x = \varepsilon(x)$, so that $h(x) - \varepsilon(x) \leq 0$, and since $\exp\{rM\} \geq \exp\{r\varepsilon(x)\}$ in this interval. Hence

$$\begin{aligned}\int_0^\infty \exp\{r\varepsilon(x)\}(h(x) - \varepsilon(x))f(x)dx & \geq \exp\{rM\}\int_0^\infty (h(x) - \varepsilon(x))f(x)dx \\ & = \exp\{rM\}(E[h(X)] - E[\min(X, M)]) \\ & = 0,\end{aligned}$$

where the final step follows by equation (9.2). Thus,

$$\int_0^\infty \exp\{rh(x)\}f(x)dx \geq \int_0^\infty \exp\{r\varepsilon(x)\}f(x)dx,$$

and hence $R_e \geq R_h$.

A key assumption in the proof that $R_e \geq R_h$ is that the cost of reinsurance is the same regardless of the type of reinsurance effected. This assumption may not always be borne out in practice. To see why this is the case, let us consider a risk for which the Poisson parameter is λ and the individual claim amount distribution is exponential with mean 1. Suppose that $\theta = 0.2$ and $\theta_R = 0.25$, and that the insurer can effect proportional reinsurance, retaining 80% of each claim. Then

$$c^* = \lambda(1.2 - 1.25 \times 0.2) = 0.95\lambda,$$

and as the individual claim amount distribution net of reinsurance is exponential with mean 0.8, from Example 7.1 we know that the net of reinsurance adjustment coefficient is

$$\frac{1}{0.8} - \frac{\lambda}{c^*} = 0.1974.$$

If we now consider an excess of loss reinsurance arrangement with retention level M where M is such that the insurer's expected payment on an individual claim net of reinsurance is 0.8 (the same as under the above proportional arrangement), then

$$\int_0^M xe^{-x}dx + Me^{-M} = 0.8,$$

which gives $1 - e^{-M} = 0.8$ and hence $M = 1.6094$. Still assuming that $\theta = 0.2$ and $\theta_R = 0.25$, the insurer's net of reinsurance adjustment coefficient R_e satisfies

$$\lambda + c^* R_e = \lambda \left(\int_0^M e^{R_e x} e^{-x} dx + e^{R_e M} e^{-M} \right),$$

and as $c^* = 0.95\lambda$ we find that R_e satisfies the equation

$$1 + 0.95R_e = \frac{1 - R_e e^{-(1-R_e)M}}{1 - R_e} = \frac{1 - R_e 0.2^{(1-R_e)}}{1 - R_e},$$

where the second identity follows since $e^{-M} = 0.2$. This equation can be solved numerically, giving $R_e = 0.2752$, so that, as expected, the adjustment coefficient is greater under the excess of loss arrangement.

Table 9.1 shows the mean and variance of aggregate claims net of reinsurance for the insurer under each of the above reinsurance arrangements, as well as the mean and variance of aggregate claims for the reinsurer. It is clear from this table that excess of loss reinsurance is better from the insurer's point of view. Not only does this arrangement give the larger net of reinsurance adjustment coefficient, it also gives the same mean and a smaller variance for net aggregate claims. In contrast, from the reinsurer's point of view, the excess of loss arrangement results in a much greater variance of aggregate claims than the proportional arrangement does. Consequently, the reinsurer may view

Table 9.1 *Mean and variance of aggregate claims payments.*

	Insurer		Reinsurer	
	Mean	Variance	Mean	Variance
Proportional	0.8λ	1.28λ	0.2λ	0.08λ
Excess of loss	0.8λ	0.9562λ	0.2λ	0.4λ

excess of loss reinsurance as more risky, and may therefore set a higher value of θ_R for excess of loss reinsurance than for proportional reinsurance.

9.3.2 Proportional Reinsurance

We now consider the situation when the insurer effects proportional reinsurance and pays proportion a of each claim. Then the insurer's net of reinsurance premium income per unit time is

$$\begin{aligned} c^* &= (1+\theta)\lambda E[X] - (1+\theta_R)\lambda(1-a)E[X] \\ &= (1+\theta-(1+\theta_R)(1-a))\,\lambda E[X], \end{aligned}$$

and condition (9.4) becomes $c^* > \lambda a E[X]$. Thus, we require that

$$(1+\theta-(1+\theta_R)(1-a)) > a,$$

which gives

$$a > 1-\theta/\theta_R. \tag{9.7}$$

Thus, the insurer must retain more than proportion $1-\theta/\theta_R$ of each claim to avoid ultimate ruin. However, when $\theta = \theta_R$, the proportion retained can be zero, as in this case the insurer can use the premium income it receives to reinsure the entire risk. When $\theta < \theta_R$, the insurer can pay the reinsurance premium out of its premium income provided that

$$(1+\theta)\lambda E[X] > (1+\theta_R)\lambda(1-a)E[X],$$

and this condition translates to

$$a > \frac{\theta_R-\theta}{1+\theta_R}.$$

However, when $\theta < \theta_R$,

$$1-\theta/\theta_R > \frac{\theta_R-\theta}{1+\theta_R},$$

and so equation (9.7) specifies the crucial condition.

Example 9.1 *Let the individual claim amount distribution be exponential with mean 1, and let $\theta = \theta_R = 0.2$. Plot the net of reinsurance adjustment coefficient as a function of the proportion retained, a.*

Solution 9.1 *In this case $c^* = 1.2\lambda a$, and so from Example 7.1, the net of reinsurance adjustment coefficient, denoted $R(a)$, is*

$$R(a) = \frac{1}{a} - \frac{\lambda}{c^*} = \frac{1}{6a}. \tag{9.8}$$

Figure 9.2 shows $R(a)$ as a function of a.

In the above example, the reinsurance arrangement is effectively a risk sharing arrangement with the premium income and claims being shared in the same proportion by the insurer and the reinsurer. We can see that in equation (9.8), $\lim_{a\to 0^+} R(a) = \infty$. When $a = 0$ the insurer has neither claims nor premium income, and hence the process $\{U^*(t)\}_{t\geq 0}$ is constant and equal to u for all t, and the ultimate ruin probability is 0.

Example 9.2 *Let the individual claim amount distribution be exponential with mean 1, and let $\theta = 0.2$ and $\theta_R = 0.25$. Find the value of a that maximises the insurer's net of reinsurance adjustment coefficient.*

Solution 9.2 *We now have $c^* = (1.25a - 0.05)\lambda$, and condition (9.7) states that a should exceed 0.2. Hence we must consider the net of reinsurance adjustment coefficient, $R(a)$, for $a \in (0.2, 1]$. From Example 7.1,*

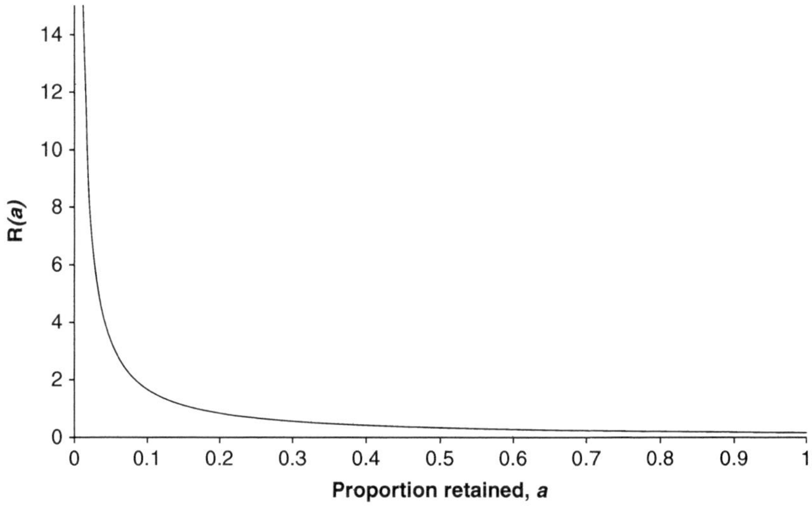

Figure 9.2 $R(a)$ when $\theta = \theta_R = 0.2$.

$$R(a) = \frac{1}{a} - \frac{\lambda}{c^*} = \frac{1}{a} - \frac{1}{1.25a - 0.05}$$
$$= \frac{0.25a - 0.05}{a(1.25a - 0.05)}.$$

Differentiation gives

$$R'(a) = \frac{-0.3125a^2 + 0.125a - 0.0025}{a^2(1.25a - 0.05)^2},$$

so that $R'(a) = 0$ *when*

$$0.3125a^2 - 0.125a + 0.0025 = 0,$$

i.e. when $a = 0.0211$ *and* $a = 0.3789$. *As only the latter value lies within the interval of interest, we conclude that* $R(a)$ *is maximised when* $a = 0.3789$ *since* $R(0.2) = 0$, $R(0.3789) = 0.2786$ *and* $R(1) = 0.1667$.

Figure 9.3 shows $R(a)$ from the above example. From this figure we note that there is a range of values for a that gives a higher value for the net adjustment coefficient than when there is no reinsurance. We also note that the same value for $R(a)$ can occur for two different values of a. For example, $R(a) = 0.25$ when $a = 0.2919$ and when $a = 0.5480$. In forming a choice between these two particular retention levels we would have to apply a different criterion to maximising the net adjustment coefficient. An obvious criterion to adopt would

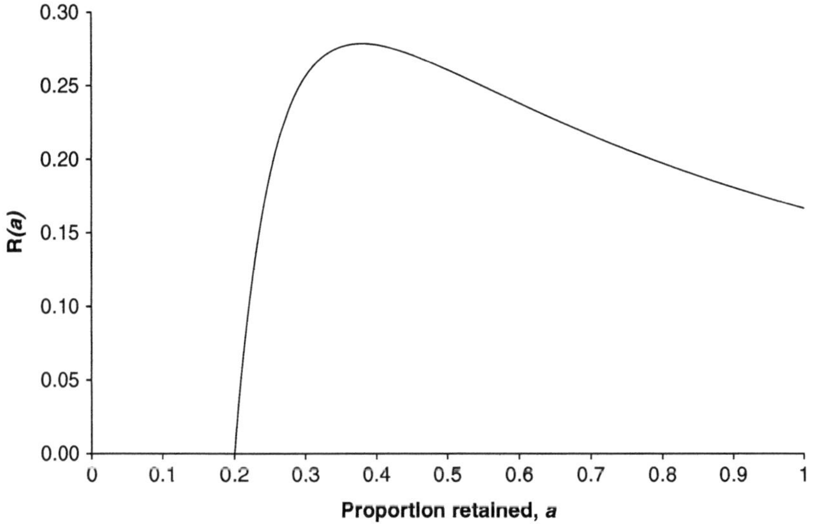

Figure 9.3 $R(a)$ when $\theta = 0.2$ and $\theta_R = 0.25$.

be to choose the retention level which gives the greater expected profit, and this is achieved when $a = 0.5480$. This follows since the insurer's expected profit per unit time is

$$c^* - a\lambda E[X] = (\theta - \theta_R(1 - a))\,\lambda E[X],$$

which is clearly an increasing function of a.

Figures 9.2 and 9.3 illustrate two possible shapes that the net of reinsurance adjustment coefficient can take as a function of the proportion retained, a. A third possible shape is that $R(a)$ is an increasing function of a. For example, if we change the value of θ in Example 9.2 from 0.2 to 0.05, then we find that

$$R(a) = \frac{1}{a} - \frac{1}{1.25a - 0.2}$$

for $a \in (0.8, 1]$, and this function is shown in Figure 9.4.

In this case the cost of reinsurance outweighs the reduction in claim variability caused by reinsurance. In particular, the insurer's premium loading factor, net of reinsurance, is small. This net loading factor can be calculated by writing c^* as $(1 + \theta_N)a\lambda E[X]$ where θ_N is the net loading factor. Thus,

$$c^* = (1 + \theta - (1 + \theta_R)(1 - a))\,\lambda E[X] = (1 + \theta_N)a\lambda E[X]$$

yields

$$\theta_N = \theta_R - \frac{\theta_R - \theta}{a}.$$

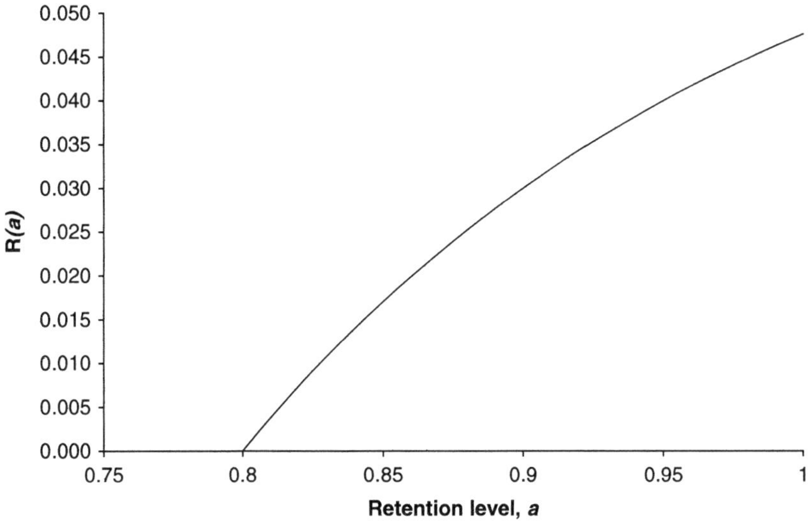

Figure 9.4 $R(a)$ when $\theta = 0.05$ and $\theta_R = 0.25$.

Table 9.2 *Optimal proportions retained.*

	$\theta = 0.1$, $\theta_R = 0.15$	$\theta = 0.1$, $\theta_R = 0.2$	$\theta = 0.2$, $\theta_R = 0.3$
$u = 20$	0.6547	0.9799	0.6356
$u = 40$	0.6494	0.9680	0.6306
$u = 60$	0.6476	0.9641	0.6290
$u = 80$	0.6468	0.9622	0.6281
$u = 100$	0.6462	0.9610	0.6276
$R(a)$	0.6442	0.9564	0.6257

Thus, when $\theta_R = \theta$, $\theta_N = \theta$, and when $\theta_R > \theta$, θ_N increases with a. In particular, when $\theta = 0.05$ and $\theta_R = 0.25$, θ_N increases from 0 when $a = 0.8$ to $0.05 = \theta$ when $a = 1$.

In all our numerical illustrations so far in this section, we have considered exponential individual claim amounts, where the mean individual claim amount is 1. For this individual claim amount distribution it follows from formula (7.11) that under proportional reinsurance with proportion retained a, the ultimate ruin probability for the process $\{U^*(t)\}_{t\geq 0}$ is

$$\frac{\lambda a}{c^*} \exp\left\{-\left(\frac{1}{a} - \frac{\lambda}{c^*}\right)u\right\}, \tag{9.9}$$

which can be treated as a function of a. In particular, we can find the value of a that minimises this ultimate ruin probability for a given value of u. Table 9.2 shows values of a that minimise expression (9.9) for a range of values of u and different combinations of θ and θ_R. In the final row of the table, the value of a that maximises $R(a)$ is shown. From these values we can say that choosing a to maximise the net of reinsurance adjustment coefficient is a reasonable proxy to choosing a to minimise the ultimate ruin probability, at least for large values of u.

9.3.3 Excess of Loss Reinsurance

We now consider the situation when the insurer effects excess of loss reinsurance with retention level M. In this case the same ideas that apply to proportional reinsurance also apply. To illustrate ideas, for the remainder of this section let the individual claim amount distribution be exponential with mean 1. Then

$$\begin{aligned} c^* &= (1+\theta)\lambda - (1+\theta_R)\lambda \int_M^\infty (x-M)e^{-x}dx \\ &= \lambda\left(1+\theta-(1+\theta_R)e^{-M}\right), \end{aligned}$$

and condition (9.7) gives

$$\lambda\left(1+\theta-(1+\theta_R)e^{-M}\right) > \lambda\left(\int_0^M xe^{-x}dx + Me^{-M}\right) = \lambda\left(1-e^{-M}\right),$$

which leads to $M > \log(\theta_R/\theta)$ as the condition for the minimum retention level. Further, the net of reinsurance premium loading factor is given by

$$c^* = (1+\theta_N)\lambda\left(1-e^{-M}\right) = \lambda\left(1+\theta-(1+\theta_R)e^{-M}\right),$$

which gives

$$\theta_N = \frac{\theta - \theta_R e^{-M}}{1-e^{-M}},$$

and θ_N increases from 0 when $M = \log(\theta_R/\theta)$ to θ as $M \to \infty$. Thus, under excess of loss reinsurance we have the same situation as under proportional reinsurance, namely a minimum retention level which depends on the relative values of θ and θ_R, and a net of reinsurance loading factor which increases from 0 to θ as the insurer moves from the minimum to the maximum retention level.

Now let the net of reinsurance adjustment coefficient be denoted by $R(M)$. Then, adapting equation (9.5), we have

$$1+\left(1+\theta-(1+\theta_R)e^{-M}\right)R(M) = \frac{1-R(M)e^{-(1-R(M))M}}{1-R(M)},$$

an equation which must be solved numerically for $R(M)$ for a given value of M. Figure 9.5 shows $R(M)$ when $\theta = \theta_R = 0.1$. This figure has the same characteristics as Figure 9.2. The reason for this is that the net of reinsurance premium loading is 0.1 for all values of M. In the case when $M = 0$, the insurer cedes the entire risk to the reinsurer and $\lim_{M\to 0^+} R(M) = \infty$. As M increases, the insurer's share of each individual claim increases and $R(M)$ decreases to a limiting value of 0.09091 as $M \to \infty$. Figure 9.6 shows three examples of what happens when $\theta < \theta_R$. Here $\theta = 0.1$ and θ_R takes the values $0.15, 0.25$ and 0.35. For each of these values of θ_R, there is an optimal value of M that maximises $R(M)$. As θ_R increases, the optimal value of M increases and the value of $R(M)$ at the optimal M decreases. This is in line with the examples on proportional reinsurance. As the cost of reinsurance increases, the insurer must retain a greater part of the risk in order to maximise the net of reinsurance adjustment coefficient.

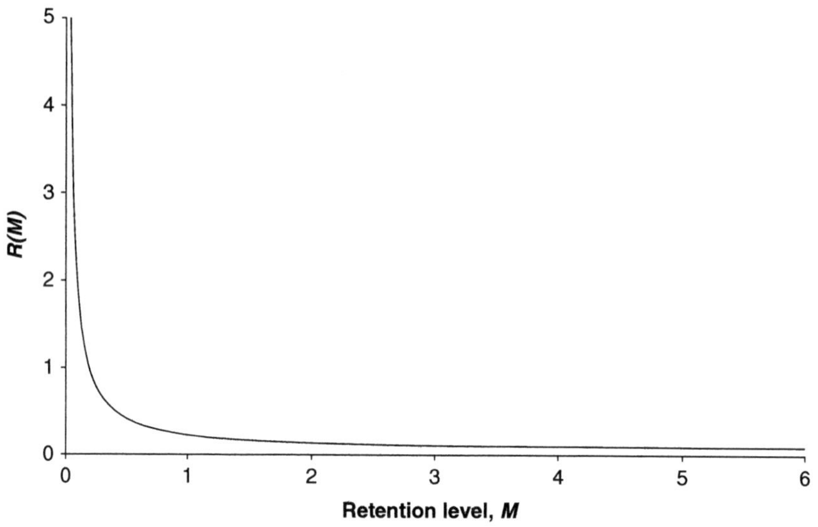

Figure 9.5 $R(M)$ when $\theta = \theta_R = 0.1$.

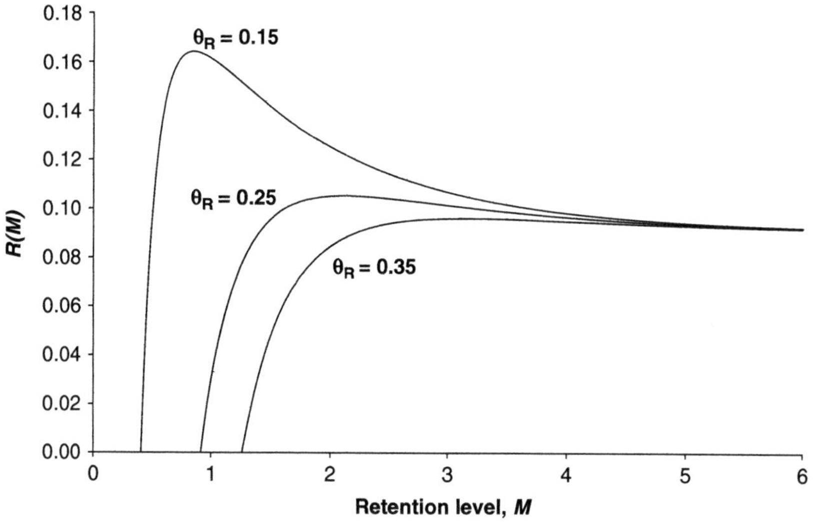

Figure 9.6 $R(M)$ when $\theta = 0.1$ and θ_R varies.

9.3.4 De Vylder Approximations

In the previous section we used the adjustment coefficient as a proxy for the ruin probability, and found optimal retention levels by maximising the adjustment coefficient. A disadvantage of this approach is that the optimal retention level is independent of the initial surplus, u. In this section we address this issue by approximating the ultimate ruin probability when there is reinsurance. Our objective is to find the retention level that minimises our approximation to the ultimate ruin probability.

In Chapter 7 we introduced De Vylder's approximation to the ultimate ruin probability. This approximation can be applied provided that the first three moments of the individual claim amount distribution exist, and the parameters of the approximation are expressed in terms of these three moments, the Poisson parameter and the premium income.

We can extend De Vylder's approximation to include the situation when the insurer has effected reinsurance. The parameters for De Vylder's approximation are given in equations (7.24), (7.27) and (7.28). All that we need to do with these equations is replace the moments, m_k for $k = 1, 2, 3$, by the moments of the net of reinsurance individual claim amount distribution, which we denote by μ_k for $k = 1, 2, 3$, and replace the premium income, c, by the net of reinsurance premium income, c^*. The parameters of De Vylder's approximation will then be functions of the retention level, as will the formula for the ultimate ruin probability. Thus, we should be able to differentiate this formula to find the retention level that minimises De Vylder's approximation to the ultimate ruin probability. However, it is usually the case that differentiation is a very tedious task. By contrast, it is very straightforward to calculate De Vylder approximations under reinsurance, and to solve numerically for the optimal retention level. This is the approach we follow.

Throughout this section we illustrate ideas when the individual claim amount distribution is

$$F(x) = 1 - \frac{2}{3}e^{-2x} - \frac{1}{3}e^{-x/2}$$

for $x \geq 0$, and the first three moments of this distribution are 1, 3 and 16.5. Further, the Poisson parameter is $\lambda = 1$ throughout.

Proportional Reinsurance

We first consider De Vylder approximations under proportional reinsurance, with proportion retained a. In this setting, $\mu_k = a^k m_k$ for $k = 1, 2, 3$, and so from (7.27),

$$\tilde{\alpha} = \frac{3\,\mu_2}{\mu_3} = \frac{3\,m_2}{a\,m_3} = \frac{6}{11a},$$

from (7.28)

$$\tilde{\lambda} = \frac{9\lambda\,\mu_2^3}{2\,\mu_3^2} = \frac{9\lambda m_2^3}{2\,m_3^2} = \frac{54}{121},$$

Table 9.3 *Optimal proportions retained.*

	$\theta = 0.1$, $\theta_R = 0.15$	$\theta = 0.1$, $\theta_R = 0.2$	$\theta = 0.2$, $\theta_R = 0.3$
$u = 20$	0.659 (0.659)	0.991 (0.992)	0.637 (0.636)
$u = 40$	0.649 (0.649)	0.969 (0.969)	0.627 (0.627)
$u = 60$	0.646 (0.646)	0.962 (0.962)	0.624 (0.624)
$u = 80$	0.644 (0.644)	0.959 (0.958)	0.623 (0.622)
$u = 100$	0.644 (0.643)	0.957 (0.956)	0.622 (0.621)
$R(a)$	0.639	0.948	0.617

and from (7.24)

$$\tilde{c} = c^* - \lambda\,\mu_1 + \frac{\tilde{\lambda}}{\tilde{\alpha}},$$

where, from (9.3),

$$\begin{aligned} c^* &= (1+\theta)\lambda\, m_1 - (1+\theta_R)\lambda\,(1-a)\, m_1 \\ &= (1+\theta) - (1+\theta_R)(1-a), \end{aligned}$$

so that

$$\tilde{c} = (1+\theta) - (1+\theta_R)(1-a) - a + \frac{9a}{11}.$$

This leads to the De Vylder approximation

$$\psi(u) \approx \frac{9a}{11\,\tilde{c}} \exp\left\{-\left(\frac{6}{11a} - \frac{54}{121\,\tilde{c}}\right)u\right\}.$$

While it is possible to find the value of a that minimises this expression, it is simpler to calculate this expression for a set of values of a between $1 - \theta/\theta_R$ and 1. In the subsequent analysis, we compute approximations for values of a that are integer multiples of 0.001. Table 9.3 shows values of a that minimise the De Vylder approximation to the ultimate ruin probability for the same combinations of θ and θ_R and values of u as in Table 9.2. It is also possible to compute the exact ruin probability in this case, and values of a that minimise the exact ruin probability are shown in parentheses. The final row shows the values of a which maximise the adjustment coefficient. We can see that the De Vylder approximations are very good and, in these illustrations, provide a better solution for the optimal retention level than maximising the adjustment coefficient.

Table 9.4 *Optimal excess of loss retention levels.*

	$\theta = 0.1$, $\theta_R = 0.15$	$\theta = 0.1$, $\theta_R = 0.2$	$\theta = 0.2$, $\theta_R = 0.3$
$u = 5$	1.022	2.132	0.995
$u = 10$	1.001	2.032	0.975
$u = 15$	0.994	2.001	0.969
$u = 20$	0.991	1.987	0.966
$u = 25$	0.989	1.978	0.964
$R(M)$	0.982	1.945	0.958

Excess of Loss Reinsurance

We now consider excess of loss reinsurance. In this case the moments of the individual claim amount distribution, net of reinsurance, are given by

$$\mu_k = \frac{2\,k!}{3 \times 2^k}\left(1 - \sum_{j=0}^{k} e^{-2M}\frac{(2M)^j}{j!}\right) + \frac{2^k \times k!}{3}\left(1 - \sum_{j=0}^{k} e^{-M/2}\frac{(M/2)^j}{j!}\right)$$
$$+ M^k\left(\frac{2}{3}e^{-2M} + \frac{1}{3}e^{-M/2}\right).$$

Table 9.4 shows values of M that minimise the De Vylder approximation to the ultimate ruin probability for the same combinations of θ and θ_R as in Table 9.2, but for smaller values of u as the minimum ruin probabilities are much smaller under excess of loss reinsurance compared with proportional reinsurance. In this case it is not possible to compute the exact ruin probability, but we can solve numerically for the adjustment coefficient, and the final row in Table 9.4 shows the values of M which maximise the adjustment coefficient. The pattern in Table 9.4 is similar to that in Table 9.3. In particular, for each combination of θ and θ_R, the optimal retention levels decrease with u, and these optimal retention levels are greater than the retention level that maximises the adjustment coefficient. Further, for the combination $\theta = 0.1$ and $\theta_R = 0.2$ the optimal retention levels are higher than for the other two combinations of θ and θ_R, reflecting the relatively higher cost of reinsurance.

9.4 Notes and References

The problems discussed in Section 9.2 are standard applications of utility theory to actuarial problems. See, for example, Borch (1990). Examples of papers discussing reinsurance and the adjustment coefficient are Waters (1983) and Centeno (1986). Table 9.2 is based on table 1 of Dickson and Waters (1996).

9.5 Exercises

1. In identity (9.2), find M when $X \sim \gamma(2, 0.01)$ and $h(x) = x/2$.
2. Aggregate claims from a risk have a compound Poisson distribution with Poisson parameter 100, and individual claim amounts are exponentially distributed with mean 100. The insurer of this risk decides to effect proportional reinsurance, and the reinsurance premium is calculated according to the expected value principle with a loading factor of θ_R. Find an expression for the proportion retained that maximises the insurer's expected utility of wealth with respect to the utility function $u(x) = -\exp\{-\beta x\}$, where $0 < \beta < 0.01$.
3. Aggregate claims from a risk have a compound Poisson distribution with Poisson parameter 100, and individual claim amounts are exponentially distributed with mean 100. The insurer of this risk decides to effect excess of loss reinsurance, and the reinsurance premium is calculated according to the variance principle with parameter 0.5.
   (a) Show that the reinsurance premium when the retention level is M is
   $$P(M) = 101 \times 10^4 \times e^{-0.01M}.$$
   (b) Find the retention level that maximises the insurer's expected utility of wealth with respect to the utility function
   $$u(x) = -\exp\{-0.005x\}.$$
4. Aggregate claims in a year from a risk have a compound Poisson distribution with parameters λ and $F(x) = 1 - e^{-\alpha x}$, $x \geq 0$. The insurer of this risk decides to effect excess of loss reinsurance with retention level M, and the reinsurance premium is calculated by the Esscher principle with parameter $h < \alpha$.
   (a) Show that the reinsurance premium is
   $$\frac{\lambda\alpha e^{-\alpha M}}{(\alpha - h)^2}.$$
   (b) Let M^* be the retention level that maximises the insurer's expected utility of year end wealth with respect to the utility function $u(x) = -\exp\{-\beta x\}$, where $0 < \beta < \alpha$. Show that
   $$M^* = \frac{1}{\beta}\log\left(\frac{\alpha^2}{(\alpha - h)^2}\right).$$
5. Aggregate claims from a risk have a compound Poisson distribution with Poisson parameter λ, and the individual claim amount distribution is exponential with mean $1/\beta$. The insurer of this risk effects proportional

reinsurance with proportion retained a. The premium for the risk and the reinsurance premium are calculated with loading factors of θ and θ_R respectively, where $\theta < \theta_R$. Show that

$$R(a) = \frac{\beta}{a} \frac{\theta - \theta_R(1-a)}{1 + \theta - (1+\theta_R)(1-a)}$$

for $1 - \theta/\theta_R < a \leq 1$.

6. Aggregate claims from a risk have a compound Poisson distribution with Poisson parameter λ, and the individual claim amount distribution is $\gamma(2, 0.02)$. The insurer calculates the premium for this risk with a loading factor of 20%, and can effect proportional reinsurance. The insurer has a choice between retaining 60% or 80% of each claim, and in each case the reinsurance premium is calculated with a loading factor of 25%. Which retention level should the insurer choose to maximise its net adjustment coefficient?
7. Aggregate claims from a risk have a compound Poisson distribution with Poisson parameter λ, and the individual claim amount distribution is $Pa(3, 200)$. The insurer calculates the premium for this risk with a loading factor of 10% and effects excess of loss reinsurance with retention level M. The reinsurance premium is calculated with a loading factor of 15%.
   (a) Find an expression for the insurer's net of reinsurance loading factor in terms of M.
   (b) What is the minimum value of M such that the insurer's net of reinsurance loading factor is positive?
   (c) Give the equation satisfied by the insurer's net of reinsurance adjustment coefficient.
8. The aggregate claims process for a risk is a compound Poisson process with Poisson parameter 1, and individual claim amounts are gamma distributed with each parameter equal to 2. The insurer's premium income per unit time is 1.2. The insurer has effected proportional reinsurance with proportion retained a, and the reinsurance premium is calculated with a loading factor of 25%.
   (a) Find the minimum value of a such that the insurer's expected profit per unit time, net of reinsurance, is greater than 0.
   (b) Show that De Vylder's approximation to the probability of ultimate ruin under this proportional reinsurance arrangement is
   $$\frac{9a}{11a - 0.4} \exp\left\{\frac{-(3a - 0.6)u}{a(11a - 0.4)}\right\}.$$
   (c) To three decimal places, find the value of a that minimises this expression when $u = 15$.

Appendix

In Chapter 8 we showed that there exists a unique positive solution, ρ, of Lundberg's fundamental equation, so that

$$\lambda + \delta - c\rho = \lambda f^*(\rho).$$

In order to obtain the Laplace transform identity from Section 8.6.2, what we need is an expression in terms of δ for $e^{-\rho t}$. The way in which we find this is to apply Lagrange's implicit function theorem, which states that for any analytic function h,

$$h(\rho) = h\left(\frac{\delta+\lambda}{c}\right) + \sum_{n=1}^{\infty}(-1)^n \frac{(\lambda/c)^n}{n!}\frac{d^{n-1}}{dz^{n-1}}\left\{h'(z)\int_0^\infty e^{-zx} f^{n*}(x)\,dx\right\}\Bigg|_{z=(\delta+\lambda)/c}.$$

Setting $h(z) = e^{-zt}$, so that $h'(z) = -te^{-zt}$, we have

$$\begin{aligned}
e^{-\rho t} &= e^{-(\delta+\lambda)t/c} \\
&\quad + \sum_{n=1}^{\infty}(-1)^n \frac{(\lambda/c)^n}{n!}\left\{\frac{d^{n-1}}{dz^{n-1}}(-t)\int_0^\infty e^{-z(x+t)} f^{n*}(x)\,dx\right\}\Bigg|_{z=(\delta+\lambda)/c} \\
&= e^{-(\delta+\lambda)t/c} \\
&\quad + \sum_{n=1}^{\infty}(-1)^n \frac{(\lambda/c)^n}{n!}\left\{(-1)^n t\int_0^\infty (x+t)^{n-1} e^{-z(x+t)} f^{n*}(x)\,dx\right\}\Bigg|_{z=(\delta+\lambda)/c} \\
&= e^{-(\delta+\lambda)t/c} \\
&\quad + \sum_{n=1}^{\infty}\frac{(\lambda/c)^n}{n!}\, t\int_0^\infty (x+t)^{n-1} e^{-(\delta+\lambda)(x+t)/c} f^{n*}(x)\,dx.
\end{aligned}$$

For an arbitrary function b, we then have

$$\begin{aligned}
b^*(\rho) &= \int_0^\infty e^{-\rho t}\, b(t)\,dt \\
&= \int_0^\infty e^{-(\delta+\lambda)t/c}\, b(t)\,dt
\end{aligned}$$

$$
\begin{aligned}
&+\sum_{n=1}^{\infty}\frac{(\lambda/c)^n}{n!}\int_0^{\infty} t\int_0^{\infty}(x+t)^{n-1}e^{-(\delta+\lambda)(x+t)/c}f^{n*}(x)\,dx\,b(t)\,dt\\
&= c\int_0^{\infty} e^{-(\delta+\lambda)r}\,b(cr)\,dr\\
&\quad+\sum_{n=1}^{\infty}\frac{(\lambda/c)^n}{n!}\int_0^{\infty} t\int_{t/c}^{\infty} c^n r^{n-1}e^{-(\delta+\lambda)r}f^{n*}(cr-t)\,dr\,b(t)\,dt\\
&= c\int_0^{\infty} e^{-(\delta+\lambda)r}\,b(cr)\,dr\\
&\quad+\sum_{n=1}^{\infty}\frac{\lambda^n}{n!}\int_0^{\infty} r^{n-1}e^{-(\delta+\lambda)r}\int_0^{cr} tf^{n*}(cr-t)\,b(t)\,dt\,dr\\
&= \int_0^{\infty} e^{-\delta t}\left(ce^{-\lambda t}b(ct)+\sum_{n=1}^{\infty}\frac{\lambda^n t^{n-1}}{n!}e^{-\lambda t}\int_0^{ct} yf^{n*}(ct-y)\,b(y)\,dy\right)dt\\
&= \int_0^{\infty} e^{-\delta t}\,h(t)\,dt\\
&= h^*(\delta),
\end{aligned}
$$

where

$$
h(t) = ce^{-\lambda t}b(ct)+\sum_{n=1}^{\infty}\frac{\lambda^n t^{n-1}}{n!}e^{-\lambda t}\int_0^{ct} yf^{n*}(ct-y)\,b(y)\,dy.
$$

Solutions to Exercises

Chapter 1

1. From the fact that $\sum_{x=1}^{\infty} \Pr(X = x) = 1$, we have

$$\sum_{x=1}^{\infty} \frac{\theta^x}{x} = -\log(1-\theta),$$

and hence

$$M_X(t) = \sum_{x=1}^{\infty} e^{tx} \frac{-1}{\log(1-\theta)} \frac{\theta^x}{x} = \frac{-1}{\log(1-\theta)} \sum_{x=1}^{\infty} \frac{\left(\theta e^t\right)^x}{x} = \frac{\log(1-\theta e^t)}{\log(1-\theta)}$$

provided that $\theta e^t < 1$ or, equivalently, $t < -\log\theta$. The first two moments can be found by differentiating $M_X(t)$. First,

$$\frac{d}{dt} M_X(t) = \frac{1}{\log(1-\theta)} \frac{-\theta e^t}{1-\theta e^t} = \frac{1}{\log(1-\theta)} \frac{-\theta}{e^{-t}-\theta}$$

gives

$$E[X] = \frac{-1}{\log(1-\theta)} \frac{\theta}{1-\theta},$$

and

$$\frac{d^2}{dt^2} M_X(t) = \frac{1}{\log(1-\theta)} \frac{-\theta e^{-t}}{\left(e^{-t}-\theta\right)^2}$$

gives

$$E[X^2] = \frac{-1}{\log(1-\theta)} \frac{\theta}{(1-\theta)^2},$$

and hence

$$V[X] = \frac{-1}{\log(1-\theta)} \left(\frac{\theta}{(1-\theta)^2} + \frac{1}{\log(1-\theta)} \left(\frac{0}{1-\theta} \right)^2 \right).$$

Alternatively,

$$E[X] = \sum_{x=1}^{\infty} x \Pr(X = x) = \frac{-1}{\log(1-\theta)} \sum_{x=1}^{\infty} \theta^x = \frac{-1}{\log(1-\theta)} \frac{\theta}{1-\theta}$$

and

$$E[X^2] = \frac{-1}{\log(1-\theta)} \sum_{x=1}^{\infty} x\theta^x = \frac{-1}{\log(1-\theta)} \frac{\theta}{(1-\theta)^2}.$$

2. As

$$\int_0^1 f(x)dx = 1$$

it follows that

$$\int_0^1 x^{\alpha-1}(1-x)^{\beta-1}dx = \frac{\Gamma(\alpha)\Gamma(\beta)}{\Gamma(\alpha+\beta)},$$

and hence

$$\begin{aligned} E[X^n] &= \frac{\Gamma(\alpha+\beta)}{\Gamma(\alpha)\Gamma(\beta)} \int_0^1 x^{n+\alpha-1}(1-x)^{\beta-1}dx \\ &= \frac{\Gamma(\alpha+\beta)}{\Gamma(\alpha)\Gamma(\beta)} \frac{\Gamma(n+\alpha)\Gamma(\beta)}{\Gamma(n+\alpha+\beta)} \\ &= \frac{\Gamma(\alpha+\beta)\Gamma(n+\alpha)}{\Gamma(\alpha)\Gamma(n+\alpha+\beta)}. \end{aligned}$$

In particular,

$$E[X] = \frac{\Gamma(\alpha+\beta)\Gamma(1+\alpha)}{\Gamma(\alpha)\Gamma(1+\alpha+\beta)} = \frac{\alpha}{\alpha+\beta}$$

and

$$E[X^2] = \frac{\Gamma(\alpha+\beta)\Gamma(2+\alpha)}{\Gamma(\alpha)\Gamma(2+\alpha+\beta)} = \frac{\alpha(\alpha+1)}{(\alpha+\beta)(\alpha+\beta+1)},$$

giving

$$V[X] = \frac{\alpha\beta}{(\alpha+\beta)^2(\alpha+\beta+1)}.$$

3. (a) We have

$$F(x) = \int_0^x c\gamma y^{\gamma-1} \exp\{-cy^\gamma\}dy,$$

and the substitution $z = cy^\gamma$ gives

$$F(x) = \int_0^{cx^\gamma} \exp\{-z\}dz = 1 - \exp\{-cx^\gamma\}.$$

(b) As $Y = X^\gamma$, we have

$$\Pr(Y \le y) = \Pr(X \le y^{1/\gamma}) = 1 - \exp\{-cy\}.$$

Further,

$$E[X^n] = E[Y^{n/\gamma}] = c\int_0^\infty y^{n/\gamma} e^{-cy} dy = c\frac{\Gamma(1+n/\gamma)}{c^{1+n/\gamma}} = \frac{\Gamma(1+n/\gamma)}{c^{n/\gamma}}.$$

4. We simply write the form of $\gamma_n(x+y)$, then use a binomial expansion. Then

$$\begin{aligned}
\gamma_n(x+y) &= \frac{\beta^n (x+y)^{n-1} e^{-\beta(x+y)}}{\Gamma(n)} \\
&= \frac{\beta^n e^{-\beta(x+y)}}{\Gamma(n)} \sum_{j=0}^{n-1} \frac{(n-1)!}{j!\,(n-1-j)!} x^{n-1-j} y^j \\
&= \frac{1}{\beta} \sum_{j=0}^{n-1} \frac{\beta^{n-j} x^{n-j-1} e^{-\beta x}}{(n-1-j)!} \frac{\beta^{j+1} y^j e^{-\beta y}}{j!} \\
&= \frac{1}{\beta} \sum_{j=1}^{n} \gamma_{n-j+1}(x)\, \gamma_j(y).
\end{aligned}$$

5. When $X \sim Pa(\alpha, \lambda)$, the kth moment is

$$E[X^k] = \int_0^\infty x^k \frac{\alpha\lambda^\alpha}{(\lambda+x)^{\alpha+1}} dx,$$

and by integrating the generalised Pareto density, we get

$$\int_0^\infty \frac{\lambda^\alpha x^{k-1}}{(\lambda+x)^{k+\alpha}} dx = \frac{\Gamma(\alpha)\Gamma(k)}{\Gamma(\alpha+k)}.$$

Then

$$\begin{aligned}
E[X] &= \int_0^\infty x \frac{\alpha\lambda^\alpha}{(\lambda+x)^{\alpha+1}} dx = \alpha\lambda \int_0^\infty \frac{x\lambda^{\alpha-1}}{(\lambda+x)^{2+(\alpha-1)}} dx \\
&= \alpha\lambda \frac{\Gamma(\alpha-1)\Gamma(2)}{\Gamma(\alpha+1)} = \frac{\lambda}{\alpha-1}.
\end{aligned}$$

Similarly,

$$\begin{aligned}
E[X^2] &= \int_0^\infty x^2 \frac{\alpha\lambda^\alpha}{(\lambda+x)^{\alpha+1}} dx = \alpha\lambda^2 \int_0^\infty \frac{x^2\lambda^{\alpha-2}}{(\lambda+x)^{3+(\alpha-2)}} dx \\
&= \alpha\lambda^2 \frac{\Gamma(\alpha-2)\Gamma(3)}{\Gamma(\alpha+1)} = \frac{2\lambda^2}{(\alpha-1)(\alpha-2)}
\end{aligned}$$

and

$$E[X^3] = \alpha\lambda^3 \frac{\Gamma(\alpha-3)\Gamma(4)}{\Gamma(\alpha+1)} = \frac{6\lambda^3}{(\alpha-1)(\alpha-2)(\alpha-3)}.$$

6. When $X \sim Pa(\alpha, \lambda)$,

$$E[\min(X, M)] = \int_0^M \frac{x\alpha\lambda^\alpha}{(\lambda + x)^{\alpha+1}} dx + M\left(\frac{\lambda}{\lambda + M}\right)^\alpha,$$

and writing $x = \lambda + x - \lambda$ we get

$$\begin{aligned}
&\int_0^M \frac{x\alpha\lambda^\alpha}{(\lambda + x)^{\alpha+1}} dx \\
&= \int_0^M \frac{\alpha\lambda^\alpha}{(\lambda + x)^{\alpha}} dx - \lambda \int_0^M \frac{\alpha\lambda^\alpha}{(\lambda + x)^{\alpha+1}} dx \\
&= \frac{\alpha\lambda}{\alpha - 1} \int_0^M \frac{(\alpha - 1)\,\lambda^{\alpha-1}}{(\lambda + x)^{\alpha}} dx - \lambda\left[1 - \left(\frac{\lambda}{\lambda + M}\right)^\alpha\right] \\
&= \frac{\alpha\lambda}{\alpha - 1}\left[1 - \left(\frac{\lambda}{\lambda + M}\right)^{\alpha-1}\right] - \lambda\left[1 - \left(\frac{\lambda}{\lambda + M}\right)^\alpha\right].
\end{aligned}$$

Thus,

$$\begin{aligned}
&E[\min(X, M)] \\
&= \frac{\alpha\lambda}{\alpha - 1}\left[1 - \left(\frac{\lambda}{\lambda + M}\right)^{\alpha-1}\right] - \lambda\left[1 - \left(\frac{\lambda}{\lambda + M}\right)^\alpha\right] + M\left(\frac{\lambda}{\lambda + M}\right)^\alpha \\
&= \frac{\alpha\lambda}{\alpha - 1}\left[1 - \left(\frac{\lambda}{\lambda + M}\right)^{\alpha-1}\right] - \lambda + \frac{\lambda^\alpha}{(\lambda + M)^{\alpha-1}} \\
&= \frac{\alpha\lambda}{\alpha - 1}\left[1 - \left(\frac{\lambda}{\lambda + M}\right)^{\alpha-1}\right] - \lambda\left[1 - \left(\frac{\lambda}{\lambda + M}\right)^{\alpha-1}\right] \\
&= \frac{\lambda}{\alpha - 1}\left[1 - \left(\frac{\lambda}{\lambda + M}\right)^{\alpha-1}\right].
\end{aligned}$$

7. The moment generating function is

$$M_X(t) = \int_{-\infty}^{\infty} \exp\{tx\} \frac{1}{\sigma\sqrt{2\pi}} \exp\left\{\frac{-(x - \mu)^2}{2\sigma^2}\right\} dx$$

and

$$\begin{aligned}
tx - \frac{(x - \mu)^2}{2\sigma^2} &= \frac{-1}{2\sigma^2}\left(x^2 - 2\mu x + \mu^2 - 2tx\sigma^2\right) \\
&= \frac{-1}{2\sigma^2}\left(x^2 - 2(\mu + \sigma^2 t)x + \mu^2\right) \\
&= \frac{-1}{2\sigma^2}\left(\left(x - (\mu + \sigma^2 t)\right)^2 - 2\mu\sigma^2 t - \sigma^4 t^2\right) \\
&= \mu t + \tfrac{1}{2}\sigma^2 t^2 - \frac{1}{2\sigma^2}\left(x - (\mu + \sigma^2 t)\right)^2.
\end{aligned}$$

Thus,

$$M_X(t) = \exp\left\{\mu t + \tfrac{1}{2}\sigma^2 t^2\right\} \int_{-\infty}^{\infty} \frac{1}{\sigma\sqrt{2\pi}} \exp\left\{\frac{-(x-(\mu+\sigma^2 t))^2}{2\sigma^2}\right\} dx$$
$$= \exp\left\{\mu t + \tfrac{1}{2}\sigma^2 t^2\right\}$$

since the integrand is the density function of a $N(\mu+\sigma^2 t, \sigma^2)$ random variable.

Then

$$\frac{d}{dt} M_X(t) = (\mu + \sigma^2 t) M_X(t)$$

gives $E[X] = \mu$, and

$$\frac{d^2}{dt^2} M_X(t) = \sigma^2 M_X(t) + (\mu + \sigma^2 t)\frac{d}{dt} M_X(t),$$

so that $E[X^2] = \sigma^2 + \mu^2$ and hence $V[X] = \sigma^2$.

8. (a) $\Pr(X \leq 30) = F(30) = 0.625$.
   (b) $\Pr(X = 40) = F(40) - F(40^-) = 0.25$.
   (c) As $\Pr(X = 20) = 0.5$, and $F'(x) = 1/80$ for $20 < x < 40$,

$$E[X] = 20 \times 0.5 + \tfrac{1}{80} \int_{20}^{40} x dx + 40 \times 0.25 = 27.5.$$

   (d) $V[X] = 77.083$ since

$$E[X^2] = 20^2 \times 0.5 + \tfrac{1}{80} \int_{20}^{40} x^2 dx + 40^2 \times 0.25 = 833.33.$$

9. As the mean and variance are 100 and 30,000 respectively,

$$\exp\left\{\mu + \tfrac{1}{2}\sigma^2\right\} = 100$$

and

$$\exp\{2\mu + \sigma^2\}\left(\exp\{\sigma^2\} - 1\right) = 30,000,$$

so that

$$100^2\left(\exp\{\sigma^2\} - 1\right) = 30,000,$$

giving $\sigma^2 = 1.3863$ and $\mu = 3.9120$.

(a) From the solution to Example 1.4 with $M = 250$ and $n = 1$,

$$E[\min(X, 250)] = \exp\left\{\mu + \tfrac{1}{2}\sigma^2\right\}\Phi\left(\frac{\log 250 - \mu - \sigma^2}{\sigma}\right)$$
$$+250\left(1 - \Phi\left(\frac{\log 250 - \mu}{\sigma}\right)\right)$$
$$= 100\Phi(0.1895) + 250\,(1 - \Phi(1.3669))$$
$$= 78.97.$$

(b) As $X = \min(X, 250) + \max(0, X - 250)$, we have

$$E[\max(0, X - 250)] = 21.03.$$

(c) We need $E[\min(X, 250)^2]$, which, from the solution to Example 1.4 with $M = 250$ and $n = 2$, is

$$\begin{aligned}
&\exp\left\{2\mu + 2\sigma^2\right\} \Phi\left(\frac{\log 250 - \mu - 2\sigma^2}{\sigma}\right) \\
&+250^2\left(1 - \Phi\left(\frac{\log 250 - \mu}{\sigma}\right)\right) \\
&= 40,000\Phi\left(-0.9879\right) + 250^2\left(1 - \Phi(1.3669)\right) \\
&= 11,828.11.
\end{aligned}$$

Hence $V[\min(X, 250)] = 5,591.59$.

(d) We have

$$E[X|X > 250] = E[X - 250|X > 250] + 250$$

and

$$\begin{aligned}
E[X - 250|X > 250] &= \frac{E[\max(0, X - 250)]}{\Pr(X > 250)} \\
&= \frac{21.03}{0.0858} = 245.02,
\end{aligned}$$

giving $E[X|X > 250] = 495.02$.

10. (a) Let $S_n = \sum_{i=1}^{n} X_i$. Then $S_n \sim B(mn, q)$ since

$$E\left[\exp\{tS_n\}\right] = E\left[\exp\{tX_1\}\right]^n = \left(qe^t + 1 - q\right)^{mn}.$$

(b) The same argument gives $S_n \sim N(n\mu, n\sigma^2)$ since

$$\begin{aligned}
E\left[\exp\{tS_n\}\right] &= E\left[\exp\{tX_1\}\right]^n \\
&= \left(\exp\{\mu t + \tfrac{1}{2}\sigma^2 t^2\}\right)^n \\
&= \exp\{n\mu t + \tfrac{1}{2}n\sigma^2 t^2\}.
\end{aligned}$$

11. (a) Using the arguments in the previous question, the distribution of $S_4 = \sum_{i=1}^{4} X_i$ is $NB(4, 0.75)$ since

$$E\left[\exp\{tS_4\}\right] = E\left[\exp\{tX_1\}\right]^4 = \left(\frac{0.75}{1 - 0.25e^t}\right)^4.$$

Then

$$\begin{aligned}
\Pr(S_4 = 0) &= 0.75^4 = 0.3164,\\
\Pr(S_4 = 1) &= 4 \times 0.25 \times \Pr(S_4 = 0) = 0.3164,\\
\Pr(S_4 = 2) &= \frac{5}{2} \times 0.25 \times \Pr(S_4 = 1) = 0.1978,\\
\Pr(S_4 = 3) &= \frac{6}{3} \times 0.25 \times \Pr(S_4 = 2) = 0.0989,\\
\Pr(S_4 = 4) &= \frac{7}{4} \times 0.25 \times \Pr(S_4 = 3) = 0.0433.
\end{aligned}$$

(b) Using the recursion formula (1.18) with $n = 4$, $f_x = 0.75(0.25^x)$ for $x = 0, 1, 2, \ldots$, and $g_0 = 0.75^4 = 0.3164$, we have

$$\begin{aligned}
g_1 &= \frac{4}{3} 4 f_1 g_0 = 0.3164,\\
g_2 &= \frac{4}{3}\left(\frac{3}{2} f_1 g_1 + 4 f_2 g_0\right) = 0.1978,\\
g_3 &= \frac{4}{3}\left(\frac{2}{3} f_1 g_2 + \frac{7}{3} f_2 g_1 + 4 f_3 g_0\right) = 0.0989,\\
g_4 &= \frac{4}{3}\left(\frac{1}{4} f_1 g_3 + \frac{3}{2} f_2 g_2 + \frac{11}{4} f_3 g_1 + 4 f_4 g_0\right) = 0.0433.
\end{aligned}$$

12. The result follows by defining random variables $\{Y_i\}_{i=1}^n$ where $Y_i = X_i - m$ is distributed on $0, 1, 2, \ldots$. Now apply formula (1.18) to $\sum_{i=1}^n Y_i$. In particular, let $\hat{f}_x = \Pr(Y_1 = x)$ and $\hat{g}_x = \Pr(\sum_{i=1}^n Y_i = x)$ for $x = 0, 1, 2, \ldots$. Then $\hat{f}_x = f_{x+m}$ and $\hat{g}_x = g_{x+nm}$, giving

$$\hat{g}_0 = \hat{f}_0^n = f_m^n = g_{mn}\,.$$

For $x = 1, 2, 3, \ldots$,

$$\hat{g}_x = \frac{1}{\hat{f}_0} \sum_{j=1}^{x} \left((n+1)\frac{j}{x} - 1\right) \hat{f}_j \hat{g}_{x-j}\,,$$

giving

$$g_{x+nm} = \frac{1}{f_m} \sum_{j=1}^{x} \left((n+1)\frac{j}{x} - 1\right) f_{j+m} g_{x+nm-j}\,,$$

or, alternatively, for $r = mn+1, mn+2, mn+3, \ldots$,

$$g_r = \frac{1}{f_m} \sum_{j=1}^{r-mn} \left(\frac{(n+1)j}{r - mn} - 1\right) f_{j+m} g_{r-j}\,.$$

Chapter 2

1. We have

$$u'(x) = 1 - x/\beta > 0$$

and

$$u''(x) = -1/\beta < 0,$$

giving

$$r(x) = 1/(\beta - x),$$

which is clearly increasing in x.

2. (a) We need to show that $u'(x) > 0$ and $u''(x) < 0$. These conditions are satisfied since

$$u'(x) = \frac{2}{3}x^{-1/3} > 0$$

and

$$u''(x) = \frac{-2}{9}x^{-4/3} < 0.$$

(b) If the individual does not insure, the individual's resulting wealth is $250-X$, and hence

$$E[u(250 - X)] = \tfrac{1}{200}\int_0^{200} (250 - x)^{2/3} dx = 27.728$$

since X has density function $\frac{1}{200}$ in the interval $(0, 200)$. If the individual insures, the resulting wealth is

$$250 - 85 - Y = 165 - Y,$$

where $Y = \min(X, 20)$. Hence

$$\begin{aligned} E[u(165 - Y)] &= \tfrac{1}{200}\left[\int_0^{20} (165 - x)^{2/3} dx + \int_{20}^{200} 145^{2/3} dx\right] \\ &= 27.725. \end{aligned}$$

Hence, the individual will not purchase insurance cover as

$$E[u(250 - X)] > E[u(165 - Y)].$$

3. From equation (2.6), the minimum acceptable premium is Π where

$$\Pi = \tfrac{1}{0.002}\log M_X(0.002),$$

and as $X \sim N(10^6, 10^8)$,

$$M_X(0.002) = \exp\left\{10^6 \times 0.002 + \tfrac{1}{2}10^8 \times 0.002^2\right\},$$

giving $\Pi = 10^6 + 10^5 = 1.1 \times 10^6$.

4. (a) The investor chooses Share 1 if $E[u(AX_1)] > E[u(AX_2)]$. Now

$$E[u(AX_1)] = E\left[(AX_1)^{1/2}\right] = A^{1/2}E\left[X_1^{1/2}\right],$$

and so $E[u(AX_1)] > E[u(AX_2)]$ if and only if $E[X_1^{1/2}] > E[X_2^{1/2}]$, independent of A.

(b) Since $X_i \sim LN(\mu_i, \sigma_i)$, we have $E[X_i^{1/2}] = \exp\{\frac{1}{2}\mu_i + \frac{1}{8}\sigma_i^2\}$. Thus, $E[X_2^{1/2}] > E[X_1^{1/2}]$ when

$$\exp\left\{\tfrac{1}{2}0.09 + \tfrac{1}{8}0.02^2\right\} < \exp\left\{\tfrac{1}{2}0.08 + \tfrac{1}{8}\sigma_2^2\right\},$$

i.e. when $\sigma_2 > 0.201$.

(c) The condition $E[AX_1] = E[AX_2]$ implies $\mu_1 + \frac{1}{2}\sigma_1^2 = \mu_2 + \frac{1}{2}\sigma_2^2$ and, under this condition, $V[AX_1] < V[AX_2]$ implies $\sigma_1^2 < \sigma_2^2$ since

$$V[X_i] = E[X_i]^2(\exp\{\sigma_i^2\} - 1)$$

and $E[X_1] = E[X_2]$. The investor chooses Share 1 if

$$\tfrac{1}{2}\mu_1 + \tfrac{1}{8}\sigma_1^2 > \tfrac{1}{2}\mu_2 + \tfrac{1}{8}\sigma_2^2,$$

which gives $\sigma_1^2 < \sigma_2^2$. The investor is risk averse, and so prefers Share 1 which has the same expected accumulation as Share 2 but the lower variance of accumulation.

5. Again using equation (2.6), the minimum acceptable premium is Π where

$$\Pi = \frac{1}{0.005}\log M_Y(0.005)$$

and $Y = \max(0, X - 20)$. As $\Pr(Y = 0) = 1 - 0.2e^{-0.2} = 0.8363$ and Y has density function $0.2 \times 0.01e^{-0.01(x+20)}$ for $x > 0$,

$$\begin{aligned}
M_Y(0.005) &= \Pr(Y = 0) + 0.2\int_0^\infty e^{0.005x}0.01e^{-0.01(x+20)}dx \\
&= 0.8363 + 0.002e^{-0.2}\int_0^\infty e^{-0.005x}dx \\
&= 0.8363 + 0.002e^{-0.2}/0.005 \\
&= 1.16375,
\end{aligned}$$

giving $\Pi = 30.33$.

6. There are three possibilities: don't insure or effect one of the two insurance contracts. Consider first complete insurance cover. The individual's expected utility of wealth is then

$$u(10^6 - 120) = k\,\log(10^6 - 120) = 13.8154k.$$

Second, consider partial insurance. If hospitalisation occurs, the individual must pay the policy excess of 1,000. Thus, the expected utility of wealth is

$$0.99\,u(10^6) + 0.01\,u(10^6 - 1{,}000) = 13.8155k.$$

Third, with no insurance cover, the expected utility of wealth is

$$0.99\,u(10^6) + \int_{10,000}^{12,000} \frac{u(10^6 - x)}{2 \times 10^5}\,dx,$$

since X has density $1/(2 \times 10^5)$ over $(10,000,\ 12,000)$. Now

$$\begin{aligned}
\int_{10,000}^{12,000} \frac{u(10^6 - x)}{2 \times 10^5}\,dx &= k \int_{10,000}^{12,000} \frac{\log(10^6 - x)}{2 \times 10^5}\,dx \\
&= \frac{k}{2 \times 10^5} \int_{\log(10^6-12,000)}^{\log(10^6-10,000)} z\,e^z\,dz \\
&= \frac{k}{2 \times 10^5}\Big((10^6 - 10,000)\left(\log(10^6 - 10,000) - 1\right) \\
&\quad -(10^6 - 12,000)\left(\log(10^6 - 12,000) - 1\right)\Big) \\
&= 0.1380k.
\end{aligned}$$

So the expected utility of wealth is $13.8154k$, meaning that the individual would opt for the partial insurance cover.

Chapter 3

1. For the variance principle with parameter $\alpha > 0$,

$$\begin{aligned}
\Pi_{X_1+X_2} &= E[X_1 + X_2] + \alpha V[X_1 + X_2] \\
&= E[X_1] + E[X_2] + \alpha\,(V[X_1] + V[X_2] + 2Cov(X_1, X_2)) \\
&= \Pi_{X_1} + \Pi_{X_2} + 2\alpha Cov(X_1, X_2).
\end{aligned}$$

Hence $\Pi_{X_1+X_2} \le \Pi_{X_1} + \Pi_{X_2}$ if and only if $Cov(X_1, X_2) \le 0$.

2. (a) We have

$$\Pi_X = \sqrt{E[X^2]},$$

and as $X \sim \gamma(2, 2)$, $E[X^2] = 1.5$, so that

$$\Pi_X = \sqrt{1.5} = 1.225.$$

(b) Let $Y = X + 1$, where X is as in part (a). Then

$$E[Y^2] = E[X^2 + 2X + 1] = 4.5,$$

giving

$$\Pi_Y = \sqrt{4.5} = 2.121,$$

and so $\Pi_Y \neq \Pi_X + 1$, and hence the principle is not consistent.

3. Consider the equation $u(300) = E\left[u(300 + \Pi_X - X)\right]$. This yields

$$300 - 10^{-3}(300^2) = E[300 + \Pi_X - X - 10^{-3}\,(300 + \Pi_X - X)^2].$$

The right-hand side becomes

$$300 + \Pi_X - E[X] - 10^{-3}\left(300^2 + 600\Pi_X + \Pi_X^2\right)$$
$$+2 \times 10^{-3}(300 + \Pi_X)E[X] - 10^{-3}E[X^2],$$

so that

$$\Pi_X^2 - (400 + 2E\left[X\right])\,\Pi_X + E\left[X^2\right] + 400E\left[X\right] = 0.$$

Now

$$E[X_1] = 100 \quad \text{and} \quad E[X_1^2] = 10,400,$$

so that

$$\Pi_{X_1}^2 - 600\Pi_{X_1} + 50,400 = 0,$$

and hence $\Pi_{X_1} = 101.0025$. Similarly,

$$E[X_2] = 102 \quad \text{and} \quad E[X_2^2] = 10,620,$$

so that

$$\Pi_{X_2}^2 - 604\Pi_{X_2} + 51,420 = 0,$$

and hence $\Pi_{X_2} = 102.5407$. Finally,

$$E[X_1 + X_2] = 202 \quad \text{and} \quad V[X_1 + X_2] = 616,$$

giving

$$E\left[(X_1 + X_2)^2\right] = 41,420.$$

Thus,

$$\Pi_{X_1+X_2}^2 - 804\Pi_{X_1+X_2} + 122,220 = 0,$$

giving $\Pi_{X_1+X_2} = 203.5460$, so that $\Pi_{X_1+X_2} \neq \Pi_{X_1} + \Pi_{X_2}$. Hence the principle of zero utility is not additive.

4. Let $X \sim P(\lambda)$. Then

$$M_X(t) = \exp\{\lambda(e^t - 1)\},$$

and so, in the notation of Section 3.3.6,

$$M_{\tilde{X}}(t) = \frac{M_X(t+h)}{M_X(h)} = \frac{\exp\left\{\lambda(e^{t+h} - 1)\right\}}{\exp\left\{\lambda(e^h - 1)\right\}} = \exp\left\{\lambda e^h(e^t - 1)\right\},$$

so that $\tilde{X} \sim P(\lambda e^h)$.

5. In the notation of Section 3.3.6, $\tilde{X} \sim \gamma(2, 0.01 - h)$ since

$$M_{\tilde{X}}(t) = \frac{M_X(t+h)}{M_X(h)} = \left(\frac{0.01}{0.01 - h - t}\right)^2 \left(\frac{0.01 - h}{0.01}\right)^2$$
$$= \left(\frac{0.01 - h}{0.01 - h - t}\right)^2.$$

As

$$\Pi_X = E[\tilde{X}],$$

it follows that

$$250 = \frac{2}{0.01 - h},$$

and hence $h = 0.002$.

6. As $\Pr(X \leq x) = (x - 5)/10$ for $5 \leq x \leq 15$, we have

$$1 - F(x) = \begin{cases} 1 & \text{for } x < 5 \\ (15 - x)/10 & \text{for } 5 \leq x \leq 15, \\ 0 & \text{for } x > 15 \end{cases}$$

and so

$$\Pi_X = \int_0^\infty (1 - F(x))^{1/\rho}\, dx$$
$$= \int_0^5 dx + \int_5^{15} \left(\frac{15 - x}{10}\right)^{5/6} dx$$
$$= 10.4545.$$

7. The weight is

$$w(x) = \frac{1}{\rho}(1 - F(x))^{(1/\rho)-1}.$$

Thus,

$$w'(x) = \frac{1}{\rho}\left(\frac{1}{\rho} - 1\right)(1 - F(x))^{(1/\rho)-2}(-1)f(x),$$

and since $\rho > 1$, $w'(x) > 0$, so that w is an increasing function.

8. We have $Y = X + 100$ where X is distributed as Pareto(2,100) since

$$\Pr(Y \leq x) = \Pr(X \leq x - 100) = 1 - \left(\frac{100}{100 + x - 100}\right)^2.$$

Then

$$P_X = \int_0^\infty \left(\frac{100}{100 + x}\right)^{2/\rho} dx$$
$$= \frac{100}{(2/\rho) - 1}\int_0^\infty \frac{(2/\rho - 1)\,100^{2/\rho - 1}}{(100 + x)^{2/\rho}} dx$$
$$= \frac{100\rho}{2 - \rho}.$$

As the premium principle is consistent,

$$P_Y = P_X + 100 = \frac{200}{2-\rho} = 400,$$

giving $\rho = 3/2$.

9. (a) We start from $\Pi_X(\beta) = \beta^{-1}\log M_X(\beta)$. Then

$$\begin{aligned}\Pi_X'(\beta) &= -\beta^{-2}\log M_X(\beta) + \frac{1}{\beta}\frac{M_X'(\beta)}{M_X(\beta)} \\ &= \frac{1}{\beta^2}\left(\beta\frac{M_X'(\beta)}{M_X(\beta)} - \log M_X(\beta)\right).\end{aligned}$$

Both the numerator and the denominator are zero when $\beta = 0$, and so to find $\Pi_X'(0)$ we use l'Hôpital's rule. The ratio of derivatives of the numerator and denominator of $\Pi_X'(\beta)$ is

$$\begin{aligned}&\frac{\frac{M_X'(\beta)}{M_X(\beta)} + \beta\left(\frac{M_X''(\beta)M_X(\beta)-M_X'(\beta)^2}{M_X(\beta)^2}\right) - \frac{M_X'(\beta)}{M_X(\beta)}}{2\beta} \\ &= \frac{1}{2}\left(\frac{M_X''(\beta)M_X(\beta) - M_X'(\beta)^2}{M_X(\beta)^2}\right),\end{aligned}$$

and letting $\beta = 0$ we get

$$\frac{E\left[X^2\right] - E\left[X\right]^2}{2} = \frac{V\left[X\right]}{2},$$

i.e. $\Pi_X'(0) = \frac{1}{2}V\left[X\right]$.

(b) From part (a) we have

$$\beta^2\Pi_X'(\beta) = -\log M_X(\beta) + \beta\frac{M_X'(\beta)}{M_X(\beta)},$$

giving

$$\begin{aligned}&\left(\beta^2\Pi_X'(\beta)\right)' \\ &= -\frac{M_X'(\beta)}{M_X(\beta)} + \frac{\beta}{M_X(\beta)^2}\left[M_X''(\beta)M_X(\beta) - M_X'(\beta)^2\right] + \frac{M_X'(\beta)}{M_X(\beta)} \\ &= \beta\left[\frac{M_X''(\beta)}{M_X(\beta)} - \left(\frac{M_X'(\beta)}{M_X(\beta)}\right)^2\right].\end{aligned}$$

From the theory of Esscher transforms, we know that if the distribution of a random variable $\tilde{X}$ is the Esscher transform with parameter $h > 0$ of the distribution of a random variable X,

$$M_{\tilde{X}}(t) = \frac{M_X(t+h)}{M_X(h)} \Rightarrow M_{\tilde{X}}^{(r)}(t)\Big|_{t=0} = E\left[\tilde{X}^r\right] = \frac{M_X^{(r)}(h)}{M_X(h)}.$$

Hence

$$\frac{M_X''(\beta)}{M_X(\beta)^2} - \left(\frac{M_X'(\beta)}{M_X(\beta)}\right)^2$$

represents the variance of the distribution which is the Esscher transform with parameter $\beta > 0$ of the distribution of X, and so

$$\left(\beta^2 \Pi_X'(\beta)\right)' > 0.$$

Thus, if $h(\beta) = \beta^2 \Pi_X'(\beta)$, we know that $h(\beta)$ is an increasing function of β. We also know that

$$\lim_{\beta \to 0^+} h(\beta) = 0,$$

and hence $h(\beta) > 0$ for $\beta > 0$. Thus,

$$\beta^2 \Pi_X'(\beta) > 0,$$

and since $\beta > 0$, $\Pi_X'(\beta) > 0$.

Chapter 4

1. In the notation of Section 4.2, $E[N] = 120$ and $V[N] = 300$, $E[X_1] = 1$ and $V[X_1] = 2$, giving $E[S] = 120$ and $V[S] = 540$ by formulae (4.5) and (4.6).
2. By formula (3.2), the premium is $\beta^{-1} \log E[\exp\{\beta S\}]$ where $\beta = 0.0001$, and S denotes aggregate claims. Hence

$$E[\exp\{\beta S\}] = \exp\{100\,(M_X(\beta) - 1)\},$$

where $X \sim \gamma(2, 0.001)$ and so the premium is $100\,(M_X(\beta) - 1)\,/\beta$. As

$$M_X(\beta) = \left(\frac{0.001}{0.001 - \beta}\right)^2,$$

the premium is $234,568$.
3. The Esscher transform of the compound Poisson distribution is also a compound Poisson distribution with Poisson parameter $200 M_X(h)$ and moment generating function $M_X(t+h)/M_X(h)$ for individual claims, where $h = 0.001$. This follows since

$$\begin{aligned}\frac{M_S(t+h)}{M_S(h)} &= \frac{\exp\{200\,(M_X(t+h) - 1)\}}{\exp\{200\,(M_X(h) - 1)\}} \\ &= \exp\{200(M_X(t+h) - M_X(h))\} \\ &= \exp\left\{200 M_X(h)\left(\frac{M_X(t+h)}{M_X(h)} - 1\right)\right\}.\end{aligned}$$

Hence the individual claim amount distribution is exponential with parameter $0.01 - h = 0.009$ since

$$\frac{M_X(t+h)}{M_X(h)} = \frac{0.01}{0.01-h-t}\frac{0.01-h}{0.01} = \frac{0.01-h}{0.01-h-t}.$$

The premium is the mean of this compound Poisson distribution, i.e.

$$200\frac{0.01}{0.01-0.001}\frac{1}{0.009} = 24,691.$$

4. By the result at the end of Section 4.3, the distribution of S_1+S_2 is compound Poisson. The Poisson parameter is the sum of the Poisson parameters, i.e. $20+30=50$, and individual claims are distributed as Z where

$$\begin{aligned}
\Pr(Z=10) &= \tfrac{2}{5}\Pr(X=10) = 0.1,\\
\Pr(Z=20) &= \tfrac{2}{5}\Pr(X=20) + \tfrac{3}{5}\Pr(Y=20) = 0.38,\\
\Pr(Z=30) &= \tfrac{2}{5}\Pr(X=30) + \tfrac{3}{5}\Pr(Y=30) = 0.34,\\
\Pr(Z=40) &= \tfrac{3}{5}\Pr(Y=40) = 0.18.
\end{aligned}$$

5. When $N \sim B(n,q)$,

$$P_N(r) = (qr+1-q)^n,$$

and so

$$\begin{aligned}
P_{N_R}(r) &= P_N[P_I(r)]\\
&= (q(1-\pi_M+\pi_M r)+1-q)^n\\
&= (q\pi_M r + 1 - q\pi_M)^n,
\end{aligned}$$

so that $N_R \sim B(n, q\pi_M)$.

6. We have $P_{N_R}(r) = P_N[P_I(r)]$ where

$$P_I(r) = 1-\pi_M+\pi_M r$$

and (see Chapter 1, Exercise 1)

$$P_N(r) = \frac{\log(1-\theta r)}{\log(1-\theta)}.$$

Then

$$\begin{aligned}
P_{N_R}(r) &= \frac{\log(1-\theta(1-\pi_M+\pi_M r))}{\log(1-\theta)}\\
&= \frac{\log\left((1-\theta(1-\pi_M))\left(1-\frac{\theta\pi_M r}{1-\theta(1-\pi_M)}\right)\right)}{\log(1-\theta)}\\
&= \frac{\log(1-\theta(1-\pi_M))}{\log(1-\theta)} + \frac{\log\left(1-\frac{\theta\pi_M r}{1-\theta(1-\pi_M)}\right)}{\log(1-\theta)}\\
&= \frac{\log(1-\theta(1-\pi_M))}{\log(1-\theta)} - \frac{1}{\log(1-\theta)}\sum_{n=1}^{\infty}\frac{1}{n}\left(\frac{\theta\pi_M r}{1-\theta(1-\pi_M)}\right)^n.
\end{aligned}$$

Hence

$$\Pr(N_R = 0) = \frac{\log(1 - \theta(1 - \pi_M))}{\log(1 - \theta)},$$

and for $n = 1, 2, 3, \ldots,$

$$\Pr(N_R = n) = -\frac{1}{n \log(1 - \theta)} \left(\frac{\theta \pi_M}{1 - \theta(1 - \pi_M)} \right)^n .$$

7. (a) In the notation of Section 4.4.2, with $M = 400$,

$$\pi_M = 1 - F(400) = \left(\frac{400}{400 + 400} \right)^3 = \frac{1}{8},$$

and hence

$$p^* = \frac{0.5}{0.5 + 0.5\pi_M} = \frac{8}{9},$$

so that $N_R \sim NB(100, 8/9)$.

(b) Let $\hat{X}$ denote the amount of a (non-zero) claim for the reinsurer, and let X denote the amount of a claim, with $X \sim F$. Then

$$\begin{aligned}
\Pr(\hat{X} \leq x) &= \Pr(X \leq 400 + x | X > 400) \\
&= \Pr(400 < X \leq 400 + x) / \Pr(X > 400) \\
&= \frac{F(400 + x) - F(400)}{1 - F(400)} \\
&= \left[\left(\frac{400}{800} \right)^3 - \left(\frac{400}{800 + x} \right)^3 \right] \div \left(\frac{400}{800} \right)^3 \\
&= 1 - \left(\frac{800}{800 + x} \right)^3 ,
\end{aligned}$$

so that $\hat{X} \sim Pa(3, 800)$.

(c) We have

$$Cov(S_A, S_B) = E[(S_A - E[S_A])(S_B - E[S_B])]$$

and $S_A = 0.7S$, where S has a compound negative binomial distribution whose components are given in (a) and (b). Hence

$$Cov(S_A, S_B) = 0.21V[S].$$

Then

$$\begin{aligned}
V[S] &= E[N_R]V[\hat{X}] + V[N_R]E[\hat{X}]^2 \\
&= 12.5 \times 48 \times 10^4 + 14.0625 \times 400^2 \\
&= 825 \times 10^4
\end{aligned}$$

gives

$$\begin{aligned}Cov(S_A, S_B) &= 0.21 \times 825 \times 10^4 \\ &= 1.7325 \times 10^6.\end{aligned}$$

8. (a) The reinsurer pays $\max(0, X - M)$ on each claim, where X is exponentially distributed with mean 100. Thus,

$$\begin{aligned}E\,[S_R] &= 10E[\max(0, X - M)] \\ &= 10 \int_M^{\infty} (x - M) 0.01 e^{-0.01x} dx \\ &= 10 \int_0^{\infty} y 0.01 e^{-0.01(y+M)} dy \\ &= 10e^{-0.01M} \int_0^{\infty} y 0.01 e^{-0.01y} dy \\ &= 1,000e^{-0.01M}\end{aligned}$$

(since the final integral is the mean of the exponential distribution), and

$$\begin{aligned}V[S_R] &= 10E[\max(0, X - M)^2] \\ &= 10 \int_M^{\infty} (x - M)^2 0.01\, e^{-0.01x} dx \\ &= 10 \int_0^{\infty} y^2 0.01 e^{-0.01(y+M)} dy \\ &= 2 \times 10^5\, e^{-0.01M}.\end{aligned}$$

Hence the reinsurance premium is

$$1,000e^{-0.01M} + 2 \times 10^2\, e^{-0.01M} = 1,200e^{-0.01M}.$$

Alternatively, the distribution of S_R is compound Poisson with Poisson parameter $10e^{-0.01M}$, and individual claims are exponentially distributed with mean 100, giving

$$E[S_R] = 10e^{-0.01M} \times 100 = 1,000e^{-0.01M}$$

and

$$V[S_R] = 10e^{-0.01M} \times 2 \times 100^2 = 2 \times 10^5\, e^{-0.01M}.$$

(b) As net profit equals premium income less claims, both net of reinsurance, the net profit is

$$1,100 - 1,200e^{-0.01M} - S_I$$

and $E[S_I] = E[S] - E[S_R]$. Thus,

$$\begin{aligned}E[g(M)] &= 1,100 - 1,200e^{-0.01M} - \left(1,000 - 1,000e^{-0.01M}\right) \\ &= 100 - 200e^{-0.01M},\end{aligned}$$

which is positive for $M > 69.31$.

(c) For each value of M, the variance of net profit is just the variance of net aggregate claims, so

$$\begin{aligned} V[g(M)] &= V[S_I] \\ &= 10E[\min(X,M)^2] \\ &= 10\int_0^M x^2 0.01e^{-0.01x}dx + 10M^2e^{-0.01M}. \end{aligned}$$

Thus,

$$\begin{aligned} \frac{d}{dM}V[g(M)] &= 10M^2 0.01e^{-0.01M} + 20Me^{-0.01M} - 10M^2 0.01e^{-0.01M} \\ &= 20Me^{-0.01M}, \end{aligned}$$

which is positive for all $M > 0$, so that $V[g(M)]$ is an increasing function of M.

9. Starting from the definition of $E[\min(Y,M)]$ we have

$$\begin{aligned} E[\min(Y,M)] &= \sum_{j=0}^{M} jh_j + M\sum_{j=M+1}^{\infty} h_j \\ &= \sum_{j=0}^{M-1}[1-H(j)] \\ &= \int_0^M [1-F(x)]\,dx \\ &= \int_0^M \int_x^\infty f(y)dydx \\ &= \int_0^M \int_0^y dxf(y)dy + \int_M^\infty \int_0^M dxf(y)dy \\ &= \int_0^M yf(y)dy + M\int_M^\infty f(y)dy \\ &= E[\min(X,M)]. \end{aligned}$$

Note that the first step in the above comes from

$$\begin{aligned} &h_1 + 2h_2 + 3h_3 + \cdots + Mh_M + M(h_{M+1} + h_{M+2} + \cdots) \\ &\quad = h_1 + h_2 + h_3 + \cdots + h_M + (h_{M+1} + h_{M+2} + \cdots) \\ &\qquad + h_2 + h_3 + \cdots + h_M + (h_{M+1} + h_{M+2} + \cdots) \\ &\qquad + h_3 + \cdots + h_M + (h_{M+1} + h_{M+2} + \cdots) \\ &\qquad + \cdots \\ &\qquad + h_M + (h_{M+1} + h_{M+2} + \cdots) \\ &\quad = [1 - H(0)] + [1 - H(1)] + \cdots + [1 - H(M-1)]. \end{aligned}$$

10. With $a = -1.5$, $b = 16.5$ and $\Pr(S = 0) = 0.4^{10}$, the Panjer recursion formula gives the following values:

x	1	2	3	4	5
$\Pr(S = x)$	0.0006	0.0022	0.0061	0.0134	0.0252

and hence $\Pr(S \leq 5) = 0.0477$. (Answers are rounded.)

11. Let X denote an individual claim amount and let $\hat{X}$ denote a non-zero payment by the reinsurer. Then, in the notation of Section 4.4.2 with $M = 4$,

$$\pi_M = \Pr(X > 4) = 0.2(0.8^4 + 0.8^5 + 0.8^6 + \cdots) = 0.8^4$$

and

$$p^* = \frac{0.5}{0.5 + 0.5\pi_M} = 0.7094,$$

so that the distribution of the number of non-zero payments for the reinsurer is $NB(10, 0.7094)$. Further, for $x = 1, 2, 3, \ldots$,

$$\begin{aligned}\Pr(\hat{X} = x) &= \Pr(X = x + 4 \mid X > 4) \\ &= \frac{\Pr(X = x + 4)}{\Pr(X > 4)} \\ &= 0.2(0.8)^{x+3}/0.8^4 \\ &= f_x.\end{aligned}$$

Using the Panjer recursion formula the respective probabilities of aggregate claim amounts of 0, 1 and 2 for the reinsurer are 0.0323, 0.0188 and 0.0210, so the solution is 0.0721.

12. (a) Start from

$$P_N(r) = \sum_{n=1}^{\infty} r^n p_n = rp_1 + \sum_{n=2}^{\infty} r^n p_n,$$

giving

$$\begin{aligned}P_N(r) &= rp_1 + \sum_{n=2}^{\infty} r^n \alpha p_{n-1} \\ &= rp_1 + \alpha r \sum_{n=2}^{\infty} r^{n-1} p_{n-1} \\ &= rp_1 + \alpha r P_N(r).\end{aligned}$$

Further, since $p_n = \alpha^{n-1} p_1$ for $n = 2, 3, 4, \ldots$ and

$$p_1 + \sum_{n=2}^{\infty} \alpha^{n-1} p_1 = p_1 \left(1 + \frac{\alpha}{1 - \alpha}\right) = \frac{p_1}{1 - \alpha} = 1,$$

we have $p_1 = 1 - \alpha$. Hence

$$P'_N(r) = 1 - \alpha + \alpha P_N(r) + \alpha r P'_N(r).$$

(b) From $P_S(r) = P_N[P_X(r)]$ we have

$$\begin{aligned} P'_S(r) &= P'_X(r)P'_N[P_X(r)] \\ &= P'_X(r)\left(1 - \alpha + \alpha P_X(r)P'_N(P_X(r)) + \alpha P_N(P_X(r))\right) \\ &= (1-\alpha)P'_X(r) + \alpha P_X(r)P'_S(r) + \alpha P'_X(r)P_S(r). \end{aligned}$$

(c) Multiply the above equation by r, then equate coefficients of r^x for $x = 1, 2, 3, \ldots$:

$$\begin{aligned} xg_x &= (1-\alpha)xf_x + \alpha\sum_{j=0}^{x} f_j(x-j)g_{x-j} + \alpha\sum_{j=0}^{x} jf_jg_{x-j} \\ &= (1-\alpha)xf_x + \alpha\sum_{j=0}^{x} xf_jg_{x-j}, \end{aligned}$$

giving

$$g_x = (1-\alpha)f_x + \alpha\sum_{j=0}^{x} f_jg_{x-j},$$

and hence

$$g_x = \frac{1}{1-\alpha f_0}\left((1-\alpha)f_x + \alpha\sum_{j=1}^{x} f_jg_{x-j}\right).$$

Further,

$$g_0 = \sum_{n=1}^{\infty} p_n f_0^n = \sum_{n=1}^{\infty}(1-\alpha)\alpha^{n-1}f_0^n = \frac{(1-\alpha)f_0}{1-\alpha f_0}.$$

(d) We have

$$\begin{aligned} E[S^r] &= \sum_{x=1}^{\infty} x^r g_x \\ &= (1-\alpha)\sum_{x=1}^{\infty} x^r f_x + \alpha\sum_{x=1}^{\infty} x^r \sum_{j=0}^{x} f_jg_{x-j} \end{aligned}$$

$$= (1-\alpha)E[X_1^r] + \alpha f_0\sum_{x=1}^{\infty} x^r g_x + \alpha\sum_{j=1}^{\infty} f_j\sum_{x=j}^{\infty} x^r g_{x-j}$$

$$= (1-\alpha)E[X_1^r] + \alpha f_0 E[S^r] + \alpha\sum_{j=1}^{\infty} f_j\sum_{y=0}^{\infty}(y+j)^r g_y.$$

Now

$$\sum_{y=0}^{\infty}(y+j)^r g_y = \sum_{y=0}^{\infty}\sum_{k=0}^{r}\binom{r}{k}y^k j^{r-k} g_y$$
$$= \sum_{k=0}^{r}\binom{r}{k}j^{r-k}\sum_{y=0}^{\infty}y^k g_y$$
$$= \sum_{k=0}^{r}\binom{r}{k}j^{r-k}E[S^k]$$

gives

$$E[S^r] = (1-\alpha)E[X_1^r] + \alpha f_0 E[S^r] + \alpha\sum_{j=1}^{\infty}f_j\sum_{k=0}^{r}\binom{r}{k}j^{r-k}E[S^k]$$
$$= (1-\alpha)E[X_1^r] + \alpha f_0 E[S^r] + \alpha\sum_{k=0}^{r}\binom{r}{k}E[S^k]\sum_{j=1}^{\infty}f_j j^{r-k}$$
$$= (1-\alpha)E[X_1^r] + \alpha f_0 E[S^r]$$
$$+\alpha\sum_{k=0}^{r-1}\binom{r}{k}E[S^k]E[X_1^{r-k}] + \alpha E[S^r](1-f_0)\,,$$

and hence

$$E[S^r] = \frac{1}{1-\alpha}\left((1-\alpha)E[X_1^r] + \alpha\sum_{k=0}^{r-1}\binom{r}{k}E[S^k]E[X_1^{r-k}]\right)$$
$$= E[X_1^r] + \frac{\alpha}{1-\alpha}\sum_{k=0}^{r-1}\binom{r}{k}E[S^k]E[X_1^{r-k}].$$

13. (a) We have

$$P_N(r) = \sum_{n=0}^{\infty}r^n p_n = p_0 + \sum_{n=1}^{\infty}r^n\sum_{i=1}^{k}\left(a_i + \frac{b_i}{n}\right)p_{n-i}.$$

Hence

$$P_N'(r) = \sum_{n=1}^{\infty}nr^{n-1}\sum_{i=1}^{k}\left(a_i + \frac{b_i}{n}\right)p_{n-i}$$
$$= \sum_{i=1}^{k}\sum_{n=1}^{\infty}(na_i + b_i)r^{n-1}p_{n-i} \quad \text{and let } j = n-i$$
$$= \sum_{i=1}^{k}\sum_{j=1-i}^{\infty}\left((j+i)a_i + b_i\right)r^{j+i-1}p_j$$

$$= \sum_{i=1}^{k} r^i \sum_{j=0}^{\infty} \left(a_i j p_j r^{j-1} + (ia_i + b_i) r^{j-1} p_j \right)$$

$$= \sum_{i=1}^{k} \left(a_i r^i P'_N(r) + (ia_i + b_i) r^{i-1} P_N(r) \right).$$

(b) By definition, $Y_j = \sum_{i=1}^{j} X_i$ so that (by independence)

$$P_{Y_j}(r) = P_{X_1}(r)^j$$

and

$$P'_{Y_j}(r) = jP_{X_1}(r)^{j-1} P'_{X_1}(r).$$

(c) Starting from

$$P'_S(r) = P'_X(r) P'_N \left[P_{X_1}(r) \right],$$

we have

$$\begin{aligned} P'_S(r) &= P'_{X_1}(r) \sum_{i=1}^{k} a_i P_{X_1}(r)^i P'_N \left[P_{X_1}(r) \right] \\ &\quad + P'_{X_1}(r) \sum_{i=1}^{k} (ia_i + b_i) P_{X_1}(r)^{i-1} P_N \left[P_{X_1}(r) \right] \\ &= P'_{X_1}(r) \sum_{i=1}^{k} a_i P_{Y_i}(r) P'_N \left[P_{X_1}(r) \right] \\ &\quad + P'_{X_1}(r) \sum_{i=1}^{k} (ia_i + b_i) P_{X_1}(r)^{i-1} P_S(r) \\ &= \sum_{i=1}^{k} a_i P_{Y_i}(r) P'_S(r) + \sum_{i=1}^{k} \left(a_i + \frac{b_i}{i} \right) P'_{Y_i}(r) P_S(r). \end{aligned}$$

(d) We can multiply the result in part (c) by r, and then write it as

$$\begin{aligned} \sum_{x=1}^{\infty} x r^x g_x &= \sum_{i=1}^{k} a_i \left(\sum_{j=0}^{\infty} r^j f_j^{i*} \right) \left(\sum_{x=1}^{\infty} x r^x g_x \right) \\ &\quad + \sum_{i=1}^{k} \left(a_i + \frac{b_i}{i} \right) \left(\sum_{j=1}^{\infty} j r^j f_j^{i*} \right) \left(\sum_{x=0}^{\infty} r^x g_x \right). \end{aligned}$$

Equating coefficients of r^x we get

$$\begin{aligned} xg_x &= \sum_{i=1}^{k} a_i \left(\sum_{j=0}^{x-1} f_j^{i*}(x-j) g_{x-j} \right) \\ &\quad + \sum_{i=1}^{k} \left(a_i + \frac{b_i}{i} \right) \left(\sum_{j=1}^{x} j f_j^{i*} g_{x-j} \right) \\ &= \sum_{j=1}^{x} g_{x-j}(x-j) \sum_{i=1}^{k} a_i f_j^{i*} \\ &\quad + \sum_{j=1}^{x} g_{x-j} j \sum_{i=1}^{k} \left(a_i + \frac{b_i}{i} \right) f_j^{i*} + \sum_{i=1}^{k} a_i f_0^{i*} x g_x, \end{aligned}$$

giving

$$\left(1 - \sum_{i=1}^{k} a_i f_0^{i*} \right) x g_x = \sum_{j=1}^{x} g_{x-j} \sum_{i=1}^{k} \left(x a_i + \frac{b_i j}{i} \right) f_j^{i*}$$

or

$$g_x = \frac{1}{1 - \sum_{i=1}^{k} a_i f_0^i} \sum_{j=1}^{x} g_{x-j} \sum_{i=1}^{k} \left(a_i + \frac{b_i j}{i x} \right) f_j^{i*}$$

since $f_0^{i*} = f_0^i$.

(e) The issue with using the formula is that it involves convolutions, which must be calculated before applying the formula.

14. The moments of the individual claim amount distribution are

$$\begin{aligned} m_1 &= \frac{0.4}{0.01} + \frac{0.6}{0.02} = 70, \\ m_2 &= 2\left(\frac{0.4}{0.01^2} + \frac{0.6}{0.02^2} \right) = 11{,}000, \\ m_3 &= 6\left(\frac{0.4}{0.01^3} + \frac{0.6}{0.02^3} \right) = 2.85 \times 10^6. \end{aligned}$$

Thus, $E[S] = 3{,}500$ and $V[S] = 550{,}000$.

(a) We approximate $\Pr(S \leq 4{,}500)$ by

$$\Pr\left(Z \leq \frac{4{,}500 - E[S]}{\sqrt{V[S]}} \right) = \Pr(Z \leq 1.3484),$$

where $Z \sim N(0, 1)$, so the solution is 0.911.

(b) To obtain the translated gamma distribution's parameters, first set

$$\frac{2}{\sqrt{\alpha}} = Sk[S] = \frac{50 m_3}{(50 m_2)^{3/2}},$$

giving

$$\alpha = \frac{4 \times 50^3 \times 11^3 \times 10^9}{50^2 \times 2.85^2 \times 10^{12}} = 32.7732,$$

then set

$$\beta = \sqrt{\frac{\alpha}{V[S]}} = 7.7193 \times 10^{-3},$$

and finally set

$$k = E[S] - \frac{\alpha}{\beta} = -745.614.$$

Then

$$\Pr(S \leq 4,500) = \Pr(Y \leq 5,245.614),$$

where $Y \sim \gamma(\alpha, \beta)$. Using software, this probability is 0.905.

15. Let S denote aggregate claims, X individual claims. Then

$$E[S] = 10{,}000qE[X] = 10^7 q$$

and

$$\begin{aligned} V[S] &= 10^4 qV[X] + 10^4 q(1-q)E[X]^2 \\ &= 10^4 q 10^6 + 10^4 q(1-q)10^6 \\ &= 10^{10} q(2-q) \end{aligned}$$

since $V[X] = 10^6$. The second assumption implies that

$$S \sim N\left(10^7 q, 10^{10} q(2-q)\right),$$

and the third assumption implies Pr(premium $> S) = 0.95$ and the premium income is 10^6. So

$$\Pr(10^6 > S) = \Pr\left(\frac{10^6 - 10^7 q}{10^5\sqrt{q(2-q)}} > Z\right),$$

where $Z \sim N(0, 1)$

$$\begin{aligned} &\Rightarrow \frac{10 - 10^2 q}{\sqrt{q(2-q)}} = 1.645 \\ &\Rightarrow 10^2(1-10q)^2 = 1.645^2 q(2-q) \\ &\Rightarrow 100 - 2000q + 10^4 q^2 = 5.41205q - 2.706q^2 \\ &\Rightarrow 10002.706q^2 - 2005.412q + 100 = 0 \\ &\Rightarrow q = \frac{2005.412 \pm \sqrt{2005.412^2 - 4,001,082.4}}{20005.412}, \end{aligned}$$

i.e. $q = 0.1074$ or 0.0931. The premium should exceed expected claims, so $q = 0.0931$ since the expected claim amount per policy is $1{,}000q$. Mathematically, $q = 0.1074$ does not satisfy

$$\frac{10 - 10^2 q}{\sqrt{q(2-q)}} = 1.645.$$

Chapter 5

1. (a) The mean is

$$100 \times 0.001 \times 1 + 300 \times 0.002 \times 1 + 200 \times 0.002 \times 2 = 1.5,$$

and the variance is

$$\begin{aligned} &100 \times 0.001 \times 0.999 \times 1 \\ &+300 \times 0.002 \times 0.998 \times 1 \\ &+200 \times 0.002 \times 0.998 \times 4 \\ =\ &2.2955. \end{aligned}$$

(b) The total claim amount is 2 if one of four events occurs:

(A) 2 deaths from the first group
(B) 2 deaths from the second group
(C) 1 death from the third group
(D) 1 death from each of the first and second groups.

The probability of event (A) is

$$\binom{100}{2} 0.001^2 0.999^{98} \times 0.998^{300} \times 0.998^{200} = 0.001649,$$

the probability of event (B) is

$$0.999^{100} \times \binom{300}{2} 0.002^2 0.998^{298} \times 0.998^{200} = 0.059893,$$

the probability of event (C) is

$$0.999^{100} \times 0.998^{300} \times \binom{200}{1} 0.002 \times 0.998^{199} = 0.133275$$

and the probability of event (D) is

$$\binom{100}{1} 0.001 \times 0.999^{99} \times \binom{300}{1} 0.002 \times 0.998^{299} \times 0.998^{200} = 0.020011.$$

Adding together the probabilities of these events gives 0.2148.

2. (a) The mean is

$$225 \times 0.95q \times 60 + 300q \times 45 = 26,325q,$$

and the variance is

$$\begin{aligned}&225 \times 0.95q(1-0.95q) \times 60^2 + 300q(1-q) \times 45^2\\&= 1,377,000q - 1,338,525q^2.\end{aligned}$$

(a) (i) The Poisson parameter is

$$225 \times 0.95q + 300q = 513.75q,$$

and the claim amounts are

45 with probability $300/513.75 = 0.58394$
60 with probability $(225 \times 0.95)/513.75 = 0.41606$

(ii) The mean claim amount is

$$45\frac{300}{513.75} + 60\frac{225 \times 0.95}{513.75},$$

and hence the mean of the compound Poisson distribution is

$$513.75q\left(45\frac{300}{513.75} + 60\frac{225 \times 0.95}{513.75}\right) = 26,325q,$$

and similarly the variance of the compound Poisson distribution is

$$513.75q\left(45^2\frac{300}{513.75} + 60^2\frac{225 \times 0.95}{513.75}\right) = 1,377,000q.$$

(iii) In each category we are replacing the binomial distribution for the number of deaths by a Poisson distribution which has the same mean but a greater variance, resulting in the compound Poisson distribution having a greater variance.

3. (a) From

$$A(r) = \prod_{i=1}^{n}(p_i + q_i B(r))$$

we get

$$\log A(r) = \sum_{i=1}^{n} \log(p_i + q_i B(r)).$$

Then

$$\begin{aligned}A'(r) &= A(r)\sum_{i=1}^{n}\frac{q_i B'(r)}{p_i + q_i B(r)}\\&= A(r)\sum_{i=1}^{n}\frac{(q_i/p_i)\,B'(r)}{1+(q_i/p_i)\,B(r)}\\&= A(r)\sum_{i=1}^{n}\sum_{k=0}^{\infty}\left(\frac{q_i}{p_i}\right)B'(r)(-1)^k\left(\frac{q_i}{p_i}B(r)\right)^k,\end{aligned}$$

provided that $|(q_i/p_i)\,B(r)| < 1$. Now $C(r,n) = B(r)^n$,

$$C'(r,n) = nB(r)^{n-1}B'(r),$$

and so

$$\begin{aligned} A'(r) &= A(r)\sum_{i=1}^{n}\sum_{k=0}^{\infty}\left(\frac{q_i}{p_i}\right)^{k+1}(-1)^k B(r)^k B'(r) \\ &= A(r)\sum_{i=1}^{n}\sum_{k=1}^{\infty}\left(\frac{q_i}{p_i}\right)^{k}(-1)^{k-1} B(r)^{k-1} B'(r) \\ &= A(r)\sum_{i=1}^{n}\sum_{k=1}^{\infty}\left(\frac{q_i}{p_i}\right)^{k}\frac{(-1)^{k-1}}{k}C'(r,k). \end{aligned}$$

(b) Multiply the identity in part (a) by r to obtain

$$\begin{aligned} \sum_{x=1}^{\infty} xr^x g_x &= \left(\sum_{x=0}^{\infty} r^x g_x\right)\left(\sum_{i=1}^{n}\sum_{k=1}^{\infty}\frac{(-1)^{k-1}}{k}\left(\frac{q_i}{p_i}\right)^{k}\sum_{x=1}^{\infty} xr^x h_x^{k*}\right) \\ &= \left(\sum_{x=0}^{\infty} r^x g_x\right)\left(\sum_{i=1}^{n}\sum_{x=1}^{\infty} xr^x \sum_{k=1}^{\infty}\frac{(-1)^{k-1}}{k}\left(\frac{q_i}{p_i}\right)^{k} h_x^{k*}\right) \\ &= \left(\sum_{x=0}^{\infty} r^x g_x\right)\left(\sum_{i=1}^{n}\sum_{x=1}^{\infty} xr^x f_x(i)\right) \\ &= \left(\sum_{x=0}^{\infty} r^x g_x\right)\left(\sum_{x=1}^{\infty} xr^x \phi_x\right), \end{aligned}$$

where $f_x(i)$ and ϕ_x are as defined in the question. The solution for g_x is obtained by equating coefficients of r^x. For $x = 1, 2, 3, \ldots$, we get

$$xg_x = g_0 x\phi_x + g_1(x-1)\phi_{x-1} + \cdots + g_{x-1}\phi_1,$$

giving

$$g_x = \frac{1}{x}\sum_{i=1}^{x} i\phi_i g_{x-i}.$$

Trivially, $g_0 = \prod_{i=1}^{n} p_i$.

(c) This follows by writing $p_i = \exp\{-\log(1 + q_i/p_i)\}$ since

$$\begin{aligned} g_0 = \prod_{i=1}^{n} p_i &= \prod_{i=1}^{n}\exp\{-\log(1 + q_i/p_i)\} \\ &= \exp\left\{-\sum_{i=1}^{n}\log(1 + q_i/p_i)\right\} \\ &= \exp\left\{-\sum_{i=1}^{n}\sum_{k=1}^{\infty}\frac{(-1)^{k-1}}{k}\left(\frac{q_i}{p_i}\right)^{k}\right\}. \end{aligned}$$

(d) Let $\Lambda = \sum_{i=1}^{n} q_i/p_i$. Then $g_0^{(1)} = \exp\{-\Lambda\}$. Further, for $x = 1, 2, 3, \ldots$,

$$\phi_x^{(1)} = \sum_{i=1}^{n} \frac{q_i}{p_i} h_x = \Lambda h_x,$$

and hence

$$g_x^{(1)} = \frac{\Lambda}{x} \sum_{i=1}^{x} i h_i g_{x-i}^{(1)},$$

which is the Panjer recursion formula for a compound Poisson probability function.

4. (a) We have

$$g_0 = \prod_{i=1}^{I} \prod_{j=1}^{J} p_j^{n_{ij}},$$

and hence

$$P_S(r) = \prod_{i=1}^{I} \prod_{j=1}^{J} \left(p_j + q_j r^i\right)^{n_{ij}} = g_0 \prod_{i=1}^{I} \prod_{j=1}^{J} \left(1 + \frac{q_j}{p_j} r^i\right)^{n_{ij}}.$$

Thus,

$$\begin{aligned} \log P_S(r) &= \log g_0 + \sum_{i=1}^{I} \sum_{j=1}^{J} n_{ij} \log\left(1 + \frac{q_j}{p_j} r^i\right) \\ &= \log g_0 + \sum_{i=1}^{I} \sum_{j=1}^{J} n_{ij} \sum_{k=1}^{\infty} \frac{(-1)^{k+1}}{k} \left(\frac{q_j r^i}{p_j}\right)^k \\ &= \log g_0 + \sum_{k=1}^{\infty} \frac{(-1)^{k+1}}{k} \sum_{i=1}^{I} \sum_{j=1}^{J} n_{ij} \left(\frac{q_j r^i}{p_j}\right)^k. \end{aligned}$$

(b) From the definitions

$$\begin{aligned} Q_2(r) &= S_1(r) - \tfrac{1}{2} S_2(r) \\ &= \sum_{i=1}^{I} \sum_{j=1}^{J} n_{ij} \frac{q_j r^i}{p_j} - \tfrac{1}{2} \sum_{i=1}^{I} \sum_{j=1}^{J} n_{ij} \left(\frac{q_j r^i}{p_j}\right)^2 \end{aligned}$$

and

$$Q_2(r) = \sum_{x=1}^{\infty} b_x^{(2)} r^x.$$

Hence, if x is even,

$$b_x^{(2)} = \sum_{j=1}^{J} n_{xj} \frac{q_j}{p_j} - \tfrac{1}{2} \sum_{j=1}^{J} n_{x/2,j} \left(\frac{q_j}{p_j}\right)^2,$$

which is non-zero if $x \le 2I$. If x is odd,

$$b_x^{(2)} = \sum_{j=1}^{J} n_{xj} \frac{q_j}{p_j},$$

and this is non-zero provided that $x \le I$.

Chapter 6

1. (a) We have $\psi_d(0) = E[Z_1] = 3q$. Then equation (6.7) gives

$$\psi_d(1) = [1 - H(0)]\,\psi_d(1) + [1 - H(1)] + [1 - H(2)]$$

since $H(3) = 1$, so that

$$\psi_d(1) = q\psi_d(1) + 2q,$$

giving $\psi_d(1) = 2q/p$. Similarly,

$$\psi_d(2) = [1 - H(0)]\,\psi_d(2) + [1 - H(1)]\,\psi_d(1) + [1 - H(2)]$$

gives

$$\begin{aligned}\psi_d(2) &= \frac{q}{p}\psi_d(1) + \frac{q}{p}\\ &= \frac{2q^2}{p^2} + \frac{q}{p}.\end{aligned}$$

For $u \ge 3$, we get

$$\psi_d(u) = [1-H(0)]\,\psi_d(u) + [1-H(1)]\,\psi_d(u-1) + [1-H(2)]\,\psi_d(u-2),$$

which gives

$$\psi_d(u) = \frac{q}{p}\psi_d(u-1) + \frac{q}{p}\psi_d(u-2).$$

(b) Recursive calculation (e.g. using a spreadsheet) gives $\psi_d(10) = 0.01003$ and $\psi_d(11) = 0.00641$.

2. The equation satisfied by R_d is

$$E[\exp\{R_d(Z_1 - 1)\}] = 1$$

and

$$\begin{aligned}E[\exp\{R_d Z_1\}] &= p + \sum_{k=1}^{\infty} \exp\{R_d k\} q(1-\alpha)\alpha^{k-1}\\ &= p + \frac{q(1-\alpha)\exp\{R_d\}}{1 - \alpha\exp\{R_d\}}\\ &= \frac{p + (q-\alpha)\exp\{R_d\}}{1 - \alpha\exp\{R_d\}}.\end{aligned}$$

Thus,

$$\frac{p + (q - \alpha)\exp\{R_d\}}{1 - \alpha\exp\{R_d\}} = \exp\{R_d\},$$

which gives

$$p + (q - \alpha)\exp\{R_d\} = \exp\{R_d\} - \alpha\exp\{2R_d\}$$

or, equivalently,

$$\alpha\exp\{2R_d\} - (p + \alpha)\exp\{R_d\} + p = 0.$$

Thus,

$$\begin{aligned}\exp\{R_d\} &= \frac{1}{2\alpha}\left(p + \alpha + \sqrt{(p+\alpha)^2 - 4p\alpha}\right) \\ &= \frac{1}{2\alpha}\left(p + \alpha + \sqrt{(p-\alpha)^2}\right) \\ &= \frac{p}{\alpha},\end{aligned}$$

and so $R_d = \log(p/\alpha)$.

3. (a) This follows from the definition of $G_d(0, y)$ and the fact that $g_d(y) = 1 - H(y)$ for $y = 0, 1, 2, \ldots$.
   (b) This follows by the same arguments that give equation (6.5), noting that the amount of the first drop below the initial level u must be at most $u + y - 1$ if the deficit at ruin is to be less than y.
   (c) From Example 6.2, $H(y) = 1 - q\alpha^y$ and hence

$$G_d(0, y) = \sum_{j=0}^{y-1} q\alpha^j = q\frac{1 - \alpha^y}{1 - \alpha}.$$

Following the methodology in Example 6.2,

$$\begin{aligned}G_d(u, y) &= \sum_{j=0}^{u-1}[1 - H(j)]\,G_d(u - j, y) + \sum_{j=u}^{u+y-1}[1 - H(j)] \\ &= \sum_{j=0}^{u-1} q\alpha^j G_d(u - j, y) + \sum_{j=u}^{u+y-1} q\alpha^j\end{aligned}$$

and

$$G_d(u + 1, y) = \sum_{j=0}^{u} q\alpha^j G_d(u + 1 - j, y) + \sum_{j=u+1}^{u+y} q\alpha^j.$$

Then

$$\alpha G_d(u,y) = \sum_{j=1}^{u} q\alpha^j G_d(u+1-j,y) + \sum_{j=u+1}^{u+y} q\alpha^j,$$

and hence

$$G_d(u+1,y) - \alpha G_d(u,y) = qG_d(u+1,y),$$

giving

$$G_d(u+1,y) = \frac{\alpha}{1-q} G_d(u,y).$$

This gives

$$\begin{aligned} G_d(u,y) &= \left(\frac{\alpha}{1-q}\right)^u G_d(0,y) \\ &= q\frac{1-\alpha^y}{1-\alpha}\left(\frac{\alpha}{1-q}\right)^u. \end{aligned}$$

(d) This follows by noting that

$$\Pr(\text{deficit} = y|\text{ruin from initial surplus } 0) = g_d(y)/\psi_d(0),$$

and as $g_d(y) = 1 - H(y)$,

$$g_d(y) = 1 - p = q$$

for $y = 0$, 1 and 2 and $g_d(y) = 0$ for $y = 3, 4, 5, \ldots$. Hence, for $y = 0$, 1 and 2,

$$g_d(y)/\psi_d(0) = 1/3.$$

4. We want

$$\psi_d(0,3) = \psi_d(0,1) + h(0)\psi_d(1,2)$$

and

$$\psi_d(1,2) = \psi_d(1,1) + h(0)\psi_d(2,1) + h(1)\psi_d(1,1).$$

Now

$$\begin{aligned} \psi_d(0,1) &= 1 - H(0) = 0.3, \\ \psi_d(1,1) &= 1 - H(1) = 1 - 0.9 = 0.1, \\ \psi_d(2,1) &= 1 - H(2) = 0, \end{aligned}$$

so that

$$\psi_d(1,2) = 0.1 + 0.2 \times 0.1 = 0.12$$

and hence

$$\psi_d(0,3) = 0.3 + 0.7 \times 0.12 = 0.384.$$

Chapter 7

1. (a) From Section 1.3.3, the individual claim amount distribution has mean $300/3 = 100$ and second moment

$$\frac{2 \times 300^2}{3 \times 2} = 3 \times 10^4.$$

Hence $E[S(1)] = 100 \times 100 = 10^4$ and $V[S(1)] = 100 \times 3 \times 10^4 = 3 \times 10^6$.

(b) Similarly, $E[S(2)] = 200 \times 100 = 2 \times 10^4$ and $V[S(2)] = 200 \times 3 \times 10^4 = 6 \times 10^6$.

(c) The distribution of $S(2) - S(1)$ is the same as the distribution of $S(1)$, so the answers are the same as in part (a).

2. By equation (7.2), R satisfies

$$\lambda + 130\lambda R = \lambda \left(\frac{0.02}{0.02 - R} \right)^2,$$

so

$$1 + 130R = \left(\frac{1}{1 - 50R} \right)^2.$$

Hence

$$\left(1 - 100R + 2,500R^2\right)(1 + 130R) = 1$$

or, equivalently,

$$325,000R^2 - 10,500R + 30 = 0,$$

giving $R = 0.0032$.

3. Replacing $\exp\{Rx\}$ by $1 + Rx + \frac{1}{2}R^2x^2 + \frac{1}{6}R^3x^3$, we can write equation (7.2) as

$$\begin{aligned} 1 + 1.05R &= \int_0^\infty \left(1 + Rx + \tfrac{1}{2}R^2x^2 + \tfrac{1}{6}R^3x^3\right) f(x)dx \\ &= 1 + Rm_1 + \tfrac{1}{2}R^2m_2 + \tfrac{1}{6}R^3m_3, \end{aligned}$$

where f is the $\gamma(2.5, 2.5)$ density function, so that $m_1 = 1$, $m_2 = 7/5$ and $m_3 = 63/25$. Thus,

$$R^2 + \tfrac{5}{3}R - \tfrac{5}{42} = 0,$$

and hence $R = 0.0686$. (From Example 7.3, the actual value is 0.0685.)

4. From equation (3.2) the premium is

$$\begin{aligned} \Pi_{S(1)} &= \beta^{-1} \log E\left[\exp\{\beta S(1)\}\right] \\ &= \beta^{-1}\lambda\left(M_X(\beta) - 1\right). \end{aligned}$$

Rearranging this we get $\lambda + \Pi_{S(1)}\beta = \lambda M_X(\beta)$, so $\beta = R$.

5. (a) With $\lambda = 100$ and $c = 125$, we have

$$\begin{aligned}\psi_1(u) &= \int_0^\infty \lambda e^{-\lambda t} \int_{u+ct}^\infty e^{-x} dx dt \\ &= \int_0^\infty \lambda e^{-\lambda t} e^{-(u+ct)} dt \\ &= \frac{\lambda e^{-u}}{\lambda + c} \\ &= \tfrac{4}{9} e^{-u}.\end{aligned}$$

(b) Again with $\lambda = 100$ and $c = 125$, we have

$$\begin{aligned}\psi_2(u) &= \psi_1(u) + \int_0^\infty \lambda e^{-\lambda t} \int_0^{u+ct} \psi_1(u+ct-x) e^{-x} dx dt \\ &= \psi_1(u) + \int_0^\infty \lambda e^{-\lambda t} \int_0^{u+ct} \frac{\lambda e^{-(u+ct-x)}}{\lambda + c} e^{-x} dx dt \\ &= \psi_1(u) + \frac{\lambda e^{-u}}{\lambda + c} \int_0^\infty \lambda e^{-(\lambda+c)t} \int_0^{u+ct} dx dt \\ &= \psi_1(u) \left(1 + \int_0^\infty \lambda e^{-(\lambda+c)t} (u+ct) dt \right) \\ &= \psi_1(u) \left(1 + \frac{\lambda u}{\lambda + c} + \frac{\lambda c}{(\lambda + c)^2} \right) \\ &= \psi_1(u) \left(\tfrac{101}{81} + \tfrac{4}{9} u \right).\end{aligned}$$

6. (a) The mean individual claim amount is

$$\tfrac{1}{2} \left(\tfrac{1}{2} + \tfrac{3}{2} \right) = 1,$$

and so R satisfies

$$\begin{aligned}1 + 1.1R &= \tfrac{1}{2} \left(\frac{2}{2-R} + \frac{2/3}{(2/3) - R} \right) \\ &= \frac{1}{2-R} + \frac{1}{2-3R}.\end{aligned}$$

Thus,

$$(1 + 1.1R)(2-R)(2-3R) = 2 - 3R + 2 - R,$$

which leads to

$$3.3R^2 - 5.8R + 0.4 = 0,$$

giving $R = 0.0719$.

(b) From above, it follows that $c = 1.1\lambda$, $\phi(0) = 1/11$ and

$$f^*(s) = \frac{1}{2+s} + \frac{1}{2+3s}.$$

Thus,

$$\begin{aligned}
\phi^*(s) &= \frac{c\phi(0)}{cs - \lambda(1 - f^*(s))} \\
&= \frac{1}{10}\frac{1}{1.1s - 1 + \left(\frac{1}{2+s} + \frac{1}{2+3s}\right)} \\
&= \frac{1}{10}\frac{(2+s)(2+3s)}{1.1s(2+s)(2+3s) - (2+s)(2+3s) + (4+4s)} \\
&= \frac{1}{10}\frac{(2+s)(2+3s)}{3.3s^3 + 5.8s^2 + 0.4s} \\
&= \frac{1}{33}\frac{4+8s+3s^2}{s\left(s^2 + \frac{58}{33}s + \frac{4}{33}\right)} \\
&= \frac{1}{33}\frac{4+8s+3s^2}{s(s+R_1)(s+R_2)} \\
&= \frac{A}{s} + \frac{B}{s+R_1} + \frac{C}{s+R_2},
\end{aligned}$$

where $R_1 = 0.0719$ and $R_2 = 1.6857$. Thus,

$$A(s+R_1)(s+R_2) + Bs(s+R_2) + Cs(s+R_1) = \tfrac{1}{33}\left(4 + 8s + 3s^2\right),$$

giving $A = 1$, $B = -0.8984$ and $C = -0.0107$, so that

$$\phi(u) = 1 - 0.8984\exp\{-0.0719u\} - 0.0107\exp\{-1.6857u\}.$$

(c) The first three moments of the individual claim amount distribution are $m_1 = 1$,

$$m_2 = \tfrac{1}{2}\left(2\left(\tfrac{1}{2}\right)^2 + 2\left(\tfrac{3}{2}\right)^2\right) = \tfrac{5}{2}$$

and

$$m_3 = \tfrac{1}{2}\left(6\left(\tfrac{1}{2}\right)^3 + 6\left(\tfrac{3}{2}\right)^3\right) = \tfrac{21}{2}.$$

Hence the parameters in De Vylder's approximation are

$$\begin{aligned}
\tilde{\alpha} &= \frac{3m_2}{m_3} = \frac{15}{21} = \frac{5}{7}, \\
\tilde{\lambda} &= \frac{9\lambda m_2^3}{2m_3^2} = \frac{125\lambda}{196}, \\
\tilde{c} &= c - \lambda m_1 + \tilde{\lambda}/\tilde{\alpha} \\
&= 139\lambda/140,
\end{aligned}$$

and De Vylder's approximation is

$$0.8993\exp\{-0.0719u\}.$$

The numerical values are:

u	Exact	Approximate
0	0.9091	0.8993
10	0.4377	0.4380
20	0.2132	0.2133
30	0.1039	0.1039
40	0.0506	0.0506
50	0.0247	0.0246

7. (a) We know from Example 7.1 that $R = \alpha - \lambda/c$. Next, we have

$$\begin{aligned} E[Xe^{RX}] &= \int_0^\infty xe^{Rx}\alpha e^{-\alpha x}dx \\ &= \frac{\alpha}{(\alpha-R)^2}\int_0^\infty (\alpha-R)^2 xe^{-(\alpha-R)x}dx \\ &= \frac{\alpha}{(\alpha-R)^2} \\ &= \frac{c^2\alpha}{\lambda^2}, \end{aligned}$$

and as $m_1 = 1/\alpha$, we have

$$C = \frac{c/\lambda - 1/\alpha}{c^2\alpha/\lambda^2 - c/\lambda} = \frac{\lambda}{\alpha c}.$$

(b) Here $R = 0.0719$, and so

$$\begin{aligned} E\left[Xe^{RX}\right] &= \tfrac{1}{2}\int_0^\infty xe^{Rx}\left(2e^{-2x} + \tfrac{2}{3}e^{-2x/3}\right)dx \\ &= \int_0^\infty xe^{-(2-R)x}dx + \tfrac{1}{3}\int_0^\infty xe^{-(2/3-R)x}dx \\ &= \frac{1}{(2-R)^2} + \tfrac{1}{3}\frac{1}{(2/3-R)^2} \\ &= 1.2113. \end{aligned}$$

As $m_1 = 1$ and $c/\lambda = 1.1$, the value of C is 0.8984, which is our approximation to $\psi(0)$, and to four decimal places the approximations are the same as the exact values for other values of u in the above table.

8. (a) As $k(x) = (1 - F(x))/m_1$,

$$\begin{aligned} E[L_1^r] - \frac{1}{m_1}\int_0^\infty x^r \int_x^\infty f(y)dydx \\ = \frac{1}{m_1}\int_0^\infty \int_0^y x^r dx f(y)dy \end{aligned}$$

$$= \frac{1}{(r+1)\,m_1}\int_0^\infty y^{r+1} f(y)dy$$
$$= \frac{m_{r+1}}{(r+1)\,m_1}.$$

(b) As N has a geometric distribution with mean $1/\theta$, $E[N] = 1/\theta$ and $V[N] = (1+\theta)/\theta^2$. Then

$$E[L] = E[N]E[L_1] = \frac{m_2}{2\theta m_1}$$

and

$$\begin{aligned} V[L] &= E[N]V[L_1] + V[N]E[L_1]^2 \\ &= \frac{1}{\theta}\left(\frac{m_3}{3m_1} - \frac{m_2^2}{4m_1^2}\right) + \frac{1+\theta}{\theta^2}\frac{m_2^2}{4m_1^2} \\ &= \frac{m_3}{3\theta m_1} + \frac{m_2^2}{4\theta^2 m_1^2}, \end{aligned}$$

giving

$$E[L^2] = \frac{m_3}{3\theta m_1} + \frac{m_2^2}{2\theta^2 m_1^2}.$$

9. (a) The rationale is that the mixed distribution that approximates ϕ and the distribution ϕ each have the same mean.

(b) As

$$f(x) = \tfrac{1}{3}\left(\tfrac{1}{2}e^{-x/2} + e^{-x} + 2e^{-2x}\right),$$

we have

$$m_1 = \tfrac{1}{3}\left(2 + 1 + \tfrac{1}{2}\right) = \tfrac{7}{6},$$
$$m_2 = \tfrac{2}{3}\left(4 + 1 + \tfrac{1}{4}\right) = \tfrac{7}{2}$$

and

$$M_X(r) = \tfrac{1}{3}\left(\frac{1}{1-2R} + \frac{1}{1-R} + \frac{2}{2-R}\right).$$

Thus, with $\theta = 0.05$, the adjustment coefficient R satisfies

$$1 + 1.05\tfrac{7}{6}R = \tfrac{1}{3}\left(\frac{1}{1-2R} + \frac{1}{1-R} + \frac{2}{2-R}\right),$$

which, after some straightforward algebra, reduces to

$$2.45R^3 - 6.575R^2 + 3.9083R - 0.1167 = 0,$$

from which we find that $R = 0.0315$.

Further,

$$E\left[Xe^{RX}\right] = \tfrac{1}{3}\int_0^\infty xe^{Rx}\left(\tfrac{1}{2}e^{-x/2} + e^{-x} + 2e^{-2x}\right)dx$$
$$= \tfrac{1}{6}\frac{1}{(1/2-R)^2} + \tfrac{1}{3}\frac{1}{(1-R)^2} + \tfrac{2}{3}\frac{1}{(2-R)^2}$$
$$= 1.28674,$$

giving

$$C = \frac{0.05 \times \frac{7}{6}}{1.28674 - 1.05 \times \frac{7}{6}} = 0.944782.$$

Next set $\psi(0) = C + A = 20/21$, so that $A = 0.007599$, and finally set

$$\int_0^\infty \psi(u)du = E[L] = \frac{C}{R} + \frac{A}{S},$$

where

$$E[L] = \frac{m_2}{2\theta m_1} = \frac{7/2}{0.1 \times 7/6} = 30.$$

Then

$$S = \frac{A}{30 - C/R} = 1.02686,$$

and so our approximation to $\psi(20)$ is 0.5032.

10. (a) Set $\psi(0)\alpha/\beta = E[L]$ and $\psi(0)\alpha(\alpha+1)/\beta^2 = E\left[L^2\right]$ with $\psi(0) = \lambda/(\mu c)$, so that

$$E[L] = \frac{\lambda}{\mu(c\mu - \lambda)}$$

and

$$E[L^2] = \frac{2\lambda}{\mu^2(c\mu-\lambda)} + \frac{2\lambda^2}{\mu^2(c\mu-\lambda)^2}$$
$$= \frac{2\lambda c}{\mu(c\mu-\lambda)^2}.$$

Then

$$E[L^2] = \psi(0)\left(\frac{\alpha^2}{\beta^2} + \frac{\alpha}{\beta^2}\right)$$
$$= \frac{1}{\psi(0)}E[L]^2 + \frac{1}{\beta}E[L],$$

giving

$$\frac{2\lambda c}{\mu(c\mu-\lambda)^2} = \frac{\mu c}{\lambda}\frac{\lambda^2}{\mu^2(c\mu-\lambda)^2} + \frac{1}{\beta}\frac{\lambda}{\mu(c\mu-\lambda)},$$

so that

$$2\lambda c\mu = \lambda c\mu + \frac{1}{\beta}\lambda\mu(c\mu - \lambda).$$

and hence $\beta = \mu - \lambda/c$ and $\alpha = 1$.

(b) We find

$$E[L] = \frac{m_2}{2\theta m_1} = \frac{5/2}{0.2} = 12.5$$

and

$$\begin{aligned} E[L^2] &= \frac{m_3}{3\theta m_1} + \frac{m_2^2}{2\theta^2 m_1^2} \\ &= \frac{21/2}{0.3} + \frac{25/4}{0.02} \\ &= 347.5. \end{aligned}$$

As $\psi(0) = 10/11$, we have

$$\frac{10}{11}\frac{\alpha}{\beta} = 12.5$$

and

$$\frac{10}{11}\frac{\alpha(\alpha+1)}{\beta^2} = 347.5,$$

giving $\alpha = 275/281$ and $\beta = 20/281$. The approximate values are shown below with exact values (from Question 6).

u	Exact	Approximate
0	0.9091	0.9091
10	0.4377	0.4368
20	0.2132	0.2125
30	0.1039	0.1036
40	0.0506	0.0506
50	0.0247	0.0248

11. (a) Starting from $h(r) = \lambda - cr - \lambda E[e^{-rX}]$ we have $h(0) = 0$ and $h'(r) = -c + \lambda E[Xe^{-rX}]$ so that $h'(0) = -c + \lambda E[X] > 0$ under our assumption that $c < \lambda E[X]$. Further, $h''(r) = -\lambda E[X^2 e^{-rX}] < 0$ so that any turning point of h is a maximum. Finally,

$$\lim_{r\to\infty} h(r) = -\infty,$$

meaning that there is a unique turning point and hence there exists $R > 0$ such that $h(R) = 0$.

(b) We solve

$$\lambda - cR - \frac{\lambda\alpha}{\alpha + R} = 0,$$

giving $R = (\lambda - \alpha c)/c$.

(c) If there is no income before time u/c, then $U(u/c) = u - c(u/c) = 0$ and ruin occurs. The probability of no income by time u/c is $e^{-\lambda u/c}$ since the time to the first event (income) is exponentially distributed with parameter λ. This explains the first term. The density associated with the first income occurring at time $t < u/c$ is $\lambda e^{-\lambda t}$. If there is income at time $t < u/c$, and the amount of the income is $x > 0$, with associated density $f(x)$, ruin can subsequently occur with probability $\psi(u - ct + x)$, which explains the integral expression.

(d) Insert e^{-Rz} for $\psi(z)$ in the right-hand side of equation (7.30). We get

$$\begin{aligned}
&e^{-\lambda u/c} + \int_0^{u/c} \lambda e^{-\lambda t} \int_0^{\infty} \psi(u - ct + x) f(x)\, dx\, dt \\
&= e^{-\lambda u/c} + e^{-Ru} \int_0^{u/c} e^{-(\lambda - cR)t} \lambda \int_0^{\infty} e^{-Rx} f(x)\, dx\, dt \\
&= e^{-\lambda u/c} + e^{-Ru} \int_0^{u/c} (\lambda - cR)\, e^{-(\lambda - cR)t}\, dt \\
&= e^{-\lambda u/c} + e^{-Ru} \left(1 - e^{-(\lambda - cR)u/c}\right) \\
&= e^{-Ru}.
\end{aligned}$$

(e) Setting

$$\psi(40) = \exp\left\{-40\left(\frac{1}{c} - 1\right)\right\} \le 0.01$$

yields $c \le 0.8968$.

12. Insert

$$K^{n*}(u) = 1 - \sum_{j=0}^{n-1} e^{-\alpha u} \frac{(\alpha u)^j}{j!}$$

in equation (7.19), as follows:

$$\begin{aligned}
\phi(u) &= \frac{\theta}{1+\theta} + \sum_{n=1}^{\infty} \frac{\theta}{(1+\theta)^{n+1}} \left(1 - \sum_{j=0}^{n-1} e^{-\alpha u} \frac{(\alpha u)^j}{j!}\right) \\
&= \frac{\theta}{1+\theta} + \frac{\theta}{1+\theta} \sum_{n=1}^{\infty} (1+\theta)^{-n} - \frac{\theta}{1+\theta} \sum_{n=1}^{\infty} (1+\theta)^{-n} \sum_{j=0}^{n-1} e^{-\alpha u} \frac{(\alpha u)^j}{j!} \\
&= \frac{\theta}{1+\theta} + \frac{1}{1+\theta} - \frac{\theta e^{-\alpha u}}{1+\theta} \sum_{n=1}^{\infty} (1+\theta)^{-n} \sum_{j=0}^{n-1} \frac{(\alpha u)^j}{j!}.
\end{aligned}$$

Now change the order of the double summation:

$$\sum_{n=1}^{\infty}(1+\theta)^{-n}\sum_{j=0}^{n-1}\frac{(\alpha u)^j}{j!} = \sum_{j=0}^{\infty}\sum_{n=j+1}^{\infty}(1+\theta)^{-n}\frac{(\alpha u)^j}{j!}$$
$$= \sum_{j=0}^{\infty}\frac{(\alpha u)^j}{j!}\sum_{n=j+1}^{\infty}(1+\theta)^{-n}$$
$$= \sum_{j=0}^{\infty}\frac{(\alpha u)^j}{j!}\frac{1}{\theta(1+\theta)^j}$$
$$= \frac{1}{\theta}e^{\alpha u/(1+\theta)}.$$

Hence

$$\phi(u) = 1 - \frac{\theta e^{-\alpha u}}{1+\theta}\frac{1}{\theta}e^{\alpha u/(1+\theta)}$$
$$= 1 - \frac{1}{1+\theta}e^{-\alpha\theta u/(1+\theta)}.$$

13. (a) $L_1 \sim Pa(3,3)$ since

$$k(x) = \frac{1}{m_1}(1-F(x)) = \left(\frac{3}{3+x}\right)^4 = \frac{3\times 3^3}{(3+x)^4}$$

as $m_1 = 1$ and $F(x) = 1-(3/(3+x))^4$.

(b) Approximations are shown below for the same values of κ as in Table 7.2.

	Lower Bounds for $\psi(u)$			Upper Bounds for $\psi(u)$		
u	$\kappa = 20$	$\kappa = 50$	$\kappa = 100$	$\kappa = 20$	$\kappa = 50$	$\kappa = 100$
10	0.47037	0.47326	0.47423	0.48001	0.47712	0.47616
20	0.26140	0.26423	0.26518	0.27090	0.26804	0.26708
30	0.14758	0.14982	0.15058	0.15514	0.15285	0.15209
40	0.08415	0.08578	0.08632	0.08966	0.08798	0.08742
50	0.04838	0.04950	0.04988	0.05220	0.05103	0.05064
60	0.02803	0.02878	0.02904	0.03060	0.02981	0.02955

	Average of Bounds		
u	$\kappa = 20$	$\kappa = 50$	$\kappa = 100$
10	0.47519	0.47519	0.47519
20	0.26615	0.26613	0.26613
30	0.15136	0.15134	0.15133
40	0.08691	0.08688	0.08687
50	0.05029	0.05026	0.05026
60	0.02932	0.02930	0.02929

Chapter 8

1. Note that when $u = b$, the surplus remains at b until the first claim occurs. Thus,

$$\xi_r(b,b) = \int_0^\infty \lambda e^{-\lambda t} \int_0^b f(x)\xi_r(b-x,b)dxdt + \int_0^\infty \lambda e^{-\lambda t}(1-F(b))\,dt$$
$$= \int_0^b f(x)\xi_r(b-x,b)dx + 1 - F(b).$$

As $\xi_r(u,b) \ge \xi_r(b,b)$ for $0 \le u \le b$,

$$\xi_r(b,b) \ge \xi_r(b,b)\int_0^b f(x)dx + 1 - F(b)$$
$$= \xi_r(b,b)F(b) + 1 - F(b),$$

we have $\xi_r(b,b) \ge 1$, i.e. $\xi_r(b,b) = 1$, and hence $\xi_r(u,b) = 1$ for $0 \le u \le b$.

2. Ruin can occur with or without the surplus attaining level b prior to ruin. Let $\Psi(u)$ denote the ruin probability required. Then

$$\Psi(u) = \xi(u,b) + \chi(u,b)\psi(b),$$

where $\xi(u,b)$ and $\chi(u,b)$ are calculated with a 20% loading and $\psi(b)$ is calculated with a 10% loading. Thus,

$$\xi(10,20) = \frac{\psi(10) - \psi(20)}{1 - \psi(20)} = \frac{0.1574 - 0.0297}{1 - 0.0297} = 0.1316,$$

and $\chi(10,20) = 0.8684$ and $\psi(20) = 0.1476$, giving

$$\Psi(10) = 0.1316 + 0.8684 \times 0.1476 = 0.2597.$$

3. Conditioning on the time and the amount of the first claim we obtain

$$G(u,y) = \int_0^\infty \lambda e^{-\lambda t} \int_0^{u+ct} G(u+ct-x,y)f(x)dxdt$$
$$+ \int_0^\infty \lambda e^{-\lambda t} \int_{u+ct}^{u+ct+y} f(x)dxdt$$
$$= \frac{\lambda}{c}\int_u^\infty e^{-\lambda(s-u)/c} \int_0^s f(x)G(s-x,y)dxds$$
$$+ \frac{\lambda}{c}\int_u^\infty e^{-\lambda(s-u)/c} \int_s^{s+y} f(x)dxds$$
$$= e^{\lambda u/c}\left(\frac{\lambda}{c}\int_u^\infty e^{-\lambda s/c} \int_0^s f(x)G(s-x,y)dxds\right.$$
$$\left. + \frac{\lambda}{c}\int_u^\infty e^{-\lambda s/c} \int_s^{s+y} f(x)dxds\right).$$

Differentiation with respect to u gives

$$\frac{\partial}{\partial u}G(u,y) = \frac{\lambda}{c}G(u,y) - \frac{\lambda}{c}\int_0^u f(x)G(u-x,y)dx - \frac{\lambda}{c}\int_u^{u+y} f(x)dx.$$

4. We have

$$\frac{g(u,y)}{\psi(u)} = \frac{(1.1589 + 1.0893y)e^{-R_1u-2y} - (0.3256 - 0.5774y)e^{-R_2u-2y}}{\psi(u)},$$

where $R_1 = 0.2268$ and $R_2 = 2.9399$, so

$$\begin{aligned}\frac{g(u,y)}{\psi(u)} &= \frac{1.1589e^{-R_1u} - 0.3256e^{-R_2u}}{2\psi(u)}2e^{-2y} \\ &\quad + \frac{1.0893e^{-R_1u} + 0.5774e^{-R_2u}}{4\psi(u)}4ye^{-2y} \\ &= w_1(u)2e^{-2y} + w_2(u)4ye^{-2y},\end{aligned}$$

where

$$w_1(u) = \frac{1.1589e^{-R_1u} - 0.3256e^{-R_2u}}{2\psi(u)}$$

and

$$w_2(u) = \frac{1.0893e^{-R_1u} + 0.5774e^{-R_2u}}{4\psi(u)}.$$

Values for these weights are

u	0	1	2	3	4	5
$w_1(u)$	0.500	0.669	0.679	0.680	0.680	0.680
$w_2(u)$	0.500	0.331	0.321	0.320	0.320	0.320

We conclude that the conditional distribution of the deficit at ruin varies little with initial surplus.

5. If ruin occurs with a deficit of y, then we require that the surplus attains 0 without falling below y, and the required probability is

$$\begin{aligned}\int_0^\infty \frac{g(u,y)}{\psi(u)}\chi(0,y)dy &= \int_0^\infty \alpha e^{-\alpha y}\frac{1-\psi(0)}{1-\psi(y)}dy \\ &= \alpha(1-\psi(0))\int_0^\infty e^{-\alpha y}\sum_{j=0}^\infty \psi(y)^j dy \\ &= \alpha(1-\psi(0))\sum_{j=0}^\infty \int_0^\infty e^{-\alpha y}\left(\frac{\lambda}{\alpha c}\right)^j e^{-Ryj}dy\end{aligned}$$

$$= \alpha(1 - \psi(0)) \sum_{j=0}^{\infty} \left(\frac{\lambda}{\alpha c}\right)^j \frac{1}{\alpha + Rj}$$

$$= \sum_{j=0}^{\infty} \left(\frac{\lambda}{\alpha c}\right)^j \frac{R}{\alpha + Rj}$$

since $R = \alpha - \lambda/c = \alpha(1 - \psi(0))$.

6. (a) With $\delta = 0$, equation (8.25) becomes

$$\varphi^*(s) = \frac{c\varphi(0) - \lambda\,\alpha^*(s)}{cs - \lambda + \lambda f^*(s)} = \frac{\phi^*(s)}{c\phi(0)} \left(c\varphi(0) - \lambda\alpha^*(s)\right),$$

where the second step follows from equation (7.12), and inversion gives

$$\varphi(u) = \frac{1}{c\,\phi(0)} \left(c\,\varphi(0)\,\phi(u) - \lambda \int_0^u \alpha(x)\,\phi(u-x)\,dx\right).$$

(b) Our Gerber-Shiu function is

$$\varphi(u) = E\left[\exp\{-s\,U(T_u^-)\} I(T_u < \infty)\right],$$

which is the Laplace transform of $U(T_u^-)$. So

$$\varphi(u) = \int_0^\infty e^{-sx}\, w(u,x)\,dx.$$

Further

$$\alpha(u) = \int_0^\infty a(u,y) f(u+y)\,dy = \exp\{-su\}(1 - F(u)).$$

Thus,

$$\varphi(u) = \frac{\phi(u)}{\phi(0)}\,\varphi(0) - \frac{\lambda}{c\phi(0)} \int_0^u e^{-sx}\,(1 - F(x))\,\phi(u-x)\,dx.$$

Note that the integral is just the Laplace transform of a function that is $(1 - F(x))\,\phi(u-x)$ for $0 < x < u$ and 0 otherwise. Also

$$\varphi(0) = \frac{\lambda}{c}\,\alpha^*(\rho),$$

and as $\rho = 0$ when $\delta = 0$ we have

$$\varphi(0) = \frac{\lambda}{c} \int_0^\infty e^{-su}\,(1 - F(u))\,du.$$

Inversion gives $w(0,x) = (\lambda/c)\,(1 - F(x))$.
Next, inverting $\varphi(u)$ we get the density of the surplus immediately prior to ruin as

$$w(u,x) = \frac{\phi(u)}{\phi(0)}\, w(0,x) - \frac{\lambda}{c\,\phi(0)} I(x<u)(1-F(x))\,\phi(u-x)$$

$$= w(0,x)\frac{\phi(u) - I(x<u)\phi(u-x)}{\phi(0)}.$$

7. (a) This is achieved by making the substitution $x = u - c\tau$ in the second integral, then rearranging the equation.
   (b) For a surplus process starting at 0, the terms on the left-hand side give the density associated with a drop in the surplus process to level $ct - u - y$ at time t. The first term represents the situation where there are no claims up to time t so that the surplus is ct at time t, then a claim occurs of amount $u + y$ causing the surplus to fall to $ct - u - y$. The second term represents the situations where the aggregate claim amount is $u - x$ for $0 < x < u$ at time t, so that the surplus at time t is $ct - u + x$, then a claim of amount $x + y$ occurs, resulting in a drop to level $ct - u - y$. Note that for such realisations of the surplus process, there is a final time when the surplus process upcrosses through level $ct - u$, and that time cannot be before $t - u/c$ (since that is the time required to reach $ct - u$ if there are no claims). The terms on the right-hand side simply give a different representation of these realisations. The first represents the case when there are no claims up to time $t - u/c$, so that the surplus process is at level $ct - u$ at that time, and $\omega(0, y, u/c)$ is the density associated with the first drop below that level occurring after a further time period of u/c (so at time t), and the amount of the drop being y, resulting in a surplus level of $ct - u - y$ at time t. Similarly, in the integral term consider $g(x, t - (u - x)/c)$. An aggregate claim amount of x at time $t - (u - x)/c$ implies a surplus at that time of $ct - u$, and $\omega(0, y, (u - x)/c)$ is the density associated with the first drop below that level occurring after a further time period of $(u - x)/c$ (so at time t), and the amount of the drop being y, resulting in a surplus level of $ct - u - y$ at time t.
8. (a) Consider $0 < x < u$. Then if ruin occurs from initial surplus u, the surplus process must cross downwards through x. So

$$\varphi(u) = \varphi(u-x)\,\varphi(x),$$

   meaning that $\varphi(u)$ is of the form $e^{-\rho u}$.
   (b) Using similar arguments to those in the solution to Exercise 11 in Chapter 7 we have

$$\varphi(u) = e^{-(\lambda+\delta)u/c} + \int_0^{u/c} \lambda\, e^{-(\lambda+\delta)t} \int_0^{\infty} f(x)\,\varphi(u - ct + x)\,dx\,dt.$$

   Inserting $\varphi(u) = e^{-\rho u}$ into this equation yields

$$\lambda + \delta - c\rho = \lambda f^*(\rho).$$

(c) If there is no random gain by time $t = u/c$ then $U(t) = 0$ and ruin occurs. As the time to the first random gain is exponentially distributed, $\Pr(T_u = u/c) = e^{-\lambda u/c}$.

(d) As in the Appendix, we have

$$\begin{aligned} e^{-\rho u} &= e^{-(\delta+\lambda)u/c} + \sum_{n=1}^{\infty} \frac{(\lambda/c)^n}{n!} u \int_0^{\infty} (x+u)^{n-1} e^{-(\delta+\lambda)(x+u)/c} f^{n*}(x)\, dx \\ &= e^{-(\delta+\lambda)u/c} + \sum_{n=1}^{\infty} \frac{(\lambda/c)^n}{n!} u \int_{u/c}^{\infty} (ct)^{n-1} e^{-(\delta+\lambda)t} f^{n*}(ct-u)\, c\, dt \\ &= e^{-(\delta+\lambda)u/c} + \sum_{n=1}^{\infty} \frac{\lambda^n}{n!} u \int_{u/c}^{\infty} e^{-\delta t} e^{-\lambda t} t^{n-1} f^{n*}(ct-u)\, dt \\ &= e^{-\delta u/c} e^{-\lambda u/c} + \int_{u/c}^{\infty} e^{-\delta t} \frac{u}{t} \sum_{n=1}^{\infty} e^{-\lambda t} \frac{(\lambda t)^n}{n!} f^{n*}(ct-u)\, dt. \end{aligned}$$

Inversion yields that T_u has a mass of probability $e^{-\lambda u/c}$ at u/c (as was established in part (c)) and density $(u/t)\, g(ct-u, t)$ for $t > u/c$.

(e) We know from the solution to Exercise 11 in Chapter 7 that the ultimate ruin probability is $\psi(u) = e^{-Ru}$ where $R = (\lambda/c) - \alpha$. Now, writing ρ as ρ_δ,

$$\varphi(u) = E[e^{-\delta T_u} I(T_u < \infty)] = e^{-\rho_\delta u},$$

so

$$-\frac{d}{d\delta}\varphi(u) = E[e^{-\delta T_u} T_u I(T_u < \infty)] = \rho_\delta' u e^{-\rho_\delta u}.$$

Setting $\delta = 0$ gives

$$E[T_u I(T_u < \infty)] = \rho_0' u e^{-\rho_0 u}.$$

When $\delta = 0$ we have $\rho_0 = R$ (set $\delta = 0$ in $\varphi(u)$ to see this), and we can find ρ_0' by differentiating

$$\delta + \lambda - c\rho_\delta = \frac{\lambda\alpha}{\alpha + \rho_\delta},$$

which gives

$$1 - c\rho_\delta' = \frac{-\lambda\alpha\rho_\delta'}{(\alpha+\rho_\delta)^2}.$$

Set $\delta = 0$. Then $\alpha + \rho_0 = \lambda/c$ and a little algebra gives

$$\rho_0' = \frac{\lambda}{c(\lambda - \alpha c)}.$$

Hence

$$E[T_u \mid T_u < \infty] = \frac{\lambda u}{c(\lambda - \alpha c)}.$$

9. (a) It was shown in Section 8.6.5 that

$$\rho_0' = \frac{1}{c - \lambda m_1}$$

and

$$1 - c\frac{d}{d\delta}\rho_\delta = -\lambda \int_0^\infty \left(\frac{d}{d\delta}\rho_\delta x\right) e^{-\rho_\delta x} f(x)dx.$$

Differentiate again to obtain

$$\begin{aligned} -c\frac{d^2}{d\delta^2}\rho_\delta = \lambda \int_0^\infty \left(\frac{d}{d\delta}\rho_\delta\, x\right)^2 e^{-\rho_\delta x} f(x)dx \\ -\lambda \int_0^\infty \left(\frac{d^2}{d\delta^2}\rho_\delta x\right) e^{-\rho_\delta x} f(x)dx. \end{aligned}$$

Hence

$$-c\,\rho_0'' = \lambda \int_0^\infty \left(\rho_0' x\right)^2 f(x)dx - \lambda \int_0^\infty \rho_0''\, x f(x)\, dx,$$

and so

$$(c - \lambda\, m_1)\, \rho_0'' = -\lambda\, m_2\, (\rho_0')^2\,,$$

i.e.

$$\rho_0'' = \frac{-\lambda\, m_2}{(c - \lambda\, m_1)^3}.$$

(b) It was shown in Section 8.6.5 that

$$\frac{d}{d\delta}\varphi(0) = \frac{-\lambda}{c}\int_0^\infty \left(u\frac{d}{d\delta}\rho_\delta\right) e^{-\rho_\delta u}\,(1 - F(u))\, du,$$

and so

$$\begin{aligned} \frac{d^2}{d\delta^2}\varphi(0) = \frac{\lambda}{c}\int_0^\infty \left(u\frac{d}{d\delta}\rho_\delta\right)^2 e^{-\rho_\delta u}\,(1 - F(u))\, du \\ \frac{-\lambda}{c}\int_0^\infty \left(u\frac{d^2}{d\delta^2}\rho_\delta\right) e^{-\rho_\delta u}\,(1 - F(u))\, du, \end{aligned}$$

so that

$$\begin{aligned} E\left[T_0^2\, I(T_0 < \infty)\right] = \frac{\lambda}{c}\int_0^\infty \left(u\,\rho_0'\right)^2\,(1 - F(u))\, du \\ -\frac{\lambda}{c}\int_0^\infty u\,\rho_0''\,(1 - F(u))\, du \end{aligned}$$

$$= \frac{\lambda}{c}(\rho_0')^2 \int_0^\infty u^2\,(1 - F(u))\,du$$
$$- \frac{\lambda}{c}\rho_0'' \int_0^\infty u\,(1 - F(u))du$$
$$= \psi(0)\left((\rho_0')^2 \frac{m_3}{3m_1} - \rho_0'' \frac{m_2}{2m_1}\right).$$

Hence

$$E\left[T_{0,c}^2\right] = (\rho_0')^2 \frac{m_3}{3m_1} - \rho_0'' \frac{m_2}{2m_1}$$
$$= \frac{m_3}{3\,m_1\,(c - \lambda\,m_1)^2} + \frac{\lambda\,m_2^2}{2\,m_1\,(c - \lambda\,m_1)^3}.$$

(c) We use the fact that $T_{u,c}$ has a compound distribution, and the counting distribution has mean

$$1 + \psi(0)\alpha u = 1 + \frac{\lambda u}{c}$$

and variance

$$\psi(0)\alpha u = \frac{\lambda u}{c}.$$

Using $E[T_{0,c}] = 1/(c\alpha - \lambda)$ and, from part (b),

$$E[T_{0,c}^2] = \frac{2}{(c\alpha - \lambda)^2} + \frac{2\lambda}{(c\alpha - \lambda)^3},$$

we get (by applying formula (4.6)),

$$V[T_{u,c}] = \left(1 + \frac{\lambda u}{c}\right)\left(\frac{2}{(c\alpha - \lambda)^2} + \frac{2\lambda}{(c\alpha - \lambda)^3} - \frac{1}{(c\alpha - \lambda)^2}\right)$$
$$+ \frac{\lambda u}{c}\,\frac{1}{(c\alpha - \lambda)^2}$$
$$= \frac{(c + \lambda u)(c\alpha - \lambda) + 2\lambda(c + \lambda u) + \lambda u(c\alpha - \lambda)}{c(c\alpha - \lambda)^3}$$
$$= \frac{\alpha c(c + 2\lambda u) + \lambda c}{c(c\alpha - \lambda)^3}.$$

10. (a) The distribution of the time to the first claim is exponential with mean $1/\lambda$, and on any subsequent occasion that the surplus attains the barrier, the distribution of the time to the next claim is also exponential with mean $1/\lambda$. Hence the distribution of the amount of dividends in any dividend stream is exponential with mean c/λ.

(b) There is a further dividend stream if the first claim is of amount $x < b$ and the surplus subsequently attains b from level $b - x$ without going below 0. The probability of this is

$$p(b) = \int_0^\infty \lambda e^{-\lambda t} \int_0^b f(x)\chi(b-x,b)dxdt = \int_0^b f(x)\chi(b-x,b)dx.$$

Should the surplus process return to level b, the probability of a further dividend stream is also $p(b)$. Thus,

$$\Pr(N=r) = p(b)^{r-1}(1-p(b))$$

for $r = 1, 2, 3, \ldots$.

(c) Let Δ denote the total amount of dividends. Then $M_\Delta(t) = M_N\left[\log M_D(t)\right]$ where N is distributed as in part (b) and D is exponentially distributed with mean c/λ, so that $M_D(t) = \lambda/(\lambda - ct)$. As

$$\begin{aligned} M_N(t) &= \sum_{r=1}^\infty e^{tr} p(b)^{r-1}(1-p(b)) \\ &= (1-p(b))e^t/(1-p(b)e^t), \end{aligned}$$

we have

$$\begin{aligned} M_\Delta(t) &= \frac{(1-p(b))M_D(t)}{1-p(b)M_D(t)} \\ &= \frac{(1-p(b))\,\lambda}{(1-p(b))\,\lambda - ct}, \end{aligned}$$

so that Δ is exponentially distributed with mean $c/((1-p(b))\lambda)$.

(d) We now have $\Pr(N=0) = 1 - \chi(u,b)$, and for $r = 1, 2, 3, \ldots$,

$$\Pr(N=r) = \chi(u,b)p(b)^{r-1}(1-p(b))$$

by the same argument as in part (b). Now

$$\begin{aligned} M_N(t) &= 1 - \chi(u,b) + \sum_{r=1}^\infty e^{tr}\chi(u,b)p(b)^{r-1}(1-p(b)) \\ &= 1 - \chi(u,b) + \chi(u,b)\frac{(1-p(b))e^t}{1-p(b)e^t}, \end{aligned}$$

and hence

$$\begin{aligned} M_\Delta(t) &= 1 - \chi(u,b) + \chi(u,b)\frac{(1-p(b))M_D(t)}{1-p(b)M_D(t)} \\ &= 1 - \chi(u,b) + \chi(u,b)\frac{(1-p(b))\,\lambda}{(1-p(b))\,\lambda - ct}, \end{aligned}$$

and so the distribution of Δ is a mixture of a degenerate distribution at 0 and the exponential distribution in part (c), where the weight attaching to the degenerate distribution is $1 - \chi(u,b)$.

Chapter 9

1. As $X \sim \gamma(2, 0.01)$, $E[X] = 200$ and hence $E[h(X)] = E[X/2] = 100$. Next, with $\beta = 0.01$,

$$\begin{aligned}
&E[\min(X, M)] \\
&= \int_0^M \beta^2 x^2 e^{-\beta x} dx + M e^{-\beta M} (1 + \beta M) \\
&= \frac{\Gamma(3)}{\beta} \int_0^M \frac{\beta^3 x^2 e^{-\beta x}}{\Gamma(3)} dx + M e^{-\beta M} (1 + \beta M) \\
&= \frac{2}{\beta} \left(1 - e^{-\beta M} \left(1 + \beta M + \frac{\beta^2 M^2}{2} \right) \right) + M e^{-\beta M} (1 + \beta M) \\
&= \frac{2}{\beta} \left(1 - e^{-\beta M} \left(1 + \frac{\beta M}{2} \right) \right) \\
&= 200 \left(1 - e^{-0.01M} (1 + 0.005M) \right).
\end{aligned}$$

Solving $200\,(1 - \exp\{-0.01M\}(1 + 0.005M)) = 100$ numerically gives $M = 114.62$.

2. We want to maximise

$$E[u(-P_R - S_I)] = -\exp\{\beta P_R\} E[\exp\{\beta S_I\}],$$

where P_R is the reinsurance premium and $S_I = aS$ where S denotes aggregate claims. Further, for proportion retained a,

$$P_R = (1 + \theta_R) \times 100 \times 100(1 - a) = (1 + \theta_R)(1 - a) \times 10^4,$$

and S_I has a compound Poisson distribution with individual claims being exponentially distributed with mean $100a$. Thus,

$$\begin{aligned}
E[\exp\{\beta S_I\}] &= \exp\left\{ 100 \left(\left(\frac{0.01/a}{0.01/a - \beta} \right) - 1 \right) \right\} \\
&= \exp\left\{ \frac{100 a \beta}{0.01 - a\beta} \right\},
\end{aligned}$$

and hence

$$\begin{aligned}
E[u(-P_R - S_I)] &= -\exp\{(1 + \theta_R)(1 - a)\beta \times 10^4\} \exp\left\{ \frac{100 a \beta}{0.01 - a\beta} \right\} \\
&= -\exp\{h(a)\},
\end{aligned}$$

where

$$h(a) = (1 + \theta_R)(1 - a)\beta \times 10^4 + \frac{100 a \beta}{0.01 - a\beta}.$$

We thus require to find a that minimises $h(a)$. Differentiation gives

$$\frac{d}{da}h(a) = -(1+\theta_R)\beta \times 10^4 + \frac{100\beta}{0.01 - a\beta} + \frac{100a\beta^2}{(0.01-a\beta)^2}$$
$$= -(1+\theta_R)\beta \times 10^4 + \frac{\beta}{(0.01-a\beta)^2},$$

and setting this equal to zero we get

$$(0.01 - a\beta)^2 = \frac{1}{(1+\theta_R)\times 10^4},$$

which gives

$$a = \frac{1}{100\beta}\left(1 - (1+\theta_R)^{-1/2}\right)$$

provided this is less than 1. Finally, we note that

$$\frac{d^2}{da^2}h(a) = \frac{2\beta^2}{(0.01-a\beta)^3} > 0.$$

3. (a) Let X be exponentially distributed with mean 100, and let $Y = \max(0, X - M)$. Then

$$P(M) = 100(E[Y] + 0.5E[Y^2]),$$

where

$$E[Y] = \int_M^\infty (x-M)0.01e^{-0.01x}dx$$
$$= \int_0^\infty 0.01ye^{-0.01(y+M)}dy = 100e^{-0.01M}$$

and

$$E[Y^2] = \int_M^\infty (x-M)^2 0.01e^{-0.01x}dx$$
$$= \int_0^\infty 0.01y^2e^{-0.01(y+M)}dy = 2\times 10^4 e^{-0.01M}.$$

Hence

$$P(M) = (10^4 + 10^6)e^{-0.01M} = 101 \times 10^4 e^{-0.01M}.$$

(b) We want to find M to maximise $E[u(-P(M) - S(M))]$ where $S(M)$ has a compound Poisson distribution, with Poisson parameter 100 and individual claims are distributed as $\min(X, M)$. Consider

$$\begin{aligned}
&E\left[e^{0.005S(M)}\right] \\
&= \exp\left\{100\left(\int_0^M e^{0.005x}0.01e^{-0.01x}dx + e^{0.005M}e^{-0.01M} - 1\right)\right\} \\
&= \exp\left\{100\left(\frac{0.01}{0.005}\left[1 - e^{-0.005M}\right] + e^{-0.005M} - 1\right)\right\} \\
&= \exp\left\{100\left(1 - e^{-0.005M}\right)\right\}.
\end{aligned}$$

Then

$$\begin{aligned}
&E\left[u(-P(M) - S(M))\right] \\
&= -\exp\left\{0.005P(M)\right\}\exp\left\{100\left(1 - e^{-0.005M}\right)\right\} \\
&= -\exp\left\{h(M)\right\},
\end{aligned}$$

where h has the obvious meaning. We want to choose M to minimise h, so differentiate:

$$\begin{aligned}
\frac{d}{dM}h(M) &= \frac{d}{dM}\left[5,050e^{-0.01M} + 100\left(1 - e^{-0.005M}\right)\right] \\
&= -50.5e^{-0.01M} + 0.5e^{-0.005M}.
\end{aligned}$$

Setting the derivative to zero gives

$$\frac{50.5}{0.5} = e^{0.005M},$$

so that $M = 923.02$. To check for a minimum, differentiate again:

$$\frac{d^2}{dM^2}h(M) = 0.505e^{-0.01M} - 0.0025e^{-0.005M},$$

which equals 0.00002475 when $M = 923.02$, confirming that h has a minimum at this value of M.

4. (a) Aggregate claims for the reinsurer have a compound Poisson distribution with Poisson parameter $\lambda e^{-\alpha M}$, and an individual claim amount distribution that is exponential with mean $1/\alpha$. From Exercise 3 of Chapter 4, the Esscher transform of this distribution is a compound Poisson distribution with Poisson parameter $\lambda e^{-\alpha M}M(h)$, where $M(h)$ is the moment generating function of the exponential distribution evaluated at h, so that

$$M(h) = \frac{\alpha}{\alpha - h},$$

and the individual claim amount distribution is exponential with parameter $\alpha - h$. The mean of this distribution is the reinsurance premium, namely

$$\lambda e^{-\alpha M}\frac{\alpha}{\alpha - h}\frac{1}{\alpha - h} = \frac{\lambda\alpha e^{-\alpha M}}{(\alpha - h)^2}.$$

(b) We want to maximise

$$E[u(-P(M) - S(M))] = -\exp\{\beta P(M)\}E\left[\exp\{\beta S(M)\}\right],$$

where $P(M) = \lambda\alpha e^{-\alpha M}/(\alpha - h)^2$ and $S(M)$ denotes net of reinsurance claims. Now

$$\begin{aligned}
&E\left[\exp\{\beta S(M)\}\right] \\
&= \exp\left\{\lambda\left(\int_0^M e^{\beta x}\alpha e^{-\alpha x}dx + e^{\beta M}e^{-\alpha M} - 1\right)\right\} \\
&= \exp\left\{\lambda\left(\frac{\alpha}{\alpha-\beta}\left(1 - e^{-(\alpha-\beta)M}\right) + e^{-(\alpha-\beta)M} - 1\right)\right\} \\
&= \exp\left\{\frac{\lambda\beta}{\alpha-\beta}\left(1 - e^{-(\alpha-\beta)M}\right)\right\},
\end{aligned}$$

which means we want to maximise

$$g(M) = -\exp\left\{\beta\frac{\lambda\alpha e^{-\alpha M}}{(\alpha-h)^2}\right\}\exp\left\{\frac{\lambda\beta}{\alpha-\beta}\left(1 - e^{-(\alpha-\beta)M}\right)\right\},$$

which is equivalent to minimising

$$h(M) = \beta\frac{\lambda\alpha e^{-\alpha M}}{(\alpha-h)^2} + \frac{\lambda\beta}{\alpha-\beta}\left(1 - e^{-(\alpha-\beta)M}\right).$$

Now

$$\frac{d}{dM}h(M) = \frac{-\lambda\beta\alpha^2 e^{-\alpha M}}{(\alpha-h)^2} + \frac{\lambda\beta}{\alpha-\beta}(\alpha-\beta)e^{-(\alpha-\beta)M},$$

and setting this equal to zero gives

$$\frac{\alpha^2}{(\alpha-h)^2} = e^{\beta M},$$

giving

$$M^* = \frac{1}{\beta}\log\left(\frac{\alpha^2}{(\alpha-h)^2}\right).$$

Also

$$\begin{aligned}
\frac{d^2}{dM^2}h(M) &= \frac{\lambda\beta\alpha^3 e^{-\alpha M}}{(\alpha-h)^2} - \lambda\beta(\alpha-\beta)e^{-(\alpha-\beta)M} \\
&= \lambda\beta e^{-\alpha M}\left(\frac{\alpha^3}{(\alpha-h)^2} - (\alpha-\beta)e^{\beta M}\right),
\end{aligned}$$

and hence

$$\left.\frac{d^2}{dM^2}h(M)\right|_{M=M^*} = \lambda\beta e^{-\alpha M^*}\left(\frac{\alpha^3}{(\alpha-h)^2} - (\alpha-\beta)\frac{\alpha^2}{(\alpha-h)^2}\right)$$
$$= \frac{\lambda\alpha^2\beta^2 e^{-\alpha M^*}}{(\alpha-h)^2} > 0,$$

so that h has a maximum at M^*.

5. The net of reinsurance premium income is

$$((1+\theta) - (1+\theta_R)(1-a))\,\lambda/\beta,$$

the individual claim amount distribution net of reinsurance is exponential with mean a/β and moment generating function

$$M_X(t) = \frac{\beta}{\beta - at},$$

and so the solution follows from

$$1 + ((1+\theta) - (1+\theta_R)(1-a))\,R(a)/\beta = \frac{\beta}{\beta - aR(a)}.$$

6. The net of reinsurance premium income is

$$1.2 \times 100\lambda - 1.25 \times 100\lambda(1-a) = (125a - 5)\,\lambda.$$

The net of reinsurance adjustment coefficient, which we write as R rather than $R(a)$, thus satisfies

$$1 + (125a - 5)\,R = \left(\frac{0.02}{0.02 - aR}\right)^2.$$

Set $a = 0.6$. Then

$$1 + 70R = \left(\frac{1}{1 - 30R}\right)^2,$$

which gives

$$10R - 3,300R^2 + 63,000R^3 = 0,$$

so that

$$R = \frac{1}{126,000}\left(3,300 - \sqrt{3,300^2 - 40 \times 63,000}\right) = 0.003229.$$

Set $a = 0.8$. Then

$$1 + 95R = \left(\frac{1}{1 - 40R}\right)^2,$$

which gives

$$15R - 6,000R^2 + 152,000R^3 = 0,$$

so that

$$R = \frac{1}{304,000}\left(6,000 - \sqrt{6,000^2 - 60 \times 152,000}\right) = 0.002682.$$

Finally, set $a = 1$. Then

$$1 + 120R = \left(\frac{1}{1 - 50R}\right)^2,$$

which gives

$$R - 475R^2 + 15,000R^3 = 0,$$

so that

$$R = \frac{1}{30,000}\left(475 - \sqrt{475^2 - 60,000}\right) = 0.002268.$$

Hence the conclusion is to reinsure and retain 60% of each claim.

7. (a) The premium income is 110λ, the reinsurance premium is

$$1.15\lambda E[\max(0, X - M)],$$

where $X \sim Pa(3, 200)$, and using Exercise 6 of Chapter 1,

$$\begin{aligned} E[\max(0, X - M)] &= E[X] - E[\min(X, M)] \\ &= 100\left(\frac{200}{200 + M}\right)^2, \end{aligned}$$

so that the reinsurance premium is

$$115\lambda\left(\frac{200}{200 + M}\right)^2.$$

Again using Exercise 6 of Chapter 1, the expected aggregate claim amount, net of reinsurance, for the insurer is

$$100\lambda\left(1 - \left(\frac{200}{200 + M}\right)^2\right),$$

leading to

$$110\lambda - 115\lambda\left(\frac{200}{200 + M}\right)^2 = (1 + \theta_N) \times 100\lambda\left(1 - \left(\frac{200}{200 + M}\right)^2\right),$$

which gives

$$\theta_N = \frac{10 - 15\,(200/(200 + M))^2}{100\left(1 - (200/(200 + M))^2\right)}.$$

(b) The loading θ_N is positive when

$$10 - 15\left(\frac{200}{200+M}\right)^2 > 0,$$

which gives $M > 44.95$.

(c) The net adjustment coefficient $R(M)$ satisfies

$$1 + \left(110 - 115\left(\frac{200}{200+M}\right)^2\right) R(M)$$
$$= \int_0^M e^{R(M)x} \frac{3 \times 200^3}{(200+x)^4} dx + e^{R(M)M} \left(\frac{200}{200+M}\right)^3.$$

8. (a) We have $c^* = 1.2 - 1.25(1-a) = 1.25a - 0.05$, and we require this to exceed the expected aggregate claims, net of reinsurance, which equal a. So we require $0.25a - 0.05 > 0$, i.e. $a > 0.2$.

(b) The first three moments of the individual claim amount distribution, net of reinsurance, are a, $1.5a^2$ and $3a^3$. Thus, the parameters of the De Vylder approximation are

$$\tilde{\alpha} = 1.5/a, \quad \tilde{\lambda} = 1.6875, \quad \tilde{c} = 1.375a - 0.05,$$

which lead to the approximation

$$\frac{9a}{11a - 0.4} \exp\left\{\frac{-(3a - 0.6)u}{a(11a - 0.4)}\right\}.$$

(c) Solving via a grid search we find $a = 0.384$ gives the minimum of the approximation to the ultimate ruin probability.

References

Albrecher, H. and Boxma, O. (2005) On the discounted penalty function in a Markov-dependent risk model. *Insurance: Mathematics & Economics* **37**, 650–672.

Asmussen, S. and Albrecher, H. (2010) Ruin Probabilities, 2nd edition. *World Scientific Publishing, Singapore.*

Borch, K. (1990) Economics of Insurance. *North-Holland, Amsterdam.*

Bühlmann, H. (1980) An economic premium principle. *ASTIN Bulletin* **11**, 52–60.

Centeno, M. L. (1986) Measuring the effects of reinsurance by the adjustment coefficient. *Insurance: Mathematics & Economics* **5**, 169–182.

De Pril, N. (1985) Recursions for convolutions of arithmetic distributions. *ASTIN Bulletin* **15**, 135–139.

De Pril, N. (1986) On the exact computation of the aggregate claims distribution in the individual life model. *ASTIN Bulletin* **16**, 109–112.

De Pril, N. (1988) Improved approximations for the aggregate claims distribution of a life insurance portfolio. *Scandinavian Actuarial Journal*, 61–68.

De Pril, N. (1989) The aggregate claims distribution in the individual risk model with arbitrary positive claims. *ASTIN Bulletin* **19**, 9–24.

De Pril, N. and Dhaene, J. (1992) Error bounds for compound Poisson approximations of the individual risk model. *ASTIN Bulletin* **22**, 135–148.

De Vylder, F. (1978) A practical solution to the problem of ultimate ruin probability. *Scandinavian Actuarial Journal*, 114–119.

De Vylder, F. and Goovaerts, M. J. (1988) Recursive calculation of finite time survival probabilities. *Insurance: Mathematics & Economics* **7**, 1–8.

Dickson, D. C. M. (1992) On the distribution of the surplus prior to ruin. *Insurance: Mathematics & Economics* **11**, 191–207.

Dickson, D. C. M., Egídio dos Reis, A. D. and Waters, H. R. (1995) Some stable algorithms in ruin theory and their applications. *ASTIN Bulletin* **25**, 153–175.

Dickson, D. C. M., Hughes, B. D. and Zhang, L. (2005) The density of the time to ruin for a Sparre Andersen process with Erlang arrivals and exponential claims. *Scandinavian Actuarial Journal*, 358–376.

Dickson, D. C. M. and Li, S. (2010) Finite time ruin problems for the Erlang(2) risk model. *Insurance: Mathematics & Economics* **46**, 12–18.

Dickson, D. C. M. and Waters, H. R. (1991) Recursive calculation of survival probabilities. *ASTIN Bulletin* **21**, 199–221.

Dickson, D. C. M. and Waters, H. R. (1996) Reinsurance and ruin. *Insurance: Mathematics & Economics* **19**, 61–80.

Dickson, D. C. M. and Waters, H. R. (1999) Multi-period aggregate loss distributions for a life portfolio. *ASTIN Bulletin* **29**, 295–309.

Dickson, D. C. M. and Waters, H. R. (2002) The distribution of the time to ruin in the classical risk model. *ASTIN Bulletin* **32**, 299–313.

Dickson, D. C. M. and Waters, H. R. (2004) Some optimal dividends problems. *ASTIN Bulletin* **34**, 49–74.

Dickson, D. C. M. and Willmot, G. E. (2005) The density of the time to ruin in the classical Poisson risk model. *ASTIN Bulletin* **35**, 45–60.

Drekic, S. and Willmot, G. E. (2003) On the density and moments of the time to ruin with exponential claims. *ASTIN Bulletin* **33**, 11–21.

Dufresne, F. and Gerber, H. U. (1989) Three methods to calculate the probability of ruin. *ASTIN Bulletin* **19**, 71–90.

Feller, W. (1966) An Introduction to Probability Theory and Its Applications, Volume 2. *Wiley, New York.*

Gerber, H. U. (1979) An Introduction to Mathematical Risk Theory. *S. S. Huebner Foundation, Philadelphia, PA.*

Gerber, H. U., Goovaerts, M. J. and Kaas, R. (1987) On the probability and severity of ruin. *ASTIN Bulletin* **17**, 151–163.

Gerber, H. U. and Pafumi, G. (1998) Utility functions: From risk theory to finance. *North American Actuarial Journal* **2**, No. 3, 74–100.

Gerber, H. U. and Shiu, E. S. W. (1998) On the time value of ruin. *North American Actuarial Journal* **2**, No. 1, 48–78.

Goovaerts, M. J., De Vylder, F. and Haezendonck, J. (1984) Insurance premiums. *North-Holland, Amsterdam.*

Grimmett, G. R. and Welsh, D. J. A. (1986) Probability: An Introduction. *Oxford University Press, Oxford.*

Hogg, R. V. and Klugman, S. A. (1984) Loss Distributions. *John Wiley, New York.*

Klugman, S. A., Panjer, H. H. and Willmot, G. E. (1998) Loss Models – From Data to Decisions. *John Wiley, New York.*

Kornya, P. S. (1983) Distribution of aggregate claims in the individual risk theory model (with discussion). *Transactions of the Society of Actuaries* **35**, 823–858.

Kuon, S., Reich, A. and Reimers, L. (1987) Panjer vs De Pril vs Kornya: A comparison from a practical point of view. *ASTIN Bulletin* **17**, 183–191.

Lin, X. S. and Pavlova, K. (2006). The compound Poisson risk model with a threshold dividend strategy. *Insurance: Mathematics & Economics* **38**, 57–80.

Lin, X. S. and Willmot, G. E. (2000) The moments of the time of ruin, the surplus before ruin, and the deficit at ruin. *Insurance: Mathematics & Economics* **27**, 19–44.

Panjer, H. H. (1981) Recursive evaluation of a family of compound distributions. *ASTIN Bulletin* **12**, 21–26.

Panjer, H. H. (1986) Direct calculation of ruin probabilities. *Journal of Risk and Insurance* **53**, 521–529.

Panjer, H. H. and Lutek, B. W. (1983) Practical aspects of stop-loss calculations. *Insurance: Mathematics & Economics* **2**, 159–177.

Panjer, H. H. and Wang, S. (1993) On the stability of recursive formulas. *ASTIN Bulletin* **23**, 227–258.

Panjer, H. H. and Willmot, G. E. (1986) Computational aspects of recursive evaluation of compound distributions. *Insurance: Mathematics & Economics* **5**, 113–116.

Panjer, H. H. and Willmot, G. E. (1992) Insurance Risk Models. *Society of Actuaries, Schaumburg, IL.*

Picard, P. (1994) On some measures of the severity of ruin in the classical Poisson model. *Insurance: Mathematics & Economics* **14**, 107–115.

Prabhu, N. U. (1961) On the ruin problem of collective risk theory. *Annals of Mathematical Statistics* **32**, 757–764.

Rolski, T., Schmidli, H., Schmidt, V. and Teugels, J. (1999) Stochastic Processes for Insurance and Finance. *John Wiley, Chichester.*

Schröter, K. J. (1991) On a family of counting distributions and recursions for related compound distributions. *Scandinavian Actuarial Journal*, 161–175.

Sundt, B. (1992) On some extensions of Panjer's class of counting distributions. *ASTIN Bulletin* **22**, 61–80.

Sundt, B. and Jewell, W. S. (1981) Further results on recursive evaluation of compound distributions. *ASTIN Bulletin* **12**, 27–39.

Wang, S. (1995) Insurance pricing and increased limits ratemaking by proportional hazards transforms. *Insurance: Mathematics & Economics* **17**, 43–54.

Waters, H. R. (1983) Some mathematical aspects of reinsurance. *Insurance: Mathematics & Economics* **2**, 17–26.

Willmot, G. E. and Lin, X. S. (1998) Exact and approximate properties of the distribution of the surplus before and after ruin. *Insurance: Mathematics & Economics* **23**, 91–110.

Index